NORDI'S GIFT

CLYDE RICE

Nordi's Gift

BREITENBUSH BOOKS, INC.

• PORTLAND •

The publisher and author wish to express their appreciation to the Oregon Arts
Commission for a grant which aided the publication of this book.

First edition. 1 2 3 4 5 6 7 8 9

Library of Congress Cataloging-in-Publication Data
Rice, Clyde, 1903–
    Nordi's gift / Clyde Rice.
    Sequel to: A heaven in the eye.
    ISBN 0-932576-77-X (cloth)
    1. Rice, Clyde, 1903–   —Family. 2. Rice family. 3. Oregon—Biography.
I. Title.
CT275.R532A3 1990
929'.2'0973—dc20   90-1948
                                                CIP

Breitenbush Books, Inc., P.O. Box 82157, Portland, Oregon 97282
James Anderson, publisher; Patrick Ames, editor in chief
Editor in charge, Gary Miranda
Designer, Ky Krauthamer

Distributed by Taylor Publishing Co., 1550 W. Mockingbird Lane, Dallas,
Texas 75235

Manufactured in the United States of America

To Virginia, Bunky, and Nordi

CONTENTS

PROLOGUE: *Page 3*

I

1934

In Which I Make It to Oregon, Make the Acquaintance of Several Stumps and Two Psychiatrists, Catch My First Glimpse of Virginia, and Solidify My Status as a Failure: Page 7

II

1936

In Which I Save and Am Saved by Acme Flavoring, Become a Misfit in Suburbia, Solve a Problem by Assaulting Some Lawn Chairs, and Begin to See Virginia: Page 51

III

1937

In Which I Build Us a House out of Rammed Earth, Grow Fatter on the Thinner Business, Have a Brief Run-in with Some Ghostly Sums, and Inadvertently Declare My Love: Page 85

IV

1939

In Which I Seduce Virginia, Bungle Things with Bunky, Get Canned by Acme Flavoring, and Become an Inconsequential Cog in the War Machine: Page 141

V

1943

In Which I Tell Nordi about Virginia, Split My Personality and the Shipyards, Go to Alaska, and Am Called Back by Urgent News: Page 203

VI
1944

In Which I Face the Family Music, Build a Boat, Lose and Gain a Wife, and Attempt to Beat Some Sense into My Head: Page 243

VII
1946

In Which I Become an Ineffectual Fisherman, Visit Nordi, Learn to Appreciate Spike Jones, and Have to Sell the Bunky: *Page 303*

VIII
1947

In Which I Become a Sawyer, Tinker with Writing, Get Alder and Deeper in Debt, and Learn of Nordi's Decision: Page 371

IX
1955

In Which I Trade the Mill for Vanilla, Settle Accounts with My Father for Good, Gain Some Familiar Neighbors, and Suffer My Greatest Loss: Page 409

EPILOGUE: *Page 449*

NORDI'S GIFT

PROLOGUE

Wᴴᴱɴ, AT THE AGE of thirty-two, I ruptured myself carrying a seven hundred and fifty pound statue to safety, I felt I had performed my duty to Aʀᴛ. That wasn't what my teachers in art school had in mind, but time didn't hang heavy on my hands in those days and I felt the effort and the injury were sufficient dues to the Muse.

But fifty years later, with another injury and time galore on hand, I felt the waft from Athena's wand, and though she didn't exactly tap me with it, my wife's urgings made up the difference. "You'll be off your feet for six months," she said. "Now's the time to get that story on paper."

And so I wrote *A Heaven in the Eye*, and tried to tell of my life on and around San Francisco Bay in the twenties. I told of the fellows and girls I gloried in knowing down by the Bay, my private Olympus where ambrosia was Dago red; of Art Coulter and his wife, Taffy, an exquisite if exquisites there be; of the brainy David Cartwright, who swam the Golden Gate in December; of the dilettantish Pushells, who wasted more talent than most mortals are blessed with, and who did it with style; of Annie Marge, who liked to do it in trees; of the many-sided Madeline, and of Hearst's headline writer, Bob Drake; and always of Nordi, the incredible Nordi.

To my amazement, the book was published. It even won an award. Some respectable people said nice things about it in print. I was happy. I'd achieved my impossible dream—to tell people of the richness of ordinary living. Soon after, though, I began to

3

receive letters. *Sure*, they said, *but what happened next? What happened to Nordi? And where's your son, Bunky? And that stump ranch you were heading for in Oregon, what happened there?*

Well, I was flattered and answered their letters. But I figured I had done a bit for ART again—this time with words, not muscle—and I didn't think I owed the world any more pages of print. But after awhile I began to believe I did. No reason; it just sank into me. You see I'd left all these readers up in the air at the end of the book. I had barely hinted at what happened when Nordi and I returned to Oregon.

And then one day I sat down and wrote: *So I decided to join the human race*, etc. What I meant, I suppose, was that this book, these people, would do very well indeed without the self-conscious strut of Californians. These people were Oregonians and they didn't need grease paint or false eyelashes to get it across.

Hey, I want you to meet Ray Neufer, master woodcrafter, who carved himself into our lives in an unpredictable way; I want you to meet his first wife, a cause-crazy virago in the Oregon manner, who once told Nordi she didn't feel quite dressed unless encased in sandwich boards demanding that certain soft-shelled clams be shifted to less rocky shores, etc., etc.; I want you to meet "the Little Lady," my father's last woman who went on to become my arch enemy; I want you to meet my Oregonian in-laws, who hated me even before I gave them good reason to. I want you to meet Nordi's niece, Virginia, to whom these pages hardly do justice. And, though it remains a wound after all these years, I must tell you what happened to Nordi.

I wrote seven hundred and twenty pages for *Nordi's Gift* knowing full well much of it would land on the publisher's cutting floor. I wish you could have gotten all of it to read, like the wild things that went on when I hired out on a fish tug bound for Alaska. (I didn't quite meet the famous Shove-Down Ole up there; a bear finished him off several days before I arrived at his diggings.) Those hundred pages had to be taken out, for my otherwise excellent publisher has the notion that the covers of a book shouldn't get too far apart. (I'm told that all publishers are similarly concerned, while we who are moved by our Muse to tell a full flowing tale, are not. Editors and publishers then, must be diplomats besides having an eye for beauty and meaning.)

After I got into the story, we had a relationship, you and I. You were somebody who'd listen and it seemed necessary to tell you how things moved along for me, and for Nordi and Bunky, and for Virginia. Along the way, I make an occasional observation about the glories and indignities of what philosophers are fond of calling the "human condition." But those letters I received from some of you who read *A Heaven in the Eye* made me a believer in the writer–reader setup, so I've tried to tell things just the way they happened and never to insult your intelligence. Oh, maybe in a few places. You'll find them.

I

*In Which
I Make It to Oregon,
Make the Acquaintance of Several Stumps
and Two Psychiatrists,
Catch My First Glimpse of Virginia,
and
Solidify My Status as a Failure*

1934

So I DECIDED to join the human race, lower middle class, Protestant, sort of, and certainly not catholic in their views. I didn't gravitate, didn't lurch, into the Smiths' and Joneses' mundane sphere of activity. No, hunger and want drove me and my wife headlong into the somewhat reluctant arms of our parents and relatives and into the bailiwick of our neighbors around the stump ranch. A couple of over-thirty waifs with child had to be absorbed by people whose own provender was none too certain. To their credit they did what they could with thinning larders and half-time jobs.

Decided, did I say? Really the lay of things handled that problem for me. Now, in late April on a Sunday morning, we ended our trek from Tiburon, but turned from our stumpland destination because Nordi demanded a long, hot bath. She maintained she wanted to be clean and rested before her encounter with a stump.

So we arrived before my father's door, truck piled high with plows and mattress, axes and saws and various oddments and, coupled to it, the trailer we had dragged behind us holding our cow and goat and the dozen chickens and, latched to it, our still dependable bicycle.

"Hello, Pop," I said, when on his crutches he came to the door. He stared at me before he said, "Clyde," expressing the word quietly, thoughtfully, then looked out at all the disarray that was our equipage. "Everything but the kitchen sink," he said with no smile on his face.

"Yes, everything I figured we could use clearing land."

"Those animals thirsty?"

"No, Pop, we watered them a couple of hours ago."

"How about the chickens?"

"Forget it, Pop."

Then seeing my wife coming around the corner of the truck, he called out, "Why, Nordi! I'm glad to see you. Come in and meet 'the Little Lady.'"

" 'Little Lady'?"

"Yes, Pearl and I divorced. Nordi, I want you to come in and meet the Little Lady."

Well, Nordi had her hot bath; we all did. We were asked to spend the night. After luncheon my father and I drove out to look for the best road to get the truck and trailer up the hill out of Oregon City, and chose one. He was serious, solemn, not at all as he had been the last time we had looked for land. That time we had driven out in the farmland on the edge of the Willamette Valley. As a young salesman, it had been part of his territory.

Here the exuberance of youth had been spent away from my frigid mother—towns like Whiskey Hill and Molalla, and Good Tidings, yes, towns like Peach Meadow, Hubbard, and Mulino. The land around these towns was rich and too expensive for me to buy. When we found that out, he still continued to drive around and began pointing out to me boarding houses and hotels where he had stopped and showing me windows he had jumped out of in the middle of night because of the sudden appearance of a husband. These reminiscences of sexual exploits seemed to do him a world of good. It was Mame here and Sarah there, and he told me an odd thing: that, when you had a quick one with the serving girl or the mistress of the boarding house and the lady was still encased in her corset, the sporting men called it a "turtle."

"Yes, I had a turtle with Josephine. Gosh! It must be four years ago." Then suddenly we drove on without words. He was never to speak to me in that cheerful manner again.

Now, painfully lame on crutches, he was thoughtful as we

drove along. Being a Christian Scientist he wouldn't speak of his injury, but eventually I found out that he had been delivering an oration about how much better his brand of bottled flavors was than his competitor's, when feeling a mellifluous phrase emerging from his consciousness and oiling his tongue, he stepped back as if to speak to a large audience instead of mutton-faced Ed Gorse, the store's proprietor, and dropped ten feet through an open trapdoor and lit standing. His hip joints took the awful blow and, since then, Mrs. Eddy's beloved practitioners could do little about it.

As we rolled sedately along he presently began talking. His business, he said, was in difficulty, for although his mainstay and best seller, a very good imitation vanilla, commanded a sensible price, the market was lately being overrun by a product in a big thin bottle that looked like a lot but wasn't, selling at less than half the price of my father's product. He rummaged in the car's glove compartment and brought out two bottles of the cheapie.

"Don't just taste these. You gotta drink the darn stuff. There's nothing subtle here." I did. "How do you figure it, Clyde?"

"There's no flavor at all," I answered, "just mild color."

"It's Mississippi River water," he said. "The coloring is mud in the water. I had it analyzed. Times are hard. People think with their purses. That St. Louis outfit is going to break me if I'm not careful."

"Is there any way I can help?" I asked.

He turned his head as we drove along and looked me over, looked me up and down with distaste. We really didn't have much room for it, sitting as we were side by side, but it worked. I had been weighed on whatever scales and found wanting.

"Hell," he said, "you can't take care of yourself, and anyway you owe me money."

We drove along silently the rest of the way, and I had time to consider and do a little summing. Here I was back in Oregon after a dozen years in California. I could not deny that my father was right, but I hadn't lost my independence sitting on my ass. In the years of the great depression I had battled miserable odds and lost. Not just once, but five times I had taken a beating. Whether it was tuberculosis while fishing off the west coast of Mexico, or a coffer dam going out around one footing of the Golden Gate Bridge, or a temporary change in the laws concerning milk in San Francisco, I got it right in the teeth. To handle the problems of a stump ranch you needed to be a big brawny plugger, and here was I, an average guy of five-feet-eight and not overly muscular. By keeping myself always in condition I had so far made up for it, but again—bad odds. Still, I could see no alternatives.

We reached his house where we had dinner and slept a troubled sleep from which I awakened hours before dawn. My mind kept going back to the little house we had built at Waterspout Point on San Francisco Bay. Losses during the depression had taken it away from us. Finally, with nothing more to lose, we left California. The long strange trip up here was not over yet.

"Are you awake?" Nordi whispered, turning slightly.

"Yes, full of questions and propounding inadequate answers." I paused. "But I can't kick. I've got you and Bunky. If I could only do better by you, merciful sleep would come."

She rolled over and drew my head down to her warm breasts. "We've made it, Clyde. We're back home! All those awful miles, hundreds of them, while you fought to keep our wreck on the road and rolling, are almost over. Sleep now, darling."

Well, she did, but I continued to go over the past remembering our early carefree years together. Time was fading some of Nordi's beauty. Ten years before she had been a rather famous artist's model. Our interest in art and painting, love of beauty brought us together when we met in art school and kept us close. Nordi's little ways of making me feel loved—her support, telling me she loved the twinkle in my deep-set gray eyes and my childish honesty. That was what kept me going, helped me roll with the punches life had been handing out.

After an early breakfast we were soon at Oregon City and the hill—Pop, in his car with my heavy rope to pull if need be, though we made it without his help. He turned back to vanilla, yeah, and twenty-five other flavors, while that little decrepit Ford engine strove clatteringly along in its last effort for mankind and, specifically, for me.

The country about was slightly rolling, but soon the road came down and out on the vast plain of the Willamette Valley, our road now following a finger of the valley as it reached in among the foothills of the mountains. We finally turned off the road and drove laboriously up into the hills—a turning road that we left at our own lane, which led into the eighty acres of stumps.

When we reached a small woodman's shack, we climbed out of our truck that was never to roll again, that had stayed in one piece for us until the journey was over. How can you love a battered piece of equipment? Well, we did. After all our belongings were out, we pushed our faithful truck into a little gulch behind the shack, where it came to rest standing. I suppose rust is still working quietly on its remains.

When everything was under cover with space for the cow and goat in the shed, we stared out over our land and it seemed each stump with its many great roots gripped the earth tighter, dared us. Then we looked long and hard at each other with Bunky staring up at us, and we laughed at ourselves and for ourselves, and because we had so little to do with and so much to do, we felt our frailty and we clung together as we girded our loins with laughter, for it was all we had.

Then Nordi started sweeping out the shack. I took my best axe and went out to consider a stump, but I looked at a hundred before I turned back to tackle one near the shack.

Smoke was pouring from the chimney as I came up. There was a pretty good kitchen range left in the shack and the smell of frying drifted to me. I rummaged among my tools for an old fashioned auger. The auger was a yard long and drilled a two-inch hole. The handle end was a crossbar of wood, which I twisted, forcing the auger into the stump while applying what pressure I could to keep it biting into the wood. One hole I drilled into the stump horizontally for over a foot. The next hole started over a foot above the first but angled down to it sharply.

I did it right the first time. The holes met deep in the stump.

I was tired but not completely frazzled by the grueling job, so I got a burning coal (in this case, from Nordi's stove) and shoved it in to where the holes met. Now I got out a tiny bellows I'd had for years and blew in the lower hole in the stump till it caught fire. Then sticking an iron pipe into the angled hole and another into the horizontal hole I had a little furnace burning, never wanting for fuel. After an hour I shoved the horizontal pipe farther in, directing the flame at the center of the stump. Several hours later I banked the stump with dirt and sod and let it consume itself down into its main roots. Sounds easy, but it demanded more from a man than I had or ever would have. "Just work slower. That's it," I said to myself, "and work more hours."

A week later we had seventeen stumps, with our help, consuming themselves. Two burned until they were only smoking craters, their deep roots still burning far underground. We turned from them to another endeavor, though still starting a new stump every day.

There were many great trees that had been left on the place, firs about four to seven feet through and extremely tall—old growth Douglas fir, they were called—too big for the former owner's sawmill. I decided to cut one down and make cordwood from it to sell in Portland. I chopped for two days making a big notch on the side toward where it would fall, then started sawing at the back side to sever the trunk. With the big crosscut saw, that was much longer than I am tall, Nordi and I were finally able to get the saw in about six inches, so that it was held in place while we pulled it back and forth.

That evening Nordi decided to go in and see her people, for she could ride in with Mr. Storter, who trucked the railroad ties from a nearby mill to the docks in Portland. So I was left with Bunky, Delia the cow, and Scheherazade, our Nubian goat of Egyptian descent nicknamed Zaddie, who, missing Nordi, followed me everywhere. Bunky kept himself busy for days damming an intermittent brook.

After many experiments I rigged two screen-door springs to a willowy sapling, which handled the other end of the saw after a fashion, and sawed through the trunk, though it took about forty rests to do it. When the tree looked to be ready to topple, I took our animals to the shack and tied them and checked on Bunky at his dam. Back at the tree, after a few dozen saw strokes, I withdrew the saw and hammered two wedges in the sawcut. Soon the treetop began to shake against the sky. I yelled, "Timber," in case anyone was near. The huge tree started to crash to the earth. There was a great whistling as the boughs that had soughed in the wind for a century screamed their way down to a mighty crash as the monarch hit the forest floor. Around the fallen tree was the debris of smaller trees it had broken and mashed into the sod. Some limbs that had been torn off in the fall and caught temporarily in smaller trees now fell here and there. Then all was quiet and in the silence I shuddered with awe, feeling puny indeed, but I climbed up on the trunk and marched down the length of it, marveling at its massiveness. I went to the shack and released the animals, who came with Bunky and me to see what the crash was about, the cow and the goat giving it a close inspection.

Next day, Tuesday, I started sawing the great log into four-foot lengths to be split up into cordwood. Starting at the butt I made one cut through. Wednesday I sawed through one and a half. I grew weary.

Thursday Nordi arrived in the morning with news that Pop wanted to see me. So, taking the same truck that she had arrived on, I argued my way into town. There my father confronted me with some facts.

"Look, Clyde," he said, "you're not built for it."

"You mean hard work? I've done it all my life. I've carried a lot of stones twice and three times as heavy as any cordwood."

"Perhaps, but you have to keep going with cordwood. With those stones you could rest between, but cordwood is a constant drudge if you expect to make enough to keep you through the winter."

"Yeah, but—"

My father waved me down. "Short arms, small hands, and an artiste. I tell you, Clyde, it won't work."

"Okay, Pop, you got any alternatives?"

"I don't know," he said, "I've been asking around. Seems nobody has a job opening in their places, and if they have, their or their wife's relatives are waiting in line to glom onto it."

"So I've got to keep cutting wood, Pop. Hell! I've got the trees. That's something at least."

"I see," he said grimly. "Come along."

We drove up in front of an agriculture equipment store. WADE said the sign on the worn building. We entered.

"Dragsaw, second hand? What have you got?" said my father to the clerk. Well, we picked one with three extra blades, files and saw set, and a splitting gun.

"A hundred bucks even," said the mechanic who had extolled its innards to us.

"A hundred and ten, if you deliver," said Pop.

"Where to?" The man was cautious.

"Near Wendel."

"Gosh, I can't deliver way out there."

"What's your competitor's address?" asked my father.

"Okay, tomorrow," the man said quickly, "but I'll need fifty dollars now, sixty on delivery. How do you get into your swamp?"

"Tell him, Clyde, if you think he can follow directions." Standing at the curb outside, my Dad, still grim, said "That's all I can do for you, son. Good luck!"

That dragsaw was a heavy wooden frame, a narrow triangle in shape, and like a wheelbarrow, it had a wheel in the narrow end. Where the handles of a wheelbarrow would be were the ends of the frame and attached to either of them were big moveable dogs—steel points. I could rest the handles on the log and drive in the dogs that would hold the rig in place on a log. Surrounded by the triangle of the frame was a simple little engine of ancient design that, through cams and levers, worked a saw heavier than the usual logger's saw. It moved the saw back and forth in the cut.

It could cut through a four-foot log in less than ten minutes. The main problem with it was moving it to the next cut. It was too heavy for me and the handles were too wide apart and, when I backed up against the log with it, I was captured until I could drive the dogs into place.

Once, when I was doing this, both dogs swung down on my wrists, imprisoning me, and my back was arched against the big log I was cutting. No one was within a mile of me. I was on my own. I made one great effort with all my strength and forced one of the dogs up, or I'd be there yet. It skidded off on its wheel, and somehow no bones were broken. It was a tool for a big, rangy man. We medium-size and small guys took on a dragsaw at our peril.

I soon learned how to use a splitting gun—a round rod a foot long sharpened and deeply drilled at one end. At the inner end of the drilled hole was a tiny hole. You filled the big hole with blackpowder and pounded it into the center of the end of the log. This compressed the powder. You put a short blasting fuse into the little hole, lit it and retreated. When it exploded, it split the log into two or three pieces, usually throwing them up ten or twenty feet in the air. The wood could easily be split into cordwood after that.

Zaddie and Delia grazed a few feet from where I worked, and when I lit the fuse and ran back, they ran back too and with me stared at the log to be split by the explosion. After it happened the three of us rushed through the powder smoke to see how many pieces had been split out. When we had studied it all and seen just what had happened, they went back to grazing until the next explosion.

Bunky came every once in awhile, but his series of dams and pools was more interesting than mere explosions. Bunky was not on the team. In fact I was the team, but the goat and the cow were excellent sidewalk superintendents.

Soon Bunky met other young boys of the scattered farms around and went with them to a two-room school about a mile away, where there was a summer session. Before long he had many friends and was enjoying himself. We too met some of our neighbors and found most all of them interesting.

From the first tree I cut five and a half cords—a cord is four feet by four feet by seven feet. The second tree was a bit bigger and it had no brush to hinder it when it fell. It leaned in no discernible way. The only place I could fall it was near two tall stumps ten feet high, cut years ago when that was the fashion in dropping big trees. It was with a certain delicacy that I placed the notch to assure that the tree would fall where I wanted it, otherwise it would plunge into the canyon. I was so confident that the tree would fall according to my plan, that I set the peg out a hundred feet to drive into the ground when it came down on it.

I worked three days on the tree and had taken out the saw and was driving wedges in the sawcut to topple it when a sudden blast of wind came from another quarter and down it fell on the two stumps. Fifty feet of the top broke off and fell in the canyon. The massive log over a hundred feet long lay ten feet above the ground.

Next day I put the car jack under one side on the stump, and working at it, soon had the log in place for cutting up. So it went. In three months I had one hundred fifteen cords of fine wood seasoning, ready for market.

Two brothers had contracted to haul my wood to town. I had gotten enough customers to sell it all in Portland and everything seemed fine, but one of the brothers was jailed and the other one left the state with their truck. When I looked for other truckers, they were all engaged in getting cordwood to town, though one agreed to haul it if I waited a week.

Very early rain came that year. For two weeks it pounded down and my road to the highway became a quagmire. I cut the bark off stumps and filled the ruts with bark. By the time the road was passable and the cordwood brought into Portland, my customers, of necessity, ordered other wood, and I had to sell elsewhere at a lower price, because it was late in the season. My net was three hundred and fifty dollars with which to face the winter. Nordi despaired. If she hadn't put in a big garden behind the shack we certainly would have starved. She took fifty dollars and rented a furnished farmhouse nearby. I had cut up enough short blocks to make into stovewood, so at least we had a roof over our heads and fuel to keep us warm, four sacks of potatoes, a keg of sauerkraut, carrots and turnips without end. Now I decided to go into the mountains to get a deer for meat in our house.

"But, Clyde," Nordi objected, "you promised me you would never hunt out of season again."

"I know, but I figure I've got a right to feed my family. Look, Nordi, if we were from one of the old settler pioneer farms like down around Peach Meadow, I'd get my venison as a pioneer's right. Of course that's a thing of the past, but it's still honored in a left-hand way. What I mean is, the law looks the other way, and I do come from such beginnings, but where's the farm—the old ties to the land? I haven't any, so I'm fair game for game wardens."

In early afternoon I hid the tools and picked up my gun. I had told Nordi if I didn't get back to come looking for me around the Red House Trail in the morning, but I strayed in a northerly direction from the old pioneer trail. I wandered as quietly as I could into an area where a tornado must have struck fifty or a hundred years ago. The big tree trunks lay in ancient disorder. Over them in some recent storm alders had been uprooted and cast about like jackstraws.

In this odd maze I found my deer—a big buck—and a head shot dropped him. As I scrambled over a log to get to the downed buck I heard a car being started to the north and down below me. It immediately backed and filled, obviously turning around, and bumped away heading north, I gathered. *Game Wardens*, I thought. They must have been parked at the end of the road.

I had wandered too far into the Gooper Creek drainage and

shot the deer above the town. The road from Wendel ended below me, stopped by cliffs, and the wardens knew that the way out of this part of the woods was the Red House Trail. They were driving around to intercept me, a matter of fifteen miles on rutted roads.

With my knife I cut off the deer's head and the scent glands on its hind legs, then opened it up and removed the viscera and heart and lungs. I lashed the left hind leg to the left foreleg, did the same to the right legs, slipped my arms in the apertures produced, and reared up with the heavy carcass on my back, grabbed my Winchester and started clambering up a log lying between me and the Red House Trail. But the neck of my victim and my family's food reached up much higher than my head. I would claw my way up to the top of a big, mossy log and start to jump down on the other side only to get that neck caught in branches or against the trunk of one of the uprooted alders, and back down I'd come with my burden breaking my fall. After this happened a few times, I knew I should have cut off the neck with the head; but now in a blind, unthinking rush to get out of the woods, I scrambled on another hundred yards or so, until completely winded, I lay down and the carcass lashed to me did too. I hadn't had time to drain it before my flight and now my back was soaked with blood and my shoes sloshed with it at every step.

As I lay with both arms numbed from the pressure of the leg bones on them, I laughed, admitting with disgust, "Clyde, you're in another mess. True to form, doing it the Rice way!" And then I thought of the waiting game wardens. (How I was certain that there were two of them, I don't know.) Anyway, thinking on game wardens I recalled that many minions of the law become plump, because theirs is not an active job. The word "Ah" was expelled from me—a very satisfied "Ah," for I saw a way out of my dilemma.

I waited for deeper dusk, so it would be hard to see through the woods, though I could still see twigs and branches that would crackle underfoot. One thing was obvious: I would not be able to carry this big buck home. I was hard put to carry him a hundred yards without resting. I must leave it to drain while I slipped past the wardens, got Nordi and a borrowed horse. Anyway, somehow we were going to get all that meat home.

I rolled awkwardly over and reared myself up, buck carcass and all, and staggering, stumbling I came to the trail, crossing it to a maple thicket where, after repeated attempts, I heaved the carcass up over two whittled vine maple crotches.

I believed I was about a half a mile from where the trail met the road. The woods were not as dark as I needed. It began to rain heavily, a soaking rain, still it couldn't wash the smile from my face, for this now seemed like a light-hearted game instead of one leading to jail. The rain brought the darkness I needed. Remembering carefully just how the trail ran, I began paralleling it by about a city block south. I figured that one plump game warden had stayed in the car at the end of the road, while the other one pussyfooted a goodly stroll up the trail to intercept me.

I had not gone far when through the trees I glimpsed the pussyfooter on my side of the trail making a hiding place from where, unseen, he could howl, "THROW UP YOUR HANDS."

He was much too close to where I was passing to make me happy. Scarcely moving, barely breathing I did finally pass him. Farther down on my parallel course, about between the wardens, my coat caught on a branch. Thank God! The branch was alive and could bend instead of breaking with a crack.

It was getting darker and I moved a bit faster to get out while I could see. After some time, when I was reasonably sure that I was past their car, I took to the road and continued down it. Well after complete dark, I heard a shot and an automobile horn answering it. I stepped into the brush when I heard them coming and watched them go by. After that I sauntered home, where I told Nordi we had meat, but I'd need help to get it. She said I was a sight, but blood is easily removed with cold water.

Half frozen, but clean once more, I sat down to a supper of bean soup with the small withered potatoes in a butter sauce.

We slept until the alarm went off at one o'clock. At Nordi's suggestion we forgot about a horse and got out our wheelbarrow.

We skinned the carcass in the barn and took one beautiful roast to the house.

A couple of days later a plump man knocked at our door. I answered. I'd been expecting him. Now the dread was over. Nordi knew too.

"Hello," I said, "won't you come in and eat with us. She just put it on the table."

The mill's whistle blew for noon. He looked a little startled from his grimness of lip. "Do you ask people in to eat with you without knowing their names?" he asked.

I laughed, steady as a rock now. "Well, in the city I didn't, but in the country I do. It's a pleasure. Come on in."

He stepped in. I took his hat. "There's a basin and a towel on the back porch," I said.

He came back washed up, his hair neatly parted. The grim expression was oddly seated on his open jovial countenance. I saw he wasn't particularly fat, but compact, short-coupled with short arms. We sat down to the beautiful venison roast and the boiled weazened potatoes and hot biscuits. After all the plates were filled I sat down.

"What's your name?" I asked, buttering a biscuit. "Mine's Clyde Rice."

"My name's Johnson, the same as the people what built this house. You renting or did they sell?" he wondered, around a mouthful of venison.

"Renting," I replied, "we were buying eighty acres of stumps back of here." I caught Nordi's eye and smiled hope. At least I tried to smile hope.

Rather quizzically, he said, "Rice? You got relatives up Salem way? My father was born there."

"My grandfather was born at Scio in 1855. Is that close enough? His wife was born in a blockhouse near where Philomath is now. Guess an Indian raid brought the settlers in."

He was smiling into his plate as he said, "My grandfather settled in Salem. I was raised on a farm near Silverton." He lifted his smile, now a grin, and regarded me.

"That makes both of us webfoots, doesn't it?" I said.

"Well, I was away for awhile."

"Makes no difference," I grinned. "I was too—California—but I always dreamed of Oregon, Western Oregon. I took a hell of a beating down there and now here too. A guy just can't cut it anymore."

"Roosevelt's in there pitchin'," he said.

I agreed. "Wonder what would have happened if he hadn't taken hold when he did."

"Why, Stalin would be chopping us up just like we was Russian citizens," he answered as Nordi filled his cup. "Which reminds me," he said. "They solved that axe murder over in Molalla. Seems these guys fought over their different interpretations of a statement in the Koran. I thought that one stumbling block was enough, but now we've got another book to kill about or for. Oh, I forget. Here's your pocketbook," he announced and, after I took it, he went on. "Looked like you fell off a log and lost it. You know I'd stay out of those woods up there before you lose somethin' else."

"It's a healthy idea," I agreed, "and I'm going to observe it to the letter." We gossiped a bit then he got up. "I got to be getting along," he said. "Mrs. Rice, thank you for a most welcome meal. You sure know what to do with a roast of beef."

On the porch before he put on his hat, he said, "Now take that noon whistle. It reminded me how hungry I was and changed things. Well, so long, Rice." He put on his hat, stepped off the porch and was gone.

●

For two days Nordi canned the meat in pint jars and hid them in stumps and under logs in case anyone else came to investigate. Added to our fare of vegetables we were in good shape for the rest of the winter.

One day I was chopping away at a stump to begin another hole when I thought I heard a car. It came toward us dodging stumps on our weebleton-to-wobbleton lane. My sister, Valerie, had recently married and was now bringing me her sisterly love and Bill, her husband, but most of all a job, temporary sure, but a job. They had work for me cleaning up the high brush growing on their several acres, and to fall and square enough trees to make a big log cabin.

In two weeks I had Bill and Val's acres cleared of brush and was falling tall firs. Eighteen trees I harvested, limbing and removing the bark. When the logs were squared and left for seasoning, Bill paid me sixty-five dollars and drove me home. Winter had now set in. When he let me out at the stump ranch, a cold wind was blowing down from the mountains. Nordi was not around, so I hurried through a deepening dusk to where we had been burning stumps.

Near the stumps that she had somehow kept burning I found her, dirty and disheveled, but triumphant—and her smile was glorious. Behind her was a strange-looking team of horses, and behind them some distance was an enormous fire fueled by small logs and other debris that had lain scattered between the stumps throughout the place. Her team had been dragging in a long narrow log and had gotten it jammed between three stumps.

The team she had hitched to the log was not exactly matched. One was a smallish saddle horse with its white hide covered with great blotches of red and brown. It was harnessed to a coal-black mare built like a dachshund, its long back dipping down in the middle, like the cables of a suspension bridge. At the moment they were standing wound up in their harness. The saddle horse had been trained western style to neck rein, while the old mare had not, so the same signal with the reins made them go in opposite directions, and they usually ended up entangled, waiting patiently for everything to be straightened out before another disastrous start. Yet, in spite of this, Nordi had cleaned off two or three acres, for the long fire was burning on mounds of ashes of a week's buildup.

The mare had been, Nordi explained to me, one of a team of hearse horses. When its mate died, the undertakers had put the old mare out to pasture and bought a second-hand Packard hearse. Being in the hill country, where farm tractors often rolling over on their owners added to demise by disease and old age, their business was good and sometimes brisk, so they let Nordi have the use of the ancient mare for a pittance.

We got the team out of the mess and led them to the barn. We spoke of going to the house for coffee and cookies, though we knew that we would not consume food till other more important matters were vigorously attended to. When Bunky came home from school, he tried to show how much he had missed me with many hugs and exuberant punchings. Until his bedtime he told tales about the people on the farms about. He was full of curiosity about a small sawmill just up the road from our rented house. The mill cut railroad ties from small second-growth logs. Japan bought ties from hundreds of small mills for their Manchukuo takeover. Horse logging of small timber kept the mill in logs and the loggers in beans and in grain for their horses, but little else. People worked for next to nothing. The depression was still very much with us.

I was still cutting cordwood—our cash crop, as it were— sawing, blasting, splitting and piling the resinous wood, and always drilling stumps and setting them to burn inwardly. Whatever the endeavor, I was watched by Zaddie and Delia, whose two offspring we had lost to a marauding cougar.

Venison stew with sauerkraut sounds strange, but in Nordi's hands it became just right by the third mouthful and you savored the rest. Her apple dorper, rich with fresh-churned butter, was hard to refuse. We were comfortable in our poverty and our lives had meaning. Nordi milked Zaddie, while I milked bounteous Delia. We had more than enough milk, so I wangled two weaner pigs for some cordwood, and they thrived on the milk and small potatoes that we got for a song and boiled for them. The little pigs were a delight to Nordi. She claimed their comments on comfort and food, annoyance and fear, were most expressive, adding, "And they belch with such bravura and confidence."

For human company, we occasionally resorted to the Nordstroms. Nordi's people were Swedes, with a great love of the outdoors. My side of the family never seemed to get farther out than the suburbs, so because I was a nature lover too, I was drawn more to Mrs. Nordstrom and her daughters and their husbands than I was to my own people. But whichever I chose I ran smack dab into religious cant. To approach the heart of either family you ran a gauntlet of different interpretations of the Bible, combined with a ponderous reserve of ignorance that each man and woman and child valiantly defended.

Nordi's folks liked to picnic on Sundays and sometimes to camp. They liked to bake lots of pies and scatter them around on picnic tables neatly segmented for casual use. They liked to swim in cold mountain streams, liked to pick huckleberries up near the snowline of Mount Hood.

Olga, Nordi's sister, played the piano and though far from a master of technique, she brought feeling and meaning out of many compositions that had been flat for me before. Mrs. Nordstrom's other daughter, Tek, had two daughters, Doris and Virginia, whom Olga had among her piano students. When we first came to Portland Olga had asked Virginia to play for me and she had burst into tears and run upstairs. I remember her long pink silk dress disappearing up the stairway, the dress in which earlier in the day she had graduated from grade school. She had my sympathy, but I took no more notice of her—at least not yet.

The appurtenances of Nordi's and Olga's home were saturated with not only Grieg and Sinding but also with MacDowell and Chopin. Sweet Nordi sang, her sister accompanied and often sang the alto part and the odor of fine cooking drifted through the house.

Mrs. Nordstrom, right from the start, knew I was a child of the devil. Years before when Nordi and I slipped away and married without her parents' consent, Nordi's mother was in a rage when we came to announce our marriage. Being a Seventh Day Adventist she knew that any day may be the world's last. She was certain in 1922 that four or five years was the most that the world could possibly carry on. She was furious with me because, she said, she wanted her two youngest daughters to go to heaven as virgins and I had kind of punctured her dream. Still, she maintained Olga would enter heaven as a virgin, and never forgave me for the trend I started, for eventually Olga too married.

Mrs. Nordstrom had fallen in love with Olga's husband, Jack Forsythe, a big Irishman who loved fun, Olga and his bottle. He was a salesman kind of fellow and liked to be seen driving a large car. They liked that too. Olga sat beside him, with the old lady resplendent in the back seat, for she too liked to go.

Her other son-in-law was Teddy Broms, a quiet, exceptionally kind man who with his wife, Tekla, and two daughters was also under the old matriarch's thumb. She ruled her three daughters, as well as a step-daughter and through them tried to rule her sons-in-law, and of the four I was soon found to be the most recalcitrant.

·

But Mrs. Nordstrom with word and gesture pointed out after they'd fed us several times that there was no real need of our company. She pulled her group tighter about her and looked her hated son-in-law coldly in the eye and we, bending our every effort to existence on the stump ranch, turned inward to our little world of Bunky and each other, Zaddie and Delia and our very friendly loving piglets.

By now, too, we knew some of our neighbors: the Lundstroms, who lived only a quarter of a mile away; Johnson, owner of the property on our western boundary; and Wilbur Kingsley, who had plowed the cleared acre back of the shanty a week after we arrived. Johnson, a widower, partook of Nordi's apple dorper at weekly intervals. A certain ease was coming into our lives. We worked to the limit of our endurance, but the results were showing. We expected to seed three acres to wheat around the craters and standing stumps that we'd finish off next year.

One late morning after I had finished drilling a stump, I

ambled over to where I was splitting cordwood and found that my tools were gone. The dragsaw had not been touched, but my several axes and steel wedges and sledge had been taken from where I had carefully hid them.

The Lundstroms and Johnson had warned of thievery. Even a very decrepit hatchet had been taken. Very little could be done without my tools. Without an axe I couldn't even make kindling or stovewood. I felt very let down. No fury erupted from me, for I knew very well that people who stole such tools were destitute, more beaten by want than perhaps I'd ever been. Because I knew that hopeless world they lived in, even denouncing them in my mind would have been traitorous to my code, such as it was. Evidently they didn't have the strength or a way to get my dragsaw out of the ravine, or maybe they only stole what was absolutely necessary to stay alive.

Pondering my loss, I remembered that soon after we arrived I had reconnoitered the near mountains, thinking of a possible trapline in the winter. The people around told me they had tried it and found there was little fur to be had up there. The fifty-dollar bounty on cougar had me thinking I'd build a bark shanty in a place where deer congregated in the winter and snag a cougar without hounds. In my tramping around I'd left an old axe.

Now I needed the axe. Hurrying to the house I told Nordi of our loss and where I was going. She gave me a piece of smoked jerky and begged me to be careful. I cut cross-country aiming to hit the trail a mile or so above where I had shot the deer. Much sooner than expected I was in snow. A mile farther on I was wallowing through knee-deep snow. The crust was rotten and wouldn't support me. For each step I rose up on the crust and, when my full weight was on it, broke through. Pushing on in that way made each hundred yards a battle. Going always higher I could finally walk on the crust and in time reached the timbered flat where my axe was hidden. Above its ten or so acres the land rose steeply.

I had hidden the axe under a small log in about the center of the area and near the trail, but the trail was not blazed, simply scuffed out by men and other predators and the deer. I had gotten to the flat because I knew the general way, but now I had no marks to go by in my search. All the towering hemlocks looked the same and, between them in corridors and small clearings, the snow hid all that was beneath it.

I scouted around. It was like hunting for the proverbial needle in a haystack. But I had come for the axe, so I went off the flat and then came back. With no reference points to help me, I had to help myself—use that other part of me. I wandered the area as a living question. Where? Where? Where? I asked the timbered flat, the trees and the snow, but quietly. With eyes half-closed I continued and finally came to a halt. No big decision. I just stopped, dug a hole in the snow and there was the axe. It seemed most natural to me, quite in the order of things.

When I climbed into this country the sky had been bleak and, once deep in the timber, a black storm, coming from the southeast, was obscured from me. I was scarcely aware of a lofty agitation above me so keen was I to what lay beneath the snow. After I retrieved the axe, trees some distance away threshed their tops as a sudden high wind reached down and harrowed them roughly and then the forest around me roared. Branches came pelting down, great falling limbs crashed into the snow. Fearing for my life I rushed away, falling many times on the slippery crust and each time I fell, I held the double-bitted axe at arm's length away from me. I passed over the area where the crust was rotten. Soon floundering through knee-deep snow, I left the timber and entered the brush of cutover land still alive, struck only once—a glancing blow that knocked me sprawling but broke no bones.

"Trapezius," Nordi said of where the falling limb had lacerated and bruised my back. It had crashed down near where I was scrambling to get up. The springiness of its outer branches had bounced the jagged end of the limb into the flesh of my back, its force still a menace in its final angular sprawl. I had jumped up and grabbed the axe that was jarred from my hands and charged on, wild to leave the deep woods. I had left a bloody trail as

I rushed along. Now I was squirming under the bite of iodine.

"It's at least three inches long, and deep," she said. "I can't pull the edges together with tape. It's got to be stitched to-gether." It was sore, sure, but her gentle hands and warm breath on me compensated for the pain.

The neighbors had spoken of a free clinic in Portland at the medical school. "I think you should go there tomorrow. This looks like a job for them," she said as she bandaged me up as best she could.

The neighboring mill was tied up for repairs, and that tied up Mr. Storter's truck, so I rode into Portland on our bike. The thirty miles went easily, though the gash in my back began bleeding again as I entered Portland. I soon arrived at the doors of the medical college and, after a few questions about livelihood and my ineptness at snaring the dollar, they stitched me up. I'll admit I yodeled in the process, for I'm allergic to Novocaine.

Afterward I talked to the doctor, a big lumbering man who I gathered was interested in everything, and told him about the axe and the way I found it. "Yes," staring at me intently, he remarked that he had an uncle with abilities along those lines.

"Uncles and aunts," I responded, happy with him but still a little annoyed. "Each family has an uncle or an aunt who displays this special kind of knowing. The family always holds them off at arm's length, as they do halfwit second cousins. Seems we never want to face up to the fact that many of us are so endowed. In fact, I'm inclined to believe that each man's brain is capable of getting results in this manner, but we really do not want to deal with these oddments when there are quick easy answers that dodge them."

"Mr. Rice," he said, getting heavily to his feet, "when you come up to have the stitches removed, ask for me. I'd like to continue this discussion. It's been a pleasure."

Well, I didn't, for Nordi took the stitches out. Those who hew wood must work ceaselessly if they are to survive.

In splitting cordwood the rich pitch smell of Douglas fir is something I never tire of. The splitting open of each plump

four-foot section of log was like disrobing a woman. You open at
once all the fresh color, grain and fragrance that has been kept
inviolate until your onslaught. The resinous tang of the virgin
wood assails you and, as you divide and divide again the beautiful
wood into cordwood, your gloves become sticky with the per-
fumed sap—the pitch of fir. One must be worn to a frazzle not to
be enthralled by such abundance.

I now had many long stacks of cordwood seasoning, ready to
be trucked and sold. I had to sell some of it wholesale to a dealer
to keep us in necessities like new shoes for fast-growing Bunky. It
was now mid-winter. Snow arrived from time to time but soon
dissipated. Each day I strove to up my production, but four cords
was the best I could ever do. Other woodcutters did much better.
I was in perfect shape. I should have been able to cut more. It was
embarrassing, but in spite of myself, gradually my best became a
little over two cords a day. We wondered about it, Nordi and I.
I was not stymied by the winter. It was just that I needed a little
chirking up, we thought.

In late winter I had to sell over half of my accumulated
cordwood, wholesaling it to a fuel dealer. I sold of necessity for I
was back one month on payment for the land, and Nordi announced tearfully that she was pregnant.

We had been so careful, for we could barely feed and clothe
ourselves, and the doctor who had delivered Bunky had impressed upon Nordi and me that she should never have another
baby, that they both would die if she did. Later I stopped in to
check with the doctor about it, but he had contracted a sinus
infection that infected his brain and killed him. He was a famous
obstetrician, so he must have had good reason to warn her.

Nordi wept, but said she must have an abortion. So I headed
for the city to scout around among friends and relatives until
finally someone, I've forgotten who, told me of a woman doctor
who was a master of the procedure. I sold the wood, borrowed
from my father and sold my set of Dickens's novels, leather-
bound and illustrated by Cruikshank. My mother had given the
books to me on my twelfth birthday and Pop had kept them for

me until now. Mr. Storter said he would be available at one o'clock to take her home and I expected to taxi her over to the dock where he unloaded.

I stood across the street from where on the second floor my darling was racked with futile pain. After seemingly endless hours she appeared coming down the stairs. To my surprise a car driven by my father drew up to the curb. I helped her into the car and, though he urged her to come to his home, faintly she begged to be taken out to the stump ranch, saying she needed to be with Bunky.

At the ranch Pop didn't come in but drove away, clearly agitated. I carried her in and made her as comfortable as I could. She began to cry softly. The doctor had warned her to be still and quiet for a few days. I asked her if I could help in any way.

"No," she said through her tears, "just hold me like you're doing. I want to hug Bunky. I need to hold Bunky. I cry for opposing reasons," she said. "I can't explain why!" and she wept on until Bunky came home. Next day I stayed with her, cuddling and comforting her any way I could. I cooked up a big venison stew and, alas, I tried to bake a pie. Before noon it started to snow. I fixed up a lounge on the porch and bundled her into it. There was no wind and from the porch she could hear the big flakes touch the ground. She was in that place between sorrow and joy, certainly not related to the usual mundane center of living, but a place where laughter and sorrow are separated by a fragile thinness. It was a place of light, not sunlight but an inner radiance of everything. She said the feeling for her was tied to the fall of snowflakes.

The snow continued. I felt I should break trail for Bunky. I met him almost halfway home from school. "Hi Pop!" he shouted and pelted me with snowballs. While we were having our fun, it grew much darker. Snow, in such a thick fall as I had ever seen, came down. The trail I'd kicked out on my way to Bunky was filling up, so we hurried back through a literal wall of snowflakes and were soon home. Delia and Zaddie seemed glad to see us as we milked and fed them. We brought in wood for the night and closed the door on the world outside.

After supper we sang for Nordi, as she always did for us, but now for a few days that was forbidden her. Nordi clung to Bunky, much to his puzzlement. "I'm getting all the affection," he said. "Poor Pop." So we bundled around her and sang some of her favorites until bedtime.

With the loss of the money and the backlog of cordwood, the only thing I could do was split more of it and stack it around. Two cords a day! It still wasn't enough to allow me to say I was in the business and now I was getting a pain in my side when I tried to step up production. It seemed that it was a fight against lethargy. My movements, in spite of myself, were slow, and try as I would I could not seem to get snap into things. Finally, I decided that there was something wrong with my insides. Something would have to be done about it.

I biked the thirty miles to Portland. I could have gone on the truck, but I was so full of shame to be a woodcutter who was incapable of cutting three or four cords that I did not want to be noticed going into town on a weekday or of leaving my chopping at all. I arrived at the free clinic of the medical college and told a pleasant young doctor my problems. After checking me over and doing a number of tests, they told me they could find nothing wrong. As I was leaving the doctor said: "You know, Mr. Rice, your problem might be in your head. If you want I'll make an appointment for you with our psychiatrist."

I told him I had read a book written by Freud on the subject and I was perfectly willing to do anything to speed me up. A few days later I did see the psychiatrist.

I was soon through the usual rudimentaries with this eagle-eyed and, from his movements and speech, decisive man. Then I tried to tell him of my problem. He held up a restraining hand.

"Not now," he said, "we'll come to it. Do you read many books?"

"Yes," I answered.

"Have you read a book lately?"

"Yes, *Song of the Lark* by Willa Cather."

"What did you like most in that book?"

"Well, I didn't like the main characters."

"What did you like?"

"There was a minister in it. I don't ordinarily favor ministers, but he had several kids and his house sat up on a windy hill. It jutted out into the wind on its open foundation and the wind howled under it. The house didn't have a sub-floor, just a single floor, between that bitter cold wind, with the kids playing on the floor in the room above. But there was a stove and love and laughter up there and somehow it was successful. They were protected, fraily, sure, but protected. I thought Miss Cather did a wonderful thing in depicting that."

He broke in. "Miss Cather," he said, "you think she's a pretty fine woman, huh?"

"Yes, I do, an excellent writer."

"You ever dream about her or the heroine of the story?"

"Why, no, not at all."

"Aw come on, be honest. You're talking to a psychiatrist. How'd you like to take that opera singer to bed?"

"Well, from the picture of her that Cather draws I'd much rather somebody else took her to bed."

"You're a pretty evasive fellow, aren't you, Mr. Rice?"

"No, I don't think so."

"Mr. Rice, listen to me. I'm here to help you, but you've got to admit to what you and I know is true. Your fantasy world is overpowering you till you can't accept the reality of the real world. Now it happens that I read *The Song of the Lark.*"

"Did you hanker to crawl in with the lark?"

"Rice, I'm the one who is asking the questions. Do I make myself clear?"

"You were, but I'd like you to answer mine now."

"Why?"

"Because it would give me a picture of my interrogator. You most probably did want to bed the lark, you know. After all we're males, and one of our greatest instincts is to impregnate. You know, I think I see my problem. I don't fantasize anymore. Reality absorbs me so completely, and I'm losing a battle with it, because I can't cut enough wood to sustain me and my family. All of me is so intent on splitting wood, falling trees, trying to be more efficient. You know, studying each move has made me a stumblebum. Do you get the picture?"

But he was leaving the room. I gathered that he was angry. I left too. I felt I was onto something that would help me. I came home on my bike feeling that perhaps I had a solution to my problem, but it was soon forgotten. For one thing I was behind a month on the land payment of thirty dollars. I tried to sell some more wood to the wholesalers, but times were hard. They wouldn't buy even at half price.

In Portland after I had left the psychiatrist I ran into Catherine McKenzie, an old friend from art school days. We shook hands but that didn't do it, so we rushed into an embrace. "Long time no see!" we exclaimed simultaneously, and we laughed. Meeting one another made us think of our mutual friend, Charles Heaney, a fellow art student—it was his favorite greeting.

Catherine and I had corresponded regularly in the twelve years I was in California. She wanted to know what I was doing now. We had coffee together and I told her about the psychiatrist and my problem of not being able to turn out enough work to pay for necessities. As always she was deeply interested. "It sounds rough," she said, "but everywhere it's rough now."

"It's rougher at the bottom," I informed her. As we parted, I said: "Stop out at the place sometime. Let's keep in touch." Meeting her buoyed me up quite a bit.

Talking with Catherine about the rough times made me realize again that I must make a payment on the land. Fearing that I would lose the place unless I saw the former owners and told them the why of it, I headed out one afternoon on our bike.

The road from Molalla to Silverton was being raised several feet with a deep ditch on each side to take care of the runoff. The unfinished surface was of heavy river gravel and round rocks as big as muskmelons. I banged around and through it and reached Silverton where the twin brothers who owned the land lived. They had closed their mill and for the time being were working for wages in a big mill at Silverton, baching there away from their families.

When I explained to them the difficulties that had kept me from paying, one of them said, "Well, we hoped you wouldn't pay. Played right into our hands. We wanted to get that land back, and here it is ourn again. You ain't carried out the contract and you're through."

"But I could pay in a month or two," I protested. "My wife has been sick and it's cost me plenty."

"Yep! That's the way it goes," the one who looked like the other one said. "It's hard on you, but it's swell for us. We found out after you took the place over that they's a big canyonside where we could quarry crumbly rock good for roadbeds. We found we could sell it to the county right off, but you was on there, so we bided our time, seein' you weren't built for the cordwood business. Now it's ourn by default!"

"What am I to do?" I wondered, believing that I was talking to myself, but the one who looked like the other one spoke up:

"You don't have to get off the place, Rice—at least not till fall. You can grow what you want on it and even cut cordwood up there where you are now in the big second growth. We want 'em off up there anyways 'cause right along in there is where our quarry is going to be, so we'll give you that break at least."

I must have looked despondent. "I know it's mean," the other one said, "but meanness will get a guy places, and mean we've decided to be from here on out. We're going to succeed in this world by using other men's sweat just like other men has used ourn, so no hard feelings. That's just the way she is. Well, so long! We got to get to a meeting."

They went toward the town's lights, shining dimly through fog that had come in with nightfall. Dully, I stood holding my bike. Some part of me was bringing stupor to my brain to shield me from the dismal facts.

Finally, I walked the bike up to the highway. Along it on both sides a few lighted houses indicated the invisible road. I pedaled down between them, but soon there were no more. I went on until they disappeared behind me in mist. I stopped, hoping my night sight would begin to improve, but it didn't. I'll wait longer, I thought, then make out the road. I waited, and what the twins told me came at me like a locomotive out of the dark. It roared into my consciousness: I'VE LOST THE PLACE! I LOST THE PLACE! I saw it all too plainly: the leaving of warm comfortable California to get eighty acres to work on, to really assert myself once more. Now I've lost it all.

I got on the bike thinking if there were stars I could guide myself with one of them—in a fog? I lit a match, held it over my head and saw that I was engulfed by fog so thick with moisture that the match went out.

I started out imagining where the road was and, sure of myself for awhile, following the road in my mind. I was sure I had the knack of it, when I suddenly plunged over the side and down into the draining ditch, with enough water in it to cover me completely. I had broken through the ice. I got the bike out of the water and somehow scrambled it and myself back upon the road. The front wheel rubbed on the forks, but it would go. I stood trying to figure out where the edge of the road was from where I fell in. I dragged the bike along the edge until I could be certain which direction it went and then, keeping that in my mind, moved slowly on.

Wringing wet and cold, I did not feel the shock of the water as I drove off the other side of the road after covering perhaps two hundred yards. I clambered up the bank and stood there wondering what in hell I should do—how could I beat this? In a fury I got back on again and rode down the center of where I thought the road was. I must have gone a half mile when one of those boulders deflected the bike. I lost my sense of where I was going and went headlong off the bicycle, crashed through the ice and bottomed out in deep mud with the bike on top of me.

I was some time getting up from this. My left hand was cut. I could feel the warm blood. I got up on the road, thick mud was on my back, my legs were encumbered with it and the cold water on stomach and chest made me tighten up against everything. The bike's front wheel had crumpled on the boulder. It would roll with a humping motion. I would have to walk to keep life in me and I must drag along the bike that my father had sent to me in California with the message that "it would keep me off the pavement when my shoes wore through." His note came to me with great clarity. I was bereft of anger toward him now.

"Keep kicking. Got about seventeen miles to go," I said, "not dead yet," and slogged along. There was nothing else to do. If it hadn't been for worrying about Nordi and Bunky, I'd have drowned myself in the ditch; but the feeling of responsibility, even in such a sodden, mud-smeared, anguished creature as I, was still in the shreds of my manhood.

I staggered on, pushing the wreck of the bicycle before me. After a mile or so I tripped and fell to my knees and stayed there, relaxed after a fashion in my icy clothes. But then I could think! I'VE LOST THE STUMP RANCH—OUR HOME!

"HOME, MY ASS!" I was yelling, "HOME FOR GUYS LIKE ME! SHIT NO!" And when the yelling stopped: "Not man enough to own a house," came quietly, implacably. "Guess that's right," I grieved and thought was silent for a small time. Then I struggled to my feet.

"Why am I always wrong?" I asked the night. "Why do I always grab the short one when fate holds out the straws?" I took up the bike again, dragging it on the edge to get my bearings as to the direction of the road.

•

Many hours later dawn made the dense fog a visible wall. I thought from my contacts with fences, signposts, culverts and bridges that I was nearing home. Soon I heard Lundstrom's hound bay off to the left. Stultified by my terrible loss and the beating I had taken from the Silverton road, I slogged on carrying or pushing the bicycle that had been given me as an insult on my thirtieth birthday. The fog and my bemused mind kept me dull to everything but the need to plug along. All night I'd kept headed toward home, toward Nordi.

Home, did I say? Homestead? Property? Land? That was far behind me now, vague as the fog. What I stumbled toward was a place to lay down my burdens, to find surcease in Nordi's presence, to sleep.

I staggered on and soon found a big gate. I felt of it. Yes! It was ours. I had made it. I felt for its yew wood bolt. Soon I found the house and laid down my bicycle and came into the house, into warmth.

When I told her many hours later of our loss, Nordi flinched as if she'd been stabbed. That part was my hell! But Nordi was Scandinavian and in a half-hour she was ready for whatever the future would bring us.

I could not work for over a week. The barbed wire that lines country roads had guided me home, but not without taking bits of flesh as payment for showing me the way.

While my hands were healing, Catherine McKenzie appeared, sans Cadillac. (Her father's firm had gone under in 1930.) A secondhand Chevy coupe was filling its place very well. She was concerned over the threadbare life Nordi must lead to qualify as Mrs. Rice. She had had a lengthy visit with Nordi before I arrived. They seemed to have some sort of an understanding, for I caught them looking knowingly at one another. "Just women stuff," Nordi remarked about it afterwards, and I didn't give it much thought.

Shamefacedly we hid the fact that I had lost the place. As Catherine was leaving, she remarked that her brother was still in excellent health. One of the two psychic healings that I did in my life was to cure her brother of something that had not responded to doctors' efforts. She always felt indebted to me because of this.

Catherine's outright honesty, intelligence, and uproarious laughter had made me seek her out as a friend in art school. She was ten years my senior. Ours was a platonic relationship, and I valued it highly. The meeting in the street and the coffee we drank together—well, I was glad that they happened.

On went the work in the big second growth woods that stood atop the quarry area. From there I could see down to the stump land, on the acre we had cleared for planting. Nordi helped me start the saw cuts on a half a dozen middle-sized trees. I laid about me with sledge and wedges and fury. Hope was gone—I'll never own this place. Anger was the force that drove in the wedges. My mouth was foul with loutish curses as I attacked each section of log. I was like some mad crusader of old amid saracens, splitting this log, chopping off limb stubs on that. Two tree trunks lay fallen next to each other. I trimmed off their limbs and sledged them open in a frenzy, often using my axe with such force it opened up log sections that I usually split with sledge and wedges. Often I lay panting, worn out, for rage drains away vitality while hope sustains it.

For several months Nordi had shown concern about my health and well-being and in spite of the doctor's opinion that I was in fine shape. Now, after breakfast, when I reached for my coat, she said: "Please don't go up there today. You've got over ninety cords seasoning. You need a rest."

"There's no room for holidays," I answered, "if we are ever to get out of this setup."

I started to put the coat on, but she jerked it out of my hands and ran out in the yard with it. Well, I caught her and she was so exciting in my arms that I agreed to do whatever she wanted.

Later, bundled up, for it was a cold and windy day, we were up in the cutover land just rambling. Sometimes we held hands as we went along, parting as brush interfered, then joining our hands once more.

"What shall we do," she said, "now that the land isn't ours anymore?" We slowed our walk to a stroll, swinging our linked hands as we went on, our glances met fleetingly.

"I don't know. They say there's infinite possibilities in this world, and I believe it, sure! But look, Nordi, I'm thirty-three years old and you know I've put everything—work, money, planning—into three big chances and now I've lost even this miserable stump ranch."

We had stopped and stood in a pocketful of clearing in the brush. We faced each other and then looked down at the sod where I was kicking into a molehill. "You know the rest. I've lost three good jobs besides, since I married you and I can't see where I screwed up on any of them."

"I'm still proud of you, Clyde."

"Yeah! You have to be off your rocker if you're proud of me. It seems I'm one of those unlucky ones. I tell you, Nordi—I'm scared! There's a good life out there somewhere, but I can't take chances anymore. Every time I bet myself against the world, I end up the fall guy."

"Maybe it's because you're not a believer. You see all the sides of what you take on. With you it's a gamble. You give it all you've got, but you can't put belief into it."

"Belief, yeah, redneck belief!"

We went on. We both felt we'd said too much, gabbled about eternal puzzles. We were too near the nitty gritty to do that without feeling terribly foolish. We tried to be light-hearted, but under the pressures of survival, carefree laughter seemed impossible, and then when we found fake laughter in our mouths, I pushed her down where last year's leaves had been blown into a fluffy pile against the fan-like roots of a fallen tree. I was rough with her, but somehow we got the impeding clothes away so that we could join, though it was barely possible. There was our clothing and the wind, and a great sogginess under the leaves, but frenzied response was our only defense against the cold, uncaring world—to hide in and to cling to one another. As we lay embraced, there was a constancy in her scrutiny, her survey of my eyes, that made me realize that her love was one of the few things in my life that couldn't be destroyed or driven away.

Next day we received a card from the owners of the eighty acres:

Dear Sir:

Don't cut anymore of that big second growth on the place. We started up our Otter Creek Mill again. Can cut and haul logs from there to the mill at a profit. Business is business,
    Louie

P.S. You can leave your cordwood where it is till selling time. It's safe in there.

I scouted around among the little farms and clearings in the woods, hoping to find some big, old-growth trees for sale. Stumpage, it was called, but none was available and the dragsaw was only a boon on big logs.

We lived for a couple of days without fantasies or goals. The loss of the land had set us adrift in many ways. Hopes, when they came, were stamped in the mud, as it were, with hoots of derision: yeah, yeah! I've been there before. It's all bullshit! Fate, I conceived of as a combination of my ineptness, my wrong choices and the difficult times and a feeling that whatever I did, or would do, would go wrong. It was a continual rage aimed at myself and the world, for now I had no work to hide in.

Nordi and Bunky and our animals were treasured, were worshipped. I mentally clung to them as fair islands in a sea of hopelessness. At night after supper I would leave the house and, looking south, would grasp the top rail of the fence and think of the less shabby conditions at the start of this degrading descent of mine. I would stare south, where far over many horizons, was our home at Waterspout Point, forgetting momentarily that I had lost it.

It became a habit. Often I'd stand there for hours. Late at night Nordi would come and lead me to bed. She was strangely silent about my vigils. Sometimes I would pound on the top rail of the fence, and sometimes I wept, but always I felt myself in the hands of fate. Maybe I'm going insane, I thought, and I would grab the rail tighter. Is fate going to try that on me? Well, it won't work! As long as I can wiggle, I am in some way my own man. But mostly I held onto the top rail of the fence because of the years of frustration, though I didn't know it.

We were sitting on the front porch of our rented abode wondering what to do. We had not spoken for an hour and were set to do more of it when Catherine arrived. We heard her coming toward us. Soon we could see the red of her coupe through the trees. A moment more and she was driving in as I opened the gate. She shut off the motor and stayed in the seat gazing at me.

"What brings you out so early?" I asked.

She still was looking me over rather severely, but her smile, always irrepressible, soon bloomed warmly, tolerantly, on me. "News," she said, "I bring some strange news," and stepped out of her car. Nordi was beside us. She kissed Catherine, who put her arms about Nordi. "For you, Nordi," she said, "it's very good news. Let's sit on your porch," she went on. "I need a glass of well water before I tell you what I've found out. Oh, my," she said, after she had quaffed the soft water. "When we were in the money (I mean Dad's land and bond business), I met and associated with a lot of people who had power in Portland, but in this particular mess I couldn't use them. Here I worked from the bottom up."

Turning to me, she said, "I found out that psychiatrist you talked to at the medical school was a phony and is completely discredited now. You didn't know that he sent a note to Nordi to come and see him about your case. You had evidently infuriated him. When she met with him he told her that from his study of you, he was sure you were a criminally inclined maniac and within three months you would go berserk and kill whomever was near and to keep axes and guns and knives away from you at all cost."

"I was furious at fate, not people," I said.

"He told Nordi that he could have you incarcerated, which he advised her to allow him to do by signing the necessary papers. He frightened her but she refused. When I came visiting she broke down and told me how things stood."

"Catherine talked me into taking one of her brother's revolvers," said Nordi, "And I hid it. Only for Bunky's sake would I ever use it."

"My God, honey!" I muttered.

"She's waited in love and terror through the last three months," continued Catherine. "This is the fourth month. There could be something wrong with you, Clyde—but, criminally insane, that's utter nonsense. Say, I brought some fixings for lunch. They're in the car. I'll get them," she said a bit stiltedly and left us. While she was gone we held each other tightly, that was all. It seemed to take care of what we needed at the moment.

After lunch she sat on the porch steps for awhile talking with us of mutual friends. Eventually she grinned up at us and said: "There's more, and I'm particularly proud of it. I wanted Clyde to have the best in assistance, and I'm almost broke. I saw I'd have to do it with the proverbial mirrors. Here's how it worked.

"I know a woman reporter—a sob sister, they call them—who owes me money. Now Sandra knows a judge, who for some withheld information (he didn't want to become news) owes her a good turn and the judge was a chum of Harry Kisdork's in college. Kisdork, in case you—well, out here you wouldn't know, has been lecturing at medical colleges across the country on the use of psychiatry on seemingly incurable cases of mumbletypeg, as seen among housewives and bird dogs. Do you understand, Clyde? Do you see what I've been up to?"

"Sorta."

"Then you'll see this really great psychiatrist?"

"I can't turn it down when you've gone to that much trouble. Maybe he can find out what's wrong with me."

"I have it all down on this card. You see him at one-fifteen Wednesday, Room 217, Medical College, and no fee, though he gets a hundred dollars an hour in his practice in Chicago. There's just one part of it that'll be hard for you, but I hope you go through with it. There's a class of about fifteen or twenty interns who've been attending his lectures and will be in on Kisdork's examination of you when you see him on Wednesday."

"Nordi and I don't even know what today is. Out here you lose track."

"Part of the 'being out in the sticks' syndrome, I'm told,"

murmured Catherine, and loudly, "Wednesday is tomorrow. Have you a way to get in?"

"Sure, on my bike. Catherine, you've brought us hope. How can I ever repay you?"

"Pay me? It's me who'll be eternally in arrears to you. Just remember what you did for my brother and shut up. Golly, though, this was one time when I worked the angles just like a real hustler."

A little before noon I was pumping up the medical school hill, my bike moving along easily on the secondhand wheels. A thick corned-venison sandwich was in a parcel lashed to the handlebars. My mind? Really I had it in neutral. I was trying not to think. To hell with opinions and beliefs. I had read a great deal of Freud and about him, and another gentleman I admired, who pushed the logic tight compartment concept. I was going to keep out of it this time, so I tried to affect more interest than I really had in the faces of people who passed by.

Eventually I was ensconced in a room with a score of pleasant looking young men, who smiled at me from behind their glasses. Then Harry Kisdork arrived with the man from the outer office. Kisdork was a squat man with long arms, big hands, a broad brow. His eyes were friendly and his lips were classic in chiseled contour, precise yet sensuous. All in all my impression was that he was one hell of a human being.

"Mr. Rice," he said, "I know about the lady reporter, my friend the judge, and how it was worked out. Your friend, Catherine, should be in business. She accosted me in the hall and told me how you helped her brother without religious cant and other things she felt I should know."

He turned to the young interns. "I'll expect a paper from you on this particular case.

"Mr. Rice, tell me about yourself. We have ample time to hear something of your life and the vicissitudes that brought you here. I understand that you were here before and were interrogated by a fraud. I'm sorry you had that experience."

"No, it was all right," I said. "I saw, while talking to him, that even my fantasies were completely involved in cutting cord-wood. I saw that was bad, but the immediacy of my problems took all my sap. I had no energy or will to become the person I once was. I was down to the simplest kind of survival."

"Would you give me a brief picture of your childhood and early years?"

"My childhood was the best part of my life. I purposely got myself expelled from high school. I was able to go to art school. There I met a girl, Nordi. I married her and quit the school, but not before I became involved with beauty and significance (what vague terms). Beauty and significance, and what you would call labor intensive work, have been the bases of my life. I have read much of the great literature of the world. I've done a few things, like Catherine's brother, that made me realize that we humans have many dimensions yet to be discovered. Religion uses these phenomena to bring in the tithe, not just the Christian religion, but all of them." Suddenly feeling myself a didactic fool, fury arose in me, but I hung on.

"Okay, here's a fair picture of what I did. After marriage we moved to San Francisco and I worked for my father there in an ill-conceived branch of his business. When his partner died, he closed the branch. He offered me a job if I would come to Portland and sell goods. He said he'd make me sales manager after one year. I loathed the idea and turned it down. Surely life could be richer than that.

"I got a job as a deckhand on the ferryboat that ran between Sausalito and San Francisco. Soon I was second mate. I did a few things that made me popular, saved some lives and other things, so that the president of the railroad came twice to chat with me. One day, walking up Market Street, I saw myself in a mirror. I was swaggering a bit, a twenty-five-cent cigar in my face. I looked self-satisfied, bovine. All I needed was a cud to chew. I quit the job at once, bought a half interest in a fifty-foot diesel fishboat and was doing very well fishing off the Mexican coast, when I found I had tuberculosis.

"The doctor told me to quit the sea and fishing. His reasons made sense to me, so I left the boat. And due to my contract with my partner, I also left the money I had in it. I was broke. Lots of food, a year's rest overcame the tuberculosis, but a year was gone from my life.

"This was in the bottom of the depression. I went back to the ferries and soon was promoted to superintendent. Then, along with most of the people in the railroad terminal's shops, I was let out. I got a job running a night launch carrying railroad crews across the Bay and eventually got bumped even from that—a seniority set-up. Two men shared my job.

"It has gone like that ever since. I've just lost eighty acres of stumpland. I thought it was my last stand. Still, I know I'll try again—something else—and lose again."

Kisdork spoke up, "Your Catherine told me what she knows about the goat milk deal. You've certainly had your share of ill luck, Clyde. Still, you're not alone with your many difficulties. Scores of my patients in Chicago were not able to cope with the depression because of temperament or accident or just facing a suddenly topsy turvy world."

"I welcomed it," I said. "It seemed a chance to meet the primitive world head on. I thought I could hold my own in a simple existence, but as you see I haven't been able to do that. That's why I'm here."

"Were there any problems in your sex life?" Kisdork asked.

"Nordi and I were virgins. I've removed a few more hymens and have been rather busy sexually. Women excite me and I love them very much. Some are unbelievably beautiful and women have a different way of looking at our problems. I think we need their viewpoint. We males have hogged the stage long enough."

"I agree with you," said Kisdork. "Clyde, what would you like to do in the future and, I mean, a future less bleak. What do you hope to do in, say, 1941?"

"Own some pleasant acres in clover by a brook and, though I'm ill-prepared for it, I want very much to be a writer."

The arrival of a very late and flustered intern broke in on what I was saying. The young men all moved around in their seats until the newcomer was settled, when Kisdork led off with: "This is what I see. Fundamentally, you've educated yourself and will for the rest of your life, but two things operate against you. In spite of yourself, you're becoming more intellectual, though still in love with the life and mental activity of sheepherders, loggers and poor farmers. I think that in a way you welcome adversity as a way of life. You feel that adversity is the true center of human activity. I don't think you can ever weld the two attitudes toward life together, at least to your satisfaction, and you'll always be at odds with yourself, and that's good.

"It's obvious your problem is not making yourself more efficient at cutting cordwood, but letting your mind range in the fields you've educated it in. Get a job. Leave cordwood production to somebody else. Your soul is complaining about the battle going on in your mind. Write out your problems in poetry. Let breadth be your way. Use your mind to its utmost. You've been short-changing it for years. If I had to split cordwood up in the woods, I know that I would come to pieces in short order.

"Now, one more question. Which would you rather have—an exquisite and remarkable wife or a bevy of beautiful willing girls—a harem? Which would you choose?"

"The other one," I answered.

"Sane!" Kisdork proclaimed loudly. "Sane, and you're also a philosopher," he said smiling at me.

There was a slight hubbub among the bespectacled young interns. Those who had them, tweaked their mustaches in approval.

Later, on my bicycle, coasting down off the hill, I was happy. But the job he spoke of? Who didn't want a job? Still, I was pleased, almost light-hearted. I phoned Catherine, but was told she was down at the coast.

At home, when I tried to tell Nordi of Kisdork's summation, she interrupted to tell me that my sister Val's husband, Bill, had been out while I was away. He thought he had a job for me. He had a contract with the federal government to make aerial photographic maps of much of the farmland of Idaho and Eastern Oregon—a New Deal wiggle of Roosevelt's. When I talked to Bill next day, he said he was fairly sure he could work me in with the ground crew, said he'd let me know in a week.

I wheeled over to Acme Flavoring and told Pop of my luck. He was sour, non-committal, and when I mentioned Kisdork, he sneered: "Materia medica of the mind!" and turned his back on me with a "Can't you see I'm busy?" He wasn't, but he was often like that.

I was glad to head back to Nordi, always to the haven of Nordi. Then, as always, I wondered why she didn't leave me—the Nordi who wanted things, the status symbol junk that her family and friends dusted three times a week.

Nordi and I were in a strange place, balancing between hope and fear, not trusting hope, because we had been so often fooled by it. Still disappointment had been ours too long and cynicism had too long been our armor to be quickly cast aside. Hope, however, like sunlight, came stealing in through the hinges and joinings of our armor and timid smiles appeared on our disbelieving countenances.

We said nothing about it to Bunky; in fact, we said little about it between ourselves. Cautiously we considered what we would do if a real honest-to-God job materialized. "We could . . ." materialized from my thoughts. Nordi looked up from her mending at the sound, but carefully did not respond to it.

Yeah, we could . . . what? Well, we could move away from here, away from the eighty acres that were no longer ours. We could sell our cordwood, say goodbye to our faithful truck where it slumbered in the gully, look sadly at the land we had cleared and find another life. Perhaps such thoughts were in Nordi's mind too, but we went to sleep keeping our hopes and plans for the future to ourselves. Which was just as well, for the future had plans of its own.

II

In Which
I Save and Am Saved by Acme Flavoring,
Become a Misfit in Suburbia,
Solve a Problem by Assaulting Some Lawn Chairs,
and
Begin to See Virginia

1936

Edla, NORDI'S MOTHER and my semi-nemesis, had been born by a lake in Sweden and could row a boat, a thing I always tried to remember when her lack of mental dimension appalled me. Before she had been married quite a year, her husband was killed in a grain elevator fire and she, heavy with child, had been left to face the world. After the birth of her daughter, Tekla, she got a job with John Nordstrom, a widower with six children, some of whom were almost her own age— pleasant, cow-like creatures—twice her size, with half her acumen. Edla fed and dressed them and taught them cleanliness, particularly between the legs, and that God frowned on too much learning. She also beseeched them to learn a trade like nursing and that men were—humph! Humph was the sound that accompanied her negative view of men. Men were, well—humph, incapable of much except drinking and pruncing. Pruncing, she would admit to the young ladies, was usually effected on a bed.

Mr. Nordstrom soon married her. He knew a good thing and, before long, she bore Olga and then my Nordi, whom, even now, they still kept calling Evelyn. (People at times are so obtuse.) Olga was prettier than Nordi; she was the perfect daughter and became in time the perfect lady who liked to picnic and camp. Slenderer than Nordi or her mother, she took after her father, the dignified Mr. Nordstrom, who Edla, after she had gained enough control, forced to smoke his cigars in the basement.

Men—humph! The strange thing about the old girl's dismay with the other half of the human race was that, though she pointed with scorn at each of our many foibles, she really felt herself closer to men than to those "prissy sit-on-a-cushion women." "I'd like to stick them with a darning needle somewhere where it would do the most good, especially those with that fat rear on 'em. Sitting on your rear end too much in the long run makes it squash out."

One Sunday old lady Nordstrom arrived with her tribe, curiosity having got the better of her. She had to know how her daughter Evelyn fared with that scoundrel. One look from Nordi and I knew I should keep quiet about our troubles.

Jack looked around cynically and snickered when he had seen where we had been working. Irish, he saw a joke in a bit of slang that was prevalent at the time: "You sure have to stir your stumps out here to bring in the beans. Don't you?"

No one got it but Nordi and I. While the rest of the family looked askance, Mrs. Nordstrom demanded if that was something dirty. Teddy, on the other hand, was very sympathetic. He'd been a woodsman in his youth. He left his family to stand rather close to me. "That's a beautiful axe you have there," he said of my swamper.

Tek and her daughters, Dory and Virginia, were gone, looking for a big pond that was on the place. Old lady Nordstrom frowned and made disparaging remarks at the house, the barn and the well, and when one of the pigs squealed, went into a tizzy about the dangers of pork. When Tek's two girls came back and began playing with the piglets, Grandma was going to leave at once and take the clan with her, but they calmed her down with some of Delia's thick cream in her coffee. It soothed her and they all had another cup.

Olga and the girls announced that they'd come out to go swimming, that the girls thought the pond looked dangerous with the sunken logs in it and a very marshy, muddy bank.

"Let's take our picnic down to Milk Creek," said Olga. "I know a Finnish family who owns property there. It's only a mile or so. You too, Ev and Clyde—a swim will do you good. How about it?"

Teddy wanted to stay and fall a couple of trees with me but Tek objected: "What are we going to do while you're doing that? Please, Teddy, come along."

I saw the look she gave him then. Good God! It was loaded with love. It's her eyes, I thought, suddenly seeing Tekla in a different light. Such loving eyes—how lucky Teddy is, I thought. Strange I hadn't noticed it before—and, turning, saw Virginia, the older daughter, glancing my way with the same long lashed eyes and was startled. Can forthright Swedes look like this, I wondered?

Nordi hustled Bunky and me into one of the cars. The Nipanens welcomed us with strawberries and had their daughters pick a fine bowl of them to put on the picnic table they had for visitors. Milk Creek ran through their hundred acres. The women had covered the table with the fixings for a fancy picnic lunch set for fourteen. After we had eaten, Mrs. Nordstrom prepared yet another gallon of coffee for when we got out of the water and everyone began getting into swimming suits behind bushes.

The creek along where we were was fast and about shoulder deep. We all swam, Grandma making slow progress with her dog paddle across the stream. I tossed in an old red tobacco can full of gravel at the beginning of a rapids and the fast current swept the can down where we could see it glimmering. Then we started plunging in to grab it as we were swept past. I was able to get down near it and hang onto some underwater rocks, but when I tried to make a pass at it, I was quickly jerked into the pool below. It was fun!

It was early summer, so Milk Creek was cold and soon everyone had given up and gone to lie in the sun, except the Bromses' older daughter and me. Now, Virginia was extremely shy, her diffidence stemming from her family's general reticence in the clan's affairs. On them Grandma's thumb was successful practically all the time, but of all the relatives Virginia loved the water most, not spectacularly, but water seemed to engulf her lovingly. She didn't plunge in, she slipped in. Anyway, Ginny and I, though we knifed in, were swept by the twisting currents past the can. There happened then a most minuscule camaraderie born of our laughing pique at the way the crosscurrents defeated us.

At last, when thoroughly frozen, we gave up and, when I lay down on my blanket on turf at the pool's edge, Virginia lay down on it beside me. Virginia's mother saw and, gathering the rest of the group around, they came over to observe this stupendous phenomenon. To the exclamation of all, she hid her head but stayed where she was. After they left, going back to their eating again and the slicing of pies, our eyes chanced to meet and Virginia smiled a little smile that admitted to herself and me that she had done a very daring thing and that she liked it. She had become a long, bony creature. Except for two small but very satisfactory buttocks she looked like a deprived child, but I liked that smile and the awakening presence that was behind it. Still, my interest was hardly more than casual. Only later did I realize that this pleasant day at Milk Creek was the beginning of something that would affect all of us in ways we couldn't have imagined.

A few days later, my sister Valerie stopped by to tell me that Bill had left for Montana. "He told me to write him, care of the Staghorn Hotel in Missoula," she said. "Looks like he's getting more territory to map. The pilot and cameraman for the Montana mapping came down really hard, Bill said. The plane is a wreck and the mapper's doing nicely in the hospital at Helena. You'll get that job," she went on. "I'm sure of it, and it'll be fun to have you near after all these years."

I absorbed the certainty in her voice. We smiled at each other. "That's great," I remarked. "I haven't had my hopes confirmed like this for a long time."

"By the way," she added, "before I forget, Pop called to say he wants to see you the next time you come into town."

I was surprised. "Last time I talked to him he showed an uncommon lack of interest in me."

"You owe him money, Clyde. I did once. He handles a mean cold shoulder."

A few days later, pedalling my bike into town, I kept wondering what Pop could want. As soon we met, however, I could see that he was in his salesman mode. My father had a strange habit while making a sale. He would work to get the proprietor away from his cash register or office and, preferably alone, into the man's warehouse or loading platform, where Pop would point out that, to both of them, "time was valuable." Sometimes he'd say that "time is money," which he hoped would make the owner feel important. If Pop had a hunch the proprietor was related to or had a friend who was a lawyer, time was always "of the essence." He'd then inform the man that, because of this, what he had to say must be brief and concise. Here he would smile the grin of a conspirator and let the proprietor in on the deal, while all the time gazing with heavy-lidded world-weary eyes at the gentleman's nose. He would step back from his stance too close to the man and size him up, as if he were going to club him with an until-then undisclosed fact; or, coming close, he would tap the customer on the shoulder as he went on with his spiel, but always continuing his weary-eyed assessment of the other's nose. His methods worked, I guess, for he and his company and his family had thrived.

So I knew he had some proposition to sell when he arranged things so that we were at the far end of the building, appraising stacks of gilt edged cartons. And, sure enough, he turned on me and sized me up.

"See here, Clyde, I want to talk to you. You haven't even paid the interest on that loan I handed you for your goat shenanigans. Now I need money, and I mean I need money! I'm going to have to buy out the Cramers' family interest in Acme or go broke. It may seem funny to you, but Acme Flavoring Company can't support two families anymore. If the Cramers are out of it, I can take bigger chances. It'll be hell, but I think I could make it if I'd cater to creameries, bakeries and candymakers wholesale. Seems it's the only way for me to pull us out. The small bottle goods for the grocer that we dealt in is through. With the depression still hanging on, people are buying cheap junk flavors. I can't compete 'cause I won't peddle crap to the public."

Pop in a jam! Acme Flavoring about to go down—the stable pillars of my childhood, toppling? My caution disappeared.

"I'll sell what cordwood's left, Pop. I could get twelve dollars a cord later; but now, well, I think I could get ten. Two dollars out of that ten goes for trucking, so I figure seven times a hundred and fifteen—say, seven hundred and fifty dollars I could get for you in two weeks, even if the peddling goes slow. And the job with Bill is coming up; Valerie was pretty sure of it. That's the best I can do, but remember we have to eat and pay rent somehow if Bill's job for me doesn't pan out."

"Jesus," my father said, glaring at me in quick fury. "They say a man will grab at a straw if he's drowning, and I believe it, but you're a piss-poor straw, son. You've only been a fart in a gale of wind since you got too good for that steady job on the ferries you had. Look," he said, the exasperation fading from his face, "don't join up with Bill yet. Sell your cordwood in a hurry. I need the money. Say! You ought to be able to peddle quite a bit of it yet today." He spun on his heel. I heard the front door slam and, though I hurried out too, he was up the street a block, driving away as I emerged to hop my bike.

Now, I've been around, but this sudden twist from the slow heavy movements of wood cutting and the slow agony of failure, this unexpected turn of things was quickening my step. Look lively, fella! But why? To pay my debt, yes, but something far more subtle and exciting were hope and a changing future. In my inner self I was at this moment exchanging the sledge hammer and blasting iron for lighter instruments. What they would be I could only guess, but I knew of myself that from now on I must be—well, brisk!

I got on my bike, sped out into the suburbs and sold people their winter's wood four months before they needed it, but cheaper, and avoided the words "big second growth," even if they started to talk in such terms. I was able to sell for immediate delivery thirty-seven cords before I turned and pumped my way toward the village of Wendel, where nearby on the Johnson place waited my family. I said little, either from superstition or fear that if I said too much, I'd tip over the applecart. Nordi, who is part me as I am part her, forbore questioning me. Our loving, after Bunky had kissed us and wended his way to bed, was not as angry as it had been; despair no longer rode our hungers.

Early the next day I saw my woodhaulers and gave them the addresses of the buyers, and explained that I was going to sell all I had at once. They agreed to deliver it as quickly as they could. On the east side and on the west side of the river I chose my customers and told them of the beautiful wood, the crashing of tall trees, the ring of steel on steel as the wedges were driven in to open up the trunks, how the wood would keep them warm come winter. Three days I peddled my bike through the streets and avenues of Portland's suburbs till the wood was sold. At the end of the week I was able to hand Pop a third of the small sum I promised and two weeks later brought the sum up to seven hundred dollars, keeping fifty dollars for food.

Bill was still in Missoula. He wrote that he had a definite place for me, and as soon as he got back, I would start earning wages. Valerie said from Bill's letters she felt certain he would be back within a week. When the Montana addition to his contract came through, he would be a very busy man in those short months when the crops would show up on photographs taken from the air, but I couldn't live long on promises.

My father turned up one morning not long after Bunky left for school. He was smiling, though again I saw it was one of those he used on customers. "You sold all your wood?" he asked.

"Sure, I sold more than I had. Come on in! It's a chilly morning."

Nordi brewed more coffee and we chatted, but it was obvious that he was looking Nordi and me over carefully, speculating as to where we fit into his scheme of things. As we sipped our coffee, he mused, "I s'pose you're wondering, as I am, why I came out here. I've been up all night going over things. I made my proposition to the Cramers yesterday, and they were not surprised. They knew it couldn't go much farther the way it's been going. We had come to some open agreements. I aim to use everything I've got and can lay hands on to swing this deal before Acme Flavoring Company, small as it has gotten, founders.

"Not so many years back I had twelve salesmen selling western goods to the East. We had a man in St. Louis. But the way of selling groceries has sure changed. The men me or my salesmen dealt with—well, over half of them have retired, and their kids have got big ideas. They talk of running three stores instead of one, and they want half of my and every other supplier's profit. Fine produce is taking one hell of a beating. How often do you see Crosse and Blackwell's pickled walnuts on a condiment shelf? These days they're trying to do it with pickled string beans, but you can't pickle a string bean and make it taste like a pickled walnut.

"Anyway, I didn't come out here to talk about that. I've got to get everything that's owed me, every last cent, to handle this deal. You're my biggest debtor. You still owe me a little over four thousand and I got a way you can pay it back. You, son, can be my shipping clerk, delivery man and maker of the extracts. Nordi can bottle, label and carton the goods. The Little Lady can take care of the office with a girl to help her. Then me and Johnny Lind, our only salesman, can meet the trade and, between us, somehow cover our three-state territory. A hundred dollars is all I can pay you two together and fifty of that will go on your debt to me and you'll have to stay alive as best you can on the other fifty. Think about it. I got to know in an hour."

"Isn't there something else?" I asked.

"Yes, you're right. If we make it, and I believe we will, your wages will be commensurate with the volume of business we get."

I looked at Nordi. "We'll have to talk it over with Zaddie. Just give us ten minutes." So we went out to the barn and, fondling

Zaddie's velvety ears, we agreed that this might be, in the long run, a tangent from the way things had been going.

Pop needed us at once, ("At once means now to me" was vintage Pop) and he provided us with a low-floored dray for our move. We were able to hitch our old trailer to the dray and, though Zaddie and Bedelia weren't wild about the idea, they could be prodded into it with a bribe of oats. A couple of fellows came to buy the dragsaw.

Again we moved our dozen chickens and all the whole caboodle that we moved up from California—we moved back to the environs of Portland—a place on Mount Scott fitted to our needs, and now we had the use of the company car to get around in. Most firms use a delivery vehicle for transporting goods but they used a Chevy sedan for their deliveries, typical of the lax way they ran their business. The understanding about the use of the delivery car was that Pop would pay the gas, not only in business hours, but also on weekends for trips of short duration.

The office and mixing room were opposite each other in the fore part of the Acme Flavoring building. There was a loading platform and an area for box material out back and a long room for the bottling and labeling. The rest of the building was a scattering of labels, bottles, cartons, glue and the stock of bottled goods on hand. The goods were put up in various sizes from two ounces to gallon bottles. Still there was a lot of space left in which to produce disarray of a high order. It was inconceivable that with a combined crew of twenty-five people, including the salesmen, they had been able to operate year after year from such a mess.

I soon saw that, beside doing my regular work, I would somehow have to organize the place, so I designed a long, complicated cabinet with compartments for every packet of labels, every bulk container of cartons, in such a manner that they were protected from dust and dampness and could be found at once. I wangled enough plywood and other lumber to construct it. Meanwhile, Nordi bottled, labeled and cartoned the grocery trade extracts, and I carried out what I was hired to do and worked every possible moment at reorganizing the place.

I'd be hard put to explain Acme Flavoring Company and myself without a consideration done in a very delicate manner of my father's third wife, the Little Lady. I've never had an enemy like her. She had married my father after divorcing her husband, who she felt wouldn't fill the bill to carry out the one goal she had in her life—to wit, to raise her baby daughter in a manner that would ready her for the good things of life. Her baby daughter was an exquisite infant in every way, but had been born cross-eyed, a condition later corrected by minor surgery. However, the intense dedication cast into the Little Lady's mind before the corrective surgery was to stay the rest of her life, even when the need for it no longer existed.

She married my father when he was on crutches and at least twenty years her senior, first because she liked him a great deal (she was in his employ) and also because he seemed stable, a platform from which to start her daughter's upward movement. Jim Rice and Acme Flavoring Company were in her hands when I turned up—an only son, a ne'er-do-well—and in her extremely conservative mind was a fright that I might also have ideas. I was conceived of as a possible danger for her daughter's well-being.

She sent away for a brother, Ernest, who was having difficulty in the town where he was employed. Ernest was a kindly man and his kindness had gotten him in a jam where he worked as a superintendent in a toy factory. The only way he could extricate himself from the situation was to leave. He was to take my job supposedly because he was an engineer, as I was not. He appeared on the scene, pencil behind his ear, two slide rules in his pocket, and began working to worm me out. Ernest's attempts to root me from my job were funny and I found that he was stupider than I.

Several months went by. We were living and paying rent with the fifty dollars a month we received. In fact, with the venison and a pig we raised, now salted down, we were adequately, often sumptuously fed. We brought our chickens in from the stump ranch, the ones we brought from California, and they and their offspring gave us eggs without end and fryers. We had planted a garden. Everything came up in abundance. We would have green peas in another week. We were providing green stuff for my father's table and the Nordstrom clan.

Nordi was in her glory. Whether at her bottling and labeling vanilla or rooting around in the rich loam of her garden, she was smiling, not just with her face but all over. The starched skirts of her uniforms were whisked around gaily as she trotted about her duties. Even her garden overalls failed to obscure her joyous femininity.

Bunky didn't like the city school as he had the single-room country one. After his first six years with only grownups to fraternize with, young companionship was what he hungered for. Now he brought his friends up home to ride a coasting wagon I'd made for him. It was made with big sponge-rubber washers in a manner that kept every part isolated from every other. Whatever ruts and bumps the wheels encountered on their long rush from way above us to the mailbox far down on the county road, the wagon literally floated. It was quite an ingenious setup. It could carry three boys, and how they whooped as they sped down the steep curves to the road. Bunky had become popular. It was good to see.

He came out to meet us one evening when we picked him up at the sitter's. I could see he had something on his mind. "Pop," he said, when at last we were in the house, "we know about being hungry, don't we?"

"Well, I don't think you do. We always had enough for you, didn't we?"

"No, Pop. When I saw you and Mom going without, I didn't eat all I wanted. I was in on it too."

"I should have gotten government help, Bunky. I'm ashamed."

"No. The way we did it was okay. Anyway, there's two girls at school need milk."

"How do you know?"

" 'Cuz I heard Miss Teazel tell the principal. They've got

Bright's Disease, she said. They're sisters and their folks can't afford milk everyday and Zaddie gives two quarts a day."

"Do you want to take milk to school for them?"

"It would get warm and sour, Pop. I figured it out. We got to lend them Zaddie."

Well, I thought I'd better check it out. After all, Zaddie was a very dear member of the family. Mr. Norton, the girls' father, seemed a respectable family man down on his luck—back trouble. For years he'd been a clerk for a firm that went broke in '29. He found work with the WPA. There he stumbled and hurt his back shoveling sand after a month on the job. That was two years before. He now received a pittance from the WPA. He still couldn't work. His wife was a zero in gingham; their daughters were sickly. I figured the wife had enough on the ball to milk a goat, so we brought Zaddie over—"as a loan," we pointed out emphatically.

Bunky came home one day two weeks later with news: the little girls hadn't been to school for several days. A sickening hunch hit me. I went over to their place after work. The house was quiet and no one answered my knock. The neighbor hailed me and explained that they'd been thrown out, for they had never paid rent on the furnished house. Before they left Mr. Norton had dug a pit in the backyard with that weak back of his. There they barbecued Zaddie for a party he threw for his friends before leaving the state.

Good God! Zaddie slaughtered! To me it was deliberate murder, but no one knew where they had gone, which was a good thing for both of us, as I could have ended up in the penitentiary. Zaddie gone! It was very hard for me to absorb, harder, I think, than for Bunky and Nordi. Zaddie, with more character than four average people, was now only a memory!

We had been working for my father over a year and it was winter again. Christmas was past; we were in the dead time before spring. Johnny Lind, our salesman, could drum up few sales. Johnny was a Scotchman and proud of his thrift and honesty. He was not on pure commission but was assured of a certain amount plus expenses. This had been cut to the bone. Now he and the Little Lady went round and round as she tried to lower the percentage of his commissions to a point where he could not operate. Johnny Lind and my father had great respect for one another and manly fondness, but because of unfair incursions that the Little Lady made in Johnny's paycheck, Pop and Johnny were at odds and the trust that they had in each other was sorely tried. The business was not paying for the buyout. My father's plan to shift the making of flavors for the grocer's shelf and the retail customer to making flavorings for bakers, candy-makers and creameries was not as yet profitable. It looked like the company was going under.

Pop and the Little Lady decided to sell the building, which was well built and in a good location. They could move out into the sticks and buy a cheaper building with some rental space in it beside their own place of business. At the other end of our block the Volunteers of America had a home and playground for unfortunate children and they were interested in expanding. The two old ladies who ran it eyed our building. Pop asked them in. The looked around but couldn't make up their minds. We were going to have to make up their minds for them—but how? I thought I had a way to handle the problem and luck was with me. Pop had gone to Salem to deal with a couple of big customers and the Little Lady went with him for the ride.

Nordi and I were left to hold down the fort. I decided to do a stunt I had done in San Francisco to get a real low price on a bunch of hardware, and being somewhat equipped for the role, to act the simpleton son of a customer whose account was in arrears.

I went around to the Volunteers of America office and told the good ladies that my father and his wife were away and, if they would come on over, I would show them the values and the defects of the building. Somehow I hit just the right tone—a stupid amiability—and they came. We went through the building with the proverbial tweezers. The defects that I pointed out were minor. The big beams that held the roof had longitudinal cracks in them, but were not weakened by the cracks. I pretended that I thought they were, but the ladies knew enough about structures to know better.

Once decided, they showed a desire to get the deal done that same day. I caught my father at Peerless Creamery and told him of the deal and that he should hurry back as the buyers wanted to sign the papers that day. The odd thing was that Pop and the Little Lady were furious. This was the first time they were to show this strange attitude. For days afterward they would barely speak to me.

Finally, out on Southeast Belmont, we found a building with a great deal of plaster fallen from the walls and ceiling because of a leaky roof. We put on a new roof and I taught myself to plaster and was able to repair the building. It had two other occupants—a shoe repair shop and a small neighborhood grocery.

Eventually, winter could no longer produce the sterner stuff. Spring came. Pop's efforts in wholesale extracts began to pay off. We still had a lot of grocery trade, but it was the twenty- and fifty-gallon barrels going out that really helped. Then we started selling pure vanilla in small three-gallon oak kegs with a plum-wood spigot. I coated the kegs with heavy dark varnish. They went over big. Each customer owned his own keg and was proud of it. From a bottle, vanilla was a flavor, but from his own rich looking little keg, it was a gift from the gods—an elixir. This helped us out of the doldrums. That year we did very well. With the rearrangements that I had made we were much more efficient, though it seemed that Pop and the Little Lady hated every improvement and, when it worked, accepted it with reservations that lasted for years. The increased wages we were to receive if the company prospered came niggardly when they did come, but now we were tied to Acme Flavoring Company. How, I still don't understand, but we were. It seemed to have a future for us. I was given to understand that I would run the business with the Little Lady taking care of the books and that he would soon retire. He was sixty-two and on crutches.

About this time, too, we had to leave the Mount Scott place, since the owners planned to do some remodeling to the house. Our next move was to a house on Interstate Avenue in Portland. It was a noisome place—bordering a main thoroughfare—and too close to the city for me, but it gave Nordi a chance to be closer to the Nordstroms. We had no garden now, and she would often walk over to her mother's house at dusk. Olga and Jack lived with her, and there were always friends in and eternal coffee klatches with gossip dear to Nordi's heart.

As for me, it was here on Interstate Avenue that whatever talents I had reached their peak. Now in the evening I had time to do whatever I wanted. I remembered the psychiatrist Kisdork's dictum: "Let your mind range in fields you've educated it in. Get a job. Write out your problems in poetry. Use your mind to its utmost. You've been short-changing it for years." And what my mother said to me as she lay dying: "Cut a broad swath, my dear."

These phrases had been imprinted indelibly in my mind. Now I was in a position to respond to their clarion calls. I responded quite timidly, I admit. Neither my materials nor my mind were equipped to make heroic responses to these urgings, but rather to make muted echoes of them.

I made my son a carpenter's bench with two vices and sufficient drawers and a heavy broad top on which to manfully smite wood. He was enthusiastic and very pleased with it, fiddling around on it with a carving set Nordi had given him, but really my son at that early age proved he was not a smiter of wood. He preferred things with moving parts—engines, if you will—so I used his bench and some wood, rather deftly if I do say so. But broad swath? Not by this midget.

We had heard of some flat crocks—bedwarmers they were, squat and nicely glazed that one filled with boiling water, corked and slipped between the sheets. They warmed the bed much longer than hot water bottles and certainly were more pleasing than hot bricks. Passing the kilns one afternoon I drove in and bought two for one dollar and asked for and was presented with some of the clay that they used in their wares.

At home several days later I began making a lounging figure of one of the pigs that we had raised, fondled, and eaten, and I got Nordi to pose for a seated figure to be a bookend. We were happy with the result and made a gelatin mold from it that came out badly. I wanted to do a rubber mold of the original, but Bunky, thinking I was through with the clay, worked it all up into a birdbath, well-designed, but too big to bake in the oven. The bookends from the gelatin mold were certainly second rate, but they got me planning to do more modeling with clay.

Also, I was up to making some intricately carved picture frames that I covered most carefully with gold leaf. They dignified three pictures that Nordi had painted while in California. Goldleafing over intricate surfaces for a guy who had never been particularly dexterous presented a problem, but when the frames were done Nordi was delighted; and where there was a gold leaf mistake I found that you could cover it with another gold leaf without the sense of impasto. Broad swath! Sweet mother! I hope you can now see that I'm not up to it.

Nordi and I had avoided our old art school friends when we came back to Portland. Our clothing was wretched. We couldn't ask anyone to have dinner with us, for we needed whatever food we had to sustain us. When Catherine hunted us up and helped us so marvelously, we found we had to be cool to her overtures for a deeper friendship, for we couldn't repay in kind. We hadn't yet found our friend, Heaney, so we were in a position where relatives from whom we couldn't hide our condition were our only social outlets; but my father and his wife were a couple of sticks. Their life was from nine to five, then they went home and hibernated. She cooked, they ate, he even watered the lawn, but they did these things as if they were operating on twelve heart-beats a minute; so to bed. In the morning he bathed, climbed into his suit, tied his tie, buttoned his vest, shook himself. His eyes brightened as he became once more J. M. Rice. They left the baby daughter with the Little Lady's mother and headed for Acme Flavoring Company and life.

They had two sets of friends who sometimes called on them in the evening. These people fitted perfectly into a framework that

I have just described. The women, Lillian and Thelma, were people with whom the Little Lady had worked before she had come to Acme. Their husbands were singularly dull, not even enlivened by a religious mania, political interest or sexual quirk. We could not fit in with their friends. When we were alone with Pop and the Little Lady one evening, they beset us with arguments about why we should become Christian Scientists, which, by the way, killed my mother and would kill my father and my two sisters, each with a different form of extreme medical neglect. We saw my parent and his lady eight hours a day—that was more than enough—so we followed Nordi's desires and flitted on the outskirts of Mrs. Nordstrom's tight little clan. We did this of necessity, for whether one likes it or not, man is a social animal. Still, for my wife and me, even semi-compatible members of the race were hard to come by.

As I've mentioned, the Nordstrom clan insisted on calling Nordi "Evelyn." I had named her Nordi way before we were married. Couldn't they see that for years she'd been queen of Waterspout Point and was a dead shot, and that, when in our small open boat we were caught in a sudden storm out in the Golden Gate, she faced it with a grin that the cut of storm-driven spindrift could not erase? She was my well-rounded lovely, my own little Pee-ang, but she was becoming in time among these Swedes that resurrected creature of the adenoidal past, Evelyn. She bore up under it with equanimity, while I, who had made her a thousand lovely names, hated the damned name Evelyn and felt I'd been foully treated. This Evelyn stuff could be legal all right, but there's something to *fait accompli*. They were taking her back as an Evelyn, not adding to but making a hole in that marvelous accumulation, Nordi.

One day I felt sullen about this—and I mean sullen—and I left them to get drunk. Having accomplished that, I drove over to my father's house and found them unexpectedly gone. What I did next I know only from the accounts of the neighbors, who were happy to inform my father of his son's drunken behavior. Apparently, I worked the screws and hinges loose from the basement window, got in and opened up the house and came out, took all the lawn furniture to pieces, wrapped it up in bundles, put it down the basement window, stored it, locked up the house and drove away. A half an hour later I came back, worked the screws out of the basement window, brought up all the lawn furniture, put it together just as it had been, locked up the basement window and drove away again. I know of no relationship between the word *Evelyn* and my father's lawn furniture, but there must be one, for after that I was able to accept the name without shuddering.

After several weekends on Milk Creek, Mrs. Nordstrom and Olga, who was her mother's lieutenant, decided that the family should camp at Dodge Park on the Sandy River. The plan was that, while the women stayed at the Park, we men would go back and forth in one car to our various city jobs. After a sweaty day in town we would return to a cool swim in the river and with ravenous appetites consume the smoke-flavored dinner cooked over the campfire, then an evening around the fire and so to our tents.

There were two pools in the Sandy River at Dodge Park. The lower one was more constricted and deeper than the other. We preferred it. On the day that it was my turn to provide transportation, I hid two gallons of concentrated red food color that had developed mildew in the bottles' necks. We were going to throw it out, but I took them secretly to Dodge Park. Hurrying before the others, I ran down and dumped the red dye in our favorite pool, then stirred it up by swimming around and splashing until the pool was a bloody-looking mess. I waited for the family to come over to the ballgrounds toward the bank of the pool. I spied on them and when they were about to look down into the pool, I dove under and stayed down as long as I could, then came to the surface yelling: "Help me, help me! Help me get him out. Man's been bitten by an enraged salmon."

They all rushed in to do what they could for the poor fellow— that is, for the half a minute before they realized the absurdity of it and ran me out of the pool and up the road.

Today if you were to dye a pool of a tumbling river scarlet, you'd be in trouble with the environmentalists. Most people leave such mischievous stunts in childhood, but I am certain I will carry the tendency to my grave. It is more than that. My great joy is to get a group of people or a single individual so prepared by shock or months of instruction that for a moment they are completely confused and accept an absurdity as truth.

Since the diving for the tobacco can, the family was forever urging Ginny to accompany me on whatever chore I set out or was set out to do: to get ice at the park store where we were picnicking on a scorching day or to drive to the next burg for more beer and ice cream or pop for those who held strong feelings against alcohol. She came along, smiling her shy secret smile, and with the family I saw that this was good for Ginny, that our friendship would break through her shyness and reserve. Sure, I wanted to help her. Some part of me, however, noticed that this skinny young girl had beautiful eyes that hinted at lavender or light purple, but were neither color. When Olga gave a recital for the parents and friends of her piano pupils, Doris and Virginia were among those who played, and I suffered actual pain when Ginny struck a wrong note. I believe I suffered more than she, but I never asked myself why. I wanted to do things for her that perhaps I should have done for Nordi.

When fall came and school started and the sun no longer warmed the mountain streams so that we could dally in their pools, I gave Ginny this verse:

> Oh, yesterday had summer air
> And though today the scene is fair,
> The wind is keen and golden leaves
> Are floating down upon the sheaves.
> And in this time of changing seasons
> With loss of rhyme and birth of reason,
> When joy is shoved back on the shelf
> And all we think is food, clothes, pelf,
> There is no hint, no hope, nor maybe
> We're going to lose our gay Broms baby.

Yes, now each night she'll spin and spin
A cocoon that is soft and thin
Around her ears and over her eyes,
Around her shoulders, waist and thighs
She winds the stuff that we can't see
And then pulls in the end that's free.
It would be awful to behold
If she had sealed herself in gold
But with the stuff she uses now
We still can gaze upon her brow
And though I'm sad, I still must say
It might be worse some other way.

After she read it, she was delighted. It was radiant in her face. With her shy smile she murmured: "I think you like to watch me." I was about to reply when she said, "Don't you?"

"Yes," I said, "you are a slow-growing flower and I watch you grow."

"Flower?"

"Yes, to me, a very beautiful flower."

Shyness and surprise supplanted her smile and she turned from me.

I had made a toboggan while we lived at the stump ranch. It was useful in hauling hay, but we also did jumps with it. Now I wanted to make one for Ginny. I used hickory and had a devil of a time, steaming and bending the curved front part. Still, I had it ready for Christmas.

After Christmas Ginny's father returned it to me saying it was too nice a gift for a kid. I got him to take it back for the use of all the kids, for he had a good place to keep it, but I told him that we must allow Ginny to be bossy about it when, after supper, the kids and sometimes we older ones too joined in hurtling down the long hilly streets that glistened under the arc lights.

The relationship that the family forced on me had now become the order of things. A great happiness came to me when Ginny was around. If she was in the same house with me, a small elation was mine. We seldom looked directly at one another and when we did, she smiled and I was in heaven. A fifteen-year-old girl, who had only a slight notion of the joy I knew when I was near her—what was the matter with me? I had a lovely wife to whom I owed several lifetimes of loyalty after the bitter poverty I had dragged her through. I worshipped Nordi and sexually she was a dozen women in one and now, since I had taken her away from Art at gunpoint, she was mine, all mine.

By this time I was beginning to realize that I could never fit in with either family or their friends, as other members were able to. I was an outsider because of my agnosticism and my radical views. Years before I'd had a brief love affair with Lenin's Marxism, but before Lenin died I was aware of one more borning bureaucracy similar to the one that was saddling Germany, but with different slogans and banners. I was still interested in the Russian experiment, though sadly. And on the other side of the fence I considered that the conservative viewpoint of reducing law's impingement on every angle of our life also seemed to have value.

Among everything else that I could lay my hands on, I read the radical *Nation* and *New Republic* and enjoyed the polysyllabic invective the "intellectool" left spewed at one another in letters, answered articles and rebuttals. One of the things that made me an outsider was that I had early on learned to dislike hates. I didn't hate anyone in particular, neither Japanese nor Finns, Bolsheviks nor Italians. Many times I could have been friends with people if I would hate with them what or whom they hated, but I couldn't and didn't. Why should I, I asked, and the reasons given usually were nonsense and I told them so. Because I associated with reds and archconservatives, the lower middle class was stiff-necked around me.

My three brothers-in-law and the Little Lady and my father and their friends soon looked on me as a dangerous person, quite possibly a traitor of some kind. "You can never tell," they would say. "He could be secretly siding with the enemy," the enemy being anything they couldn't comprehend and so must hate. As I said, I was not liked and I knew it. To be disliked by bigots, however, gave me stature in my own eyes.

In the eyes of my father, who was able to put all the people of the world into far fewer groupings even than Mrs. Nordstrom, I was in a category with vaudevillians, the soloists at church, acrobats and pickpockets, shell game operators, band leaders, and people who were surprisingly good at what they did. We were all sheltered in his mind under the category of "artistes." Bum painters, bad writers and impossible actors were piled in with the great of the world and looked down on as people who didn't have enough sense to pay their bills and get the two-percent, ten days' discount. Salesmen, however, were the princes of the realm. My father noted that to be a politician you had to kiss a lot of hind ends, and wasn't politics an honored calling? Well, sort of—so salesmen, with the same problem, could be looked up to as are leaders in government. Pop looked down on me, for as Kisdork had said, I welcomed adversity as a way of life. I liked it rough. Pop had a barber shave him, a manicurist do his nails, seven of his suits hung at his tailor's. Though we loved each other, father and son, we looked with distaste at each other's life style. Still he hoped, recklessly, that I'd turn into a salesman.

You would think he would start me out with something easy: a benevolent candymaker or some simpleton with a doughnut shop where I could point out how remarkable was our strawberry flavor and how characterless, really flat, were those of our several competitors. No, I got the big one, the difficult one, the one neither Johnny Lind nor my father could convince to see flavors the Acme way; but luck, it seems, was now on my side. It hovered around me, where heretofore it had always leaned back, and each time I brought home the bacon, Pop and the Little Lady accepted it in bitter silence.

This reached a high point when neither my father nor Johnny Lind could close the deal with a national chain of creameries. Pop finally turned it over to me as a poor possibility, but something that should at least be tried.

I don't know what I said but the company buyer sensed I wasn't a salesman. Perhaps he became certain that, though I didn't know the territory, I was an expert on vanilla. Anyway, after a few trials with different combinations, the company agreed to use our imitation vanilla "V" nationally. Pop and I would have to go to Chicago to sign the contract, and he would have to hire another shipping clerk, for I'd have to spend all my time producing the "V" vanilla, though it was an easy product to make. Without giving any reason Pop turned this wonderful deal down. The funny thing was the Little Lady backed him on this foolishness. I should have left this small-time madhouse then; but if they could keep the thing going in that manner, then even a dullard could do very well with it indeed. That and vague promises of complete control if I would stay on. Sure my chances were slim (promises are only promises), but looking back over the goat ranch and stump ranch and the boats, *Princess* and the *Sonoma*, I clung to this innocuous and ill-paying job. It represented security, and my ambition was dulled by the happy weekends with Nordi and her family. My old debt to my father was almost paid. Nordi found I was a better lover than when I'd been cutting down immense trees and making them into cordwood. Then I had very little energy left for anything else. Now, though not exactly amazed, she was definitely appreciative.

But for me ease seems to take something out of life and in this period I was bored, for we at Acme were never really hard pressed. We had built up a very good stock and kept it up. In the winter business slacked off somewhat, and then I helped Nordi much more with her jobs of endless repetition. I painted and repaired the building. I did all the shipping, most all of the making of the flavors and extracts, helped Nordi with the bottling and labeling and delivered all the Portland orders; so I had to move right along—still, it seemed to me like waltz time, the tempo enlivened only by the occasional family crisis.

One of these involved Bunky, who by this time was good friends with Olga's son, David. Much to Olga's annoyance, David had been born a boy. She decided to make a girl of him. His clothes were girlish and she curled his hair and once had done it so that one great curl came down over one shoulder. Had he been a girl it would have been quite fetching. She worked hard at her project, but by the time he was five she was becoming discouraged, for he was a big child for his age and clumsy in a way that couldn't be construed as feminine. Big boned, the lines of his face were already quite masculine. Poor Olga! Bunky liked David, however. Olga and Grandma took care of Bunky after school until we arrived a little before five, for we got off half an hour early by giving up our lunch hour. One evening when we came to pick up our boy we found a bit of excitement going on. There was a party next door to celebrate the birthday of the little girl who lived there. Bunky and David still had colored paper hats on. One of the party favors was a kind of whistle dressed out in colored paper streamers that whipped out when you blew it. Bunky, drawing in for a really big blow, had dislodged the miniature whistle and inhaled it, but could not cough it up. With the thing caught somewhere inside, he whistled at his every breath, though he felt no pain. He was surrounded by the children, all marveling. I took a more serious view and took him in to see some doctors I knew of. The put him under a fluoroscope and found no whistle. Just a sore throat, they said, from too much exuberant yelling. By now it made only the slightest whisper when he breathed. Okay, I believed them. Within a week he began to look sallow. When we put on the boxing gloves, he tore in at me as usual but faded almost at once, exhausted.

"It's the whistle, Pop," he said. "It's got to be the whistle."

At the doctors—and they were reputable, well-known doctors—they listened to my story, but weren't persuaded. "Kids imagine all kinds of things," one of them insisted. "I tell you, it's all in his head."

I explained about the boxing, how we had barely started and how he reeled with exhaustion. "Look for the whistle with X-ray," I said.

Both of them started using placating words. Fury came into me. I jumped up to take the place apart, but before I could rip anything out or even say anything, they were hustling Bunky into the X-ray room. Ten minutes later they contritely admitted the tiny brass whistle was well down in his right lung and that the lung was collapsed. There was a new technique, they said, and they would bring in the expert.

I got one of the whistles left at the party and took the little brass part out. It was much like the ferrules on a wooden pencil. The specialist made a very small instrument that would enter the whistle and could be made to expand to grip the whistle from within, and with his instrument reaching down the tube into the lung, bring it out. This was done, the lung inflated, and Bunky was soon as good as new.

It was about this time that we renewed our acquaintance with another Catherine—Catherine Eastham, now Neufer. We had become acquainted with her while we were in art school together and had corresponded fairly regularly with her when we lived in California. Blonde, and with the type of resiliency found in truck tires, she was an inciter, a firebrand for whatever cause and in this world of massive injustices she never lacked for causes. She liked to wave banners or wear sandwich boards, demanding rights for sick cats or money for the removal of clams to less rocky shores. She never ran out of injured parties, though her horror was that she would. Ranting was for her a way of life. She once confided to Nordi that she didn't care what the uproar was about if she could howl out demands. That was a word she loved above all— demands.

Shortly after we left for San Francisco, Catherine married Ray Neufer, a Mormon turned Marxist. They were well-suited to be partners. He was heavy with theory while she took care of the shouting. Art school, then, was a haven of sorts for young people who were beginning to question the mores of Main Street.

One day we were quite surprised to meet Catherine Neufer on the street in front of Acme Flavoring. We had not known that they lived just a block away from the factory. Nordi and I chatted with her for a time, then she asked us to dinner later in the week to meet her husband, Ray.

The dinner, though excellent, I've otherwise forgotten. I came only to meet Mr. Neufer, whom Catherine's letters had often quoted. After a few moments of heavy chit-chat while I glanced about the room at treasures in carved furniture, he came across as a broad-palmed, short bodied, no-nonsense sort of fellow. The lines in his face were engraved by thoughtful conviction. I was reminded of Marx and his posture at the time of the French communes. This uncompromising front completely hid the real Ray Neufer I was to know—a very kindly man who held no grudges and had trouble with praise. He was the complete artist, an instinctive technician. His medium was one of man's most versatile materials—wood. All the grace he so patently lacked could be found in his creations, in exquisitely carved panels and furniture.

As we ate we talked of those we had known in art school and where the intervening years had placed them. Catherine had most of the answers. It was I who had couched the question as if time itself flung people about. I did it unconsciously, informed by my experiences. I sensed Ray disapproved, though he concerned himself only with what on his plate, until over coffee he started questioning me about my beliefs.

I told him I was leery of beliefs: I didn't want to catch myself carrying a banner concerning yesterday's conjectures. For years I read a great deal, I said, about men's beliefs, but recently stumps and cordwood had been my facts and that I had no sweat left to expend on belief systems, and that now I was resting easy away from cordwood and opinions.

"What do you know about communism?"

"Enough," I said—*Das Kapital* and what I'd been able to glean from our periodicals and Russian propaganda magazines, and I told him I knew and talked at great length with a man who had been close to Trotsky. Ray didn't respond, but soon left the table and laid down on the sofa in the livingroom with his back to the room and went to sleep. Thumbs down! I had been found wanting. Okay! We spent the rest of our short visit talking with Catherine and staring at her husband's back.

Well, we wangled another evening with them and after dinner, I beat him to the couch and was able to sleep until Nordi

woke me and told me it was time to go home. It seemed to amuse
Catherine. In time, this little game of "musical couches" that Ray
and I played turned out to have more symbolic weight than any
of us could have foreseen.

The winter of the toboggan was a long one. Three times snow
came, each time it lasted long enough for sledding. We visited
often with the Broms family. Virginia's father, Teddy, and I got
along very well. He was a lover of the outdoors, an ex-woodsman
who had worked in the logging camps of Wisconsin, and he came
out west as a hewer of railroad ties. With his great muscled arms
he was a master of the broadaxe. We spent the winter evenings
planning the spring camping we would do. We agreed finally to
a two-family hiking trip with backpacks over the three-day
Memorial Day weekend.

For Christmas I had made a pack frame of spruce for Nordi. It
was carved and stood on two goat's feet, and the tops of the
uprights were carved into two nudes, one with the arms over her
head, the other with arms at her side. People admired it as
beautiful and practical. I had my heavy packboard that I'd made
a few years before in California for prospecting in the Siskiyous.

For Virginia I steam-bent very heavy rattan into a packboard
and for Teddy I made a frame similar to Nordi's, only much
stronger and without carving. On the backs of these frames I
lashed canvas packbags with covers. For Dory and Bunky and
Tekla we borrowed three small packbags.

The night before we were to leave, the weather was uncertain
and it did sprinkle a little. When Nordi, Bunky and I reached
their house the next morning at five o'clock, the time set, they
weren't even up. Dory finally let us in, but Teddy and his wife,
from deep in the covers, answered they had decided not to go.
With Dory and Virginia urging them up we got them out of bed
and through breakfast and out to the cars. There was no smile on
Teddy's face. Tekla looked highly disturbed, for Tek and Teddy
hadn't much drive, nor did they like to be pushed.

After several hours on the road we were almost to where we
would park, when I saw off to the left on a small mountain a quick

snowstorm covering it with white where no white had been before. Ours was the lead car, and I parked behind a bank where the white mountain could not be seen. They drove in behind me and I kept pointing down into the canyon where lay our destination. I hurried them along, saying I wanted to have lunch in an established camp, because I was hungry.

Teddy, pack on back, hit the trail first, the kids followed him, then Nordi. As each hiked off, Tekla in an anguish of indecision followed them a little way, then hurried back to the cars. She was torn between the desire to stay with the cars (that implied civilization) or to follow her husband and children into the wilderness. As I put on my pack and went after them, I saw Tek, now thoroughly agitated, grab her pack and trot after us where we were strung out and disappearing down the trail. No one had looked back to see the snow-covered mountain. Fine! I felt that they should not draw summations from one occurrence, at least not yet.

The trail curved down beside what would have been a brook in more sedate country, but now we were in a world of dashing water, rock and conifer forest. We were heading southward and down. Looking up I saw a great mass of clouds crowding south too and, like us, they appeared to be freighted. As we hiked down the zigzag of the trail, I considered a probable scenario when we got down to our camp site.

A cloudburst or a heavy fall of snow would arrive with us. Setting up a camp under any conditions was Nordi's and my specialty, but four other people would be standing in the rain or snow while we did it! We brought along a tent and canvas fly for the lean-to that we planned to back with boughs where Teddy and Bunky and I would hunker down. Though I hadn't figured on doing it in snow or a puddle of water, so that while we were setting up our camp everyone would be getting soaked to the skin. Good God, what sort of a Caliban was I? Wet and sickened people, pneumonia or worse—Jesus, what can I do about it! I looked up at the clouds hurtling overhead. Hell's fire, I thought, what have I done?

Teddy grunted, "What does your pack weigh, Clyde, on a guess, I mean?"

"About seventy pounds," I answered, "and I figured yours at forty when we arranged them last night."

We trudged the downhill trail through countless zigzags, each switchback seemingly piled atop the one below as we dropped down into the canyon. Bunky and the girls were below us, stepping along at a good rate. Our wives followed.

"Let's trade packs," Teddy said, and we did.

After a bit he remarked, "That pack you made for me is the best I've ever carried, and I cruised timber for six months when I first came to Oregon. We used the old style packbags—you know, narrow shoulder straps and a tump strap—but those bags pried at your back. These don't. This one of yours is a dilly. You figure on things, don't you?"

"Not enough," I answered, thinking of the jam I could be walking these people into.

"No," Teddy went on, "I've noticed it. You plan ahead more than other guys. It ain't paid off yet, but I bet it will."

"Yeah," I answered, sick with worry about the clouds scudding over the top of the canyon. "Yeah! Say we better catch up with the kids."

We did. Soon we came around a turn to see before us a small waterfall and, near where the trail passed it, a bit of turf with grass, close cropped by deer. Virginia and the kids had flung themselves on it, calling out that there was room for the rest of us too.

I believed we were about halfway down to where Roaring River meets the Clackamas. I longed for a rest for I had taken my pack back and seventy pounds wears at you going downhill. The holding back business is hard on legs; still, I stood with my pack on, as the rest lolled in ease.

"I'm hungry," I said, "let's keep right on to camp and cook up a big mulligan."

"Well, I don't know about the rest of you," said Teddy, "but I came on this trip to loaf, and here's the place to start it."

He propped himself against his pack now laying on the grass and pulled his hat over his eyes as a fellow does against the sun and produced an imitation snore.

I went along the rest of the way to our goal, and when I got there a few large raindrops sent me hopping about. The tent and fly were in my pack, but in the bottom a great slab of bacon in waxed paper was over it with bags of beans and rice, hotcake flour, raisins and prunes. The raisins were in a paper bag and I tore it. With my mouth full I looked around. It had gotten quite dark, a cold wind came down the canyon as Tekla, leading our little group, syphoned from the mouth of it. They laid their packs helter-skelter about our camping spot and stared help- lessly at the awesome cloud above us; then with a bellow, a sword of lightning struck down over across the river. We could see tor- rents of rain coming down over there, but here on our side only a few drops tapped us on the shoulders. Though I knew I shouldn't, the situation was such that I gave orders.

"I'll get the boughs for the bed," I said. "Bunky, you bring in firewood and make a hearth and start the fire. Nordi, get the tent up and stow all our stuff under it. Teddy, we're going to need six slender poles about twelve feet long for our lean-to and two short crotched ones for our cooking setup.

"Look," I said, "unless we get shelters up and the boughs under cover, we could be in for a nasty night, so step on it."

Teddy was angry and moved very slowly to do what had to be done. I climbed a bushy fir and, coming down, hacked off all the limbs. It didn't hurt the tree and, though I was chopping care- lessly within an inch of the great artery in my thigh, there was no mishap. Bunky helped me drag them into camp near where Nordi had pitched the tent. I trimmed off all the small boughs from the big ones and, when I had the pile complete, threw the fly over it and turned to help Teddy put up the poles for the lean- to. Less than an hour later, with a big stew bubbling in the pot and everything taken care of, the lean-to primitive but adequate, I relaxed and looked up. The sky was now clear, and I looked away from the resentful glances of Tek and Teddy.

Camp breakfast—well, Tek didn't actually shoulder Nordi

aside from the fire, but over a nice bed of coals and with her long handled camp frying pan she was completely in her element. Delight shone on her face as she turned the flapjacks with her own special turner. The big blackened coffeepot, eggs frying in a smaller pan and crisp bacon tangled into everything—wow!

"Careful with that syrup jug, Clyde," she said, "it's all we have with us. Pour Ted another cup. You're handier to the pot."

Everywhere we looked, if we looked closely, we saw deer. The area where we camped was a meadow, and the land that lay about the confluence of the two mountain rivers was gentle. Only the stream's beds were rocky with some great boulders tossed from God knows where, and the distant "when" of it obscure to such a mind as mine. They were now moss-covered and seemed to me homey after trying to envision those awful ages when great masses of stone were hurtling about. Were there men then, I wondered? Were there any beasts at all? Now in winter this place was a deeryard, a place where they congregate, nibbling twigs and moss and sometimes the bark of young trees until spring brought out the buds as it warmed the land.

We started to hike up a deer trail by Roaring River, but soon found the river had cataracts so steep and continuous that it was really the free falling of water somewhat impeded by extruding rocks. We struggled out of it without mishap and looked for terrain less difficult to explore.

"Lord," said Nordi looking up, "have you got something on the kinder side of perpendicular, something only as steep as stairs, something in a gentle forty-five?"

Tek scowled. "That's blasphemy," she said. "I'd rather you wouldn't talk that way in front of my daughters."

"Okay, Tek," laughed Nordi, "and I'll try not to start your daughters thinking."

"Oh, I dunno," said Tek, "I think they can get all they need to know from the Bible."

"Most of the world gets along nicely without even that," said Nordi. "Say, we're talking too much. Have you noticed how beautiful the day is?"

"I wish there were some berries to pick," mused Tek.

Dory had brought an indoor baseball in her pack. Teddy made a bat from a dry piece of driftwood he had found under a cliff's overhang where a flood had tossed it some winter before. It took a lot of whittling, but after that it was fun playing in the meadow and watching Virginia's coltish grace—an awkwardness mixed with long-line flows that was tremendously appealing to me. I felt it in my chest. It made me want to leap about. Disturbed by it, I looked away, but saw it again and again as we played around camp. Finally I fought it. What significance can it have for me, I asked myself, and looked with love at my Nordi, dressed like a gypsy in a gown she had secreted among the essentials in her pack. She was lovely. I found myself staring at the way the light draperies conformed to her thighs, while in my mind's eye Virginia's coltish movements superimposed themselves, disturbing me until I arose and stamped away, taking a quick hike up the trail. There, I turned and looked down on things, and the beauty of the day and the rivers and our camp stole me from that unwelcome mood.

That evening we sang around the fire. We had made several hikes up and down the Clackamas in our time there, and Ginny and Nordi swam, braving undertowing currents as they were swept along by the river's icy waters. We brought them their clothing and shoes where they landed some distance below, oh, a quarter of a mile, and they were pleased with themselves when, in dry clothes, they quit shivering. We all realized that we were enjoying ourselves much more than we had dreamed we would, and planned to spend more time together in the future.

But I also realized that much of my enjoyment was in Virginia. The awareness of her dragged my gaze to her almost constantly that day. By the fire I got them talking about birthdays and learned that she would be sixteen in the fall. Sixteen! But it isn't sex, I told myself, sleeping beside gentle Nordi. It's just an interest that I must hide. All this could wait until, once more at home, I could think things out.

III

In Which
I Build Us a House out of Rammed Earth,
Grow Fatter on the Thinner Business,
Have a Brief Run-in with Some Ghostly Sums,
and
Inadvertently Declare My Love

1937

FOR SEVERAL YEARS, in fact within six months after our retreat from the sticks, I longed for a place of our own in the country. I never spoke of it to Nordi, but I envisioned some kind of a subsistence place by a river. It seemed absurd—how could I when there never was a dime left after paying for our food, rent and clothing?

I don't know what would have happened, but the powers-that-be took a hand then. One power said to the other: "You know we've leaned a little heavy on Clyde Rice up in Oregon."

The other power said: "Which one? We got a lot of Clyde Rices in Oregon—pioneers, the Rices. They began breeding like mad up there from 1850 on. Has he got a middle name?"

The first power said, "Yep, it's Harvey."

Well, they talked it over and saw they'd been a little heavy handed on me and agreed to let up a bit. Not too much though. "He's the kind of guy we have to keep tied down, at least one hand and one foot."

"I don't agree, but I suppose it's orders from the Lord."

"No, it isn't that. It's for his own good. It's kinda left in our own hands to keep guys like him tethered."

So I chanced on an article about rammed-earth houses in one of those little magazines of short but potent life. I showed it to my father, who hated to step on grass. He would not step off the sidewalk to water his lawn. He hated picnics, was as citified as one could be and, though he despised the lives of farmers, Pop was an avid reader of *Organic Gardening*, which he had subscribed to for twenty years, and could talk ecstatically and somewhat learnedly about mulches and friable loam. In other words he liked the good earth in the abstract.

After he read the article, I handed him a pamphlet on rammed earth that I had gotten from the Agriculture Department of California. When he was through with that and was enthused armchair-wise, I approached him with my dream.

"Pop," said I, "Nordi and I can barely keep body and soul together on the wages you can afford to pay us. Now if I had a subsistence place where we could grow most of our food and not pay rent, we could get along nicely."

All this fit the mores of his magazine. He brightened up, but his laconic, "How?" showed he was not yet in the trance state of armchair hobbyists and sadly I couldn't push him into it. I was vague about this even for myself.

The Nordstrom family's talk around the picnic table the following weekend was full-stomach desultory. There were chunks of cake, bits of pie strewn about, coffee cups with only the dregs in them sitting here and there. I've forgotten what kind of conversation we were dragging along, but when it died, I filled the silence with an announcement.

"I'm going to get a place of my own," I said, and then I added to it, "where I can raise stuff."

Silence—we were too full with every sort of viand except pork. The gorgeous feeling of being a slob was on me. I'd just been a pig with food, and now felt that I was lounging around sloppily in several directions. Even so, I was still caught up in my announcement.

"Bottomland with a place up out of it to build on," I continued.

That last assertion brought Jack out of his lethargy—not really, for he didn't deign to turn and look at me, but enough so he could murmur, "Swell," he said, "what you going to use for money?"

"Yeah," added Teddy not laughing but concerned. "How do you figure to do it, Clyde? If you was a gambler, you might latch onto enough to make more than the down payment, but you're no gambler."

His earnestness startled me and I replied in kind. "I don't know how," I said. "Maybe I'm going to play the fool once more. Look, you guys," I said, "maybe I'm just going to try."

"With what?" asked Jack, who along with old lady Nordstrom, was the pragmatist of the group.

"I don't know," I answered again, "but I know I'll not be at another picnic this summer. I'm going to be looking."

Albert, Mrs. Nordstrom's son-in-law, awakened from a nap by this, sat up and looked at me with a startled expression. Teddy was perturbed, but Jack had been around. A horse shoer before World War I claimed him, he came out a salesman.

"You don't claw your way out of a situation where the odds are wrong. You act reasonable." That was Jack. "If you haven't got the money," he said, "you shouldn't talk," and the three of them stared at me, rather as if I had insulted them.

But I had a plan, sort of. Near Portland three rivers course down their gorges from mountain summits and then for a score of miles wander through flatlands before merging with more stately waters. On one of these rivers, preferably the Clackamas, I wanted to acquire a bit of land (say five acres), one boundary of which would be the river.

Friends asked me, knowing our dearth of money, if I was going to do it with mirrors, but I explained to them the use of rubberbands and left. Because of my affinity with the Clackamas River, I drove roads that followed the Sandy, warily centering in on my beloved stream.

Two weekends I (half-heartedly) bothered people from the Sandy's mouth on the Columbia to the steeper foothills. No one wanted to sell river frontage for a pittance. Vaguely glad, I next tried my act on people who owned land along the Molalla, both sides. It took me a weekend and a half to drive through their derisive negatives and mumbled *unh-unh*s, to where the Clackamas pours its pristine waters into the silt-laden Willamette. As the homing salmon swimming in that turbid water searched for swirls of Clackamas nectar, so I too loved the river of my childhood. I had been drawn to its banks soon after I learned the technique of running away, and not too long after I learned to bring food with me and then a fishpole. My father was heavy-handed, but my childish mind decided a sore butt was worth it and now, wonder of wonders, fate in the shape of the "powers-that-be" was going to allow me to look for land along its banks.

Sunday night, full of the knowledge that the question would end where I wanted it to end, and in the coming weekend, we ambled over to Nordi's mother's. There the old lady held close her covey of daughters and their captured husbands, but though doubly captured, we men didn't complain too much.

Coffee is largely just coffee, sure; to drink it anywhere is pleasant, but at Mother Nordstrom's it took on more than a tinge of all right, and often she would bake a batch of apple dorper for us. Now apple dorper and coffee is a combination that belongs "in there" with peaches and cream, turkey and cranberry and the root beer float. I could speak of headier sauces but feel that, though Mother Nordstrom has been dead for many, many years, we shouldn't speak of them when praising her prowess with pots and pans.

Anyway, sipping hot coffee and munching the dorper, my brothers-in-law prodded me gently about the land I didn't seem to be getting, and with my admission that no sale had yet been consummated, offered me free beer if I would accompany Nordi to the picnic next Sunday. This I refused, looking, I hoped, mysterious and resourceful.

In the evening in the middle of that week I found a place on the river that answered my needs. It was offered on very liberal terms if I could get a small bank loan, but the house, for it had one, sat on a plain of some extent, bereft of trees. And there were several houses in plain view. The river below a bluff had a small field of river bottomland along it, but a house sitting directly across the river destroyed it for me. It was all wrong esthetically. Still, nobody was snapping up property in those days, so I put it on hold.

Next evening up-river from the crossroads of Carver, I parked in the mouth of the lane I had walked as a boy. A short distance down it I worked my way through a still familiar barbed-wire fence and plunged on through brush grown there since my childhood visits. I crossed a narrow swale and was out on the meadow. Grazing cows took no notice of me, completely involved with knee-deep clover. This was the place. Far back in my mind I had held it as too good to be true and would not let myself think about it.

Now I tried to eat some of the clover myself, as I wandered over to the river. The shore hadn't changed so much there either. Except for the brush this was childhood revisited. I found some flat skipping rocks and skimmed them across the flowing waters, and then turned sadly to find the owners, ready for the rebuff that would put me once more in my luckless world. I climbed back through the barbed wire and on reluctant feet walked farther down the lane.

I soon came on a brown cottage sitting neatly under two immense maples and on the porch of the cottage a little woman of uncertain age rocked slowly as she smiled. It wasn't real. This was the stuff daydreams are made of, or I should expect stage scenery, but there was no rattle of it when a waft of cool air fluttered the russet skirt of the woman in the rocker.

"Good evening, ma'm," I enunciated between stiffened lips. "Do you have any land around here for sale?"

"Why yes," she answered, "we have some. Each acreage has river frontage."

"I used to come here as a boy," I announced, "and now I can't stand living in town any longer. What does your acreage cost?"

"Two hundred and fifty dollars an acre in five-acre tracts. Each tract touches the river and the road."

"Is there any drinking water on it or a well?" I asked, my astounded mind still able somehow to be practical.

"Some," she said, "some."

"Well, I haven't any money here with me now."

"I know," said the woman, continuing to smile.

"I have thirty dollars," I said, which was a lie. "Could I take a thirty-dollar option on the land? If I can't make a down payment in a year, the thirty dollars will be yours."

"Is that all you've got?" she asked, looking at me pertly like a robin. "An option can't hurt us, and the thirty dollars I'll spend slick as a whistle—like gift money."

I was startled. Where is it, I thought, where is the fumble that will bring dismay and reality? Still, I felt suddenly freed (from my past, I suppose). I felt as if I could fly. I wanted to sing, but the only sounds that left my lips were muted ones, "I'll be here tomorrow with the money."

I borrowed thirty dollars from my father and got a slip of paper for the money from the lady. She said the first of the month we'd go to Oregon City and make the option legal. I've never been reticent, but suddenly I was. I tiptoed around my miracle as if it were a house of cards. I talked to Nordi of it in whispers. I took her out to what the owner agreed would be our part of the meadow, our brush, our swale and, yes, our shack, for buried in the brush of our part was an ancient fisherman's shack of the late eighteen hundreds. The roof was all but caved in; still, fix the roof and you were snug from the weather. There was a chimney, but no stove. (How is it the song goes?)

I did my work at Acme with great dispatch and precision, for the job in the end must support our miracle. My reticence screwed up my strutting, when I told the Nordstrom clan of my great achievement. I let it be known around that a change had occurred in our life style, and that we were gladly divesting ourselves of our waif status.

Strangely, it was my father who first asked to see the acreage. He took me with him to make the delivery of a five-gallon oak keg of vanilla, said it was too heavy for him and he wanted to talk to the man. Then instead of returning after his talk he drove away declaring he hankered to see what kind of land I was able to get for thirty dollars down and two hundred and fifty dollars a year.

We soon passed Carver and drove down the lane to a gate near the cottage. We stepped out into tall grass where he turned up his trousers cuffs and by that gesture became, it seemed to me, the Jim Rice of his youth. He followed me to where the stakes were driven awaiting the surveyor's accuracy. Four acres of meadow and an acre of upland for house and barn, including the narrow swale we subsequently drained. He sized up the brush around the house site.

"Bill said you slashed brush like you enjoy it," said this strange man beside me.

"Yeah," I answered, "but I'm going to leave a band of it to hedge the lane. Water from the spring is piped along there. I'll connect to it when I'm ready."

Going back we were silent, cogitating on the lay of that beautiful meadow. When we arrived at the plant, he announced: "Twelve miles. It's closer than I thought."

The Nordstroms' matriarch let it be known that we would have a picnic by the river on Nordi's and Clyde's place come Sunday.

"I want to see for myself what kind of a brush heap he got for my Evelyn to slave in. How could he do it, Olga? He hasn't got a cent to his name."

"Well, all he's got is an option and he borrowed to get that," Olga replied.

Evidently that hog-tied swagger I mentioned got through to the ladies. With my father I had to be more circumspect, for I had vague plans in which he would fit.

Sunday old lady Nordstrom arrived with the rest of her clan, in which Nordi and I were beginning to be accepted as members. I had made a trail from the gate to our area. The surveyor had set the corner pegs, and we knew definitely what would be ours if we continued to pay for it for five years.

On the trail Mother Nordstrom's, "Well, I don't like all this brush," was said with her usual mettle, but when she had crossed the meadow and sat with her feet in the river, placid there, she smiled and as usual ordered Olga around.

"See that the men," she said, "bring all our fixings down here. I don't want to have to move to eat."

I went with my father on another delivery—another man he had to talk to. I was beginning to realize these people he had to see was a way for him to have a conversation with me away from the eye and ear of the Little Lady. Though the place where we were making the delivery was close, he went a roundabout way, so I was certain he was going to mention the rammed-earth house, as I believed that both of us had been thinking about it since our conversation a month or so before. I was set to be extra agreeable, but he started out with:

"Now, Clyde, I want you to understand that if I do this for you—oh, maybe a little for how it looks—I do it out of curiosity, my own curiosity. The Little Lady—well, for how it looks. She likes to look easy-going and kindly."

"Too late," I said, "maybe if you moved to another city and tried it again."

"I could fire you for that."

"Yeah, I know how irrational you can be! Your setup with Nordi and me is perfect for you, but you might destroy it for no good reason. Remember the Pembler account. I half believe you will."

We drove on. Pop's hands clenched on the steering wheel. After several blocks of silence, I said, "Well?"

"You know," he said, "I'm aware of what you're doing. We've both been thinking about that rammed-earth house. I was in a good mood and you knew it, but you like to do things your way. Give help, sure, but you can't take it. Now you ruffle me up because I want to help you, though, as I pointed out, it's for my own reasons. I know your failings as well as you know mine. Now let's get down to business."

"Okay, Pop. Have you found anything more on how they do it?"

"Nobody I talked to even knew about it," he said. "Sod houses and adobe, yes, but not pounding dry dirt in forms. What did you find out?"

"Hannibal—the general with the elephants in the Alps— know of him?" I asked.

"Yes, vaguely. Go on," he said.

"He made some forts in Spain of rammed earth, and they were there two hundred years later. Pliny, the Roman historian, tells how they were made. It takes dry dirt, dug in late summer, and you must protect the dirt you get from rain—damp, it's no good."

"Look, Clyde," said my father, "you thinking of making one out there where you got this option?"

"Yes, I am, but it takes time—months, I think. I can't do too much on my vacation time in August; in fact, I've got to work my vacation for you or Hoody Peanut Company. I was going to ask them tonight after work."

"Well, we got to be getting back," Pop said. "You and Nordi come and have dinner with us tomorrow night and let me do most of the talking. You need some kind of roof over the dirt to keep it dry while you're building, and for Christ sake, Clyde, don't get on your high horse with me in front of the Little Lady."

It wasn't apathy or disinterest that produced the quietness with which Nordi accepted the new factor in our lives. Perhaps she viewed it as an inevitable prelude to another small disaster. As things stood, we were out of debt and, though we had never a cent left over, we did exist with adequate food and clothing, the rent paid; but it was becoming a pale existence for Nordi. Still, as we drove to Pop's, she was weighing the excitement of something new against placid security and coming up with no immediate answer.

Pop answered the doorbell with a pleased smile. As he accepted our hats and slickers, wet with a summer shower, the Little Lady saw fit to signal that she was cooking a dinner with a great to-do in the kitchen. Besides being a fine bookkeeper, the Little Lady, under my old man's tutelage, had become a sound cook. I don't mean the usual frippery (a hundred variations on old themes). She prepared the old classics, bringing them as near perfection as possible—I mean the broccoli, the roast and the Yorkshire pudding with the green peas in vinegared butter sauce.

We talked of the problems we'd been having of late with the

bottle manufacturer, but Pop interrupted it: "I didn't ask you over here to talk about bottles, but the way you can build a house out of dirt."

"Dirt—what a filthy way to live!" said the Little Lady.

"Yes," said Pop, "wouldn't it get crummy in spite of you?"

"No," I answered, "the earth of the walls is pounded solid like brick, and the wall is covered on the outside with stucco. The inside will be plastered like this house."

"Well, that article you showed me in *Pageant* magazine interested me," said my father. "I've never built anything except this business. Still, if I was young, I think I'd get a lot out of building something like they showed in the magazine. I never was any good with a hammer and saw, but this goes right along with organic gardening, which I believe in."

"Seems to me," said his wife, "that you'd have better things to do than that."

"You mean sell vanilla or something to make money?" he asked.

"Yes, you're a businessman."

"What if I just wanted to be a man once in awhile, more direct?" he answered.

"Jim, that isn't like you."

"Look, Little Lady, you married a business and with it a businessman, and incidentally a man. You don't know my hunches or urges or what I'm talking about.

"Now, Clyde, the Organic magazine that I take has kept me kind of tied in with the basic world that everything else is built on, so I got you over here tonight to talk, and I don't want to be interrupted by you or the Little Lady. I know how you got that land and I've seen it. Hang on to it anyway you can! Most of it is bottomland. I tell you, as I drive through the country selling whatever I'm selling, I look at every bit of bottomland I pass, jealous of the guy who owns it.

"See here, what you're thinking is that in the winter we haven't much business and Nordi could take care of her work as well as yours if she worked hard; and if I would take care of your deliveries or hire it done, you could go out to that place you got the option on and build this dirt house, and I'd get a lot of satisfaction out of being in on it. If Nordi did both jobs I'd pay her for both jobs. Well, Clyde, aren't we thinking along the same lines?"

"The same, Pop," I answered quickened by his outburst.

"Well, speak up," he said. "What have you got to add to it?"

"I'd have to live in a tent this winter while I build it, but I can't ask Nordi to live in a wet tent."

Nordi spoke up, "I could live at my mother's in the yungrubarn."

"Yungrubarn!" said the Little Lady. The tone in which she said it implied that a yungrubarn was on par with a slug or a dead rat.

"It's the maiden's house. It's very cozy. My father, as long as he lived, painted it every other year. It's like a big toy. I'll eat with the family. Bunky's the problem. He's not doing as well in the city schools as he did at Wendel. That shack out there! Could we repair it, because then Bunky could stay with you and go to a country school?"

"Makes sense," said my father. "I think we'll be taking a long noon hour tomorrow, the three of us, and go out and see what can be done with that shack."

Under that suit (I never saw Pop without his vest), under the superficial polish of a salesman, was Pop, my father. I am because of him. I could see somewhat, watching him, why I am as I am. He had never before presented anything of himself but a head sticking out of suiting. This now was something I was finding hard to absorb.

"Little Lady," he said, "bring that bottle of 'Grandad' I just opened and four glasses. No chasers."

"Three," said the Little Lady, "if you'll excuse me. And you could hire my brother, Ernest, to take Clyde's place."

"Ernest, my ass!" said my father.

Next morning Pop told me that I hadn't a job with him until my earth house was liveable. "Nordi and I will be out at noon," he said.

I hurried out to Carver to be met on the trail to the shack by my landlady. She said she couldn't give me an option after all, admitted she'd acted impetuously, said her daughter didn't want her to sell the land, and gave me my thirty dollars back, remarking she was glad we hadn't signed papers.

"Uh, what?"—she was gone—she'd left. "Hey! I—"

Good God! I'd forgotten that I always get this in the end. Resigned, I accepted it. Okay, okay! I'll move my tools out and put them in the car. I did. But I sat on a stump by the shack, loath to leave.

Later I was to remember that moment as being in the posture of Rodin's "Thinker," nursing a knuckle. My mind blank, I was trying to dredge up some value, some onwardness, if nothing else a horizon, when she appeared again in a slot in the brush, a small youngish old lady in a faded flowered housedress peering intently into my eyes. We stayed staring at each other, it seemed for quite a long moment.

Then again like a bird, she asked pertly: "You like this place *a lot?*" From her question it appeared that her instinct, not her mind, told her of the depth of my need for this particular spot against all others. She conveyed it with the emphasis she placed on "a lot."

I answered unconsciously from deep within me. "Yes," I said, "with this place I can be the guy I want to be."

I could not see this knowledge go into her at first, for neither her eyes nor her expression changed. But then they did, for empathy pervaded the moment and we knew each other. Her smile was warm as she exclaimed: "You can have it then. We'll fix it up at Oregon City tomorrow."

With that she vanished. The brush closed the slot with leaves, and I had no doubt, no doubt at all as I brought my tools back to a stiff piece of canvas I'd shoved under a bush.

Later in the day when Pop and Nordi came to look at the

shack, it appeared to be an impossible ruin. Nordi poked around inside then came out and looked at the bushes and vines that all but obscured it. She was excited. "We can make this liveable. Let me stay and see what can be done with it."

The mess was a catalyst to her home-building instincts. I went back with Pop to the city and did her work that afternoon. In the evening when I returned to Carver she had cleared away the fallen roof, the brush and vines around it had been slashed and removed. "For two dollars and seventy-five cents I bought these salvaged two-by-fours that were lying all but rotting in a pile near our landlady's cottage. Maybe you can repair the roof and use these for rafters. What do you think?"

The repair of the shack was a matter of a few days and, when Bunky and I were ensconced with a little campstove and double bunks in one end, we grinned at each other like idiots.

I began to wonder if I could gather enough earth of the kind I needed before the rains came. The dirt would be compressed to one third its usual mass in the walls. I saw I could not gather enough of it before the rains, for the big structure I planned, so I decided to pull in the dimensions and build a two-hundred-hen chicken house that we could convert and live in until the house at the top of the property could be built. Pop and Nordi agreed, Nordi reluctantly.

In thick brush and bramble we found a place where we could build a hen house. Twenty-two feet and twenty-six feet were the length and breadth of the plan. The plan said it would hold two hundred laying hens. I believed that I could handle that many chickens while working for Acme. We cleared away vine maple, hazel bushes and berry vines and made the foundation of rock and twelve dollars' worth of cement—a poor foundation by a poor man. As I was supposed to, I tarred the top of the foundation but heavily—tar is cheap. Within the foundation's confines I began laying up my supply of dry dirt. There were several large hummocks about. I leveled them, and all I took away was soil, no stones. Soon I had my wheelbarrow trails going farther and farther for the earth I garnered from banks and small knolls on the adjoining properties. My clay and sand hoard was now stacked high within the foundation.

Then I took fright. Some anvil shaped thunderclouds appeared on the horizon and came our way. The sky soon became dark, angry wisps swept under the thunderheads, soon they were over us. There seemed to be no wind, but those great clouds slowly, majestically, moved on until we assumed that they were over Portland where "they let go," Pop said, drenching the city. Gutters overflowed everywhere. My luck had held. Our magnificent dirt heap was not even dampened. I rushed wildly about next day. I borrowed from Pop and bought enough shiplap for a roof and some long two-by-fours. From a big stand of tall fir saplings nearby I got out about twenty poles and hauled them down to my place. Neighbors said the owner of the pole thicket lived in the East: "They grow faster than we can take them—help yourself!"

Soon I had the roof over my precious dirt. It stood on the poles, propped and braced every way. I papered the roof with tarpaper and tarred it. It would have to do.

One more week of August left. Behind me were two weeks of labor that had started at dawn each day and ended around midnight. I took five kerosene lanterns from the loot I brought up from California and strung them along my wheelbarrow trail and at the place where I was digging. I was able, though I spilled many, to bring countless loads to the mass of earth that now flowed over the restraints of the foundation and loomed dark under its roof. For several days a heavy rain beat down and I knew in my bones that I must rest.

Then the weather cleared and on Sunday early in the morning we went calling on Grandma and Jack and Olga to find the clan poised for a picnic up the Washougal River. Their invitation to come with them brooked no refusal. We now, it seemed, belonged to the clan and must not refuse.

Mother Nordstrom commanded us to go in two cars instead of three, pointing out that the depression was still with us. Our car was chosen as the one to stay home, and I ended up sitting next to Virginia. I had resolutely kept her out of my thoughts after Roaring River, scarcely noticing her at picnics since then, but now I was occupying the back seat of Teddy's car with the sisters and their dog, who wouldn't stay on the floor but kept forcing its way between Dory and Virginia.

Dory kept up a chatter, Ginny was silent. It was raillery about Ginny's birthday in October when she would be sixteen and never been kissed.

Teasing her sister, she watched her, "Clyde will kiss you," she said to see her blush and remarking it. I glanced sideways—yes, she was blushing. Her sweet confusion was delightful to see.

Tek, in the front seat, admonished Dory. "Just wait till you're sixteen. We'll see how you take the teasing."

"Nobody will want to kiss me," Dory said. "I won't be pretty like Ginny."

Sixteen, huh. I decided that when we swam, I would look for the filling-out on the long lines of her.

We found a fine pool, a falls at its head with the stream above it narrow and deep. We discovered, that is Ginny and I, that we could slip into the current well above the falls and come sailing down over its rounded lip and plunge into the deeper end of the pool. It was a drop of about the height of a man and the falling water drove you way under, but the pool there seemed bottomless, though at the lower end it grew shallow for timid swimmers. After much play in the water (even Mother Nordstrom pushed me over when I wasn't expecting it), we all lay on the sand until the sun had warmed us satisfactorily, then attacked the food like hungry lions dining on early Christians—well, not exactly. Swedes, no matter how famished, are a decorous people and stay off the table.

When we had eaten too much, we dawdled over more pie (peach this time). Nordi was feeding it to me, the peach I mean, as if I were a baby, much to Tekla's annoyance.

Later we swam again. No one else wanted to try our plunge, and again that sense of camaraderie came to us, as Ginny and I helped each other up over the rocks of the low cliff. Farther and farther upstream after each plunge we went until the shouts and laughter at the pool seemed distant, when we would slip into the natural sluice of the stream and glide to the brink and over. We grew tired but climbed back for our final plunge. This time we went much farther on the deer trail that ran beside the swift water and found a sun-splashed patch of moss. I flung myself on it, then moved over to make room for Ginny. She hesitated. I wondered what she was thinking, for then she lay down very deliberately and close to me. Somehow I was distracted, a sense of portent was in the moment. It hit me.

"You know," I said, "we make a team." It came faltering from my lips. There were long seconds of silence before she quietly said: "Yes." It was as if she had given her agreement some consideration before uttering it.

On the way back that evening we passed several summer homes, modest ones, but artfully made to fit their roof angles and warm shingled sides into the various greens of the maples and firs about them. As we passed a small one, Teddy, said admiringly: "I'd like to own one just like that."

"O-oh!" scoffed Tek sarcastically, "there you go again, imagining stuff. You'll never own anything like that. It takes know-how and money. Quit dreaming," she went on, "that job of yours will never get us a cabin. We're lucky to have our house."

The girls followed their mother's lead, belittling their father. It hurt Teddy, for he was silent the rest of the trip. I decided to somehow prove them wrong.

•

We moved our furniture and household goods into the big loft over Mother Nordstrom's garage and Nordi bedded down in the yungrubarn. Bunky and I filled our shanty with our clothing, tools and housekeeping things, which included a large galvanized tub for bathing.

Bunky marched off to school, secure in the knowledge that like the one at Wendel, this was a country school. I was left ecstatically alone with a long, hard job to do. I made the forms as the pamphlet described, then bolted them to the foundation and was ready. As I was considering them, a man appeared across the forms from me surveying them too.

"Don't you build a form all around your building?" he asked, letting his inquiring glances take in the form, the roof, and the mountain of dry dirt under it.

"Not in rammed-earth," I replied. "You just move the form along after you've rammed a section till it's hard. It is finished then to stand on its own and will support the next layer when I come around again with the form."

"Hope I'm not butting in," he said, "I'm Mr. Giesek, your landlady's ex-husband. I live over past her house. Welcome to a part of my philosopher walk. Could I see those plans?" he asked, reaching out for the plans that I had in my hand.

He took out his glasses and put them on like some men do in a careful manner, as if it were quite an operation. As he studied the plans, I looked him over—a squat fellow about sixty, I guessed, a face not craggy but deeply indented, grey eyes set far back in their sockets, the brow over them furrowed. His mouth was wide and taut. He glanced up from the paragraph in the pamphlet that described the tamping tools used by the ancients.

"These tools," he said, "I can have them made for you. I'm a foundry worker. I can bring you the cast iron heads it shows here for, maybe, three dollars. What will you make the long handles of?"

"Hazel," I answered without the slightest doubt.

"Yes, that would work all right. Say, what's your first name?" When I said it was Clyde, he was pleased. "May I call you that? I think we're going to be friends."

I believed we would too, though I was always to call him Mr. Giesek. On the whole that deeply indented face had an air of foxiness, though I was to find later that it was not one of his characteristics.

"Nellie didn't tell you about the Fosters' lease on the pasture, did she?" he asked. "It runs for five more years. I hope you can come to some agreement with him, but first the house. I tell you I'm all for it. I like odd things. It isn't a new idea is it? It isn't something the government has laid on poor folks, is it?"

"Hannibal made a fort of it in Spain."

"Way back there! Huh—that would be a little before Christ, wouldn't it? Say, how did you talk Nellie into letting you do this on a thirty-dollar option?"

"I pointed out," I answered, "that if I didn't come up with the two hundred fifty dollar payment after twelve months, what I build here would be all hers."

"Well, it'd be her dirt anyway."

"Her earth, sure, but my sweat and that roof for a starter. What in hell you trying to get going here? I'm here to stay. We'll make all payments on the dot."

"Time will tell," he replied. "Anyway, I wish you luck!"

"Thanks," I said. "Here's the three dollars for the diamond and flatty irons. If it's more let me know. Say, this Foster—where does he live?"

"Up the road, Clyde. Back of that big house on the turn."

When I told Foster what I proposed to do, he was pleased to have at me. "You guys from the city," he grated out, "moving out into the country is hard on real farmers."

I started to reply, but he overrode me with, "Yeah, guys like you what snag a couple of acres, get a cow and some chickens, put up a shanty, and make a garden that'll just carry you and the kids. No, it's worse than that. You grow enough stuff on those acres to provide for your sister's family and your wife's folks and their family back in town."

"I can't make it in the city," I said.

"Uh huh, so you steal the livelihood from real farmers by taking three whole families out of the market. It's one more stinkin' outrage. You ought to come to some of our grange meetings and hear what we're up against 'round here."

There he rested his case, short of breath—a medium size guy like me but with a long handsome face of leather. Nature had tanned him but good. He wore clean, finely striped overalls and a cap of the same material. He looked more like an engineer on a Southern Pacific freight than a dairyman. Hard work had not yet torn him down. He looked alert.

I told him of the goat ranch and the stump ranch and he saw me in a slightly different light, and when I told him about the rammed-earth house, his air was apologetic about including me with "them others." He wanted to know more about the rammed-earth house and he came over with me to see where I would put it and was a bit impressed by my magnificent mound and the roof that topped it.

Finally he said, "I hope your bad luck changes on this house. You build it and I'll move the cows off, and your share of the meadow will be yours to work as you see fit." We shook hands on it.

While I was waiting for the cast iron heads, I made one of oak much larger and shaped like a pear, drilled it for a handle in the big end. Handles I made of hazelwood from bushes that, growing in tall timber and holding up their leaves to what light there was, were very straight. I made the handles as tall as a man, and when Mr. Giesek brought me the cast iron diamond shape and flat finisher, I was ready, after putting handles in them, to start a long experimental job that was to become my home.

Fifty years later the daughter of Mrs. Giesek still remembers the pounding that went on when the house was a-building. The thudding, tamping grew louder as the earth in the forms became more compacted until a cubic foot of it weighed more than a cubic foot of concrete, until the four-by-four crossbeams on the forms bowed between two foot boltings.

From seven in the morning until midnight my neighbor was aware that Rice was intent on making a house of materials normally under foot—rammed earth! Yeah man! You pitched about four inches of dirt into the space between the forms, an area a foot wide and ten feet long. Then you got in there and thumped with your long handled tools: first with the pear shaped one to sort of knead the dirt, then with the diamond shaped one to further consolidate it and work out any air spaces, and then with the flattie you tamped until the earth within the forms rang, not like a metal bell, but it rang, and you could jump out and throw in another layer.

All day while it rained and rained, you pounded dirt in the forms or moved them farther along on the foundation to have at it again. It was a dull kind of work, an inefficient way to build a home, but for me it was the only way available and I loved it. It was one of our old ways, and I felt related to mankind going back into antiquity.

And while the long, ecstatic days roll by what of the world? I was blissfully unaware of it. Far from radios and newspapers and talkative friends, I thought only of Nordi and Bunky, and yes, Virginia. Bunky, living with me, was having a very happy time. He had a marvelous teacher, one of the kind that happens to a person only once in a lifetime. Under her, little scholars absorbed more than their lessons. They learned how to think.

Bunky grew in all ways that winter, as he never had or would again, and he had a chore. Every afternoon when he came home he cut off one section of a log that lay at the top of our place. With a sharp saw almost as big as himself, he severed the piece from the log and then, with a whoop, started it rolling downhill where it ended up near our shack. There I would upend it and split it into our firewood and kindling. In winter rains it became damp, but by splitting it into small and smaller pieces, we were able to dry the wood by standing it around the stove.

In a way I helped Bunky with a problem he had at Carver school. In that strange winter the bully of the class had taken Bunky's gym shoes from his locker and, because he was bigger than Bunky, would not give them back—in fact, wore them to school. He'd been wearing them a week before Bunky told me about it.

"How can he wear your shoes if he's so big?" I asked.

"I don't know, Pop, but he's bigger than anyone in our class. He's being held back a class because his folks let him stay home whenever he wanted to and he didn't pass."

"Has he got small feet?" I asked.

"I don't know," Bunky replied, "but I won't tattle to the teacher, and when I try to take them away from him, he holds me off with his long arms and laughs at me."

"You do as I say and you'll get them back," I promised.

"I sure will, Pop."

"All right. Get that gunnysack of sawdust that I brought home to scatter over the mud at our doorstep."

I hung it on a rope under our great roof and taught him to get the most out of a punch by trying to punch through it. In short order he became a quick heavy puncher and learned to hide any sign he was going to strike out. I told him to ask for his shoes at a very muddy, slippery place.

"Say: 'Please give me my shoes,' and Bunky, when he says, 'No!' let him get the *n* out, but try to punch his nose out of the back of his head while he's trying to get the *o* out for 'no,' then haul off and hit him on the nose harder. The second one you can take your time, but hit harder, then get ready to fight him, but Bunky, I don't think you'll have to. I think he's going to be down in the mud taking off your shoes. If he isn't and he's down, try to get him on the nose again. Well, try that punch on me," and he did time and again.

Next day he came back at noon grinning broadly: "It worked, Pop," he called out before he got to me. "I only had to hit him twice. Guess his nose is still bleeding. A bunch of the guys saw it. He had to go home barefoot and get his own shoes." Bunky handed me his gym shoes. They were pretty dirty and squeezed out of shape.

"I can clean them up tonight," he said. "Got to hurry back."

It was a fall and winter of rain and more rain. No colorful autumn leaves brightened the scene. There was no chill in the air. Dead slate-colored leaves stayed hanging on the trees until heavy rains bore them to the ground. Mud was the order of the day except under the big roof.

At first I speared suckers in the river with a pounded nail at the end of one of my long hazel handles, but they tasted so muddy that I gave up using them as a source of food. There were salmon in the river, but I couldn't afford the tackle for such fishing, neither could I spare the time. Twice the Clackamas flooded our meadow. The narrow swale between our rocky upland and the meadow became a river hurling driftwood at the trees in passing. The new year, when it came, did so with windstorms from the south and the east.

With some weird contraptions that I devised myself and two of the blocks and tackles which I'd brought along in our trek from California I moved the heavy forms without help.

Each weekend Nordi came to stay with us bringing freshly laundered clothes and taking away our mud-smeared ones. With her in the shack, even in such a boar's nest as ours, it took on a home-like air. Perhaps it was curtains at the windows or the twigs of cedar with which she covered the floor, but it seemed there were ten different reasons why both Bunky and I found it necessary to spend time with her when we should be out at our chores. We got more done when she wasn't there, though she helped Bunky pitch dirt up to me where I pounded in the forms. I was coming around on the wall on the second pass and two weeks later on the third. The bark on the hazel handles was a polished brown like the shell of chestnuts, as rich a brown as those seen in the paintings of Rembrandt and Van Dyke. The bones of my hands were beginning to ache from the jar of ceaseless pounding.

One Sunday a windstorm came roaring in after dark. It was from the southwest and brought with it one heavy downpour after another. A week earlier I had finished a protective wall on the south side of my structure made of a pole frame covered with what canvas I could scrounge and burlap sacks stitched together with marlin and nailed to the frame. It held through the storm else my earth wall would have been soaked by the heavy rain driven horizontally by the wind. We were out within the earth walls, Nordi with us, expecting disaster of some kind, perhaps the whole roof would be lifted from its poles and sail away.

Bunky climbed up on the mound, now much diminished, and stepped into a sloppy hole of soft mud. We found a section of tarpaper blown from the roof. It took the three of us to hold down a great patch that the wind tried to jerk from our hands but, all sitting on it, we got it nailed down and tarred, though we were soaked and blown silly by the storm.

Monday I kept Bunky home from school, and we carefully dug out the mud. It was the shape of a cone that got bigger the farther it went down in the mound, but by evening we had every bit of it removed, and I felt sure we had enough dirt left to finish the walls. Then just to be sure, I nailed down another layer of tarpaper over the roof, tarring it down beside tacking it and felt secure.

In such times there was something almost manly in the way Bunky worked with me, though I only used him in the pinches. He was a great comrade to me. Years later I found out that in no way had I been a comrade to him, though he tolerated me. One had to be in the age group between ten and eleven to be accepted as a true companion. One of the things we did enjoy together was the antics of a mountain boomer—a coney-like creature about the size of a medium size rabbit. We kept missing kindling from behind the stove, so one night we waited, taking turns listening till we heard a tiny sound. Turning the flashlight on the kindling pile, we found the boomer hauling kindling across the room to a hole that he had made in the floor where, after much maneuvering, he got the kindling stick down and then went after another. He had no use for them, but somehow he had to steal as much as he could. We fed him rolled oats, and Bunky, though he tried, could never make a pet of him. When we tore down the shack much later, there was the kindling in a scattering pile.

So it went, and one day the walls were done. On the side facing south was an opening for a big window, six by nineteen feet to be exact. Above it we placed a built-up hollow beam set in cement on the rammed earth at either end and supported in the middle by a column. We placed one end of the long joists that would support the floor of the upstairs bedrooms on the beam and the other end on top of the back wall. I trussed them apart and trued everything up and was out gathering any kind of board

I could lay hands on to make a temporary floor for the upstairs. We planned to live there while we waited for the dirt walls to really dry out.

There were innumerable things I could do as I waited out the drying. I could remove what was left of the mound, but felt that there was a need for me at Acme. We should build up our stock for the coming season, at least of vanilla and the main flavors. There was a bus line from Carver to Portland, so Bunky never missed a class while we were in town. I made hundreds of gallons of vanilla, forty of strawberry, lemon in four different forms and an excellent maple flavor that had never been near a tree.

Pop was still enthusiastic about rammed earth, though he refused to come out and see what we had done: "Until the roof is on," he said.

In February we waited, my friends, relatives and I, for a weekend of fair weather. I had sawn out the rafters, and they were ready to be put up in place. On the third weekend it came— three days of near summer sunshine. Before sunlight brightened the land around Carver, we were at it, all six of us, tearing down, though saving every board of the great roof that had protected the mound and the walls, for now it stood in the way of the permanent roof of our house. Soon it was reduced to a stack of lumber.

With help from Teddy I raised the rafters while the others were at lunch. Then, as a crew, we nailed the old roof's shiplap on the new rafters, following that with heavy composition shingles. We were very busy till Sunday evening, when my good friends, smiling wearily, drove away and left us with *fait accompli*.

Nordi looked up at the sky, "Spill down your rains. Flourish your storms," she called out but could not finish with more brave words and rushed into my arms weeping with happiness.

Monday noon Pop and Nordi drove out. He had bought a pair of galoshes to put over his shoes and, with trouser cuffs well up, viewed the scene. After pushing here, pulling there, after driving a nail into the hardening wall, he said, "What you have here is only a shell. You'll have to work on it for years, but Clyde, I know

now that you've got the spunk. You're not very smart, but then I suppose that helps you to be an artiste. Too bad you've got no business head; still, the world needs suckers to support the sharpies. It seems life's rigged that way. It strikes a balance.

"Well, your vacation that I worked up for you ended an hour ago. I've got a long list of things that need to be done. Starting at one o'clock I'll see you at the factory."

He got in his car and drove away while Nordi and I made quick but ecstatic love in the old shack.

After Mr. Foster's kind offer to relinquish the land if I built the house, I got my father and the clan and their friends to buy the produce that they would normally buy in town from Foster. Lockers could be rented in refrigerated warehouses. Pop and I shared one, so we were able to buy a pig all packaged for freezing, half a dozen chickens and a hindquarter of a beef when Foster slaughtered. We also bought potatoes, cabbage and squash from him—fine! Jack, Teddy and Albert, as customers of Foster, bought much the same, substituting veal for pork, of course. We saved money dealing with him, besides showing him our esteem for the way he proposed to treat me.

Bunky and I had been talking about Nordi as we ate supper one evening. He said one thing, I said another—all reminiscences concerned with the way she walked, the way she gestured in arguments and the way she peeled potatoes for supper. Just chatter, really, but we built such an image of her before us, that the desire to see the real Nordi grew strong in us. Suddenly Bunky jumped up and began to clean himself up for town and so did I.

An hour later we found the yungrubarn empty and only Mother Nordstrom at home. Olga and Jack had taken Nordi along when they went to visit his sister in Beaverton. The evening became drear. We had coffee and doughnuts, but the old lady without her favorite daughter was sadly glum.

Bunky wanted to see a movie now that we were in town. *Ruggles of Red Gap*, which I had seen before, was playing at the Rio only four blocks away. I felt we couldn't leave the old lady, without her Olga, in such a lost mood. Bunky then asked her to come to the movie with us. She rattled off the taboos that were basic in her church's dogma, but not, I noticed, with her usual vehemence. Knowing her love of a joke I told her how hilarious the movie was, and I appealed to her patriotism too, telling how Laughton, the hero of the play, recited Lincoln's Gettysburg Address in one part. She didn't mention the taboos again, but said she really shouldn't go; still, in her mood it was obvious she felt the need of something to buck her up until the return of the "sainted" Olga. Fifteen minutes later we helped her into her coat and took her to the show.

She asked to be seated next to the aisle where she could jump up and leave "if they showed anything dirty," but a moment after the start of the film, she was completely enthralled in her first movie. I say "in" advisedly, for it was obvious that she lived every part, became every character; her face grew radiant, illumined. She continued to glance first at Bunky and then at me, as if the three of us were sharing our joy in the happenings on the screen. Ruggles was her son and she gloried in him.

At first from her aisle seat she could leap out into the aisle, arms waving above her head, when the need to react physically was on her. An usher asked us to put her in between us, where she sat on the edge of her seat, while her whole being absorbed *Ruggles of Red Gap.*

It's difficult for a profile to convey much. What was flaring from her face must have been in the glances she bestowed on us—sort of, "Did you see that?" "Look at that!"—seated as she was, leaning toward the screen as if to garner what was happening before it quite got to her. Yes, it must have been that. Whatever it was, I came to realize what a passionate being old lady Nordstrom was and felt that the late Mr. Nordstrom and the husband of her youth must have been dolts in bed, else why was this passionate woman so provoked with men?

In Carver I was able to get some used lumber, cedar luckily, from which I built the gables at either end of my roof. They had big windows in them. Then I floored the upstairs and brought in electricity and piped water, installed a big kitchen range and we moved in, reveling in our new abode on the second floor of the rammed-earth house.

Nordi's family's love of the countryside drew them out often to our building. Teddy and Jack helped me pour the massive cement front windowsill, and they were salient in our crew who put on the roof.

One day Jack asked me if I would mind having a neighbor, and shortly after Teddy put the same question to me. On finding that it would be my pleasure and Nordi's delight, they arranged to buy land on each side of us. Jack had succumbed to the urgings of Olga and her mother to sell the house in town and with the money received had a house built on the property alongside us.

The land that Teddy bought was the four acres of bottomland that was below Mrs. Giesek's house and her bit of upland. I gave him enough of my upland to build the house and barn that he planned, and a way through our place to get out to his bottomland.

Between the rise that we built on and narrow wash that separated us from the meadow was a wide strip of rich loam that ran across both Jack's land and ours. On Jack's there were big clumps of hazel that I dug out, roots and all. On our part there were some old maple stumps that I blew clear out of the ground with lucky blasts, for I had a hope that we were going to have a community garden later in the strip.

The bones in my hand were sore, stone bruised, it was called. The incessant jar of tamping I found is much more debilitating to bones and tendons than swinging out with axe or pick. I could do my work at Acme, but the heavier stuff, well, I'd simply have to give it up for awhile. I began catching up on my reading and the radio.

It was during these years that I, an idealist, became increasingly a cynic. Strangely, this came about somewhat through Prokofiev's music. As all semi-thinking people, I felt dismay at the ease with which a leader can inflame his group to give up their lives if necessary, attacking another group designated as the enemy by their leader. History is monotonous with it. For years my sometime interest in religions and governments and their wars had been global. Our predatory natures, greed, and unwillingness to accept the boundaries that other conflicts of the past have placed between nations, and the fiendish torture and warfare with which different sects within the Mohammedan, Buddhist and Christian religions attacked each other produced in me a dim view of our human race. I had seen pictures of bas relief plaques produced by the Babylonians and other ancients and later photographs of similar stone work from India. The ancient histories I read were full of kings and their armies.

In San Francisco I heard music that made me see their activity in a larger, but still more personal way. It was Prokofiev's *Scythian Suite* that brought into my mind a vast picture. In it I saw an army going across a rather arid country—long columns of armored foot soldiers, trudging ten abreast with spears, helmets gleaming in the sun. They marched to a cacophony of trumpets, drums and cymbals and were led by their king in a bejeweled chariot pulled by lions. When they came upon a habitation, they massacred the people, leveled all the buildings, took what they wanted and marched on—Timor, Sargon, Alexander, the Mongols, the great Cuspidor and Admiral Klangwitz, ashore.

After some time, with the din of the marauding army growing dim in the distance, with the smoke of the burning village fed no longer with flame, when at last there was quiet, timid people who had hidden in the reeds or canyons crept out and began to bury the dead and raise reed huts against the wind. They copulated and began to create order.

Several moons later they would hear distant fanfare as the returning king and his columns and the trains of booty passed them far out on the plain. They came out of their hiding places again and thanked their Gods for saving them and built simple temples to them, though why their Gods had not saved them the first time, did not enter their minds.

Now our civilized world was preparing once more for destruction and murder on a gigantic scale. Immense shoulder-to-shoulder columns, twenty abreast, marched through Russia's Red Square, their cannons following. Hitler staged huge rallies where deep block on block on block of troops lock-stepped before their dictator. Stalin attacked neutral Finland, and the Germans dismembered Poland. Mankind was ravening at the throat of mankind, and those of us aware enough to love humanity wept. The evil, ever-recurring pattern was upon us again.

After all the help that Pop had given me on the house, he became surly again without reason, for I brought him an account he had never been able to get, a baker who used more lemon emulsion than all the rest of the town. Our lemon emulsion was made from a brand of Italian lemon oil named Messina. It was the best that could be procured. I conceived the idea of adding fourteen drops of a powerful aldehyde of an orange-lemon cast to twenty gallons of Messina lemon oil emulsion. The result was a livelier fresher lemon flavor than the less rounded tasting material used by the competition. Anyway, Pop and the Little Lady, as usual, grew angry not because of the aldehyde, but about bringing in an account that he had never been able to bring home. I think he was jealous and she egged him on. He snarled around finding fault with everything I did. In fact, my father and I were never to be so close again after the dirt house became a fact.

Still, we wangled another concession from him, not as far reaching as my free winter to pound dirt, but he allowed us to come to work at seven, take a quarter of an hour for lunch and to leave at three fifteen. Of course the two of us together didn't receive the wage of one union factory worker and it was evident to all we should get breaks of some sort.

Nordi liked the work she did at Acme, never appearing bored or wearied. The trouble was we were together too much. I could not make enough money to let her quit, and she said she'd be bored stiff staying at home.

Now that no lover interfered I felt overly secure in my love life and was beginning to take Nordi too much for granted. In my mind Nordi and I were one, Nordi less an individual and more a part of me, like, say, my left arm. I should have caught the lie in this asinine sophistry, but it slipped by for it was easy.

I bought a pair of large leather gloves and stuffed them with sponge rubber in such a way that my misused hands could grasp the handles of the axes and shovels without undue pain. Spring came late that year. In March the river rose, and while it didn't flood the meadow, it did pour a torrent down the swale.

June was full of fragrances that the breezes mixed somehow so you weren't certain if it was from this bank of flowers or the flowering bushes growing up the hill.

In June, Ginny graduated from high school and, when Olga put up a tent on their land but quite close to our house, Ginny and her sister came to spend the summer with her. Bunky had a companion in David, who was now almost as big as he was.

Downstream from us a part of the river came in and made a small island. At the lower end of the island was a deep pool with a sandy bottom and big rock on one side to dive from. We made a path down to it and swam there either before supper or just before dark, for the water out of the current was warm there. Here it was that I noticed that Virginia's slender frame was filling out. She was no longer skinny, but still wonderfully slim in those places where slimness is admired.

With the new arrangement at Acme, we could be swimming at four. Nordi swam nude unless strangers were about. After a quick plunge she hurried back to cook supper, while I loafed a bit by the pool with Ginny and the kids and sometimes Olga, before attacking my endless carpentry.

The women of the family continued to arrange things so whatever the family chore, Ginny and I did it together. With Nordi, I think she was pleased to be rid of me for awhile.

Finally I had to face how deeply Ginny's smile permeated the secret life of my mind. What was it that kept putting her so insistently in my reveries? Certainly it was not her intelligence, nor wide experience or great beauty, nor her curiosity about life, nor a hunger for it. Even in the hidebound thinking of the clan, her parents were recessive and self-effacing, and she, their product, was instructed by their actions—or should I say, by their lack of volition. They were moles who loved the outdoors so much they would leave their burrow on Sundays. I saw how small was her view of the world, how limited her enjoyment of it, and I wanted to broaden her outlook on music and art, to bring her new tastes, new food. I, oh—I hungered to show her the beauty of certain relationships and wide groupings that seemed to me significant.

At the borning house, things were rolling along nicely. The downstairs windows and doors were in on the house, and it was time to build the fireplace. I had massed in the foundation for it and bought the bricks when Bob Drake appeared.

Mr. Giesek was with me at the time. I was explaining to him why the foundation for the fireplace was set out into the room. "Nordi wants the stairs to the bedrooms to go behind the fireplace to wrap around it ascending. The fireplace will be big and, except for its great mouth, encased in a stucco shell. Heat will come out at several different places besides from over the hearth."

"You talk it badly," said Giesek. "Make me a sketch. Here's a smooth board."

I was making a sketch when—"Clyde," someone called from outside. "Clyde, where are you? I haven't much time."

We came out to find Bob Drake shuffling around on his game leg; as usual he was in a hurry. After a handshake, most welcome, though it all but wrecked my hand and arm, he said:

"I wasn't sure from Nordi's directions, until I saw your house. Only a fool like you or I would tackle such a setup. Congratulations!"

"It was a chicken house design, Bob, but I wouldn't do that for all the chickens on God's green earth. It's going to be our home."

"You're a neighbor, I assume," Bob said to Giesek. "Well, I was too once. Not bad, not bad at all. Say, Clyde, do you realize it's been six years?" And to Giesek again: "On account of me, Clyde had to go without food for four days. You'll treat him better, I hope. You are a neighbor?"

"Bob," I broke in on his chatter, "where's your lightship?"

"Later," he said grabbing my shoulder and shaking it. "I've got to see a guy in town. Have dinner with me tonight at Henry Thiele's—six, huh? His food is famous clear down to Frisco. Got to go. You're looking good," and he hobbled up the road to his car. Giesek gave me a funny look. "You have many friends like that, Clyde?"

"Nobody has," I answered. "Wonder what in hell he did with his lightship?" We went back in. I wanted to be sure I had the foundation just right.

"That friend of yours has a lightship, you say? Did he own some shares in a blimp? I almost bought into a fraud like that once myself."

Well, I tried to tell him about it, but he knew nothing about ships or shipping. "Look," I said, "anchored out from our main harbors are government ships, floating lighthouses, built to take any weather."

"Anchored out?" he grumbled. "What do you mean?"

"Anchored out about ten miles from the harbor with a light and a foghorn to steer incoming ships to the harbor. Get it? Bob bought one that the government had retired. Hell, Giesek, it's a long story, like Bob.

"What do you think of this for a foundation?"

"It's all right," he said. "Say, if any more of those friends of yours come up from California, let me know. I'd like to be around. Sort of a sideshow for me."

But I kept quiet. I didn't want to talk about Bob and his U.S. lightship. He had had the engines and boilers removed, found there was a sheet of lead an inch and a half thick pinned to the ship's timbers underneath the boilers and engine. He ripped that up and sold it. It paid him enough to hire a diver to rescue a diesel engine from a yacht that had recently sunk on the coast of Southern California at Point Arquilla. Rigging it so it would turn the ship's propellor through a series of gears, then with some sails and a crew of young fellows, half of whom had never been to sea, they headed for Alaska.

Next I heard he had rented a three-masted codfish schooner and again headed for Alaska for the Kuskokwim, a river that paid off in salmon once in five years. It was a disaster.

But now he was in the money, in the paint business. He stayed around for a day or two visiting and trying to talk me out of my job.

"Look," he said, "this isn't for you. There's no spark here. It isn't chancey. Your wages are way below what I pay my help. Your old man is using his relationship with you to keep you as a serf, and I believe Mrs. Rice hates you and fears you. Come back to California with me and make four times better wages, and, Clyde, you've got friends down there. We've missed you."

I demurred. "I'm going to see this Acme thing through."

"That's foolishness, Clyde. The old fart has got you mesmerized. Well, anyway here's how you can make some extra dough. A couple of years ago I bought a bunch of stolen paint business formulas. Well—sort of *boom!* and I'm in the paint business. There's one angle of it you could use. Look, I'll send you a drum of lacquer thinner that I make and sell down south. You put out some samples. See what happens." I agreed, figuring I had nothing to lose, and turned my attention back to building my fireplace.

I had all the materials ready the morning the bricklayer arrived a bit drunk to build my fireplace and chimney. "This fireplace," I said, "will have an arched opening, a heavy steel back and sides in the firebox itself, an opening in the brickwork on each side to let out heat from the three plates, and it's going to have a smoke chamber in the flue."

"My fireplaces never need that kind of thing. Just let me do it my way," said the bricklayer.

"On the phone," I reminded him, "you said you would build it any way I wanted it."

"Okay, okay," he said. "Let's get started. You got the slaked lime for the mortar?"

"A hundred gallons of it. I slaked it last night."

We were well up to the arch of the fireplace opening when I

saw that he was deliberately building the back of the chimney without the smoke chamber. "You're not building it the way we agreed."

"Ain't no need of it," he said. "I build fireplaces and chimneys every day."

"This one's going to have a smoke pocket."

"I don't go for these new fangled ideas," he said. "Bring me some more bricks."

I handed him ten bucks. "Pack up your kit and get the hell off my place," I said.

"I don't take that kind of crap offen guys your size," he said.

"This is one time you're going to. Now get started."

He was a big man and mean, but for some reason he did leave. Maybe it was too early in the morning or something.

"I got the laugh on you," he said as he picked up his tools. "You don't know how to lay bricks and that hundred gallon hogshead of slaked lime will set up before you learn how to handle it."

After he left I remembered carefully how he had buttered, as he had said, each brick, tried it myself, kept trying and, by God, I got the arch in and the smoke pocket just like I wanted it. Plastering the chimney on the inside as I worked up, I put the chimney through the roof by dark. It was one hell of a workout—the chimney big enough for a fat Santa Claus to enter. I was proud of it.

Next day, Sunday, I had to repair a stairway into the basement at my father's. When I got back home I found Nordi had put up the kitchen chimney from its foundation below the floor up through the roof, an unbelievable job for a woman, but then one of Nordi's few annoying tricks was to beat me at my game, whatever it was. The two of us finished our chimneys Monday night, topping them off well above the ridgepole. The fireplace was an unparalleled success with its heating chambers and arched opening.

Bob Drake did send me the drum of lacquer thinner. When it arrived I ran it into five gallon tins and passed them around in the

various paint shops of the automobile dealers in the area, naming
the price and my phone number. Within a week there were ten
outfits who wanted to deal with me, for I sold it a bit cheaper than
the paint companies. Bob sent up another drum and a formula,
saying "make your own, but give me a cut."

A month later I was making my own.

"Pop," I said soon after I saw what I had. "We could do all
right on the wages you pay us if I had a sideline that would net me
a little spondoolicks to jingle in my pocket."

"How?" my old man asked, all interest.

"Well, take these deliveries I make for you," I answered. "I
could deliver something of my own while I was out there. I'd pay
for the gas."

"All of it?" asked my old man.

"Yep," I answered, "all of it."

"Done," my pennypinching father said quickly and laughed.

I put up a shed where I could make the thinner. The process
was simplicity itself. A few months of increased sales and I built
a larger place with plenty of space to work, with racks for twenty
drums and a roof over all. The walls I made shoulder high and
screened above to let in any drafts of air that might disperse the
fumes of the materials Just a spark or someone coming in with a
cigarette while I was working with these explosive liquids could
blow us sky high.

From then on, with the building of the big thinner shed and
increased sales, I began to live a life without any definite schedule, sleeping when I could, eating when I could. One thing was
fairly constant in those years: from ten-thirty in the evening until
twelve or two, as needed, I worked making and packaging the
thinner. I sold a lot in twenty-gallon drums. The other constant
was my work at Acme. I went at it with a rush and was able to stay
ahead on supplies.

It was during this time my father traded the company car
for a panel. Coming around a turn one day I saw a farmer in
the middle of the turn fixing his tire out in the road and another
car coming toward me. I slammed on the brakes. The three

fifty-gallon drums I was carrying slid forward and pushed me and my seat into the steering wheel. Jammed as I was against the wheel, unable to steer, I dared not push the brake down farther. Instead I skidded between the car and the farmer in the road, luckily without mishap. I headed to town and bought a pickup. I wanted to be in a cab separated from my load after that.

I now had a locked shed behind the factory, as Pop and the Little Lady pompously designated our place of business, where I stored several days' supplies. For Pop I did all that was required of me and more, making his extracts and emulsions and packaging the finished product for shipment and making the city deliveries. On Mondays I went to one end of my territory and worked back the following day. My route extended from Eugene on the south to Olympia in Washington, well over two hundred miles.

I love the Willamette Valley with a native's sense of ownership. With the peaks of the Coast Range and the Cascades rearing up on either side, I sang and sang again, as I headed up the valley for the next town and the lone painter, who, face caught into a breathing mask, sprayed blue over the faded red of some aging phaeton.

Pop could not understand how I did so well with the lacquer thinner. "There has to be a gimmick, Clyde," he said coming in and staring at me as if he had two sons, and at present was talking to the one he could accept. "Let me in on it."

So I did. "Pop, the people who paint automobiles are loners. One man does the painting and all the work of getting the car ready for painting. Oh, he might have a kid around after school, but I talk to a lonely guy, poorly educated, and isolated by the danger to others of his job. Booze is his solace. The salesmen who service him from the big companies are well-paid, overweight, cigar smoking, rather important-feeling men, at least when with mere car painters. They know nothing about their product and recite the line their companies drill them in. Then I come on the scene. I'm a little guy too, like the painter, a little guy who's trying to make an honest buck, pushing his own thinner, and I do know what is in it. I tell them enough, so that they sort of understand, feel they're in on the facts.

"I say: 'It's got less amyl acetate in it these summer months,' and 'I'm holding the toluol steady and keeping the butyl alcohol about the same,' and 'From what you fellows tell me, my mixture of three diluents hits it right on the nose.'

"And, Pop, I use just a shade more true solvents than is called for. It's a cost, sure, but with the national firms cutting, say two percent, and getting by all right, until some atmospheric condition or a mistake in application by the painter turns in a botched job. The body shops notice there's not nearly so many botches using my stuff, so when a representative of a big paint company tells them: 'This "707" is a new thinner. We're getting heavy sales on it up and down the coast,' the painters ask if the thinner has amyl acetate made from fusel oil or from a petroleum derivative. When the salesman doesn't know and starts another spiel, the little guy lords it over him feeling wonderful and buys my material. We're friends, see—a couple of little guys getting by."

"That cut you pay Bob Drake is uncommon high," announced my father jealously.

"Oh, it's all right," I answered, but in truth I was sick of Drake's nagging. He had an idea of sailing to Java to buy tin and zinc at the mines. It was used extensively to make body solder with which the dents were filled before painting a car body. He was really going to make a killing, so he doubled the size of the cut that I paid him and was now trying to double it again, which would make me sell at quite a loss. He was doing this with all of his customers trying to get enough money quickly to carry out his plans.

I had stopped using his formulas. I made my own based on what I saw in the paint shops, the things that were happening there. My thinners were very much better than those made with Drake's bootlegged formulas. I found myself peculiarly adept in the manipulation of thinner formulas. The aim, of course, was to make the paint start drying slowly, to gradually increase the drying tempo and then to slow the drying toward the last: this, to avoid the hated pebbling—"alligator," they called it. I had eleven different materials, each had its use. It was like working with extracts and flavors. I enjoyed it. How this affected that. How this blend toned the main ingredient. Here was mystery, nuance, subtlety, and one side of me felt completely at home while delving here.

But of Bob, I sent him back his formulas. I liked Bob, I had for years, but the dunning letters he sent me twice a month, a month before they were due, I found very annoying; but then helping him with his schemes had been more costly in the years we had lived side by side at Waterspout Point, so I kept quiet. The cut he originally demanded was unrealistic, but his later demands were insulting. Finally I sent him what I felt was the proper amount, and he quit bothering me; in fact, I received a pleasant letter apologizing for his annoying ways before he took ship for Batavia.

Our money problems were now over. I was really doing well with the lacquer thinner. I made another thinner for synthetic enamel that gave me three times more profit than from the lacquer one, and I was selling lacquer thinner in one-gallon tins for resale in hardware stores.

I was busy, but always played with the kids on Sunday and either afternoon or evening was with them at the swimming hole, and often we lay on beds of carefully placed flat pebbles and soaked up the sun, and Ginny lay beside me on the pebbles, always beside me.

One day my father greeted me with fury when I came back from city deliveries. He had discovered that my profits for the month were much more than his. True, the row between the Little Lady and Johnny Lind was hurting Acme sales. Johnny really knew that he was being cheated, so the zest for new sales was hampered.

"What's the use?" he lamented to me.

As I said, my father was madly jealous and in a fury, because my setup was showing more profit than his. Instead of being pleased that his son was doing well he came at me, his face white with passion. "Clyde," he yelled, "you quit that thinner business right now and never see any of those painters again."

I calmed him down, but he went in and talked to the Little Lady and she got him worked up wilder than ever. He stared me in the face for an agreeing answer. It was silly.

"Hell no, Pop," I said. "I won't destroy my business for a whim of yours. I do my job here better than anyone you've ever had. You've told me so. Fire me if you want, but quit my business, nonsense!"

"You heard me," he gritted out, still glaring at me.

"I'm curious, Pop. What makes you think I'd dump a growing business at your jealous whim?"

They went home and stayed away for a week.

Next day I received a phone call from an auto paint shop in Roseburg. He wanted a drum of synthetic reducer, one of lacquer thinner and one of a new wash thinner that I was now putting up. That is, he would take it if I could deliver it to my customer, Cable Bros., in Eugene before five o'clock, the same day. He would pick it up there. Wilbur Cable had convinced him that it was the best he could buy. He would haul it home, as he was up in Eugene with his truck for supplies.

I hurried back to Carver for the thinner. As I hoped Ginny was in front of Olga's tent sewing something. I asked her to come along. I had just worked that territory, so it would be a quick trip down and back. She agreed, telling Olga she was going and putting on a housedress, all loose, free and flowing. She looked quietly pleased. It was wonderful having her beside me. The air was unbelievably clear all the way to Salem and the contours and colors of the world came directly at us with intense definition, challenging our eyes and minds.

I showed her where my lookout had been on the eastern skyline, a little south of Soosap Peak, which we could see, and I also pointed out Table Mountain and Mary's Peak in the Coast Range. I showed her where my grandmother had been born, as we entered Corvallis for a late lunch.

Over a milkshake, straw in mouth, she regarded me, and in the moment I was wildly happy, but my joy in her was not sexual. Perhaps deep down where I didn't know it, it was, but now it was that I wanted to pet her like a kitten, caress her like a pet rabbit and revel in her beauty, for a beauty she was becoming before my eyes. I just couldn't keep up with the changes. I stared entranced before her enigmatic regard of me, until she took the straw from her mouth and, smiling deeply into my eyes, said:

"Strawberry is my favorite milkshake," and returned to the straw. Strange, this filled me with delight, though I wasn't aware of the why of it until next day when I could figure things out. My delight was that she was so childlike—a page on which there was as yet no writing.

Coming home in a steady summer downpour steam arose from the pavement. I had to keep the windows slightly open to dispel the continual fogging of the windshield. Ginny became chilled. I got out a blanket from behind the seat and wrapped her in it. She leaned into the far corner of the seat, but the rain came in there from the wind of our passage.

Finally I said, "Lean against me. I could use a little warmth myself. The air is saturated. I've got to leave the windows open."

She moved over and leaned against me and a warmth built up between us. Ginny fell asleep, her head on my shoulder. We arrived at Carver with my arm around the warm burden of her. It was already dark. She moved when I pulled up to stop.

"Here we are," I said softly. She burrowed into my side.

"Wish we were only half way home," she murmured. "I liked that rain. Thank you," and after several seconds, "Clyde." She said it tentatively like trying on a hat. I waited, feeling she liked it. "No rain here, huh?" she added almost bruskly.

Did she need this tone to break the spell that had held us silent the last dozen miles, when I knew she had awakened and she knew I was aware that sleep no longer gave her license to press so close? Or was she still just a child, still unknowing of the raptures of pressing or touching? After she left for Olga's tent I stayed seated in the pickup, the warmth of her seeming still against me.

I stayed with the tender turmoil that she was becoming to me, needing time to accommodate to the workaday world.

When I did, I got out and walked through the dark to the brightness of Nordi's kitchen and her welcoming kiss. I lapsed into another beautiful existence and examined a scene Bunky was making in clay of Indians hidden behind a bush and rock, waiting for a covered wagon that was approaching with dogs alert and mounted outriders, rifles nestled in their arms. Over his absorbed head I looked at Nordi and smiled. Ah, yes, the family man! The transition was effortless and complete.

.

When Pop and the Little Lady returned, they looked battered. They were both working hard at it. In a subdued voice that he tried to make sound weak, he asked me to step with him into the office. Then he turned to his wife:

"Little Lady," he murmured, "will you leave us. I want to have a talk with Clyde here about the future."

The Little Lady was a short, compact woman, but she was able to convey in the dozen steps she took to leave the room that she was being put upon, but was handling it with the innate dignity of a tall angular English aristocrat. It was a hard act to follow, and Pop was immediately aware of it.

"Clyde," he said, "both the Little Lady and I were deeply hurt by your (she says savage) reply to a simple request made by your own father. Not only that," he quickly went on, "but you impugn that our (I mean the Little Lady's and my) combined thought is piss-poor thinking. That's hard to take, Clyde, and me sixty-four."

"Where did you get the 'impugn,' Pop?"

"Why, the Little Lady got it out of the dictionary."

"Well, look," I said. "We've got some things to talk over, sure, and I don't believe jealousy is still prodding you to make unreasonable demands. What can we work out?"

It was soon evident that I was too useful for him to follow his desire to fire me. And there was Nordi, the queen of the intricate business of the backroom. We made a deal. I agreed to do just what I had been doing, but my monthly wage would be only one hundred dollars. Still, the Little Lady would keep my books, make out my statements and answer my phone as part of the deal. Fine! We shook hands on it, and he was smiling again. In fact, we went across the street and he bought me a beer. In our brief discussion he hinted several times that he would soon retire and turn the business over to me and the Little Lady, but he grew evasive when I tried to clarify his vague promises.

One day, just back from my bimonthly trip to way points and Olympia, I was sitting on the settee in front of the cold fireplace jotting down which hydrocarbons and how much of each I would order to finish out the month. I was alone. Ginny and her sister had gone home for a few days. Bunky was visiting a school friend and Nordi had not yet arrived on the bus.

Having finished my calculations, I stared thoughtlessly into the fireplace, at peace with myself. I lounged back and gazed with equal thoughtlessness at the wall on my right. After a bit, a perpendicular line appeared on it, a line about as long as my arm and where no line had been before. Strange, I was not startled, but continued to stare at it, as a horizontal line appeared and touched it at the lower end. I thought there should be numbers, and then there were, along both the horizontal and the perpendicular lines. Each number was made of three numbers, like 234 or 395—about twelve numbers on each line. Still I was not amazed. Looking at this odd thing on my wall, I thought: I'll bet I could use that to answer arithmetic problems. So I wrote on the pad, below my scribbled order for solvents, the numbers 391 and 727. Then I forcefully thought the 391 on the perpendicular and the 727 on the horizontal line, and they appeared superimposed on the other numbers.

What type of problem, I wondered, shall I do here, and decided on multiplication. I stared at the junction of the two lines and, superimposed on the two numbers, another number appeared. It was 284, 257. I wrote it down, then worked out the problem on the pad. It was right!

I tried it two or three more times with other numbers. Multiplication or division, it always came out right. I remembered the finding of the axe, the healing of Catherine's brother. Yes, it was something psychic. Okay, so I'm psychic sometimes, though rarely.

When Nordi arrived, I told her about my experience. I gave her the pencil and pad and repeated the performance staring at the wall while it all materialized. The numbers I named appeared over the others. Then I read the answer. She worked it out on the pad. "Correct," she said, "how did you do it?"

I asked her if she saw the numbers on the wall. I pointed them out, but she saw nothing there. We did it many times and I was always right.

I tried it out on Jack as a game to see who could figure on the answer first. He was very clever with figures, but I beat him time and again. He figured it akin to a card trick—an angle, he said. Next day I tried it on my father, who was a very fast calculator, but beat him at each problem. He could see nothing on the wall and became angry.

It lasted about a week. Then, as it had appeared, it left me. I wish I had exhibited this phenomenon before experts in the field of psychic happenings, experts in mathematics, but I didn't. What do I think of it? If it hadn't been for the true answers, I would have considered myself nuts.

Nordi advised me not to tell the members of the families about the strange happening. "They're touchy about you as it is," she said. She came to me and hugged me. "You poor outsider," she said, "I know how you'd like to belong, but honey, with your many corners and angles, where could you fit?"

The following week I went about my work in much the same rush as before. The figures that had been on the wall would have faded in my mind like last week's baseball scores had it not been for my father and Nordi. She felt that I needed protection because of my oddities, and mothered me when she was not considering me very thoughtfully, as if I were a column of figures she couldn't quite add up, while Pop urged me to do it again.

"I saw you do it five times," he said, "and if you can do it five times, you can always do it. Get your thinking cap on son. We need a mathematician in the family a hell of a lot more than an artiste." But the visions or whatever never came again, and when I tried to force them to reappear the feeling was all wrong and vulgar. I turned away from it with relief.

When Saturday noon closed the usual week of vanilla and lacquer thinner, Nordi and I hurried home. There, unbuttoning our clothes as we ran, we dove into the pellucid pool, frightening a pair of otters who disappeared from the pool in a headlong down-river exodus. We waded out to take off our shoes, for in the race to be first in, we hadn't allowed for the usual niceties. We were full of the joy of being together and in this paradise. We swam and cavorted till, tired, we lay on the flat pebbled basking places, ("like elephant seals," Nordi said) and talked through our noses, playing we had proboscises until we fell asleep in the sun.

We awoke to find Bunky about to pour a swimming cap full of water on our bare buttockses. We hastened to put on our swimsuits that he'd brought.

"I saw you when you ran past," he laughed. "Here come the Bromses."

Happy summer day. No garden to hoe, no stock to care for today. The work of finishing the house seemed eternal, but it was pleasant working slowly as an amateur should.

I hired Neufer to put down the hardwood floor in the front room. He looked over my circular stairway behind and around the fireplace and asked what was my method for figuring the change of the hypothetical center as the steps rose.

"I'm afraid I just blindly started out without any definite plan, working it out as I went along."

"Well, you seemed to have turned out a professional looking wrap-around stairway. I'm impressed," Ray said.

Neufer was not one to hand out compliments, so I glowed a little. We worked together on the floor and I learned a lot, for Ray had a natural affinity for wood. The most cantankerous piece of twisted flooring became cooperative once he put his hands on it. Not so under my hands and hammer. I like to believe a difference in temperament was the basis of this, but I guess we should mention, in passing, the lack of expertise on my part. Nordi was pleased with the floor when, after four coats of varnish, I left it for rougher chores.

The warm nights of late summer found us swimming after dark, or rather in the moonlight. Nordi was trying to induce the others to swim nude: "That's the only way you can really feel the water. Try it and see," and when no one moved to take off their suits, she laughed at them. One of her rare angers found voice: "This is an August night but, before you know it, you'll be wearing overcoats and hugging fires. We came to swim in the moonlight, to dive and swim in the soft intimate water, and you wear stuff to destroy the velvet of it. It's a darn dull way to enjoy what August offers."

The poetry that I knew was usually somnolent in her spoke out against this waste of a moonlit night. "Okay, you slow nymphs and weary fauns, come out of your duds and feel the flow of the water as you dive. Hurry, don't waste a second. Winter is coming."

They stripped off their suits at her talk of time a-wasting, plunged in, and at once admitted Nordi was right. There was, after all, a sleekness in swimming without encumbrances that had to be felt to be evaluated.

Teddy had a flashlight with him and with little flicks of it he was our lifeguard keeping count of heads. In the dim moonlight our nakedness was clothed in tree shadows, so that even Tekla's extreme prudishness was not offended.

Several days later I made a light that would slowly sink to the bottom of our pool. It was a fruit jar with a lamp and several flashlight batteries, and enough lead embedded in paraffin to make the bottle sink, but quite slowly. We battled in the pool over who could force it down so that the next person had to go deeper to retrieve it. It made the bottom of the pool seem like a far away mysterious place and the bodies of the swimmers appeared clothed in black against the glow from below, and Teddy kept track of our heads to be sure we were all accounted for.

•

The Forsythes sold the house where Nordi and Olga had been raised and soon after got a former contractor friend to build for them on their acreage beside us. Teddy built a shack at the top of his place and they camped in it until he could build his house.

My life was full from four in the morning until one the next morning. I used my time well and always had some time to play, as I never seemed to tire. My reading was suffering; still, I felt if I could keep up the pace until winter when fewer cars were painted and the flavoring business slowed down, I would have time for a great slug of reading in all the fields that interested me.

I came home from The Dalles on a late Saturday afternoon, half a day ahead of schedule. No one seemed to be around. The whole family was off on what I assumed was church business, and the old lady evidently had roped in Nordi and Bunky (that, in my calculations, took some doing, but they were gone). I was left to spend the evening by myself. I had eaten on the way home, so fancy free, taking an old blanket, I had just started an amble to the upper end of the meadow where I planned to lie under the sky and consider the stars, when Virginia appeared on the trail from the pool. When she saw me, she seemed almost to stop, then came on.

To my questions she explained: "A famous missionary of theirs is speaking at the church. Grandma got everybody but me," she said. "I wouldn't go. I kept thinking about each day nibbling at what's left of August. Well, something like Nordi said at the pool. Anyway I decided to get all I can out of what's left of the month."

Good Lord! I had never heard Ginny add one sentence to another before. I marveled so much that I almost forgot to reply. In fact, I didn't. I said: "Ginny, won't you come along? I'm going for a stroll to the upper end of the meadow."

"Wait till I get out of this damp suit," she called over her shoulder. She came back after a bit in a light flowery print. Quietly we wandered over the pastures through the warm evening air. It soon became a deepening dusk, and that flowery skirt caught all the light that there was and contained it. I found her hand, and we swung our caught hands a bit as we strolled along. It was too dark to tell, so I asked her if she was smiling.

Again that hesitation as if she had to ask herself first, and with a barely heard giggle, she said, "Yes," and then, "you know, this is just right."

"What is this?" I asked. I felt her make a gentle inclusive gesture with her other hand.

"The trees, the meadow and the sound of the river," she murmured. "But you know that, Clyde. I think you know it more than the rest of us, except Nordi."

"I doubt that," I said, "but it does mean a great deal to me. Well, I'll add it up. The blur of the cottonwoods by the river in the dusk, the lisp of the Clackamas against its banks, the warmth of your hand in mine."

"And the weedy smell of the meadow," Ginny surprisingly added, "and the stars too." I squeezed her hand in joy and a faint reply came back to me.

The upper meadow ended in an abrupt knoll above the river. I cast the blanket over the grass on its flat summit and waited for Ginny to lie on it. She didn't.

"No," she said. "I can absorb it better standing."

I knew what she meant. She was breathing slowly and deeply. I lay on the blanket and looked up at her.

After a bit she said, "Daddy would say I've got myself 'chock-a-block' with the river's sounds and the smell of the grass."

"And the surrounding darkness," I added.

"Yes," she replied. "Usually I don't care for darkness, but tonight I do."

She lay down beside me, and we both stared up at the stars. I pointed out several I knew. A falling star blazed a brilliant mark down across the western sky.

"Ginny," I said, "I shouldn't tell you this. I haven't any right to, but I love you and I always will."

Good God! There it was, declared—though certainly not

bidden by me, at least by the me I know. Sadness was in me at the great harm that could come of this. She didn't reply, nor did I say more. We looked up at the stars and after awhile we got up, folded the blanket and wended our way through a ground mist that now floated over the grass.

At the house I mumbled, "Good night," but she moved on as if she hadn't heard me. I stood where she left me in sad fury. Not man enough to hold it in, I despaired.

I sat in the empty kitchen, that was fragrant with the spices of fruit soup, too dismayed to turn on the light. I must have dozed, for I was bemused by actuality when Nordi or Bunky turned on the light. I awoke lounging in a kitchen chair. They both bustled over and hugged and kissed me, chair and all. With happy smiles and, in her pert way, Nordi was trotting about the room.

"I bought some sweet rolls at Pfeiffer's," she said. "He uses your flavoring, and he ordered through me a gallon of lemon emulsion. Quite a business woman, I are," she added, laughing. "I'll have coffee for you in a jiffy, and Bunky, eat this roll and then to bed with you. You're going fishing with Johnny at sunup tomorrow."

She brought us cups of coffee, but we were without milk for Bunky. "When are we going to get that cow, Clyde?"

She reached impulsively across the corner of the table that separated us and fondled my hand. "Remember, Clyde? She was closer to us than a cousin. Do you think you could find another cow as sweet?"

I didn't answer. "Nordi," I said, "how'd you like to pull up stakes and go back to Tiburon where we belong? I could join Drake with the thinner."

"Good Lord, why, Clyde?"

"There's good enough reason," I answered. "I think too much about Virginia when I should be thinking only about you."

"You're good for her, Clyde. Everyone says it's been a God-send. Don't let your romantic mind misinterpret. You're not loving me any less are you?"

"No, always more. All right, skip it. I'll look for a cow. What kind do you want?"

"Why, a Guernsey, just like Delia!"

On Sunday I talked to Foster when he and his family came back from church. We visited a bit, and then I told him I was getting a cow and I'd be fencing in my five acres as we had agreed. "No," he said, "I'm sorry but I can't let you do that."

"I don't understand."

"Well," he continued, "since you came out here you've bought milk and meat and garden grub from me, and you got Broms and Forsythe to buy out here too, and now they're good customers. Not only that, but some of your folks in town come out for a ham or a couple of sacks of spuds."

"But you promised not only me, but Forsythe and Broms, to give us the land if we settled here, and we bought from you and got our friends to buy from you because of your gentlemanly promise to us."

"Yes, but I'm doing well," he said rather grimly, "and I ain't about to tip over no applecart. Put yourself in my place, Mr. Rice. I'm doing real good now. You guys get a couple cows and make gardens and, well, you see how it would be, and I need that pasture now with the improved business. No, I'd be crazy."

When I told Jack and Teddy they were flabbergasted, then angry. They went to see Foster, but he was adamant. I remembered that Foster rented our half of the bottom from Giesek— Giesek, whom I'd found much more intelligent than his neighbors. I went to him to tell him how things stood, but he'd already heard and was disgusted.

"If he's ever a day late, Mr. Giesek," I said, "rent the bottom to us instead of him. Can you?"

"I can and will. He's two months past due now. Give me eight bucks a quarter?"

I did, so we gained twelve acres more than our three holdings combined.

"Serves him right," Giesek said, and he told me if I would

patch the roof of his big barn that was adjacent to the bottom but off the flood plain, we could use it too.

So suddenly we were in a position to each have a milk cow, and between us five or six head of whiteface and a horse or two, for Giesek told where we could get twenty acres for growing hay just for its upkeep.

Jack and Teddy were jubilant. I had bought barbed wire to fence my part. Now we used it to separate our part of the bottom from Foster's. When I was away the next Saturday (paint thinner, of course), Teddy and Jack, with the help of the boys, used Jack's brand-new posthole digger to good effect, making the posts of available cottonwood. They let me in on putting it together Saturday evening. By nightfall we had a four-wire barbed wire clear across the middle of the bottom.

The next day Foster turned up with his son and asked the meaning of the fence. He wouldn't speak to Jack or Teddy, just to me. He was angry, and I could see he wanted to fight, which would have been a mistake, for I could take him easily and he knew it. However, he had just cut off a finger in some farm machinery accident and was still in shock from that, and now to lose the land! I felt terribly about it. He asked me again why I put up the fence.

In the most deploring tones, feeling as I did, I said: "Let no man be any nicer or any meaner. You asked for it." (Why is it I feel so badly every time I win?)

It was a week before I could patch the barn's roof. I traded some thinner for some shake bolts. With my froe from the stump ranch days I rived the needed shakes and mended the roof. When Grandma and the three families came to look at our newest acquisition, Ginny, who of late had been presenting me with a stern no comment look, smiled around the edges of it and sort of at me.

It was while I was driving across the Burnside Bridge that an idea struck me. I drove on to the Oregon Liquor Commission, which handles all the alcohol that is used in the state. Acme

Flavoring was the state's biggest user, outside of the hospitals, who used it like water. The federal tax on ethyl alcohol was our single biggest expense in producing extracts and flavors, and most of that was in pure vanilla extracts and imitation vanilla flavor. The two comprised four-fifths of our total output. Though Pop didn't use prune flavor in his vanilla, he should have, for it makes the imitation taste much more like pure vanilla.

When I got to the right man, I said, "Look, we're going to bring a bunch of prunes into our extract plant, ferment the juice, then use it in our flavorings, so it will come out imitation vanilla. I can raise the alcohol high enough in the fermented juice to keep the vanillin and ethyl vanillin in solution in the finished product. The prune wine we make is not taxable since it is part of the contents of the flavor."

Well, they got their top men and lawyers, looked over the proposition and finally said: "Before we could work the law around to tax that alcohol in the processing plant, you'll have enough to retire. Yeah, you figured out one for the book. Not only that, we'll help you, through the local agricultural college. We've got more prunes in the state than we know what to do with."

At the factory Pop and the Little Lady were both in the office when I came in. I handed them an order for twenty-five gallons of imitation vanilla. He smiled. "I'll make a salesman of you yet," he said. "How's tricks?"

"As you see," I answered. "Pop, why do some firms put prune flavor in their imitation vanilla?"

"I don't know, son. Some of the great tasters of the essential oil houses say it makes for a more complex flavor like pure vanilla. One taster—Dr. Katz—said that with a small amount of pure vanilla that is put in the imitation, one without prune flavor is like a man running for a home run without touching all the bases. The way I make mine, though, is good enough for me."

"Acme flavors are the best money can buy," piped the Little Lady, and went on with her typing.

"Anyway, Pop, I've come on something that will save you money and improve your vanilla. Do you want to hear about it?"

"No, I don't, Clyde. I perfected my imitation vanilla twenty-five years ago. It's as perfect as man can make it."

"Well, I want you to hear me out anyway," and I told him the story of the inspiration and the attitude of the Liquor Commission.

Before I was through, he announced vigorously that it was all nonsense. "What do they know about producing a fine imitation vanilla? I put lots of good pure vanilla in it."

"Not enough to really enhance it like you should. The more you put in the more your profit goes down. A prune wine will improve your product and lower your costs. We've plenty of room here to handle the job and I'll do the work."

The Little Lady now saw a place to put in a word. She stood up from her desk. "Jim," she said with theatrical emphasis as if she were reading a line from a play. "I can't stand by and see a fine old gentleman bullied. Let me take you out of this."

He rose to the role. "Thank you, Little Lady," he said, and with a great bustle they left.

Though he had never ordered more than one drum of alcohol at a time and was very stingy in the use of it, seven fifty-gallon drums of grain alcohol were delivered to Acme next day.

"I got a deal," he said, which was a lie. "With all this alcohol I haven't time to fool around with prunes."

I took the silliness of it, for somehow Acme Flavoring must not falter. It was one of the verities of my childhood, and I must put up with absurdity upon absurdity until the day that I could deal with its problems. By now I knew how to improve our strawberry and half a dozen other flavors that were twenty years behind the times.

At home, Teddy and Jack planned to rest and share a bottle, for it was Sunday. The Little Lady's daughter, Marilyn, had come Friday night to spend the weekend with us. We were fond of her and admired her for her fortitude, because Pop and the Little Lady were a hard team to live with. It skipped into my mind to give her a hayride to remember. I loaded plenty of hay in the back of the pickup, talked Tek and her daughters into bringing lots of lunch and to be ready in half an hour. Nordi was going to help Olga make a little pool in Olga's flower garden.

Marilyn was, of course, delighted with such a romp, as were Bunky and David. Nordi hurried together some lunch for us. We left with an axe and a shovel under the hay and an extra can of gas and a couple of coarse blankets. Away we went, Tek with me in the cab and Marilyn, Dory, and Ginny in the hay with the kids, who were singing and laughing and cheering.

Soon we passed through Estacada and headed on up the Clackamas River, deep into the mountains of its thousand sources, the springs and seeps that come down as brooks until, as creeks, they rush along to join the Clackamas. We passed the North Fork and the South Fork, always winding higher. We left the main river, traveling up the Oak Grove Fork. From there we followed a long ridge to come back eventually to the Oak Grove Fork at Clackamas Lake.

We were now at the backbone of the Cascades. We headed east on a little-used lane leading through a deep forest toward Warm Springs Indian Reservation. I stopped and we listened to the silence. We resumed the noise of our travel and ended up in a small Indian encampment. Three or four log cabins were hidden deep in the timber. We talked to a young man and his wife. I could see that they were annoyed with our coming into this place, still untrammeled by whites. Ashamed of this part of my heritage, I sped our hayride ten miles farther, till guilt faded away. Eventually we headed back on a different road through the mountains. Tek wanted to ride in the hay.

"Used to," she said, "before I got married. I liked hayrides." She climbed in between Marilyn and Dory where the cab protected them from the wind. (Marilyn told me years later that the ride was one of the high points of her childhood.) Ginny came to ride with me in the cab. There was a long silence as we swept along.

I broke it hesitantly; the long moment was sweet with her

presence, "Do you prefer to ride in the mountains or in the valley?" I asked her, feeling very awkward in referring to our former closeness.

"It's prettier here; still, this is their trip. Going to Eugene was ours."

"Neither of us is really a good group person," I pondered.

Again the considered, "Yes."

"I wish it were raining." It stumbled out in spite of myself.

She laughed and said, "This is a hayride."

"Of course," I agreed, "but I mean, if it wasn't."

I heard her utter a very faint, "Yes," under her breath, but she moved circumspectly to her corner of the seat.

"Ginny, our summer will soon be over. Will winter take you away from us—like the poem said—remember it?"

"Yes, I do. I don't think any other girl in school had a poem written about her."

"Did it help?" I queried, feeling boorish and proddy.

" 'Course it did. When I'd feel so out of it at school, I'd say the poem in my mind and know I was—well, important to somebody."

"Don't you ever forget it," I mumbled.

"Oh, I couldn't," she answered, "but we shouldn't talk like this."

"Guess you're right," I said. I felt confused. "Ginny, would you rather ride in the hay?"

"No, I want to be here with you, but please don't talk that way. You know what I mean."

Flustered, I posed a question I didn't want to ask. "Do you mean we mustn't talk—well, sort of intimately?"

"Oh, I like it, Clyde, but I keep thinking what about Evelyn?"

We drove along with our freight of happy people, while Ginny and I, so far apart in every way, yet so close, considered my beloved Nordi.

IV

In Which
I Seduce Virginia, Bungle Things with Bunky,
Get Canned by Acme Flavoring,
and
Become an Inconsequential Cog
in the War Machine

1939

THAT WINTER CAME ON US as if making up for recent mild ones. We had one more fine swim before it started to rain, and rain alternated with freezing weather. Oh, well, we were snugged down for it with our fireplace heating the whole house. We reveled in the warmth and security we felt within our thick walls. The Forsythes too were happily established in their new home now.

I paid Bunky and David to chop down willow trees that were crowding out the cedars of the wash. They had trunks about half a foot through and the boys sawed them into nine-foot lengths that I could get up on my shoulder and stagger with uphill to the house. Cut in three pieces they would burn green if properly placed in the fireplace. The boys felled each tree with a trium phant yell of "TIMBER!" They were workmanlike about the falling and their pride in their accomplishments was, I believe, worth more to them than the wages.

We now had a cow, another Guernsey, an advanced registry Guernsey with a registered name spelled "Delite." Bunky learned to milk in due time and took the chore off my hands. Nordi refused to give up her job at Acme. Even now I can only guess the reason. Everything she did there was done with precision and joy. Our house was kept neat and with the addition of a washing machine, she felt that at last a big garden could be planned—an explosion of vegetables as had been at our California goat ranch garden in '33.

Though I still had lots of building to do, after our new privy with the half moon cut into its door, I allowed myself time to catch up on neglected reading, but gave that up to make a low deep settee. The arms were carved from exceptionally big blocks of cedar. They splayed out like great thick leaves. This, from a casual remark of Nordi's that she would rather, in the winter at least, make love before a fire than in bed. We found the settee eminently suited, but we also sat on it a lot in the daytime and before Bunky climbed the stairs to bed.

I did get in some of the reading that I had dreamed of. Steinbeck's *Grapes of Wrath* tore me up for several weeks after I'd read it. I'd seen a little of that and the torment of Steinbeck's people became my torment. I couldn't forget them.

Winters were always dull at Acme particularly after the Christmas season. We would hurry through the inventory, then make a great stock of the best selling items and do small stuff. We'd paint and take things apart, clean them and put them together again. We would take barrels to the barrel mender and then till spring we would just move stuff around. But no matter what the season, we had to call on our customers—"Keeping contact," my father called it. So I ranged through my car-painting people from one end to the other of my small territory, selling them both lacquer thinner and enamel reducer made to be used in coldest weather.

In Corvallis I first called on my favorite customer, a young fellow whose shop was built on the front of his lot with his home setting well back under tall elms. A free thinker, he engaged me in arguments over current happenings in Europe.

One of his men met me at the door. "Hi, Mr. Rice," he said, "bad news here. Jim died shortly after you were up last time. It was expected, for he had a very bad heart. I run the shop now. His sister is the new owner and does the buying. You should call on her up at the house. She knows we're low on both thinners."

Approaching the house I heard piano music through the open door, music that I had not heard before. An obscure classic, I guessed, but I didn't ring the bell or knock, for the music was rich with a second airy melody slipping through the stateliness of the dominant one. I stood there entranced until the music stopped, and a young woman appeared in the dim lit doorway. "I saw you coming and I hoped you like music. Do you?"

"Well, I couldn't ring the doorbell," I answered. "It would have been obscene. Normally I'm not an eavesdropper, but that music! Was it Bloch or Richard Strauss?"

She laughed and I had a hunch that she was her dead brother's twin.

"Business first," she said. "What brings you to my door?"

"I sold your brother lacquer thinner and reducer."

"Oh, yes, you must be Clyde Rice," she ventured. "Jim liked to pass the time of day with you. He mentioned it several times."

"I was fond of your brother," I said. "I always tried to arrange my schedule so that I could have lunch with him."

Tears appeared in her eyes. She brushed them away and presented a difficult smile. "We'll take our usual order. Have you got it along?" And then faking grimness, "Two percent ten days, thirty days net?"

We both smiled. "Will you have lunch with me as your brother did?"

"Thank you, but I'd rather you'd have lunch with me. I've just made a pot of stew with lots of green pepper and garlic and cumin. Jim would be pleased."

The steady rain that had been my companion all the way from Portland had stopped as I came into Corvallis. Now sunlight peeked past a cloud, and the young woman came out on the stoop with me to look at the clearing sky.

She was slender, though very much a woman rich of breast, sleek of hip, yet a sense of fragility like a hidden perfume was there. She reminded me of her music and of hyacinths. I made my hurried glances but didn't meet her eyes.

"Take your time, Mr. Rice," she murmured and then laughed but gently. "As a male you must survey. From you I don't mind. Oh, I've heard of your stubborn views. Jim used me as a foil in planning his next attack on your belief in the necessity of honesty."

We ate the fine stew at the kitchen table. Nordi would have put in a cabbage leaf and more onion, but as I said, it was a fine stew. The girl, really a young lady of thirty-two, said her name was Emma. "Do you know of the English painter Romney?" she asked.

"Sure," I answered with a small swagger, "and Lord Nelson, and I read somewhere that Lady Hamilton had big feet." I looked under the table and assured her that it wasn't a requisite for Emmas, at least not in the Corvallis area.

"How kind of you to let me under the wire. Won't you have another dollop of stew?"

With such foolish banter we got acquainted. Her company was exhilarating but I forced myself to leave. She came to the door with me. As I left I explained that I covered the southern end of my route every two weeks. "May I visit you when I come this way again?" I asked.

"You can, sir. Today you've driven sorrow from this house. Next time I'll play another piece by the same composer."

I forgot to call on my other customers in Corvallis and soon found myself in Eugene, still musing over Emma. I had to really face myself then to get to work on the business at hand in Eugene. There wasn't much of it for some odd reason. Everybody seemed long in the mouth. The winter, they said, was "draggin' on too long." And spring, one painter said, was having second thoughts about coming to Oregon at all, at least the Willamette Valley. As a result I carried quite a bit of thinner I had brought with me back to Portland.

It was during this time that the desire to make a jewel box for Ginny came to me. I should, I knew, make it for Nordi instead. I fumbled with my conscience and my desires and the hunger to make something new. One day, much annoyed at myself, I wandered into a cabinet shop and ordered a tiny hinged lidded box of hard Alaska cedar. I explained that I was going to finish it myself. I sized it and let the sizing settle in, or so I supposed, and then slowly, carefully I painted four scenes on the ends and sides of the box. I did them with brushes of one and three hairs and, of course, a large magnifying glass.

There were mountains and trees and people done in much detail with lots of light and color. I outdid myself and was very surprised at the result. Then I painted another elaborate scene on its top of a revel of the Gods in all the splendor of mythical Olympus. The gentleman gods were nudgling the goddesses while having some more ambrosia. After the tiny scenes had dried and hardened, I goldleafed the rest of the box, then covered all with a fine varnish of oriental gums. Contemplating it I was unable to believe that I, woodchopper Clyde, had produced it. All this in a month of after-hours craftsmanship in Acme Flavoring's shipping room. Nordi believed I was studying chemistry at the library.

On my next trip down the valley Jerry, who ran the shop for Emma, informed me that she was away on a business trip to San Francisco. I was upset by this, as I was eager to hear her piano and enjoy more of her strange personality that had kept me wondering.

One night, a former customer who had skipped town owing me three hundred dollars, phoned me at home. Said he was passing through and wanted to pay his bill. "You always treated me right," he said.

"I'm staying the night with my sister out in Gresham. Come on over." He gave me the address and I took Ginny along on the drive. He was gone when I arrived, but his sister gave me the money and asked me to count it. She wished me well.

Going home it started to rain heavily. My headlights had difficulty finding the road. There was, however, no traffic, so I drove slowly along, peering out into the night through the deluge. The roar of the rain on the roof made being inside a haven, a refuge. I tooled along, barely able to discern the road. Ginny moved over close and a shy hand slipped in and around my right arm and stayed there with friendly pressure. So we drove. I was ecstatically happy but made no move to express it.

I dropped Ginny off at Forsythe's where she was spending the night. When I arrived home I saw that Nordi had been baking. Loaves of crusty bread were piled on the counter and their fragrance filled the house. She gave me a great buttered slab of it and held my hand as I ate. She was studying my eyes, searching, it seemed, for her husband, and looking deeply into me, the composite. She saw that in essence I was good and wanted me, and I, caught in the spell, wanted her. I laid down what was left of my bread, picked her up and carried her to the settee by the fire. The sex fragrance and the bread scent permeated my brain. Nordi's searching gaze was still hunting for the very center of me, when her eyes closed and her tumultuous breathing told me that she was caught in the same whirlwind that had found me. After a lifetime or a moment our eyes opened. Though we had passed through fire and surely weren't the same people, or so it seemed, reality claimed us. Nordi's hair brushed my mouth. Softly she murmured a very pet name, then said matter of factly: "Let me up, darling. I baked a little something special for you. I suppose it's cold now, but the oven's still warm, so if I put it back in it'll soon be just right."

Early spring found me working on the barn. As soon as sap flowed in the trees I was bringing in poles and peeling them. There were about thirty of them and, when peeled, they were left to season. I needed them to make stanchions, stalls, and many other appurtenances for our animals. Then I did one more thing to make my relatives hate me.

The level strip of rich ground that was about a hundred feet wide and four hundred feet long—the one that crossed ours and Forsythe's place—was where we planned to have a garden. It lay fallow for the plow and fallow in the minds of all of us, but no one made a move to do anything about it, so I did. One Sunday when we were all together I got everyone to agree that they wanted a garden, and that, yes, they would work in it and share alike in the food that was produced. If there was no rain the following Sunday, we would spend the day working on the land as we had it plowed.

The plowman came with his tractor. He looked at the old fern stems and residue of the horsetail rush and remarked that we had our work cut out for the next four years, but I had a plan. I lined everyone up, each one had just forty feet to look after. As the plow turned up a furrow and exposed the fern roots each of us were to pull them out and stack them outside of the perimeter of the garden, then move to the other side where the plow was making its furrow coming back and repeat the process, back to the other side, and so on.

Jack and Teddy said no. The harrowing after the plow would take care of that. Why do this heavy work when it's unnecessary? I told Grandma that we had harrowed after plowing at Wendel with the self same rushes and ferns, and that we had a really bad time all summer long.

"Trust me, I know what I'm talking about."

Virginia's mother, Tekla, was adamant. She wouldn't do it. Grandma was inclined to think I knew what I was talking about and as matriarch said, "Do what Clyde says."

I think the farmer made fifty furrows before it was plowed and old lady Nordstrom saw to it that no one, including herself, shirked the job.

When it was harrowed, they saw how little the harrow could get. We had about twenty-three stacks of roots around the edge of the garden and made these into about ten high piles to burn when they were dry.

The kids, Nordi and Olga and I pulled up the wire-like roots of the rushes. Though it wasn't as spectacular, late summer showed it to be rewarding. As we planted the garden we thanked our lucky stars that we got the miserable work done together as a group and had it behind us.

This was the year that the big national paint companies like DuPont and Sherwin-Williams became aware of me through their local branches. Then there was Nasons and an outfit that made the paint for Ford Motor Car Company—Seymour. The car painters of the region used DuPont and Sherwin-Williams paint, but they used my thinner, and there was more profit in thinner in a given dollar than in paint. Each month I sold more thinner and enlarged my territory. There were other outfits—Rodda, soon to become the leading paint supplier of the area. Anyway, here I was, one lone fellow making his own thinner, milking the profit out of the automobile painting business, and it would have to be stopped.

Various tricks were tried. One DuPont outlet in the Oregon City area said they would take care of my customers with my thinners and charge me ten percent to distribute my thinners in that area. I agreed. We made all the arrangements, then nothing happened. I hadn't called on my customers because of this. But the DuPont people did call on all my customers and explained that hereafter they would be my distributor and that to start the relationship off they were going to sell DuPont thinner at below cost.

When I came by the DuPont place of business to put in my stock of thinner, I found twelve drums of their own brand: "All's fair in business," they told me. They were not going to use my thinner and they had my customers.

I went around to various paint shops and offered to sell mine below the cost of DuPont. All of them, when they got the picture, said, "Hell no! We'll use your thinner at your regular price. We like dealing with you, you've got good material, and we don't like stunts of this sort being played by the big companies."

Two years later the tricky outfit had not been able to sell a gallon of thinner in their area. Then Nasons offered me a fine deal—selling for them, really a nice setup, except that I'd have to quit selling my thinner, so that was out.

Seymour came to me to accept a dealership for all of Oregon and Northern California. The manager for them hung around for about three days. I was a little bit interested in it till I found that there were quotas to be met, sales competition with their outlets in other states. I declined, saying, "Freedom means a great deal to me." They were really insulted. But the high point of this sudden notoriety of my thinner came when a Union Oil chemist came up from Texas to talk to me about thinner.

By now I had about six types for different conditions, surfaces, and changes in the weather. He came out to the house for two days. He said, "In the tests your thinner came out far the best, whatever the paint. How did you come about making them that way?"

I finally had to tell him how it was. "I just know in these mixtures what will happen. I avoid trying to solve the problem of countless isotopic mixtures. I seem to know my way. It's like instinct, but it's some obscure thought process with which I come to conclusions, and they always seem to be right. Just in this field, you understand."

"Can you use it satisfactorily in flavors?" he asked me.

"Yes," I admitted. "There's usually five to seven ingredients in thinner, the way I make it, and this is certainly true in flavors. Still, my hunches are right. I don't know why."

"Are you psychic in other fields, Mr. Rice?" he asked.

"Yes," I agreed, "but never on cue."

"I thought so," he said. "Several of our many researchers are, and the results they get are hard to deny. I myself don't exactly deny them. There'll be a breakthrough in this someday. Mark my words!" he said and bid me goodbye.

Something I had seen lately had built up in me the desire to make a big statue, slightly over life-size, of a naked woman purposefully striding along. Ginny's sister, Dory, five years younger, had been a skinny little kid. The only thing outstanding about her were her airs of a middle-aged schoolteacher (she taught Dave and Bunky—what, God knows!) and her enormous shoulder blades that seemed to be ready to burst out from under the skin as two splendidly befeathered wings. She heckled the poor kids, but they loved it. I passed them one day as they played in the water too shallow for swimming, but excellent for water fights. She had grown into last year's too loose bathing suit, and as I passed, she reared up to catch the waterball they were playing with, and there before my eyes was one of the classic gestures of us Caucasians—the back arched, the body twisting somewhat, as she came up out of the water reaching as high as she could to catch the ball. It's a posture seen in males in the game of basketball. It happened perhaps not over a second, but with that hunger for beauty that's mine, it became etched in my mind for life. I wanted to do a statue like that with the same utter sleekness. These poses have been done thousands of times—that irritated me—but I wanted to do one of them—which one I couldn't make up my mind.

Anyway, I rented a room in the old Worcester Block where our group in art school had once taken a room. I didn't get the clay in yet, but made arrangements for it, and I came to this place early in the morning (usually about four) and worked on a big fancy workbench I was making, a model stand and the stand for the statue. I made these fixtures of heavy stuff and as if they were to be works of art, really indulging myself in the shaping of these curved things.

Nordi seemed to take my going and coming for granted. By now I owned three alarm clocks and found it difficult to sleep in the time allotted for sleep, which was never more than four hours, so I took a bedspring down to the river. In those days the river, as it passed our place, ran under bushes of overhanging vine maple growing horizontally, reaching out sometimes twenty feet over the water. In one place not too close and not too far from the shore I lashed the bedspring into the vine maple, not over three feet above the water. A mattress, a few blankets and a pillow and I could sleep to the rill sound, the liquid blending of waters. This was the second year I had it. When I started twisting and turning at home, I left sweet Nordi's warmth, trotted across the meadow and fell asleep at once to the soothing murmur of the Clackamas.

In that strip between the uplands and the bottom, our gardens were growing. Nordi had seen to it that they were planted with everything that could be grown in the Willamette Valley. There were ground cherries, Jerusalem artichokes, garbanzo beans, soya beans and leeks in profusion. The corn was planted with several different varieties that matured at different times so that we always had sweet corn on the table. The Forsythes acquired a cow—a Jersey. Between the two of us we had more than enough butter for the three families, and Nordi was experimenting with various soft cheeses.

I had found that tied into the properties we owed jointly was a piece of ten acres with an upland of two acres. The house had burned on the property, but it had an eighty-foot well, a spring, a small orchard, and the best soil on the bottom. It was offered for two hundred fifty dollars an acre. If I hadn't built my house I would have grabbed it myself. It was really an excellent place. I got the price down haggling with the owner, for I realized it was just the place for Teddy and Tek. The setup he was buying in front of Mrs. Giesek's had no place for a house or barn, and what I had given him on our place was really not adequate nor could we make it so.

I knew that Teddy, a very conservative man, would not make the move to buy it. There he could have something far better than the rest of us with less expenditure, but how to get him to move? I decided to act as if I was sorry I made my agreement with him. I got Jack and Grandma to say that I was regretting the deal I had made. When he felt that he wasn't wanted, they let him know of the possibility of buying the Baehm place. Finally, very exasperated at me, he bought it, but the five acres that he was buying next to mine he still held. I offered it to Jack, but Jack declined it, so I bought it and Teddy was free with all the advantages of the new place. He at once went out and bought the lumber needed for building a house and while it seasoned he started the digging of a full basement.

Jack and I helped him as he had given both of us help in the digging of the lanes from our houses to the road. I dug early in the morning every other day in the time I usually allotted to my project—the planned large statue of clay. I put in one hour of very vigorous digging before I had breakfast.

Next, with the thinner made the night before, I took off for Acme to make whatever extracts were on the day's schedule and, after shipping out the flavoring orders, left to make deliveries of thinner and extracts in the city and the outlying towns about.

It was on such a jaunt that I was able to see Emma again, for she had returned from a lengthy visit in San Francisco. I sat in her parlor and once more enjoyed the beauty of the strange music that she had promised to play.

I sold her a drum of lacquer thinner and a small amount of synthetic reducer, then took her to lunch in memory of those I'd had with her brother. It was a cold miserable day for spring, and we had soup to start our luncheon. We had not finished the soup before I felt that maybe I had found a kindred spirit. Emma's was the kind of beauty that is seldom noticed. It was hidden even while displayed, as in this restaurant. If she smiled casually, it was not there, but if something said sparked her, it changed. She bloomed somehow, and she transformed you with her wide-eyed appraisal. You were made aware of your innermost being through her offices. Then she looked down at her chop and became a pleasant young lady—one unrelated to the fervor of the moment before. But more than that, there was a delicacy about her, almost a sense of fragility that was strangely unsettling.

"No," she was saying, "I don't ski or ride horses, but I used to do some hiking. Now I live through music."

"It means a great deal to me too."

"How wonderful," she murmured. "But where are you in music?"

"I don't play an instrument," I answered, "I listen."

"To whom?"

"To records," I said. "I haven't been able to afford the concerts for years."

"What composers?" She was still intent.

"At the moment, Moussorgsky and Respighi—yeah, and Stravinsky."

I was tingling alive, for she was again smiling deeply into me. We stood up at our table awkwardly. It wasn't the place for it, but it was imperative that we stand and shake hands.

"Pleased ter meecher, Mr. Rice," she beamed.

We sat down to food we no longer tasted. "Respighi is mine at the moment," she remarked. We both laughed to relieve the intensity that was between us.

"With what is happening," she said, "I can't wait the two weeks before I can talk to you again. As you come back from Eugene, couldn't you stop and have dinner with me so we could continue?"

I agreed, for I was going to mention the same possibility.

Eugene was waking up from the last time I was there. Spring had been slow, but Eugene can be slow. Anyway I sold more than the usual amounts of materials, arriving back in Corvallis with ample time to give those customers there who I had been shirking plenty of consideration.

The meal at Emma's was adequate. She was not a great cook. She didn't need to be. After we'd eaten and done the dishes together, she started the evening's conversation by saying that she wanted to talk about herself first.

"My doctor in Australia and the specialist I just visited in San Francisco both chide me not to do any more hiking or have sex or any undue exercise, because, like my brother, I was born with a very defective heart. I do love the outdoors and have the same emotions as others. Still, there's music and now I've found that I must make do with it. I composed the two pieces of music I played for you."

I was enthusiastic about her music, but she would play no more for me. "Next time," she said. We talked of the joy of life, of music, of war. We talked of thinner and our friends. I told her of Nordi and Virginia, of the statue I intended to make and of the desire to someday write and tell all about it, and I began to understand her. She was like an orchid. She had the short-lived delicacy of a flower.

When I got home I sent Emma the jewel box. I tried to put my interest, my sexual interest, in her, feeling that perhaps an infatuation with an older woman might weaken my love for child-like Virginia, which I knew to be wrong and unfair to my beloved Nordi. Giving it to Emma would, I hoped, end the problem of favoring either Nordi or Virginia.

I received no note of thanks, and two weeks later on my usual trip down the Valley I learned why. A bad spell with her heart had precipitated a trip to her doctor in San Francisco. He told her to prepare herself for death and advised her to go back to her people in Melbourne, and not by plane. So with hope of seeing her parents once more, she left on a steamer and succumbed to her ailment before the ship reached Honolulu.

I had known her only a month or so, but somehow I had known her in great depth. Her death struck hard at me. I turned and drove back home. That did no good so I took a small pack and headed into the timber, ending up on Soosap Peak. A couple of days staring out over the world, and I could accept her death as part of the inevitable way of things. That was many years ago, but I still wonder sometimes where and on whose dressing table the box now rests.

With the loss of Emma and the subconscious hope that somehow our relationship, no matter how platonic, would ease or avert my extreme interest in Virginia, I was shorn of the only subterfuge I had to fend for my patched integrity.

Gradually, the reserve that being told that I loved her brought about in Virginia, disappeared. It was summer again and her parents moved into their shack on our place, while Teddy built the forms for the pouring of basement walls at his new property. One evening Ginny informed me that she and her sister were going to sleep in a tent nearby when her father had time to put it up. Why did extremely virginal Virginia offer that information, and I, seeing the statement as a trap for my integrity, why did I take the bait, for I responded against my will?

"Might I visit you there?"

There was one of her potent silences, that she ended with a very softly spoken: "I thought you might."

Nature, the powers that be, God or whatever subverted our moral senses in its eagerness to produce one more, or in case of twins, two more carriers of the genes of this our many-shaded species.

Our eyes didn't meet in this exchange. We stared at the

ground, but it came to me overpoweringly how fond she was of me. We were both aware, I assumed, that love surrounded us as did the dusk. Words would have only been in the way. It was a moment of knowing.

In the week following, Teddy put up the tent, and in that week I met Tek and her daughters at the bus station in Portland. I don't know why I was there. Perhaps to pick up some parcels too big for them to carry. It doesn't matter. What matters is that I looked into Ginny's eyes. She had on a smart little hat, its brim low over her forehead and beneath it, I looked into her eyes. Her eyes were warm on mine, not staring, not curious, surely then loving. I looked back with love too, I thought, for a delicate smile appeared on her lips.

Her mother spoke up, "Say something to Clyde," she said, "has the cat got your tongue, Virginia?"

And Virginia said, "Will you take this parcel of mine too, Clyde?" When I did they moved off.

Out on the street going to my car her eyes still looked into mine, repeating the shock of that moment when love was no longer shielded but was suddenly blooming between us as our glances held. A great crashing tumult was in me.

"I've got to have her!" I almost shouted it there in the street. I stopped. Like a balking horse I stood the pavement while hurrying pedestrians swept around me.

"She must be mine!" I spoke out loudly again, the enormous fact that was blotting out everything else. I must possess her. Sex! Yes, but more than that, adoration. Just to be in the world with her. What a wonder! We two are in this world together, I marveled. That assimilated, I continued up the street.

I drove to the next customer on my route and sold him the usual amount. It seemed strange. A great change had happened in my mind, an acceptance of things I should not even tolerate, yet here was I, selling thinner, as if nothing of moment had happened. Her hat continued to float in my memory and beneath it her loving glance, a bit dimmed by time, still controlled me.

I stopped by a park and sat in the car and tried to bring Nordi into things, but I couldn't. My mind rebelled at anything but fondly remembering Ginny's loving smile.

I drove on, but stopped again in belated consternation. God! I said to myself, considering things, reason once more a tool of sorts. Nordi and I must pull up stakes at once and go back to Marin County. Let Ginny learn to love another man, someone her own age. I'll talk to Nordi, bring back some memories of Waterspout Point, but I didn't. I had tried all that many times before. It was useless. She wanted to stay here with her mother and her sisters, and really deep down Oregon was our home.

That evening I made much of Nordi, praising her cooking, the pink of her cheeks, a recent painting of hers, hugging her each time I passed behind her chair. I loved her. She was my Nordi, a definite part of me, but now I didn't feel I was also a part of her. What was going on in my head? Anger shook me, for I was weakly letting things happen. Some grim, fatalistic corner of my mind agreed with that, sneeringly. It's already happened, that part informed me. There were ways to avert it. You went at it, as you usually do, dividedly. Now Nordi must reap what you've scattered. Nordi broke in on my thoughts. She was talking about the war in Europe.

"Clyde, I know how you hate the pattern," she said, as she sat peeling early apples for pie. "I know that you find the details strung over the pattern changing only in magnitude. I've heard you before on the battle of Crécy and the one on the Marne. War perverts the very tenets of civilization. Okay, okay, and you loathe all wars, but you can't lean away from this one, Clyde. Your favorite commentator spoke of it as an ancient rite on global scale, and he's been reprimanded—assailed as weak. Weak-kneed, I think the term was, for not being more assertive, more involved. Newspapers should express more cleavage, Leonard Cranston rumbled, show differences as well as likenesses, while Jeffrey Penerk maintains we need more vehemence in our tribal yells, but global: 'Are you with us or against us, but keep it global.' "

"Sure," I said, still thinking of Ginny. "Our leaders are arranging us to be better cannon fodder."

"But where will it hit us, Clyde? Will you join the army?"

"I'll be damned if I'll go out to shoot somebody on the other side who's filled with the same damn hokum in a different language and not eager to kill me either. The schooling on either side is inadequate for turning my sort of people into murderers."

At four next morning I crept out, not wakening Nordi, had my breakfast and loaded the pickup with three fifty-gallon drums of thinner and an assortment of smaller full containers, but before I left I quietly approached the tent where Virginia and Dory lay sleeping. In the faint light of dawn I looked down into Virginia's face. Dory, on her other side, presented only a profile. I knew I was spying and slipped guiltily away and drove through town and finally into Olympia on my Washington route. Starting at the capital I worked my way back and, by late afternoon, sold my last customer in Vancouver, my truck empty.

Dropping by at Acme I found that Nordi had left at noon for a trip to the coast with Olga, taking Bunky and David with them. They were going to see their bachelor half-brother at Tillamook. Neighbors had called saying he was very sick. It turned out that he was not as bad off as reported, still the sisters phoned Grandma that they would stay a few days and clean up his bachelor digs and also enjoy the surf.

It seemed silent at home without them. Bunky was always on some noisy project, either inside the house or out. I was able to spend some time with the Broms sisters and had a chance to murmur: "I would like to come see you tonight," to which Virginia nodded, looking away and continued looking away.

Night, it seemed, would never come. Twilight lingered as the sunset had. I tried to eat my evening meal, but couldn't and left the house to walk the meadow. The moon was very bright, soon it would be full. After much small wanderings I sought my bed over the river and fell into a troubled sleep.

I dreamed I was on a mountain top. Far away over the rim of

the world were the faint emanations of light from cities. I yearned toward these faint radiations hundreds of miles away. Between my mountain and the cities I somehow knew was a limitless waste. I stumbled down the mountain toward the faint glowing I believed to be San Francisco. Food, I thought, what will I do for food? I stared about me. I was walking on dried grass between meager groves of pine and cedar. The moon revealed that the groves were as parched as the grass. I wondered where I could get water to drink on my trek. A young doe deer stood before one of the groves. I saw where I could corner her. I'll kill her and make jerky of her flesh, then I'll have food for a twenty-day trek. When I cornered her and came close enough to make the capture, her eyes didn't plead. Instead she sought my eyes with a glance that was so friendly, I couldn't harm it and walked away. The deer came not following, but beside me and again its eyes sought mine with an expression that said we would be companions. I put my arm over its neck and it came ever closer. As we continued it pressed me and so guided me to a spring. I awoke with the rill sound of the Clackamas flowing beneath me.

The moon's different position in the sky indicated that I'd slept several hours. Now, I thought, but how to keep the dog, Tana, quiet as I approached? I think I'll talk to it so low no one will hear but me and Tana, who knows me.

I came some distance from the tent door and began speaking to the dog, so that even I could barely hear it. "Tana, it's me. Tana, you know me. Come here, Tana." After a bit Tana appeared in the moonlight and came to me quietly wagging her tail. I slipped into the tent and, easing to Ginny's side, touched her in the darkness. A warm hand reached up and clung gently to my fingers. My hand found her cheek and stroked it. She moved her head and pressed my hand between her cheek and shoulder. What rightness! I caressed her hair as her hand came out. I kissed her palm and fingers and her arm all the way to her shoulder covering it with kisses. Her hand was rumpling my hair and then softly she was pushing me away, for Dory, lying beside her, was turning over in bed. Was she awake? Did she hear us? With great care I crept away. With only our hands we had declared our love. I walked across the meadow, the splendor of life was full upon me.

A couple of evenings later, with Nordi and Bunky still away, I was about to cook a rib steak for supper when Dory came bouncing through the door.

"Ginny's cooking our dinner on the outside stove. Daddy and mother are spending the night at our house in town. She wants you to come and eat with us."

"I'll be delighted," said I, purposely leaving the steaks behind. Ginny was frying sliced zucchini in olive oil and the potatoes were hot. She was about to fry some eggs when I mentioned the rib steaks and asked Dory to run and retrieve them from our refrigerator.

"Save the eggs for breakfast." When Dory disappeared down the trail, I turned and Ginny and I smiled at each other a rather conspiratorial smile.

"If I wake you tonight, will you come with me to the river," and as an afterthought, "Ginny?" though I said it as a caress.

Her "Yes" did have consideration behind it.

"How about Dory?" I asked.

"You have to actually shake the bed to wake her," Virginia answered. "Still, be quiet when you come."

After the meal I weeded and hoed in the garden until late dusk, when I wandered down and swam in the still pool.

Much later I awakened Virginia by stroking her hair, and she met me outside the tent, her nightgown covered with a cream colored kimono decorated with a design of large flowers. The bright moonlight delineated them well. The beauty of them was part of the hour so that I would never forget it.

I whispered to her, "You lead and I'll follow," so we started out, but soon she stopped and asked me to lead the way. In the full moon's radiance I led her, and though she faltered sometimes, she followed until we entered the narrow grove of alder by the gliding river. There in a patch of moonlight within the grove I turned with opened arms, and she came into them and clung to me. She was quivering. We stayed in that, our first embrace, until her trembling quieted and she ceased using me for support.

"Come, my love," I murmured and took her hand and led her to the way to get out to my bed. With a small flashlight I stepped on the vine maple forks that led over the river to my bed, and she came, trembling, across and lay beside me and, as a child, responded to my caresses:

"I love you," I murmured. "I'll always love you."

"I know," she answered, "and I've loved you, I guess, since that summer when you wrote my poem. I know I liked you an awful lot anyway."

She wrapped her arms around me and we began kissing, much to her delight. Her family didn't kiss. It was new to her and she loved it, but for both, the miracle of our loving each other and not having to hide it from each other any longer was the wonder. She wriggled with joy in my arms, as I kissed her throat and shoulders. I tried to kiss her breasts, but this she told me I must not do. Still, when I folded her arms about her head and kissed her armpits, she was certainly not averse to it, but I was not allowed to raise her nightgown. After an hour or so of great happiness, when we were about to leave, she began crying.

"What will I say to Nordi? She is my dearest relative."

"Ginny," I answered, "I'll try to explain this to you someday. Love sometime motivates us against our codes, and we try to obey both. It's a paradox. Anyway, don't say anything to her or anyone else. We have to let on to the world that we don't belong to each other, when you and I know we do."

I went with her to her tent where with the warmest of kisses we parted. Consternation, however, accompanied me down the path. I thanked God Nordi wasn't home to confront me. Then my mind took another slant, looking for excuses. Nordi and I both had lovers in California, but we had promised each other that when we left there we were leaving a permissive world. From then on in Oregon we would be true to each other. What's so different about this? But I wouldn't be beguiled with such stuff.

How I felt about Ginny, what there was between us was certainly not comparable to my romps with Ethel Crippen or Madeline or Annie Marge. For four years I had adored Ginny in spite of myself. Certainly it wasn't her youth, and she was slender, and slender women did not interest me. Certain attributes that I found interesting in women were certainly lacking in Virginia, yet I dreamed about her constantly, trembled inside, when by chance I drove near her school, church or house. One of her smiles stayed with me for weeks. Maybe it was her eyes. They gave me the feeling that they were violet. They weren't, but her merest glance was warm. Maybe her eyes had been telling me how much she liked me. I fell asleep. Morning found me sprawled sleeping in a kitchen chair.

Still half dozing I turned on the radio. War news, then last night hit me. Guilt and joy buffeted me. Pictures assailed me: her slender grace as she walked across the meadow before me, and the beauty we had shared when, looking down into her dear face, I kissed her lips.

Nordi came back from the coast next evening, a buxom pretty full of high spirits, and I didn't have to act the part of husband. I very simply was. Nordi's energy immediately turned the house into our living vibrant home. She built a small fire in the kitchen range.

"I'll make these rooms realize their sulking time is over," she announced and brought out a great clam chowder she'd made at the beach and put in more pepper, "for you darling," and allowed me to kiss her ear as she worked up some dough for scones.

I fitted myself into this marvelous bustle: this putting our world back on the tracks, as it were. Her high heels clicked as she trotted about. Even in that small kitchen she trotted.

To make up for lost work time I made lacquer thinner and reducer until past midnight. Then when I tried to go to sleep, I couldn't. Nordi complained about my ceaseless turning, so I ended up lulled by the river and sweet memories of Virginia's warmth as she had lain beside me in my narrow nest.

The next night I went to bed and slept until late in the

morning, and the rest of the week was kept exceedingly busy. A torrid spell of weather had brought vanilla sales up, the result of many ice cream specialty shops that had recently sprouted up throughout the state, and four drums of the stuff went out to our big accounts.

I saw Virginia only in groups of the family where we both acted stiff and didn't meet one another's eyes, but I found from talking to old lady Nordstrom (as I continued to address her in my mind) that Tek and Teddy would be in town for the weekend still preparing their house for sale.

We were having coffee on the Forsythes' porch one evening. Tek and Teddy were sitting on the edges of their chairs, past ready to leave for town. Olga stepped inside for another plate of cookies and Nordi left her coffee to weed in Grandma's flower-bed that almost surrounded the porch. Grandma was reproaching her: "Ev-a-lyn," she said, "can't you sit for a minute like the rest of us?"

"I can't rest looking at weeding that needs to be done. It vexes me," was Nordi's answer.

Lolling against a porch pillar across from Virginia I nodded my head, as if agreeing with Nordi's sentiment, while looking at Ginny. With the smallest of movements she shook her head, but I persisted with almost imperceptible nods, and each time she answered with slow and tiny negatives. Olga opened the window and the door and played for us MacDowell's "Scottish Poem," a favorite of mine. In the coming dark the pleasant get-together broke up. At home, bedded down, I twisted and turned until Nordi said she was going to sleep with Bunky.

"No, I'll take my insomnia to the river," I told her and was halfway there when the urge to visit Ginny came, in spite of her many petite refusals. I changed my direction. With the dog now taking my visits as a matter of course, I stole easily into the girls' tent and touched Ginny's hand as I had before. I pulled, though gently, as if to pull her out of bed, then left and waited outside. When she emerged, I led her down to the meadow. I asked her to lead then, because she was so beautiful in her kimono. This time she didn't falter. She told me later of the first time, that she had been so frightened that her legs barely supported her and she had to fight for breath. Now, though fearful, her fondness for me brought her to the grove and to my bed over the murmuring water. We lay side by side and looked up at the moon. I kissed her cheek. She kissed back, a peck, no more.

"Clyde," she murmured, "I'm scared."

"So am I, Ginny, but we can't go back to be like we were. I should have known that what was hidden would burst out some day, didn't you, Ginny?"

After a thoughtful interval, she whispered, "I like you, Clyde, but you love me so hard." Another long pause in which I gloried in her nearness, then reluctantly, it seemed to me, she said: "You're always teaching me. I can tell. A long time ago you told me that as a flower you watched me grow, but that's not all of it. You've helped me grow."

I played with her fingers as I said, "It's only because I want you to know the richer patterns of life."

"My folks are ignorant. Grandma rules all of us through ignorance," she said. "They're afraid of books that don't agree with what they want to believe."

"Their stumbling block is the Bible, Ginny. It isn't mine."

"Please don't stop teaching me, Clyde," she pled, kissing my cheek, "if your loving me is part of it, I'll try to like you back all I can."

"You're a darling to tell me that," I whispered in her ear. "You know with you this close, talk is absurd. I'll have to kiss your mouth or have a conniption fit."

She met my lips with a kiss so ardent (at least I believed it to be ardent and demanding), that the questions troubling us disappeared. We turned to one another and embraced and contentment was ours. Soon with kisses and tighter embraces I sought to express my hunger for her. She seemed taken aback, but then responded as best she could. Remembering how she had enjoyed having her throat kissed, I did it again and her armpits I kissed as before, and though she would not let me uncover her breasts, I was able to kiss the swell of one where its lovely curve was a bit uncovered at her armpit. I was in heaven.

"You kissed my ear last time," she murmured, "I like that." Then I was whispering in them and kissing them, to our great pleasure. I sought to fondle and massage her feet. She didn't approve of such bold address and showed her reluctance by fending my hands away, as she protected her breasts. I began caressing her arms and shoulders, rather massaging them, and then abruptly put my hand down over her Mount of Venus and her flower. Instantly she grabbed my hand with both of hers, but I held mine where it was and after a bit of silent tussle, she ceased struggling and I was able to caress her flower with the very tiniest of loving movement.

Three more times I inveigled Virginia to cross the meadow to my hideaway, twice with no moon to show the way and once, because she wanted it so, without my accompanying her.

As soon as she entered the grove, she cast aside her kimono as I asked her to, and we met nakedly and embraced nakedly in the warm night air before we sought my nest above the rippling flow of the river. There Virginia tasted timidly of the flavors of forbidden fruit.

"It's not as if I'm still a child," she whispered, in my breath-warmed ear. "After all I've been eighteen for more than three months now."

But by the third rendezvous she savored the forbidden secretiveness, the fun of our deception of the family, but most of all our open love for each other when we were together.

"Our bodies turned my liking you into loving you," she said in tones that fitted the river's song. "Here, Clyde, kiss my breasts once more before I leave," and after that moment the idyll was over. And the murmuring water that had flowed under us as we loved coursed on downstream in cataracts and pools, scented perhaps with our love.

When Virginia reached her tent the third time, she found Dory wide awake and, though not the least suspicious, wondering, and Virginia, the most truthful of people, concocted a tale of sleeplessness and a walk under the moon to the promontory that broods over our bottomland by the river.

"Don't tell mama," she begged, "or they'll not let me have coffee after supper."

She was shocked at the ease with which she lied, but really frightened that we might be found out. This, she told me, as she rode into town with me some mornings later. The unsuspecting clan still went out of their Scandinavian way to see that Ginny came with me on whatever chore or expedition, providing many delightful moments and sometimes even hours for us.

As for my day-to-day work, it pleased me that, though I'm not a meticulous person, my arrangement of things in general at Acme allowed me to speedily fill and pack big orders of many small items in such a manner that we seldom had breakage en route: this, much to my father's annoyance. He liked to make a great to-do about everything. After the thinner making and packaging of it—a hefty job done before eight o'clock in the morning—I took on the Acme problems and the sale and distribution of both flavoring extracts and lacquer thinner. I don't know how I got away with it, but I was able to carry it off after I closed down the studio and brought home my new workbench and the turning base I had made for the statue. The idea of the great statue gradually receded from my mind.

Life was a hammock for me that year. I couldn't seem to fall out, try as I might. I worked hard and loved hard, and Lady Luck took me by the hand.

.

Word of mouth increased my business. By the simple act of making my product a bit richer than government precepts while the giant national producers cut theirs around two percent and got away with it—that is, until the weather or a painter's carelessness produced a botched up job on a car and a howl of outrage from the operator. Soon all knew to use "Rice's Thinner" and avoid such messes. I was in a jam to handle the new orders, until

I offered a discount on any two fifty-gallon drums—a hundred-gallon order. It reduced the necessity of smaller packaging and effort. I was able to market through another outlet fingernail polish remover and other items like it and found more places to vend my various combinations of solvents and diluents. I needed an assistant badly and was looking for one.

In the meantime, I acquired a horse—a saddle horse—on the bad debt of a thinner customer. We had had horses in California, three of them, and an enormous Belgian draft horse, the Frank of our fond memories, but none quite like Ace, the horse that had paid off two drums of thinner.

Ace loved children, tolerated women, and hated men. He had been a famous stallion leader of a band of wild horses. The ranchers, on whose lands he ran his following, tried to capture him with relays, but to no avail. Men in the area eyed him as a great mount if he could be caught. Others hated him, and far out on the dusty plains he had been shot at many times. Once he was wounded and still got away and recovered, but eventually, bogged down in deep drifts of snow, he was captured and gelded. Some said, mysteriously, that he'd been cut too high. Perhaps it was true. Still, from then on he was useless as a stud. Otherwise the gelding of him was not a success. Breaking him to the saddle must have been a long and arduous task. Now in the pasture he confronted us with flaring nostrils and haughty mien. Jack Forsythe, Olga's husband, came from a line of Irish horse dealers and had a lifelong interest in them. Before World War I he had been a horseshoer at the Fashion Stables in Portland. He knew the difference between a spavine and a spasm. When he spoke of horse's stiffles he meant it as a noun, not as a verb, and was wont to bring up the problem of the gleet in mules. But not even Jack Forsythe, who had shoed thousands of horses, could put the back shoes on Ace. Still, we heard that whoever had owned him before us had a young son who taught him such tricks as rearing up and walking on his hindlegs. Ace evidently had loved the boy, for though his controlled hatred for Jack or Teddy or me was barely concealed, he was not averse to Bunky, who was nurturing a bit of wildness in himself.

Bunky would be thirteen years old in October. Milking our Delite twice daily was producing for him the big powerful hands that I lacked and envied. I could see in the set of his shoulders and from his walk what sort of a man he would be. He was still plagued by what we thought were epileptic seizures. He had the spells at two- or three-month intervals and always at night in his sleep. They were mild, but I learned to sleep lightly because of them and knew the moment one started. I would hurl myself from Nordi's side and in his bedroom catch his tongue between my fingers (as this, I was told, one should do) and bundle him up after the spell was over with all the love that was in me. God, how I doted on my boy.

Bunky was inventive in his play, full of mischief, and sometimes he played tricks on me. There was much that I was in the dark about that he and Dave worked up in their play. I kept dynamite caps, dynamite and a coil of fuse in a small shed well away from the house. I used it now and then to blow out stumps or to break up boulders too large to move in one piece. Bunky exploded stolen dynamite in the river for a spectacle to be seen only by two boys. Telling me about it years later, he said that when he had the cap buried in one end of the dynamite stick and the fuse firm in the cap, he would grease the whole thing in axle grease, except the other end of the fuse, which he supported on a board. After lighting and floating this lethal contraption out into the fast current with the dynamite several feet below the surface, he would stand with Dave, his constant companion, on the bank and with bated breath wait until, downstream from them, a mighty column of water would rear up with a roar, the board blown sky high. Then with the roiled waters calming gradually and passing beyond their sight, Bunky would turn to Dave with a "How was it?"

And Dave, much younger, would squirm with delight and report that it was "kinda scary."

I had trained Bunky in the care of rifles and this year he was going on his first hunt with me. We planned to set up camp near a certain brook in the Maury Mountains of Central Oregon. We drove west early on the morning of a very late season hunt in the Maurys.

Bunky hated the brushy timber of Western Oregon, perhaps because I loved it. It was a way to assert himself. After all he was nearly thirteen, wasn't he, so he was not much interested as we drove through the brush and timber to Mount Hood.

When finally we came over the crest of the Cascades at Blue Box Pass, his disgust in what I loved gradually disappeared from his face. Still, he held it in neutral. Then suddenly we came out on the rolling sagebrush hills of the Warm Springs Indian Reservation. Bunky popped up from his slouch with amazement.

"Hey! Pop, this has gotta be Lone Ranger country. Wish Dave was here. Look! Look at the arroyos! Yeah, and the mesas! Betcha anything this is wild horse country." And he was right.

A half-hour later we drove through a band of fine looking horses, their hides mottled with big patterns of black, white and red, Indian ponies, but leggy. Bunky was in a rapture. We were driving down a mere track of a road that would surely be a quagmire in the winter, when someone, braving our dust, honked from behind us. It soon became apparent that they wanted us to stop, so we did.

It was a new car that came up, and out of it stepped a splendidly accoutered old Indian and his wife, both heavily ornamented with silver. He introduced himself as the chief of the Warm Springs Indians and his wife and son and his son's wife in the back seat. They were coming in from Portland in a shiny but dusty new Packard that they had just purchased. After comments on the weather, he said he wanted to race us, but I had no money to wager and told him so. Anyway, how could we race with only the wheel ruts of the very narrow road swerving around knolls, weaving through sagebrush country? That would make no difference, he said. Finally, to placate him, I agreed to race.

I started out on the road with him behind me, eating our dust which would quit the ground on only the slightest of invitations. We had not gone a half a mile when he swerved off the road from behind us and tore out through the sagebrush, finally passing us and then returned to the road again. Soon after, he stopped. They were all beaming with triumph when we came up to them.

"I won," he said, pleasure on his wrinkled old face. "If you'd bet anything, you'd 'a lost it." Then he looked us over rather imperiously, I thought, and asked if we rode horses. We spoke of our Ace. "Lotsa bottom?" he asked, but paid no attention to my boasting of Ace's tirelessness. "Look! I like you. You raced me," he said. "You come on to the reservation some time, I give you two halter-broken young stallions that are half thoroughbred. Our stud is fancy thoroughbred with papers. We run a hundred head of horses. Too much! I want white-faced cattle instead."

"I'll come next summer," I answered. "I know a trail through the mountains up above Warm Springs Meadow."

He grinned, "You got Indian blood?"

"Yes," I answered happily. "Cherokee blood from way back."

We shook hands, everyone grinning, and they drove ahead of us toward the village. None of us said anything about the Packard, still gleaming under its dust, for it would never be the same again. The fenders were torn and ripped up by the heavy sagebrush, and I was surprised to see that his radiator held cooling water in spite of the beating it had taken riding down the heavy sage as it swept over it, but that's the way he wanted things. In spite of the childishness of the act I found I had plenty of respect for him.

Well, we went on our way to the mountains. We set up our small tent by the brook, made a hearth and, hiking out, found deer scattered about everywhere and saw one marvelous rack of antlers. Bunky was going to hunt with my old 25-35, and I was going to use the new Savage 300.

We bedded down early in anticipation of a big day tomorrow, but were awakened at midnight by three pickups and a car full of drunken hunters with their women. They set up their tents around us, built a big bonfire and proceeded to pass bottles, shoot at the trees, trade women and howl at the moon. At dawn they were still firing their guns with exuberant imbecility. I knew we were jinxed. We couldn't drive away and get another spot. This was the only way into the Maurys that I knew of, outside of coming through the sage of the high desert that surrounded them. We decided to stick it out. I opened a can of corned beef and offered half of it to Bunky. He declined vigorously.

"Come on," I said over a big mouthful, "with some crackers and this beef jammed down in your innards, we can hunt all day away from these jokers and drag what meat we knock down over the snow that came down last night and froze. No brush here to get in the way."

"Swell," Bunk said, eyeing me disgustedly, "but, Pop, I can't stand greasy corned beef."

"Look here, Bunky," I said, "it's all right to toady your stomach in town, but we're out here in this man size country, and we can't wait to cook you a dainty breakfast. We got to get out of here before these guys pile off their women and start doing their hunting, blasting jaybirds on the way. Put lots of mustard on it and get it under your belt and we'll be out and going."

We got about a quarter of a mile away before the camp behind us woke up, with shootings and the distant bellowing of a Willamette Valley farmer.

"They come from over west of Albany," I mentioned to Bunky. "One of them I know slightly. I'd recognize his twangy voice anywhere. He works in a paint shop in Albany in the summer when you'd think he'd be out on his place hoeing the spinach or whatever it is he raises."

"Okay, Pop," Bunky said sullenly. "Where's all the deer we saw yesterday? Did your Albany farmers spook them this far?"

"Guess we'll have to give it another quarter of a mile. That's a hell of a long drag, I know. If these swacked assholes hadn't turned up, we'd be heading for home with a couple of nice bucks scattering their ticks all over the pickup bed, but we'll get 'em. You spot any sign yet?"

"None on the snow, Pop. Guess they lit out as soon as the farmers started banging away last night."

"You're hep to how it is all right, Bunky. Funny, from things they were howling about last night, I know they've been doing this campout right here for the last eight years."

We skidded along over the broken plains of crusted snow. "We won't like this overlong drag," I said. "Let's split up. We're far enough out now for some action. I'm going up this draw. If I don't raise anything I'll go on to the top and come down the next draw and meet you at the bottom. Careful with that gun now, and remember to lead on your deer." I watched him go.

The sky was lightening. It must have been about eight-thirty. It was going to be a clear autumn day.

Well, up this ravine you go. Remember you're not used to this Savage 300 yet. The old 25-35 seemed to think and aim itself. A team we were! Now Bunky's got it. Come on, hunt, damn you. We came to hunt, not maunder.

I scrambled up a steep pitch, then peered around at ridges uselessly. Snuffled my gaze through the brushy draw, spotted brush robins scuffing up dry leaves, a sound like deer walking. I know their ways, still I fool myself once in awhile. It turned out to be a buck, but too late.

Every towhee can be a deer! Paste that in your hat, Rice! Yeah man! Wonder how Bunky is making out. One more scuffle with this pucker-brush, make the ridge, have a look around. Hey! That's a leg, not a puckerbrush stem coming down out of that twiggy mess. Safety off? Yeah! took it off down at the bottom. There—it moved! Damned if it isn't a runt fawn. Its big eyes are on me. It won't make it through the winter. Wish I could help!

"But you can't help." I said aloud. "You know damn well you can't. Say!" I said not to me or to the fawn, "You'd make a nice old woman. Well, at least sometimes," I intervened, protecting my masculinity. Then furiously: "Save the fawn, defeat the way of things! Are we hunting?" I asked myself delicately through my mounting annoyance and stated, "We're looking for something to shoot. Christ! Shut up! SHUT UP!" I snarled and plodded higher.

On the ridge I looked around. Far off to the east I could see Steens Mountain. Closer I saw the high desert reaching out to the south, but no sign of deer. The clearness of the day allowed the sun to bring its full brunt upon the land. The snow had all but disappeared. I looked about for Bunky, but didn't see his red hat down below me. Cautiously I came down in the next draw, hoping to drive a couple of deer in Bunky's direction. . . . No shot!

Soon I was at the bottom. No Bunky! Still with hunter's caution I worked back toward the first draw where I had left him and there found him sprawled on the ground. When he heard me coming he raised himself and showed the face of a very sick boy. Around him were vomitings.

"Pop, I told you I can't eat lard," he murmured and vomited again. "Get me out of this, Pop, I'm sick."

Yes, this is all my fault, I admitted to myself, and guiltily I helped him to his feet. He had befouled himself and the front of him was besmirched with vomit. Now only green water poured from him as he heaved.

God! Oh, God! What have I done? "Son," I said in a way that I hoped he could lean on, "Son, I'll get you back to camp and some hot soup will tide you over till we can clean you up. Thank God I brought extra clothes for you!"

I went over and picked up the old 25-35 where he'd left it and, cradling the two guns under one arm, tried to support him. After several hundred yards we knew we were in trouble, for the ground that was frozen when we came was thawing, at least the first three inches of it, and I sadly observed that the soil in the Maurys was black gumbo. At each lunging step forward the muck seemed to grow deeper. There was fright in Bunky's weak voice. "Help me, Pop! I can't raise my feet. They're stuck!"

"But I am helping all I can," I muttered as I lunged along. Each shoe, as I drew it with supreme effort out of the mire, was a great adhering mound, a black snowshoe. Bunky, in his weakened condition, had to be pulled to help him drag his feet from one step to the other. I looked toward the aspen grove of camp.

How did we get so far from camp when we planned to drag our big buck to camp? Got to keep going! Got to keep pulling him along, though he falters every few steps. Got to keep him on his feet. Wow! I'm getting cramps in my upper legs. Come on, Bunky! Hot soup for you if you keep pulling each mud-gowed foot out to move it forward and sock it away again in the mud ahead. Now the other one. Progress! Well, we're not losing ground, but hardly gaining. Come on kid! I got you into this, now I'll get you out—but hell, I'm playing out.

"The weight of the guns, this gumbo and Bunky are wearing you down, Mister," I said. "Right! Got any ideas? Left foot, right foot, what else?

"You all right, Bunky?"

He didn't answer—too weak to answer. I'd soon be too weak to ask, but we were getting closer to the grove. Then my left tennis shoe pulled off in the mud. Trying to get it out I lost my balance and stepped into the mire barefooted. It was icy cold, but when I pulled my foot out only a fraction of what had clung to my shoe came out with my foot. I saw a chunk of log to sit on and floundered to it and took off the other shoe. Then I could walk after a fashion, so I sat Bunky down there and removed his shoes and we staggered on. Our feet were freezing and a bit cut up but we were getting closer to camp. I was becoming so weary I couldn't support Bunky, and I had him sit down on a log while I made my way into camp.

The farmers were gone, but their huge bonfire was now a mound of coals. I put a can of soup in the coals and thawed my feet near it, and was heading back with soup for Bunky when he stumbled into camp and lay in the warmth given off by the embers.

I got the tomato soup into him and another can for me. Then I was able to remove his filthy clothing and sluice him with brook water and had him lie near the embers' heat, while I made a bed for him in the back of the pickup. The soup came up. After that was tended to, I dressed him in dry clothes. He looked like a cadaver, eyes deep in their sockets, his face sunken in, lips blue and his skin a delicate green. I lifted him up and lay him down in the bed and covered him as best I could, wrapped the whole bed in a tarpaulin.

I was terribly frightened, believing him close to death. Still, the next soup stayed down, two bowls of it. I believed he had a chance. With him wrapped up, tarpaulin and all, I bore out of the Maurys and headed in a frenzied trip toward Portland and St. Vincent's Hospital. After hours of mad driving I stopped at Government Camp. He was asleep, the greenish tint gone from his face, so I drove on through, not so wildly. And when we reached home, he was able to step from his bed without support and showed great interest in the hotcakes he demanded and got. He was not, however, to show much interest in exploring the great outdoors with his father after that first hunting trip, and who could blame him?

•

Several weeks before the disastrous hunting trip, Ginny entered a business college in Portland. The Bromses' house in town hadn't sold as they'd hoped, and they decided to spend one more winter there. Dory loved it, for she could go to school with three friends whom she was certain she could not live without.

Shy Virginia, who did not make friends easily, was dismayed. Her inability to face the bustle of the everyday world held her back. In fact in the give and take of things she always came out second, and worse, always expected to come out second. High school had been quite difficult for her. My attention and love for several years and the past happy summer had buoyed her up. She had blossomed into the person her daydreams sometimes envisioned.

Fall brought that to an end, and she was in school again, competing, but with a shadowy sense of loss—an extending melancholic mood peculiarly Swedish. It was much worse than my poem to her had described. In it her cocoon had been transparent; now it was bleakness in which she wrapped herself. She avoided my attempts to rendezvous with her. She did admit once as I drove her out to visit Olga that we couldn't possibly ever again know such enchanted hours as had been ours.

The weather turned colder then and we had an early snow. After that it was a glum winter, but I didn't mind, for from the first of November I saved most of my evenings for study.

Somehow even in the worst of times, I had been able to find a library within biking distance where I could feed my mind with layman science, politics and the somewhat recent studies on the brain of man. This fall I went over the studies that interested me when I was under my old friend Pushell's tutelage. I had been seventeen but really I was still very much an adolescent. Nietzsche, turning the world upside down, had appealed to my youth. Nietzsche—what a world of strutting men that would have been, but now it was happening.

Freud was still difficult for me, and Marx seemed too correct for words. The lock-step of a rational view of the future. I doubted any pattern that projected itself into the future in absolutes. My experience had been that in all endeavor—art, science or life within a family—we fumble along. You can see it best in retrospect and at thirty-eight I'd piled up a little bit of that. I had been interested in the early twenties in the Italian poet, Gabriele D'Annunzio. Now reading him again, I saw how he was infected with Nietzschean audacity. He was a flaunter of banners, still I had liked his stuff, though he belonged to a school of poets I despised. They couldn't make a statement or even imply one without bringing in Ishtar, Zeus and the Colossus of Rhodes. Also, D'Annunzio's writing reeked of patriotism, which was one of the necessary ingredients of wars.

I had taught myself to think of man in the broadest of terms. The activities of nations after World War I, and the fiasco of the peace conference had seemed to me like the acts of grasping children. Now, the dictatorships that Russia and Germany espoused were one more fiasco. But the concept of one world

government—the integration of peoples—still struck this idealist as perhaps a way for people to think and act. Patriotism, in the
context of the way I viewed things, was a poison dangerous to
mankind, for it was used by power-hungry leaders of whatever
kind, in battling neighbor nations on whatever pretext. Still, I
had to admit that I had a deeply patriotic urge in myself for
Portland, for Oregon, the Pacific Coast region and our own dear
United States, and our ties with England and France.

Love of art drove man worldwide to create art. The hunger
for excellence knows no boundaries. Art, science, the accumulation of knowledge: these are the aims of mankind. In spite of this
I know that we are predatory like the weasel, with a body similar
to that of the ape, and a brain capable of unconceived miracles or
indescribable vileness, and that our belligerence is the product of
the danger that man is to man.

And then one day, as we dawdled over lunch, news came from
the radio of the attack on Pearl Harbor. I reared out of my chair,
furious, enflamed, the elemental man in me raging. We had been
attacked. I saw Nordi viewing me with amusement.

"And where is my pacifist now?" she murmured.

"I—I—I," I spluttered, "those God-damned Japs!"

"Sure," she went on, "I feel the same way, but you—? For
years I've heard you on your one world, on the duplicity of
leaders. Has fury replaced your thinking? Look, Clyde, I'm
raging inside too, but at the same time I see something. I believe
this is how it always happens. Proffered manhood is the perfect
tool for the most insignificant of leaders. But forget that! Sit
down, Clyde. We have to think. Our lives are being changed."

This was one of the Nordis I didn't know. She stepped ahead
of me into my own thinking. "You're thirty-eight and some
months old, Clyde. Will they take you?"

Next morning we drove to work in silence, our fury at the
Japanese instinctive. We had been attacked; still, I wouldn't let
my feelings come between me and my worldwide view of the
useless destruction and slaughter that is war. "The plague that

comes from within, not a plague that comes from without," I had read somewhere.

"I'm dead set against it," I burst out.

"What are you talking about?" asked Nordi.

"Power hungry leaders. Jesus! It seems any job-lot of us must have a leader."

"At what point is a leader's usefulness compromised by his hunger for power?" Nordi asked, staring out at the commuting traffic as it swept with us toward the city.

"Do you mean at what point should a leader be shot?" I asked her.

"Perhaps when he first starts to swagger," Nordi answered facetiously as we drove up to Acme.

"I'm serious, Nordi. This is no time to be joshing."

"Don't be a hypocrite and prove your manhood by enlisting."

"It's going to take all my will not to."

Pop drove up then, got out of his car. "Hi, Clyde," he said. "I tell you it was a shock to the Little Lady and me! Never did trust a Jap! I get along all right with Chinks. Look, how old are you, really, son? Are they going to get you?"

"I'm thirty-eight, Pop. I don't think they will." They didn't.

"Say, Clyde," he went on, "I want you to make a hundred gallons of "V" vanilla today. I'm going to build our stock up for this war, and you better stock up on your thinner material."

That day I filled out preliminary forms for buying solvents during the war.

"You're clear of the army with your thinner," they said at Union Oil. "They ain't going to be any more new cars until the war's over. Everybody'll have to paint the old car. You're going to make a pile. You signed up yet for your solvents and chemicals? Better get your contract going today over at Chem Distributing."

After several days of some turmoil and confusion, things started out in what seemed to be the new mode, and I was able to buy enough needed supplies to last me at least two months.

Most young men were enlisting or arranging things at home, knowing they would be drafted. The Axis nations were winning on all fronts. Terrible news, it seemed, was all the radio had to offer. It became increasingly difficult for me to keep my wits about me. I ached to be a soldier, to fight the hated Hitler and Tojo, to put on a uniform and have my thinking done for me. God! It seemed you had to fight to protect yourself from tyrants. You couldn't fight the tyrant nor his henchmen, but only people much like yourself in the opposing army, bamboozled as you were into doing the tyrant's murdering for him. You couldn't win, you were merely a tool in some glorified asshole's control.

•

It was a month later. "Lost in the mail," said the minor official of Chem Distributing. "Too late to correct it now, and yours is the only one so lost." The "so lost" gave him away. What he was telling me, he was told to tell by his superior. He was quoting some prissy guy in the upper office.

"Can't you send a tracer on it?" I asked, beginning to realize that the boom was being lowered on me.

"We did," he answered. "Now no more contracts are to be let out. There is a war on, you know."

"You mean it's too late to send a duplicate back to Washington?"

"We go by the regulations," he answered coldly.

"Good God! Where do I stand then?"

"Rice," he said, "I'm sorry to tell you, but without a contract you can't get materials."

"Seems I'm without recourse," I muttered.

"Yes, Mr. Rice, it's too late to straighten this out. Take the situation to your lawyer, but I think you're out of business until the war is over. Still, if I were you, I'd have a lawyer see what he can do."

I found out that he couldn't. I was out of business for the duration.

It was a strange look that came on my father's face when I told him my war contract for solvents had been lost in the mail, and that I was out of business for the duration: his eyes seemed to be looking into the back of his head. Next morning he fired me and would give me no reason for doing so.

"I don't have to have a reason," he said.

I left thinking that he was getting even for my refusal to quit my business last year at his jealous whim. Looking back at it now, I believe that the Little Lady, using his jealousy, manipulated him into getting rid of me. In her way of thinking I was a hazard for her complete control of the Company.

But what of Nordi? He wanted her to stay and Nordi was vehement about it. She would stay come hell or high water. At home that night she said: "Your troubles stem from the Little Lady. Whatever you do she has time and cause to put it in a bad light. I get this from little things he says as we work together on his butter flavor or the grape flavor he can't get quite right and fusses over eternally, and Clyde, he is hating himself for firing you. He really knows how she worked it, but he loves her."

"How do you fit in with all this?" I asked.

"Your Pop treats me like a daughter, and I like to do this kind of work. You make the flavors, but outside of the barrels and kegs, I turn it all into a finished product, bottled, labeled, cartoned, ready to ship out. I really don't know why it appeals to me so. You know, I'm an artist of sorts, who isn't particularly interested in painting and I'm not wild about dusting and doilies, but getting up stock for this little firm—why, Clyde, I love it."

"It's beneath you, Nordi."

"You miss it, Clyde. It's my strange satisfaction and, darling, I'm glad I've found it."

I had enough solvents to still carry on for another month, except toluol. Toluol was a by-product of gas made from coal, and I was able to get three drums of it.

"That's all for you," the superintendent said, "unless you can show me your right to it by war contract, and I hear by the grapevine that yours is lost or whatever."

One more month of thinner—seemed silly even to think about it with Corregidor in the news. Everywhere I went old men were taking the places of the young ones I knew, cranky old guys, all thumbs even in their heads, and hard to deal with. But what would I do when the last of the thinner was sold? Go back to the woods and cut cordwood?

Besides shoeing saddle horses, Jack Forsythe had been a salesman for Clorox, and was getting along fine. But when a chance came to become a guard at Oregon Shipyards, he made the change and stood around in a guard's uniform and wondered if it had been a good move. His talk, however, of the yards interested me. The Kaiser Company was enlarging their facilities as fast as they could acquire materials and men. Surely I could find work in such an operation, even though I had none of the skills needed. . . .

So I was caught with both arms in a big truck tire. There were too many of us. We hindered each other in the work. Our job in the shipyard tire shop was to keep the rolling stock rolling. All through the vast area of docks, ships and shops, towering traveling cranes and heavy equipment of all sorts wheeled about on immense tires rolling over a carpet of metal bits, welding slag, and spikes that were ground into the roads and alleys and into the thick planking of the docks. The sweeping machines got some of it, but I believe the rubber tires got more.

With that excess of manpower you would think that someone would notice my predicament, but none did, and I'm certain it was not planned. They were so busy climbing over each other trying to get to the bunged-up tires, to get a hand in on the job somehow, pressing forward in ranks, they seemed unaware of a mere individual in distress. I was loath to ask for help, though my arms were becoming numb, but when the harried foreman passed by, I called out: "Look," I said, "I'm not much use to you this way." He came over and stared.

At last he said: "Yeah, in the fix you're in, you can't fumble things or screw 'em up. Hey, Joe," he yelled to an old timer on the job. "Come 'ere! We gotta get this guy here loose from this tire, so he can dive in with the rest." And to me, "How'd you get caught in there anyway?"

"One of the guys jerked my spreading tool out of my tire to spread that tire they're all scrambling over."

"How come they aren't all over this tire?"

"I warned them off."

"How?"

"With the spreading tool."

"Threatening with a weapon, huh? You're fired!"

"Don't worry about it," I advised him. "I'm quitting!"

I left him and wandered about the yard past shops where trip hammers shaped glowing ingots into heavy ship parts. In amongst the growing hulls I cruised, awed by what I saw, deafened by the noise of construction, as thousands of men forced ringing steel to conform.

I walked the length and fell in love with the long outfitting dock. There, after launchings, the ships were equipped and finished and their great steam engines were broken in and readied for the sea. To work there I had to have a marine machinist card, so I got a job as machinist helper and studied four hours after each shift in a school that trained us inept ones to be of value.

Several months later I climbed the gangway to the deck of the *Benjamin Sempter*, a heavy toolbox on my shoulder. I'd made the grade. I was a beginning marine machinist. Down into the engine room I clambered and turned my awed stare at the simple massive engine that was slowly spinning its mighty shaft and propellor.

My leadman (straw boss to you) came over: "Is this your first shift in this tub's innards?"

"Right," I replied, trying to give my answer what I thought was a machinist-like twist by being heavy on the *t*.

"Well," he said, "look around and ask questions of the guys down here. What you good at anyway?"

"Me? Guess I'm pretty good with a sledge." I was looking at a big slugging wrench shaped to fit around a large nut, like the ones I saw on the studs securing the journals, though I didn't know they were journals yet.

"If that's so," he remarked, "we can use you down here."

That was the swing shift's crew that I worked with, but they were too numerous for their own good. Like the tire shop they got in each other's way, like flies on a piece of tired meat they practically covered the job with their bodies. That was not for me, but I stayed on until I knew my way around the ship. When I felt secure as a machinist, I quit the swing shift and got on the graveyard shift—eleven P.M. to six A.M.—and, with no herds of fellow machinists about, started earning my wage. Our crew of six machinists and three helpers got a lot done and still had time to stand by while the engineer ran the three-cylinder engine and its great crankshaft settled microscopically into its journals, and we brought the capping half of the bearing down three thousandths of an inch at a time to follow the wearing-in and seating of the main parts of the new engine.

Our leadman, Chet Kelly, must have been demoted at some time in the past for he was much more knowledgeable about ships and this particular type of engine than his foreman or superintendent. A chunky, graying fellow, he was a strong union man, but he didn't believe in leaning on it. Under him, we gave the Kaiser Shipyard more than they paid us for. I liked him. He could quote a little Shakespeare, hum a little tune as he added up his job sheet. He took a dim view of me, however. He sensed that I was a maverick, wasn't a Catholic or even a church-goer and could quote more than he could on occasion. What he liked was my work. With my partner we were the lead team in everything. At least he could understand my partner, Ran Durston, who was as Scotch as Chet was Irish and fuller of blarney than three Irishmen.

Ran was me with some more added and twice as clever. He loved a joke as much as I did. When I was unsure on a job he would step in and give me the support I needed. But with the short-handled twenty-pound hammers we worked with, I could strike a much harder blow, so I'd hold back so that both big nuts encased in slugging wrenches that we were hammering on came loose at the same time.

Of course he sensed this and approved of my ways. Confidentially Ran told me that in Scotland he had been a poacher, a professional one he said, and an excellent pickpocket, which he proved to me time and again by handing me back my keys and purse at the end of the watch, so I could go home. He was also, he said, a dognapper and with his ferrets had made a fair living harvesting rabbits raised on large estates in his corner of Scotland.

"You had to keep your wits about you, I can tell you," he remarked. I was beginning to notice that Ran was eternally conscious of all who were about him. Not only that, but he made a fair surmise of their character and what they were doing. He grinned at me, "I been in a lot of tights, but never been really snagged and housed." His grin grew wider, "Never did like their kind of windows."

The other men in our crew don't loom as large as Ran in my memory. One, Lendel, a quietly competent middle-aged fellow, hadn't one prominent feature in his makeup. Even buckteeth would have given him a handle of sorts. He wasn't particularly self-effacing, but was there on the job with Ran and me, opinionless, showing no joy or exasperation, but others besides us machinists were there completing and servicing the ships. There was the chief engineer, a former river steamer man, a crusty but democratic fellow, and there was his fireman, Gortel Schnappser, a dependable humorless old man from Clatskanie and his oiler. There was the pipe-fitter foreman, Craig Seldish, and his two buddies, Curt, the heavy-weight wrestler, and Jake, who had an impoverished farm on what was soon to be the most expensive land around Portland for homesites. Craig was quite a guy any way you wanted to look at it, intelligent, big, strong with a benign smile on his face. He and his crew did their work with such ease they seemed to be loafing.

Last, but certainly not least, the general superintendent of not only this shipyard but of two others as big—Abrams, who saw fit to come and work on the night shift with Ran and me and Lendel and our leadman, usually in the adjusting of brass bearings on the crossheads. This was indeed an honor. He told us once that our little group, six machinists and two helpers, did sixty percent of the work of the three shifts in getting the engine in shape.

We took these bearings out to see that their fit was as good as man could make it. We did this on the guard rail of the first grating up from the engine room deck. One man held the bearing on the rail while his partner scraped the finest of scrapings from it. Ran and the leadman and Lendel had big hands that could grip the bearing to the rail like a vise. Abrams's hands, like mine, were small and, when he held the bearing for me, it wobbled, but, as I did not scrape as hard or as heavily, we teamed well, but were slower than the other team, who waited for us to finish. This was terribly embarrassing to me. There was also a pin, a shaft of steel several feet long and slippery with lubricating grease that one had to grasp to lift it to the grating with one hand, bracing yourself with the other. Its diameter was such that big hands could grip it easily.

One night, Abrams with us, it happened that I was the one that reached for the sixty pound pin as we rotated the jobs. Scraping brass bearings is not like the usual scraping of the babbit bearings of the mains. If your hands were not rested, the scraping might chatter in the strokes and do more harm than good. I reached down, grasped the pin and holding it perpendicularly started to lift it, but my small hand, now tired from the scraping, was inadequate. I couldn't seem to get my fingers far enough around the pin to control it. It was slowly, very slowly slipping through my hand. I gripped till my eyes bulged. If it fell—good God!—if it fell into the machinery below, it might be dented besides doing harm. I was about to lose face. (Rice hasn't got what it takes.) I gripped despairingly, then Ran's voice was close in my ear, "I need help on my bearing. Here, I'll take that pin." He did and I was holding the bearing he was working on, and his helper, rebuffed as suddenly inadequate, was staring at us. That was my friend, Ran. In his continual scan about him, he had seen the situation and saved face for me. We went on as before, but others had seen and would remember.

While studying at mechanic's school I had been able to skip a class and take Virginia to lunch. She wore a dress that suited beautifully her long lines. It also emphasized her saucy bottom. After we were seated and had ordered she looked deeply into my eyes and smiled.

"I caught you looking at my bottom," she said. "Did it make it—you know—? Did it?"

"Of course it did," I answered.

She smiled a most childish smile, but made a small voluptuous gesture with her body. The food came and we ate, but after a few mouthfuls, she said, as she buttered a bit of bread:

"I've grown up very quickly, haven't I?"

Wild with desire I blurted out: "How's school?"

"Nothing's the same anymore," she said. "Oh! You mean my grades? They're good enough. I'll make it all right. Be looking for a job by spring."

The next time I saw her she was subdued. The grades weren't as good as she hoped. She was almost glum. "Clyde," she murmured, "what can you see in me? I'm really a dope."

The family was about us. She had used the only chance we had to speak together. We were having coffee klatch in the Bromses' new house, and after coffee we sang a bit before Nordi, Bunky and I headed for home through a low mist that the moon made fantastic. Nordi sensed my mood, for I was very worried about Virginia, would have given anything to be able to comfort her.

"What's wrong, Clyde?" she asked when we got home. "I thought it was a nice family get-together."

"I just feel down, I guess. Maybe it's the war," and rubbed her back as we lay in bed, and I told her of Abrams's working with us.

"He sounds like a real person. A little higher on the shoulder blade—there, that's it. Fine, that's made me sleepy. Good night, dear husband." But I didn't go to sleep. I stewed uselessly about Virginia's problems at business college.

On the job the chief would often run the engine for an hour

and then, if there weren't things to be fixed like pressure reducing valves, leaky faucets on deck, trouble with the thrust bearing, I was free to stare as the big crank shaft was turned by the connecting rods, as high pressure steam forced the pistons up and down in the great cylinders. All I saw of this were the connecting rods turning the crankshaft while the oiler on duty, with deftness timed to the movement of the rods, filled little open cups with lubricating oil.

Often my companions were working in other parts of the ship and I would be the only machinist on hand with the chief. We would talk a bit and then he'd be immersed in his log describing what had been done: stopped engine at 11:36 P.M., removed one three-thousandth shim from the number four bearing, started the engine at 11:59 P.M., thrust bearing warming up to be checked next stopping of the engine.

Of me, well, on those long runs I'd become mesmerized by the rhythm of the machine, the beat of it, as mentally I marched to it in sand and over mountains. It was the quick flip of my paddle on some hurrying river of Quebec. It was me pulling to shore from my sinking trading schooner. I made music to its direction, I listened to the famous marches of the world—Sousa's stirring ones and Tchaikovsky's "Great Slav March," all tied to the beat of the engine, my mind freed by the beat.

I was staring at the powerful movement of the new engine, the *Benjamin Sempter* now only a brief memory. Five such ships we had worked on since I came. We were one of three crews who, around the clock, sought to bring these ships to a semblance of perfection.

Sometimes the engine room was empty of visitors, but even on our graveyard shift we would sometimes be besieged with strangers, visitor tags in their lapels: haberdashers who sold vests and socks to minor officials in the front office, pimps and poets out for a change of scene and inspectors of all sorts, and always politicians, obsequious here, demanding there, and men of power who in that small crowded space strutted it somehow—in immaculate uniforms, impeccable top coats, they watched the engine do its thing.

One night I had a dream about the visitors. I dreamt that the ship was about to leave our ministrations for its maiden voyage, and I was the only machinist present among half a dozen strangers. The young lieutenant colonel with whom I struck up a conversation while we stared at the slow whirl of the ponderous machinery said: "I'm supposed to keep quiet on this, though it's not exactly a state secret that they're traveling incognito, but that smallish man near the chief engineer is the Narkus of Boalee and right next to him, whom you would assume to be a boy, is really his wife, the Narkee.

"They're inseparable, it seems for religious reasons. She had to dress like a boy. There has never been a woman allowed at the hot end. If you get a chance, that is, without staring, you can see in her various Asian influences. She hasn't the almond eye of the Japanese. They're really more pecan, but she's a most lovely Oriental.

"Their nation is being swarmed over by the worthless Flee-bams from the south. Now there's even a traveling Swede or two in their kingdom. They had to install parking meters for carriages. I find that vexing. The march of progress, they call it. I understand that it's intolerable to the Narkee."

The chief stopped the engine, and Ran, who had just returned, and I and the other four fellows got down in our pits to beat on big nut-loosening wrenches. When at last we had taken out the shims and hammered everything into place, we got out and wiped the oil from our backs that had dripped copiously from the slide above the LP's pit. I looked around for those interesting people. Both they and the lieutenant colonel had left the ship. I was curious and hurried up on deck only to see an unornamented closed carriage drawn by two small white horses disappearing down the dock.

When I came back the chief again stopped the engine and we took another six-thousandth all around this time. The chief said: "She's bedding herself at a pretty good rate, huh?"

Then we ran her for another hour, and I was standing watch-ing the oiler fill the various cups on the moving parts when a fellow I hadn't noticed, a tall one with quite a bulbish head that stuck out of his fringe of hair like a mushroom's nighttime bursting from the forest floor, said: "I saw you talking to the lieutenant colonel. He watches out for the Narkus. Theirs is the sensitive region in which we share an interest, and I'm assigned to check on the colonel. Did you happen to see a bulge in the colonel's pants pocket?"

"Why yes," I said, "I thought he had sequestered a nice apple, perhaps to consume later, or to throw at attack dogs."

"No," he said, "that's a good guess, but what he carries with him is a small but very effective atomic bim. When activated it has an effect on the eyes of all the people adjacent to the Boa-lee party. They themselves take a little pill with meals that protects them from its effect. Those not protected see triple, and a killer marksman sent out by Hitler would, we believe, prove ineffective.

"Their kingdom lies beside the great Asian lake, Nagabgak. That translates in English to torpid waters. In French it's slug-geesh watteair, I think. Britain desires to make a tunnel from the Boalee side of the lake under and into the country across the lake, which is practically a fiefdom of Hitler Germany. But the Narkee, who is up on such matters, wanted to know what they would do with the dirt from their borings. The English have agreed to make a great breakwater out into the lake with the material to where it is deep, so the royal yacht will not have to be dragged down the shore and into the water each time the royal family wants to go boating."

The chief started the engine and asked me to put my hand on number three journal and see if I could find vibration in it. I couldn't, but when I looked around after doing that, the mushroom-headed fellow had seemingly disappeared.

"Here," he said, popping out from the other side of the engine, with a kindly smirk, "I notice that you notice my tandem mustaches."

He was right. Above his upper lip he sported a fine narrow mustache with very pointed ends that would have given him a devilish look, except that he had another one of the same design beneath his lower lip, and on the whole these tandem masculine attributes moved with unrelated twitches as he talked.

"They're all the rage in Dwank, the capital of Boalee," he said. "I'm courting Hip Lips, the not too plump daughter of the Narkus and Narkee. At least," he went on to say, "I do when I'm at the capital."

He did look not so much devilish as peculiar. I drew myself away a bit, so that others who watched the engine would know that there was no fraternal relationship between us. Then I woke up and wrote down as much as I could remember about this strange encounter.

●

When I finally finished the course at machinist school I didn't tell Nordi and had some time to take Ginny out to lunch and to search out odd places on secluded roads where couples in parked cars spooned, agreed to marry or screwed in cramped quarters. Around the places there sometimes lurked people with warped minds. There with an arm about her, holding the wet warmness of her longingly, I kept banging my nose on hers, as I kissed and kissed again her mouth's sweet lips.

Virginia continued to have a bad time at business college. She became proficient at typing and shorthand, but the other phases of office work she learned slowly or not at all. I began to see that Virginia was perhaps only fourteen years along in her mental growth, a slowness and a backwardness I attributed to her family's fear of the new. In the Bible and in their church's use of it, they found phrases and whole sentences affirming stagnation as a proper stance while awaiting Armageddon.

My God, I thought, I've molested a child! I cast back over our relationship and knew definitely that it was a sweet wholesome young woman I had bedded. No sin had been committed in my bower above the Clackamas, whatever her bookkeeping grades.

That winter, one of the high waters flooded our fields. I got out the rowboat I always keep handy, fitted the oars and pushed out into the current to see how the vines had fared. The flood ran swiftly over the meadow. It was like the rushing tides in the gate, the Golden Gate of San Francisco. I put force into my rowing, the light skiff sped across the current and in my mind I was back once more in Tiburon. Old friends and girlfriends crowded about me, manly hands thumped my shoulders, breasts and hips brushed me as many womanly and girlish kisses found my cheeks.

Oh God, what a welter of happiness surrounded me. Bob and Harwood, Madeline, Annie Marge and sumptuous Miss Crippen. I was caught for a moment in the net of her remembered perfume. Christ! Such longing came, rowing along, just like it was 1927 or 1928, a long yesterday ago.

My plan to turn back across our submerged fields forgotten, living memories of my wild rows out into storms, I plunged on down the river buffeted by eddies, jerked by subterranean currents, I rowed down the middle of it, whooping with joy, still back, it seemed, in the raging salt tides of the Gate or the storms of the Bay. I got out of it eventually in a backwater miles downriver from our place, feeling I'd lived a year in a couple of hours.

Nordi helped me get the skiff into the trailer to bring it home. I told her the turmoil of memories that assailed me once the keel of my skiff felt fast water.

"I know," she said, as she kissed my cheek where those vaporous ladies had kissed. "I know, Clyde, and can you guess where memories haunt me most? Well, it's when I have hundreds of bottles of vanilla ready to put in their cartons, opening each carton to slip the bottle in and tucking it shut over and over again, then memories come—such memories! Funny, not so much you, as it should be, but of Art.

"The other day I thought of the time that you promised to come up some night on the *Sonoma* and serenade me while the engine of the *Sonoma* went chug-a-chug out there on the dark waters, and when you did, I slept through it. Such a waste of love." She came close, almost touching me. Electricity came across, but we didn't touch.

"You know, Clyde," she said across that tiny chasm, "I want to camp out over a weekend, sometime this winter and in bad weather, snow maybe, like we almost had at the Roaring River camp and twice at the stump ranch. Bunky could use some roughing. What was it like when you camped that winter when you were prospecting, Clyde? No! Tell me about it when we're camped. Come on, let's do it now. I'll get out the packs and camping gear."

"Yeh," I ruminated, "now that you mention it, I realize that there's been a need in me for a rough go for some time. After that fiasco Bunky and I had in the fall, well, maybe this will clean the slate."

Bunky, however, refused to accompany us. "I've had enough of that," he pointed out, "to last me next hunting season and even longer."

It was a still cold Saturday. We drove out into the hinterlands above Estacada, placed the chains on our car wheels after a look at the sky and, leaving it, plunged into the brush. A hundred yards of that and we came into a grove of big second growth fir with here and there an expansive maple. We made camp, got a week's worth of fallen limbs in around us and made a bough bed. Then we set up our tent over it, got out our piece of pitch brought from home and laid a fire ready for the match, covered it with a bit of plastic. Nordi wanted to wander.

It was rough country—that is, the going under foot was stumbly annoying. There was puckerbrush waist-high and innumerable clumps of sword fern raised up on knots of dead stuff. Through this tangle, Oregon grape was wrapped, and all of it sewn together with wire-like blackberry vines, and here and there young fir or alder finished the cover of that broken and rocky ground, and yet the expression on Nordi's face was pleased as if she was at her ease and eating chocolate éclairs.

"It'll be better farther on," she said, but it wasn't, still both of us agreed we weren't suffering.

A few big flakes of snow came down as we made our way back to the road and to our car and so to camp. It was getting very dark and a bit early for it. We assumed it was from depth of cloud cover.

"This wandering," she said as we neared camp, "reminded me of the rambling we did when we lost the stump ranch. Remember?"

"Yes, I do," I responded, "we were beaten down pretty badly along in there. I couldn't have carried on except for knowing you were backing me come hell or high water."

Suddenly she was in my arms. "Oh, Clyde," she said, "we've come a long way." She laughed a little laugh. "Still haven't gotten the fine furniture that I yearned for and moaned about as we crossed the Ross Island Bridge on our return to Oregon. Do you recall? Who cares? I've loved every bit of it as we came along." She'd been kissing me while she talked, quick ones all over my face, with hugs and burrowing into my clothing.

It was snowing again, scattered big flakes. I held her tightly a long moment and then we hurried to light the pitch kindling, and carefully stack the damp wood around it, so it would burn.

By the time our strip steaks were smoky and edible and we bit into the white mealiness of the charcoal-covered potatoes, the snow was scattering down amongst the trees and bushes. We dragged our reserve of dead branches closer and sat down to another cup of coffee staring into the flames as we smoked the Bull Durham cigarettes. Then we made love, almost placidly, our minds still entangled in the past we'd been examining together when the urge to join insinuated itself into our recollections. Contentment was ours.

We awoke in the morning to find that our little tent was pressed down almost on us by at least eight inches of new snow. The fire was long out and smelling of wet burnt wood. We dressed and pushed our duffle into our packs and on the way to the car I tripped on one of those fern clumps and fell heavily, bruising a knee.

Monday night I limped to the job. I was unable to join Ran in the pits. Instead I went to work on two pressure-reducing valves, a job that I had taken over for my own as each ship was moved forward alongside the dock, becoming more complete, until it arrived at the hot berth. There its boiler was fired and with steam up and the engine activated, the shaft slowly, ponderously turned the propellor.

By Thursday night I was back with Ran swinging my hammer with all my might. Ran seemed to prefer me as a teammate. We were always ahead of the other two teams that worked in the pits of the high-pressure and mid-pressure rods.

I had worked up a bit of foolishness that appealed to Ran's enthusiasm for the ridiculous. When the engine was stopped, so that we could remove shims from the bearings of the rods on the crankshaft, we jumped down into the pit that housed our particular bearing and throw, then we stood straight as if in salute and sang the chorus of a song I had made up called, "Dear Old Hammerduncks High." We let on to one and all that we were from Kalamazoo and had both gone to Hammerduncks High School. It was our shipyard version of the old school tie. As the other paired teams slugged at their wrenches working ahead of us, Ran and I would be lost in emotion about that dear school and then we tied into the job with such fierce expertise (I had taught Ran the slugging trick so that we always finished first), but try as I might I was never able to put the ardor into my expression and singing that Ran could. What a guy! Sometimes we did this regarded by only the oiler, the fireman and the chief, but usually there was a crowd of strangers. The military would be represented along with men of industry, but whoever viewed our fervor was impressed.

A few more months and Ginny would be out of business school, supposedly able then to face the world of offices. I must not think of it. The glimpses I had of her at home were tantalizing. I could see right through her most composed expressions, right through her clothing, no matter how layered, and see the real Ginny. She of the gazelle-like movements when we played alone in the moonlit meadow on our last rendezvous before chill winds brought an end to Indian summer. Ah, slim creature in my arms or dancing for me in the moonlight, where are your graces when among other people? Why is your self-consciousness then devoid of poetry and often awkward?

Nordi and I saw less of each other, working such odd hours. Still we managed to spend time together each day from four in the afternoon until eight in the evening. Working at night I had daylight time to keep up the place and had planted the field in alfalfa.

The arrangement with a neighbor farmer to cut it twice each summer, giving us half, some twenty tons, baled and in the barn was more than satisfactory with me.

Nordi was planning to have a big garden in the coming summer. We fussed with seed catalogs and each other and that too was good. I often dropped by at Acme to talk to Nordi and continued to speak to my tricky father and his trickier wife. Business was good. Pop had one salesman, who did well for him taking care of most of the Oregon territory and Boise and Spokane, but refused to call on Coos Bay or Olympia. In each of them I had been able to acquire several big vanilla accounts. This I had done while I was covering the towns for my thinner. Now Pop didn't want to lose them and was willing to pay double the commission and all expenses. I visited them every other month. It cost me a lost day a month at the shipyards, as I went down to them on a Sunday and came back Monday night. It did get me away a bit from the welding fumes that were beginning to play hob with my sinuses.

Nordi was steadfast. I knew how she would be in a given moment. Ginny was different. She was usually quite reserved, but her happy sense of humor didn't fit that picture nor her childish but right-on wisdom—a group of lisped profundities and shocking decisions she had made about life from her small field of reference. Lisping or not, she was right many more times than not. When I say that my darling lisped, I hope you understand that she really didn't. What I'm trying to convey is that, though her summations of the world, in spite of high school teachings, seemed abrupt, they were very well thought out. They spilled from a mouth still soft as petals and pink as a baby's, and I thought the "lisp" would do the job. I could say "her delicate lips molded at times to firm resolves," but I have to live with myself.

Old lady Nordstrom was drawing her brood about her. It was Sunday. Jack was off shoeing horses, but the rest of us, Teddy and I and our families and Jack's Olga and David, were all there, scattered through the house while the old lady worked vigorously on the great baking of enough apple dorper to stuff us all come evening.

Under the disapproving glances of Mother Nordstrom, Teddy and I were comparing bottles of the two beers we had brought with the home brew that Albert, daughter Anna's husband, had continued to make since prohibition days.

After a great quaff of beer followed by two more, Teddy wiped the foam from his upper lip and asked me what it was like working on the ships.

"Too big a question for me, Teddy," I answered. "But I can tell you a little bit about what it's like at the hot end."

"Sure, the hot end," agreed Teddy.

"Well, I like it there. One thing, it's about ninety degrees. You sweat, I tell you. There's always some work being done, besides the running-in of the engine. Small additions are made, a bracket here, some structures there, the last catch up of what goes into building a ship. The pipe fitters still have things to carry out, the painters, whole crews of them, are busy throughout the engine room and shaft alley, and always the running and stopping of the engine for adjustments and sometimes the replacement of parts.

"One morning we were rushing to deliver a ship on our shift and a part in the starting engine broke. Just as the horn blew for the graveyard shift to go off and the day shift to come on, six of us hurried down the dock to the next ship and robbed it of its starting engine, dragged it back and installed it much to the indignation of the day shift's multitude now all around us. A few hours later the *C. B. Dufur* was heading down the channel."

"Sounds like it was sort of a game that your shift was having with the job," Teddy said.

"It's the only kind of competition I can enjoy. Not competition with people, but doing the best job I can," I answered. "The relationship is between me and the job. It's always been that way for me ever since I learned in basketball and other games that I'm a poor team player."

"But you got to compete sometimes. It's the American way," muttered Teddy.

"Oh, Ran and I compete with the others, and we try to see who can take a bearing down, do what needs to be done and get it back in the shortest time. You're right! But it's the job I fight."

Here Teddy broke in, "When I was hewing ties up in Goldendale and back in Wisconsin, it was the same with me. I know exactly what you mean."

I continued: "There was a chief engineer on the ferries when I was a deckhand, who taught me how to get the best out of a maul by aiming past the striking point and in the last split second pulling in on my swing, curbing the curve of the swing to a smaller radius and gaining a harder blow. A simple thing knowing that trick, like knowing how to handle heaving lines and hawsers, axes and grubbing hoes, even wheelbarrows. It's where I get my satisfaction."

"Yeah, you and I are alike in that," agreed Teddy.

"They offered me a leadman's job recently, but I refused it," I went on. "It pays a little more and you don't have to work. You order others to do what's necessary. I once had a crew of thirty men under me when I was second mate on the ferries, but it doesn't fit me now, and it would destroy my usefulness at the hot end. They've got more than enough God-damned polished tin hat leadmen."

Jack had returned as we talked and Teddy and I tapped the bottle of whiskey he offered.

"What's this I hear about you turning down a leadman job?" he said settling himself in a chair opposite us. "I can't believe it.

You think you're too good to be a leadman, huh? That'd be like you."

"Yes, I do. I'm too good a worker to be trotting around telling guys to do what they're already doing. Too many tin whistles in that category. I don't want to join them."

"With your wife working," said Jack, "I figured you'd take it on for the money. Then you can work up to a foreman and make enough dough so that Eve could quit working and take care of the house like Olga and Tek."

"When I was making plenty with the thinner, she refused to stay home. Anyway, she gets home before school's out and has a snack ready for Bunky when he comes along. Sure, your women have an easier life," I said, "but Nordi's reasoning is that men have the best of living. Times have changed. If some women prefer to coast along at home, okay. She doesn't aim to loaf and she just pities women who do."

"Look here, Clyde. Mark my words in this!" replied Jack. "After the war these green new ways will disappear."

"The old ways are the best ways, huh, Jack? Rot! You should look around you. Enough of this. I'm going for a walk. I don't think the snow has slushed up too much."

"It was turning cold again when I came in," Jack said. "Why don't you stay in where it's comfortable. You'll be freezing on your night shift soon enough."

I put on a heavy coat and stocking cap and struck out across the bottoms. In fantasy I'm high above myself, looking down. I see myself as small and dark against the thin snow, a mere dot on the land, a thing of no significance. Is it my need to consider myself so? I don't know. It's mostly because I dislike the postures of power. I'm beginning to see power, whoever gets it, as one more minor disaster for mankind. *Ah, cut it out!* Stop fussing with half-thought-out ideas. Well, I'm only groping. Yeah, and you're talking to yourself again. Who else is there to talk to? Nordi's tired of my palaver.

On I trudged. It had gotten colder. The snow was crunchy under foot. It's dead of winter, I reflected, and the sources of the

Clackamas are frozen in. The river here has dwindled to its summer level, and I can walk its banks and see out in the overhanging branches the bedsprings that last summer carried such a freight of happiness and now appear so forlorn. And standing here in the snow I feel a warmth creeping in from some fartherest reaches of me, for late winter heralds spring.

Summer is coming, my heart tells me. Remember the fluttering and singing of the birds in the bushes, the warmth of the sun, the greening of the countryside, a chance for me, who has spent the winter with dear Nordi, to press once more lithe Virginia to me, so slight, seeming always able to cling or slip away. I'll not hold her lightly this summer. No! I must not lose her. But what of Nordi—good God! Though I should, I cannot think of Nordi now.

For a sensitive guy polygamy has its hells, and one is that a lady can obscure another momentarily with her presence, even while absent. Sometimes I miss monogamy with its simplicity. No! No! I take back the thought. Dear luck! Protect me from the loss of one of my darlings.

I walked on displeased by my frittering stance. "Come on, you ass," I mumbled, "come out of it." Watch the flow of the river, feel the good earth under this thin cast of snow. Accept what you sought as priceless. It rather sought me, I thought reflectively. In sudden fury at myself I yelled my rage out across the river. It came back from the cliffs on the other side as meaningless shouts bereft of anger. I don't know why but I was dumb before it. Then defensive words came with a certainty I seldom possess: DUALITY IS ONE OF GOD'S WAYS. Simplicity is a tool that we use to avoid understanding the complexity of everything about us, to keep down the clutter that increasing awareness brings.

Irritated by my dipping into the metaphysical morass but partially shrived of self-hate, though despairing of ever finding a way out of my dilemma, I headed back past the just completed Broms house overlooking the meadow and our own darkened house to Forsythe's and its lights shining from in amongst the trees.

I was wondering once again about the war and noticing a light in the barn. I hoped that Delite had given birth to the long-awaited calf, but decided it was Bunky and Dave milking our cows.

One day, Nordi and I were considering our taxes and insurance. It was Saturday and Bunky was off with Dave for the day. Looking our situation over we could almost be content. True, the war was a terrible thing, but today the knowledge of it struck us only a glancing blow for our big worry was Bunky. The first year we came to Carver he jumped two classes. He had a wonderful teacher, but his leap moved him out of her domain. He was not doing well in school. We attributed his changed attitude and drop in grades to the loss of his favorite teacher and to his epilepsy.

We took him to a doctor, and I described his attacks—always at night while he slept, lasting about two minutes. He was unconscious and trembled, making light groaning sounds. Then he had a chill and was dull, not aware of his mother or me. He awakened in the morning wondering why there were extra blankets over him and the hotwater bags at his feet and back, and he had a hard time believing that he had had a spell. They came at about two-month intervals, sometimes two in one month. The doctor confirmed the diagnosis as a mild form of epilepsy and cautioned us to watch him closely and to keep him away from machines.

I thought it over. For years I had wanted to write, to tell of the beauty and significance I saw about me, about the people I'd known, of Bob Drake and Pushells and Crescentia Majoris and Madeline, and I wanted to make poems about friends, distillations of well-lived lives. The time of my life to do this was now, before I was into my fifties. But now I saw, from what the doctor said, that I should work out a good life for Bunky first. He was my son. He had helped me when we lived that first winter in the old hovel. Every other day he had labored with a saw much too big for him so that we would have fuel for the fire in our boar's nest. He milked the cow and took care of it. He'd been a continual help around the place. There must be no poems, no writing, until Bunky's future was a good one and Nordi's perfume was no longer vanilla, but from flowers in her garden. These were the dreams that I told Nordi as we sat by the fire in the evening.

Sometimes when I was up in Seattle after special material or on one of my trips down to Coos Bay and I turned finally and started back, it was always a heady moment. The hunger for home would be in me, and I'd remember those I would see when I got there, imagining Nordi and how she would look, the way she walked, her sweetness and her capabilities at Acme, at home and as a lover. I'd speed down the long highway.

Then with that eagerness full upon me I would suddenly feel I was being unfair to Virginia: Virginia who meets me at odd places, Virginia's smile and awkward leggy grace would be waiting for me there. I'd be in a turmoil to be fair to my two lovelies. I'd wonder endlessly what I could do about it. There was no way out, and when I was finally with either one, desire would make it all right.

It must be inherent in some men to have more than one mate. Life urges most of us to seek out one more woman. There are men who are not affected by this urge. Which is the norm? Which way does God want us to be? And the only thing that I can see is that God wants both conditions, always both and infinite variations, a God not bound with our race's varying logics. There may be innumerable answers to any situation. When we draw aside the concealing garments of a girl or woman, I think we're urged on by the same power that produced the explosion of the universe and the condition of pattern. Enough! Enough of excuses or eternal reasons!

So I'd drive on, passing slower traffic, intent on getting home to see the sweet faces of my ladies.

V

In Which
I Tell Nordi about Virginia,
Split My Personality and the Shipyards,
Go to Alaska,
and
Am Called Back by Urgent News

1943

IT WAS ONE OF THOSE almost unbelievable nights in the shipyards. It had been snowing heavily, and the mantle of snow and the earliness of two A.M. seemed to quiet somehow the frenzy of the gigantic constructive effort that was being expended there.

The ship at the hot end glowed in men's minds as they stood in the slush and snow and looked through a whirling storm of snowflakes to where, far up the dock, the gangway of the end ship invited them to come aboard and down into the hotness and light and opened warmth reflecting from the upturned faces of people as you came down the ladder into the engine room. You became one of many visiting strangers who stood on the flat before the engine and with open coats absorbed the heat of the place and watched the slow spin of the engine.

There was usually a military man or two among them, a resplendent general perhaps, power-drunk and testy toward a svelte superbly suited man of business, equally testy and both glaring as they rubbed shoulders with my foreman and straw bosses of every kind, who had slipped away from their crews out on the ways to seek this glowing place. Hypnotically involved with the engine and its rhythmic beat, they seemed unaware of the gangs and crews of half a dozen crafts who labored there.

Between the crowd of strangers and the engine was a manhole and out of it now spewed the sweepers—the lowest craft in the yard, old aproned grandmothers, farm wives, their hair contained in kerchiefs dirty with rust and dirt. There were men too in the group—simpletons and twisted people, mentally or physically, and incipient Einsteins, intellectuals, unequipped to handle tools, who had learned to master the broom. They scattered in amongst the crowd viewing the engine, making it a motley crew indeed.

They had been down in the double bottoms—an extended tank for fuel oil under the engine room floor, a space four feet in height and maybe thirty by thirty in extent. It was baffled into a complex labyrinth to strengthen the ship and baffle the movement of the fuel oil so it would not have the power to smash about when the ship rode stormy seas. They had been down there scraping, cleaning up rust with steel brushes and with the usual tools of a sweeper. They had scoured it so that it was ready to be painted, a mad place—a claustrophobic nightmare—but here they came, those courageous old ladies and simpletons, out of the maw of the catacomb, dragging their extension cords with them, and finally they drifted up the ladder and were gone out into the storm.

Next down the ladders from above came the painters, two score of them with their buckets of paint and their extension cords, disappearing down the manhole to paint every surface of every cell in that steely maze. And all the while the engine above them was being run, stopped and started as our crew under the chief's direction worked on the bearings that were slowly seating themselves to an adjustment where the engine's great shaft could spin the propellor and force the ship over oceans and seas endlessly.

The chippers still worked there in an agony of racket, cutting away the temporary brackets of construction, and on the other side of the engine a welder and a shipfitter made showers of sparks and confusion while they welded yet another bracket for a fire extinguisher, and the pipe fitters were involved with something back of the boilers.

In all this, I, Clyde Rice, worked with my hammer or stood momentarily aside and gloried in the colors, the activities and meaning of the scene, and was definitely a part of it—I, an oddball? Who knew or cared? I was a member in good standing, one of the main actors on this stage with my sledge and my partnership with the other machinists. I'd been swept by the wide hand of war out of the pain of my uniqueness into a broader grouping that I exulted in—a shipyard worker.

As the long winter continued I found ways to meet Virginia for lunch in some obscure restaurant and then would take her to one of those places on seldom used roads, where impropriety reigns and marriages are born. One freezing day we were at such a place. We had been able to shift her heavy coat and other clothing so that I could caress her eager young body. She was silent but trembling and I was in heaven to be holding her, when I became aware of an enormous middle-aged face peering in the car window. Rage possessed me. I must have blood for this! As he drew back I flung the door open and spun on him. My feet slipped out from under me for we were standing on a large iced-over puddle. I lit on the back of my head with terrific impact and saw millions of stars. With my brain slowly clearing I realized I was lying on my back with him standing spread-legged over me. All the fight had been driven out of me. I looked up where far above me, it seemed, was his stupid face. He was muttering, "I got just as much right as you to this place."

I wiggled my head around and looked for his car. Mine was the only one. "Do you come to this place often?" I asked. It seemed we had need to share stupid inanities.

"As often as I want," he said. "I got as much right—"

"I know," I said, "and I agree. Will you help me up? Something's wrong with my back."

"Why shore," he answered and tenderly put me on my feet. "Any time," he said seriously and walked away.

I was able to hobble into the car. I wanted to laugh, but my head hurt so much I couldn't take the chance. My neck was so sore I couldn't even turn to kiss Ginny.

"That man was a giant," she said. "I'm glad you didn't try to fight with him."

"So am I," I answered still unable to take a chance on laughter. I broached the subject of going to motels, but to her that seemed more vulgar than parking out and she refused to ever consider it.

In February Virginia finished her courses at business school and began looking for work. It must have been hell for shy Ginny. No one wanted an inarticulate girl without experience. In my mind I was hovering about her trying to go with her through the tribulations of a greenie looking for her first job. I remembered the torture and the endless dismays that had been my lot back there when I was a greenie too. *At least she doesn't have to wear a bag over her head* boiled up in me, but I pushed it aside with distaste.

Then one day my worries were dispelled. Teddy informed me when we met at our mailboxes that Ginny had a job working in the office of the firm for which he had worked for years. True, he had to wangle things slightly. She, he added, was staying this week in town with her cousin, who would help her shop for suitable clothing, for he said, "She's a big girl now."

I thought of my shy lovely who on occasion could be strangely frank about intimate things and held my face in neutral.

"That's great," I stumbled out and then, once more master of myself, changed the subject by asking him how his cow's injured hoof was coming along.

After dark I went out into the center of the field and looked up (heaven you know). The runes were still available for me, the non-believer. God—I didn't say it out loud—but my mind did, and still looking up, I called out "Thanks! Thanks, God!" I found on going back to the house that I'd put so much into the thanks that I was used up. Nordi didn't notice this, but at dinner she remarked about another sudden change in me.

"You've seemed haunted, or something, for weeks. Now I see it is gone." She smiled delightedly and said archly, "I truly believe you were worried about your surrogate daughter's trouble in finding a job. Could it have brought memories of your own troubles as a kid?"

·

Work continued to be a ready distraction from my mounting troubles at home. We, the machinists, had a lunchroom built out over the water, at the hot end of the dock. It was usually pretty boisterous when we were eating. There were about seven of us who worked on the last three ships on the dock. Our crew was from all over the nation. A couple of toughs from Chicago had obviously been mobsters. In fact, quite a few were from the Midwest, but the ones who always ate together were the ones from the South, and their talk was always bravado incidents with blacks—"Negras," they said. On the whole they were good guys, but poisoned by the bigotry in their background.

The talk went like this: "And then I shot at this Negra's feet, a big one he was, but was he skeered of that gun! I itched to shoot him, and he knew it, but I just let up on him so he could last for another day. They're big, those Negras are, but are they afeered of a gun! Jest aim into their guts and they cringe."

The one-sided picture they produced disturbed me. What chance had the blacks? One day I started boasting about my hatred of midgets in much the manner that they spoke of the blacks. "And especially," I pointed out, "I hated weak midgets, ones that can't fight back."

There was not much of a point to it, but it syphoned through their heads eventually that I was talking about the lack of bravery needed to pick on oppressed people. Nothing was said.

One night I was standing at lunchtime among our shift workers when, from behind me, came a fellow, who put a hammerlock on me that pretty nearly broke my neck and then jumped away from me, smiling in the most friendly fashion. He was supposed to be quite a tough guy, a wrestler, they said. He'd killed a man, so went the tale.

There was a long table that went through the lunchroom, and two nights later he did it again, throwing me upon the table, but I had a hold of him now and whirled us across the table and smashed into some lockers on the other side, with his head under me and against a locker. He wasn't hurt badly, but he didn't come out unscathed, and I helped him up with the same amiable laughter he'd used on me.

I don't know what the rest of the crew thought about it. I wondered what would come next. I didn't have a chance using any wrestling holds on a wrestler. How could I let him know that I meant business, and I decided, no matter how awkward, I'd have to fend him off in an unorthodox fashion when he came at me again.

Well, he did three nights later. I was working on a minor job on the port side of the engine, where there's a flat like the starboard side but most of it is taken up by the condenser and fuel pump and the big squat low pressure cylinder exhaust pump, when he tackled me intent, it seemed, to break my neck. It was a quiet night. The crew were fixing something on deck. There was just the chief, the fireman and the oiler, I thought.

He came at me from behind as usual, had that death grip on me almost before I could move, but I did move. I tripped him, even as he applied the pressure and down we went, me on top. What to do? And it would have to be strange. I soon had his arm pinned out wide and I ran my sharp-heeled rigger shoes down his shins, the high arch of the shoes imprisoning them. Then with all my might I spread his legs. Those cruel bruising shoes did the work for me. I had him spread-eagled and butted his chin a couple of times, then I slipped down and, holding him spread, I butted him right under the heart, my injured neck agonizingly painful, but it had to be an unorthodox battle. I did it about seven times. He begged me to stop, but I drove the wind out of him and when he was inert, I got off of him. I pulled him around, pushed his head between the bottom of the squat pump and the deck. There I left him and went about my work. I saw him around later. We didn't speak.

A few nights later while I was working alone below the fiddly, a heavy wrench came crashing down from the top. It hit my tin hat a glancing blow. It didn't even jar me—one of those strange deflections that send force on its way. That was the nearest thing I had to a fight in the shipyards. I remembered my assailant for years afterward though, because of the continued pain in my twisted neck.

Nordi and I found, to our dismay, that Bunky had been skipping high school. He would take the school bus to school, they said, but once there he'd leave for the river and work on tugs without pay and be back at school for the bus so he could take it home. How he got away with it unnoticed was never clear to me. We confronted him with this one evening.

"Pop," he said, "I can read and write. My arithmetic is fine, geography okay, history okay, but algebra is Greek to me and always will be. Look, I've found my limits, so now I'm a man, I guess. I'll make out fine. Don't worry. I'm going to be a fisherman. Someday have my own boat. It's all I want. No desk job for me."

We talked to the school's counselor. "He's a difficult one for sure," the counselor said. "It's his slowness of thought, not the lack of it. In some ways he's deep. You see, he sees the frustration of teachers trying to move the class through the materials in the time allotted. They get impatient with him and he feels it. It's happened so much in the years he's been in school, that now he's given up. I can't say I blame him. By the way, I like him. He comes across as genuine in the talks I've had with him."

We talked it over as we drove home. Nordi remarked about his ability with clay, of the tiny dramas he produced: scenes of Indians hidden behind rocks and bushes about to attack a settler and his prairie schooner with its oxen laboring up a rise off of the plain. "But an artist's life is a meager one and Bunky's not voluble."

"Windy, you mean," I put in, seeing what she saw. "A guy belaboring the air all around him with words, trying to explain what his work of art means. He would never be able to chatter endlessly about the fringe of things or else the very center. These are the fields for geniuses."

"Yes," Nordi said, "to prepare him for such a life would be a mistake we must not make. Let him fish, have a constant grip on reality."

"Fishing is dangerous," I put in.

"But not to the soul," Nordi said. "Let him find honest frustrations, not the nebulous ones of the world of art."

Next evening after supper he looked like he was cornered—some sixth sense I suppose. "We visited your counselor yesterday, Bunky," Nordi led off.

"Yeah," said Bunky and looked the new scene over but coolly. "He's a mouthy bird," he added to his yeah, and added to that, "but I think he knows his stuff. I leveled with him, how I fit in with things. Did he level with you, Mom, or try to get technical?"

"He's a very understanding man," Nordi replied.

"He gave us the picture," I said, "so we could understand it. We'd like to hear anything you'd care to add to it."

"I guess not," Bunky answered. Then he said sadly, "I know I let you down—no words for it. I'm sorry. Seems I'm always sorry about something. Look, even if I'd made it, I'd leave it, Pop."

"You mean the desk?" I asked.

"Yes, the desk. There I was trying to educate myself for something that would be a jail. Now I'm going to tackle something more to my liking."

"You mean fishing?" I asked.

"You did it once. Outside of getting TB, how was it?"

"Best time I ever had in my life," I answered. Clearly, it was my move.

When Saturday came we started early and were down looking at the fishing fleet by ten. Astoria looked prosperous. As we wandered the floats seeing how the boats were rigged, Bunky was in his glory. Some were old boats, some spanking new, but all were curved to fit the sea. Bunky fell in love with one, a forty-two-footer, with flared bow—not too much, but enough to keep the deck clear of slosh going to windward in a small chop. The owner saw how we admired his boat and asked us aboard for a cup of coffee and served it with some of his wife's delectable sweet bread.

Bunky acted rather reserved, I thought, but when, on the way home, he began talking, we found that he absorbed everything about the boat, even to the size of the ribs, the thickness of the planking and how it was caulked. He had figured as far as he could into the rigging and gear. One way or another, it seemed, boats were going to be a part of his future.

At work, the usual chief engineer's place had been taken for a week or more by a man new to us. He had a bad burn on the side of his face and neck and the steadiest grey eyes I've ever seen. He was about my size, just a bit heavier.

"I'm just temporary," he said. "Kelly had to go down to L.A. to see his daughter get her medal for bravery under fire. She's on an ambulance."

Our foreman told us this guy had a Liberty like this one torpedoed from under him. "Two of the fish hit her back from the bow and opened her up. It's the third time for him."

"Yeah, what's he doing here?" asked Lippy, one of the helpers.

"Why he's resting up. Gonna take a Liberty out of here after this shore leave he's giving himself."

I soon took a liking to the new chief. He was solid—maybe a little bit on the too-serious side, but he put a lot into readying the engine, more careful than Kelly, it seemed to me. He'd finger and flip for sound each shim we took out of a journal, not meaning to be insulting, but just being certain.

One night when the crew were up topside working and I was on standby, he came over, definitely friendly, to stand with me as we watched the engine roll. Finally, he said:

"I'll bet, between us, we could clean up the worksheets for the three shifts."

"I'd like to have at it," I answered.

"Yeah," he went on, "I've noticed how you like to tear into things, like you know there is a war on."

"Say, I've quit this place three times, because I couldn't find enough work to keep me busy."

"This bunch you're in are workers and proud of it," said the chief. "I was on the day shift and swing too, for a short while, then they gave me the chief's job on this shift, so now I've quit writing letters to the management." He looked at the clock and then at me with that steady grey regard. "Think I'll stop the engine and we'll check things out. No need to call the crew. She's very near up to snuff as is."

After a bit, finding all perfect, we were back looking at the engine again as she rolled. The fireman was there and the oiler was quietly doing his stuff.

"Ah, come on, Rice, let's do it," the chief said, "I don't see why we have to call your leadman. Let's just start doing the list," and we went at the six or seven jobs that were to be done, not bothering to stop for lunch even. As we marched down the gangway in the morning, passing the last of the day shift coming on, we were plenty pleased with ourselves.

Next evening we heard about it. Our superintendent and foreman were in trouble—with the union and the brass. The massive crews of the day and swing shifts had nothing to do. Somehow with what we had done they could have fiddled around, stretching out the work and gotten by. Really they could have done everything over again and perhaps did, but we'd over-stepped protocol and both of us were dressed down, me, by my leadman, my foreman and superintendent. I suppose the powers-that-be had chewed at them too.

How can a serious, middle-aged fellow, who'd long wielded the scepter of authority, smile roguishly? Still, when I came down the ladder after my dressings-down, his face showed the pleasure he felt at having shaken up one simple pattern of waste, if only one time.

A week later I was on standby again and the chief and I stood talking together once more in front of the running engine.

"Well, Rice," he said, "I'm going out as chief on this one. Guess you know from the talk around about me being chief on three ships that were sunk by Hitler. Jesus! If we could only get a shot at a sub. There we sit slowly sinking and the U-boat has come to the surface waiting for the lifeboats to get away so they can blow the ship to hell, and we don't fire back. We could, but we don't. There ought to be a way that we could carry a small plane with a torpedo of our own in its undercarriage that would leave the ship the moment it's hit with the bomb and hunt out the submarine and sink it. That'd even things up a bit.

"The *Samuel Decker* will be carrying a load of wheat from Portland here down the coast, wide open to Jap subs, then through the canal so the German bastards can have at us all across the Atlantic. If there were only some way we could bomb them after they bomb us, but there doesn't seem to be any way to do that. Turn out more ships, I think. Got enough people in these yards to make twice as many. They say the problem is materials. Huh! I wouldn't know. Still, the way they're working here you'd think there wasn't a war on, but I know there is, and I'm going to do whatever I can.

"Why don't you join up? You could try for a gunner on a Liberty and maybe get a shot into a sub before the skipper hauls down the flag. Why don't you get out there and do something about it?"

Three days later he sailed as the chief engineer of the *Samuel Decker*. I thought of him, how he always looked at everything dead center. A week later the news came: A Jap caught the *Decker* off Cape Blanco with a torpedo into the engine room. Twenty five survivors reached Port Orford three days later through heavy seas. My friend with the steady grey eyes was not one of them.

After the news of his death, his importance in things began to grow in me. His half-considered remarks unsupported by facts bowled me over, and in my daydreams I saw myself in the gun tub high above the bridge, the skipper hurrying from the bridge to lower our flag (in this instance, the stars and stripes) and our lifeboats, well away from our sinking vessel. The sub surfaces and before it delivers the *coup de grâce*, I from my hiding place rise up carefully and blast the whole superstructure off the submarine. She sinks followed by a great belch of oil and debris on the surface. Ah, yes, the scene came to me many times. The chief was right. It should be done. I talked about it to Ran. He pointed out the impossibility of such a chance of getting even. "In this mixed up world," he said, "we're at the bottom and they don't like us poking our heads up in their business."

The more I thought about it, the more twisted was my view. That such a steadiness of eyes should be gone from the world! One day I told Ran that I was going to enlist Saturday. On that day I did drive out to my draft board in Estacada.

I opened the door and stepped into the presence of four or five old guys smoking the short end of cheap cigars. It stunk in there of the burning of the long ends of the butts they now mouthed. There was a sardonic twist to their expressions. They were officials of a sort and lolled in it. They wordlessly considered me. Finally one of them moved the stub of his cigar to the side of his mouth and said: "Name?"

"Rice," I answered instantly, making the word completely abstract. It was not even related to the grain. That was quite military, I thought.

"Given name?" said the man, who had moved that malodorous cigar butt to his other cheek, while I ruminated about my military bearing.

"Clyde," I answered, "Clyde Harvey Rice," but somehow I couldn't say it abstractly. Instead I grinned at them like a mere human and added, "I'm from Carver."

"So you're Clyde Rice of Carver, graveyard machinist, huh? Now you're gonna be a hero too, that it?"

"Well, no."

"Speak up! Tell us what you want to do in this war."

"A gunner on a freighter, preferably on a Liberty."

At that they all snarled a laugh around their cigar butts. One choked on his. They forgot me for a moment, watching him strangle until he coughed up the rope end of his cigar butt and tried to light it.

"Look here, we got too many of you older guys figuring Uncle needs you in foreign parts. The way we hear it, there's too damn many loafers in the shipyards. Yet they're turning out a hell of a lot of ships, so to make up for the bums there must be some guys in there really stirring their stumps. From what we hear you're one of them. You gotta always be doing something. Yeah, we got ways of knowing. Now you get your ass back over to that shipyard and stay there."

Somehow that draft board turndown pasted me into the job in a way I had to accept. We were old hands now who knew our work front and back. We swaggered a bit. Professionals? Why sure! But the work in the yard seemed repetitious lately, and stale.

Spring came one day. Man! Grand! Then it hailed and blew for a couple of days and hailed again. I was scarcely aware of the shipyards because spring came again and again and breezes were not so cold. The plum trees blossomed. One morning I came out to breathe the freshness of the season. The cottonwood buds were bursting and the waxy honey on the sheath of the bud swept through the air with an overpowering fragrance. No wonder the natives call the tree the balm. Nordi came out beside me and inhaled the sweet air and kissed me a kiss as sweet, then drew me in for waffles and eggs in her new sauce.

As we ate, we spoke of Virginia. She'd lost two jobs since she left business school. Her extreme timidity resulted in a lack of communication, otherwise she was quite competent, at least both the small firms who had turned her back to the hiring agency had so maintained.

"Now she's working for Madame Zinger, an aggressive person, Olga says. Olga knows of her through her music teacher. Ginny is being intimidated, not only by the Zinger woman, but by her coterie of actors, singers, vaudevillians—people with tremendous egos who parade about in Zinger's large studio. She teaches speech and drama and has quite a following. Poor Ginny flits about among these supercilious people as receptionist, aide (ha ha) and secretary."

Nordi left for Acme and I dawdled before sleeping my main sleep of the day—loitering and thinking of Ginny, who, for various reasons, I had not talked to or even seen for a week or more. I was going over fond, though somewhat shop-worn, memories: how she walked and ran. I saw her in my mind's eye trimming rosebushes. She was wearing heavy gloves to protect her hands from the thorns. Yes, I'd seen this several years ago at their home in town. I remembered how she loved the perfume of roses. Yeah, and she was thrilled by the scent of cottonwood buds when they burst. I could—yeah, I would!

Down by the river, from among many there, I chose a four foot high balm tree, one not yet bursting its buds and unusually limby. I also brought another small balm along for spare parts.

At the house I made a neat stand as one does for Christmas trees, drilling holes in the small trunk here and there. Forcing the tiny limbs of the spare tree into them, I soon had a well-shaped Christmas tree of balm with buds ready to burst as soon as it was taken into a warm room. I placed it outside Madame Zinger's studio door later in the day and said nothing to anyone. That was Tuesday.

Thursday I took Ginny to lunch brazenly, not to some hidden scruffy place, but to the Bohemian where I took Nordi on occasion. While we waited to be served, Ginny turned her full radiance on me, a smile so impish and so happy. "They thought she had a shy admirer," Ginny said. "They all loved the tree. You should have seen Zinger. She just simply bloomed. I moved among them so mousy, but I was bursting to tell them: 'It's from my secret lover, my Clyde.' Of course, I didn't, I couldn't. Clyde, the buds opened up this morning and made the whole studio smell, well, sort of—sensuous? Did I use the word right—teacher?"

Oh, God, if only one could keep such moments fresh forever.

And in much this manner my life ran full as the days and weeks and the months crowded by, but in November I was demoted, not fired but sent back to the ship being readied for the hot end. It made me sick inside, trashed. The leadman had said, "Rice, take your tools and go down on the next ship and do what you can to get her ready for her engine's first turnover. I'll give you Dodd and Gunson to help you."

With my toolbox on my shoulder I boarded the *Phoebe N. Tucker*. Down in the cold dark engine room I went and looked about me. Nothing was painted. Steel or rusty steel—that was the scene. It was all right, but after the hot end, it was demoralizing—an unrelenting gloom that several small lights dimly illuminated. Well, work would help. I started doing all the things I'd long felt should be done at this berth. We arranged a few more lights to see what we were doing. Everything was open for improvement here. The harrowing sound of the chippers rang through the ship. It could not distract me further.

Why—why? Why? I'd worked harder at my job than Ran or anyone on the crew. I'd turned down a leadman job to work there.

On I went with this job, tightening bolts, testing the packing on the big valves, giving the great gland, fitted around the propellor shaft where it goes through the after bulkhead of the engine room, a final tightening of bolts. I looked for small sabotage, where cranks asserted their meanness—ground glass in the oil holes, loose bolts stood on end in the low pressure pump which had ruined three pumps that I knew of. Now I inspected it with a small mirror. Some German's act of lingering loyalty to "der old country."

We were busy. I rushed at the job, trying to keep my mind too busy to seek out where I had failed at the hot end. Those who worked there had been special in my mind, though I was irritated at the union concept that separated us. Every craft down there I saw as only the group, the one group, bringing the ship as near to perfection as we could before it sailed away. Unionism, I felt, interfered with the camaraderie I had felt so strongly.

Wondering, working on the cold ship with the loss of status rankling me, I reasoned with myself that I was doing much more, getting the ship ready to be delivered, than I possibly could at the hot end. There was so much that demanded attention here. There were no waiting periods when the engine was run and you stood by waiting for a change to materialize that would require your efforts, and yet I did find time to play hooky from the job.

There in the shaft alley I would join temporarily a team of pin drivers where my ability with a fifteen-pound copper hammer on the long handle was appreciated. The shaft, from engine room down the shaft alley and out through the packing and lignum vitae bearing to the propellor, was the field of the pin drivers, for the shaft was made up in several sections and their great flanges at each joining were held together by five pins as thick as a woman's forearm driven through the machined hole in both flanges and taken up with an over-large nut. The pins had to be so tight that, in driving them in, a minute shaving would be taken off them as the pin was sledged into place. This was done by the pin drivers, hammering them through the flanges with their copper hammers. You put everything you had in each blow. There I poured out all my frustrations, my fury, everything I had into driving the pin. There were four in the crew and I made five, when I could sneak away and be with them.

I quit driving pins when Nordi noticed that the last joints of my toes were turning blue and getting bluer each night. This, from the primeval gripping I did within my shoes on the shaft alley catwalk, as I poured all into the blow that was my ecstasy. I never let my fun interfere, though, with the chores I allotted to myself and my two helpers.

Nordi's father had been sixty when she was born, eighty when I married her. In many ways he was a remarkable man. He had built a big shop on the back of their lot around and over the garage. In the years since he died Mother Nordstrom had not changed a thing there. He'd been in his grave for years and yet, if you were in one room of his shop, you felt his presence in the next one. An essence of him still permeated the place. Perhaps it was the meticulous placement of things on the shelves and in cabinets—his bag of fids, the strange tools he made for certain things he did—and the flowers that surrounded each of the several buildings that included the yungrubarn, the maiden's house. Mr. Nordstrom had built it beautifully, kept it carefully painted and, from time to time, repapered its inside walls.

Teddy, when he built his house, also made a yungrubarn, maiden's house, nearby. It was not quite as finely constructed as the one produced by Mr. Nordstrom, his father-in-law (that had looked like a large toy), but it was something he could point to with pride when visitors came. Though he built a bedroom for the girls in the house, once ensconced in the maiden's house, they never left it, until Dory in the war years decided to become a nurse and left to start training. So Virginia slept alone in the yungrubarn.

I came when no one was about and waxed the hinges of the door. No telltale oil for me. I'm not meticulous about much, but I pride myself on the consideration I can give to small details.

I didn't appear at my job in the shipyard one night. Instead I opened the door of the yungrubarn, pleased with its lack of comment on the appropriateness of my entering this small edifice to virginity. To my dying day, and I mean it as a fact, I'll remember and celebrate the welcome I received in Ginny's room. That night her joy in me and love of me were expressed with arms around my neck and her mouths eagerly tasting of the delights that only love can bring. She gave me, unknowing, that one rare hour that we men search for all our lives.

Before I left she turned on the light and looked me in the eyes in a way she hadn't before. "Dear," she said, "twice lately you've told me that someday you were going to marry me. Do you mean it when you say that?"

It startled me. I felt it as a pivotal moment, even though I still only half understood what she was telling me and I couldn't remember ever saying that to her, but I knew I must have. Ginny is incapable of lying.

"Yes, I do," I replied. All I knew was that I meant it.

A few days later, on my day off, I was fishing for trout down along the Molalla River. I passed the cabin of an eccentric old man whom I had encountered four years earlier when I was looking for trees to use for cord wood. At that time he had demonstrated his eyesight by blasting a blue jay off a limb at a hundred feet with a 30-30. Now I got the same 30-30 jammed into my stomach, with the wild old man behind it.

"I knowed it was you all along, you dirty bastard," he said, "you set those frogs agin me. I been living here for years, and all we had was normal frogs that didn't drive you crazy. Then you sneaked in here and put these big grunting bastards all around. I know'd you did it. My neighbors said you did when I blamed them for it. Now you get them big bullfrogs out of here right away or I'm gonna blast ya. I oughta blast you anyway for such a stinkin' trick."

All the time the gun, pressed against my belly, was at full cock and half-cocked, as he thumbed the hammer. Talking him out of it was a hard thing to do, because every time one of those big frogs croaked, he eased back on the hammer. Finally I made him realize that the last time I had been there and seen him was over four years ago and that we'd always been friends. He got over his rage.

He said, "I'll find out who done 'er and when I do, they better be making tracks." Then he wanted to know about the war and I told him a bit about the shipyards and left, deciding not to fish in his vicinity for, in fury, he might change his mind and shoot me.

"Cabin crazy," I told Nordi, as we were getting ready for bed. "He's too much of a loner. He's got about, oh, say fourteen head of scroungy cattle that he moves around the county. He knows where all the abandoned farms are. He runs his stock in at night and they graze the land, sometimes a week, sometimes a couple of months before the people on farms nearby realize that he's not there on a legitimate grazing contract and bring in the sheriff."

Nordi laughed. "Sounds like quite a rascal," she remarked, "though I thank him in my heart for not shooting you."

That much of our conversation I recall. I remember she was getting into bed when I confessed, inadvertently, of my relationship with Ginny. I wish I could forget her face as she absorbed what I said. She asked a strange thing: "How long?" she whispered, no breath behind it.

I blundered on, "About two years," I said and wished that I were dead.

She screamed then, as if some of her flesh was torn from her to shred through her anguish. She pushed her face into the pillow and in between the pillows, as if searching blindly for the peace and certainty that had been raped from her happy world by the very one who gave it meaning.

"Oh, Clyde, how could you? How could you?" She raised her sorrowing face and regarded me with streaming eyes. "Don't you love me anymore?"

"I'll love you just as always until I die. Oh, Nordi, for years I saw it coming and I tried to avoid it. If only you had been willing to go back to Tiburon with me while there was still time. If only I were interested in money. Perhaps that would have helped. If I—if only . . ." —etc.

She listened to my shabby excuses but lay silent, her dear face averted from me. I still stood in the crouch her guttural shriek had frozen me into. After a long empty time—so long I had come to accept it as my new reality—she turned her head and with a weary gaze, said, "Come to bed, Clyde. It's a chill night for both of us." That reflection started her to weep, but she bit her lip and lay as if in her coffin on her side of the bed.

We both lay in this manner, awake and still. Hours went by. Toward dawn I felt her turn her head toward me. We moved with one impulse and wrapped ourselves together in a knot, our arms and legs pulling the knot tighter, as if to bind us together from attack, as if we feared the world, as if I were not the culprit and the interloper was poor Ginny. Oh, God! How we clung, strapped as one by our twining arms.

"Whatever happens, Nordi," I murmured into the hair at the nape of her neck, "we are one. If one of us dies, the other will carry on our love in spite of it." We gripped even tighter, then slowly relaxing as Nordi quietly wept, we gently slept.

At breakfast several mornings later, the sun brightened things. We palely responded to it. She ventured a smile.

"Ginny had no chance against you," Nordi said. "In fact, as I see it now, neither had you. Tell her I forgive her, even accept, after a fashion. Really it's comical how the family acted, me particularly, for I know how inflammable are we who search for beauty. And a girl of eighteen—well, Mother Nature has plans for her unless she is swamped or strangled in cult-thinking, and

Ginny's church has not been able to snare her yet, just as it couldn't trap me. Me! This makes that time seem so long ago. I'm frightened, Clyde. Hold me a moment before I run to catch the bus."

The following week I told Ginny. It was not Memorial Day, but the clan had gone with piety, remembrances, and tools to curry around Mr. Nordstrom's grave trying hard to forget what an outspoken atheist he had been. Ginny stayed home, unable to carry on more than one hypocrisy at a time. We are built to carry out the one that Ginny and I supported, but when I divulged the fact that Nordi knew of us, she grew ashen and began trembling. I held her tight. We were out by the river, unaware of the beauty of our surroundings, still colored by the last of the fall leaves, our minds racing scatteringly over possibilities. Fear was there and, for her, dim hope. She still trembled.

"Why?" I foolishly asked her.

"I hate lying," she answered, "but I love you so much. Oh, Clyde, I've hurt Nordi badly! Of my few friends, I've cared for her the most."

"You didn't hurt her, Ginny. I did. You accepted a long courting as girls are constructed to do."

I told myself my problem was simple in the abstract, complicated somewhat by custom, extremely complicated by how the clan had drawn around me where the Clackamas talks of love, of freedom, of sweeping around whatever stands in its way. It poured, trickled, or hurled past, then melded its scattering into tranquil pools. It hadn't memory as I had of just why and how I had distraughtly come to this point in the lives of Nordi and Ginny and Bunky. I'm no river using gravity a thousand beautiful ways on its glide to the sea. Any way I move now I'll hurt one of these three I love. If I were just a bit less loving, perhaps I could find the answer to this dilemma.

So I ruminated as I drove to work down darkened roads until, converging with others, we reached the blaze of the lighted shipyards where work gave me surcease from this—my impasse.

Heading homeward in the morning with the new day

warming the world, I could think selfishly and remember and find it hard to believe that one man could receive so much joy from his loved ones and not be struck down (this probably from some earlier reading of the Bible).

At home Nordi made me my breakfast before she left for work, joined me in a cup of coffee, staring quizzically at me. On such a morning she said quietly, "I have forgiven you, Clyde, I've studied what I couldn't see before. Strange, none of us saw what we arranged to happen. So blind!

"Oh, that woman who died, the one in Corvallis. You hoped there would be a way out of this through her, didn't you—a romantic interlude that would make you look cheap to Ginny? Now you love the two of us, each profoundly, as I did you and Art once. I see that. I remember how it was—the apprehension, Clyde, the eternal feeling of guilt for spending my passion on one, while the other dear one waited for days, even weeks, to share in my joys. Good God! Say something, Clyde. Change the subject. Let's be silent for a moment!

"Now how about finding ways we can help Bunky to be a fisherman?"

"I want him to be his own boss," I said. "Not the epileptic they hire to cut rotten fish bait, but the guy who calls the turns."

She smiled at me as if I were a child. "Okay," she said, "what's your formula to beat the usual climbing of the slow ladder to captain?"

"Well it's a wild idea, dear, but if both Bunky and I become fishermen and on our own boat, say a four-man fifty-footer, I could be skipper until he gets the hang of it. Then he can take over and I'll come ashore to write, as I must, before it's too late."

"Write what?" asked Nordi.

"Tell what it's like to live and work in Oregon, green Western Oregon and on the sea that pounds its headlands."

"Save that until you're putting it down on paper," said Nordi. "And where would you get the money to buy such a boat, dreamer?"

"I'm not so much of a dreamer as a wild planner," I answered a bit huffily. "Bunky and I are going to build the boat, that is, if he agrees."

Nordi, who had been applying lipstick, slipped into her coat. "I've got to catch the bus, Clyde. Let's continue this tonight before you go to work."

"Not in front of Bunky," I said. "I want to be more certain before I wave this in front of him."

Our evening talk resulted in a trip to Seattle to look at boats there. I had six thousand in war bonds tucked away and some of the auto body paint shops, now doing well, that I'd carried in lean years paid their old bills—money I had kissed goodbye.

Bunky had gone back to school to appease us now that we were at last seeing things in his realistic way. I took a west coast fishing magazine and pored over each issue's revelations. Nordi and I hadn't had a vacation this year, so now we gave ourselves one in a leisurely trip to Seattle. We took a pleasant room in a hotel there. Arriving before noon, we wandered down and had lunch in a restaurant amid drying nets and fishboats. We roamed the docks and floats and saw one boat that made us think of the *Delite*, the fifty-footer that Cordoza and I had owned and, sure enough, it had the lines of a Southern California tuna boat. It reminded Nordi of Tiburon and she patted my arm.

On two different boats we were granted permission to come aboard and both owners graciously showed us around their boats. When we spoke of Bunky's desire to be a fisherman, they said his was a bad idea, that fishing in the past had been good but for the last several years, what with government regulations and the many boats coming up from California, etc., it was something to stay out of. I agreed, but I know of no industry or craft that doesn't deplore its method of making a living. It's really a protective posture, as well as a chance to snarl at whatever regulation they chaffed against.

Chatting with the fishermen about the design of their boats, the name of Edwin Monk, naval architect, kept popping up. We decided to see him next day. A breeze wafted in from the

Sound, reminding us of the salt air of San Francisco Bay and of Waterspout Point. Hungry again, we left the wharves for a seafood restaurant and dined on fried razor clams.

Nordi didn't want to take a cab back. It was a long walk back to the hotel but really a stroll, for we were in no hurry and it was a mild day and not raining. Nordi kept close to me clinging to my arm, rather insistently. It seemed we were moving back in time with each block, her arm in mine, a reminder to me that each activity of mine had been with her close by, sharing in the small triumphs, as well as the losses. Scenes of times of both went through my head as we moved along.

"What are you thinking of, Clyde?" she asked as we crossed an intersection and started a new block.

"Our past," I answered. "Nordi, why did you stay?"

"What a question, silly," she replied. "I was wishing we could do it all over again, to be young again and as free as we were when we lived on Laguna Street."

In the middle of the block, of one accord, we stopped and hugged, and our kiss was as sweet as those when kissing was new to us.

After freshening up at the hotel we went out for a movie, but left before the end. It was composed of hackneyed cliches strung together; nothing for the poor actors to work with. Outside Nordi would rather not have a drink, so we ended up in our room where we jotted down some of the answers to our questions of the day about boats, gear, engines and fishing practices. In the phone book we found Edwin Monk's number and street address, also the name of another architect in case Monk turned out to be the wrong man for us.

In the hotel room Nordi acted rather shy. Maybe it was the strange room or our thinking of the past we'd shared, but her showering and readying herself for bed was a bit tentative and hadn't had the certainty of movement, of direction usual to Nordi. When we finally met in a cool embrace beneath the covers, there was a virginal honeymoon quality to her responses that made me certain she was back in time to our loving encounters before our marriage.

Afterward, lying beside her, I mused that this was not like her, for in the sex act there came about in Nordi a splendor that, though intrinsically Nordi, yet made her seem related in the heated moment to the great bed dames of the past—Phryne, Lady Hamilton, Lola Montez—an elusive goddess quality that thrilled but eluded me.

Breakfast over, I called Edwin Monk's office and netted us an invitation to "come right over." We liked him, a quiet pleasant man. He asked us where we would fish and who was going to build the boat. We were brief about Bunky's problem and said that Bunky and I were going to build it. "I built my house," I explained, "built several skiffs and repaired a thirty-footer."

"Have you ever used a steambox?" he asked skeptically.

I told him of the thirty-foot steambox I had when I lived on San Francisco Bay. "Well," he said, adding up what I had told him, "I believe you can do it. I'll sell you a plan that I made last year for an Alaskan fisherman, a chunky forty-six-footer. That's as big as an amateur should tackle on his first boat. The complete set of plans will cost you one hundred dollars, and I believe the boat you'll build from them will fill your needs to a tee."

We looked over the plans and gradually the boat came alive to us. It would be heavily made and looked able, in its sweeping lines, to baffle the sea. He told us its hold could carry eight tons of iced fish or twenty-five tons of sardines or pilchards, and the eighty horse Cat diesel would push her along at nine knots. "She sleeps two in the deckhouse," he said, and four in the fo'c'sle."

Nordi smiled at me, so I handed him two fifty-dollar bills. Monk eased back into his office chair, asked Nordi's permission, then lit a cigarette, after handing me the pack.

"Where are you two from?" he questioned.

"Oregon," I replied, "up the Clackamas River."

"That makes three of us," he said. "I was born on Sauvie Island. Where are you going to get the oak for the ribs?" he inquired, puffing out smoke and watching it climb to the ceiling.

"I believe we'll use local oak. It's a white oak."

"Yes," he nodded, "there were groves of those big oaks where I was born. It's a fine rib oak, though famous for the rotting of its sapwood. But trim that off and you have rib wood superior to eastern oak. Some homemade boats use yew wood, you know, but it's hard to come by and for much smaller boats than the one you will be building.

"By the way, that gum timber I specified for the stem is brought over green from Australia and kept soaking wet until sold. Wrap it in wet sacks and water it each day until you use it. Dry, it's cantankerous stuff, practically impossible to work with, cross grains on cross grains. Makes ideal stem wood though."

He didn't get up from his chair, but he made some tiny moves that let us know that he had other things on his mind. "Let me hear from you," he said, "you'll have questions as you go along. I want to hear them and help where I can." He stood up. We left.

Outside with our roll of blueprints, Nordi looked harried.

"What's bothering you, Pee-ang?" I asked her. She remained silent until seated in the car. "What is it, dear?" I asked again.

"Clyde, I'm just remembering about the *Princess*, that you had to leave it because of your lungs. Won't it happen again?"

"I'll cross that bridge when I come to it," I muttered.

"And," she went on, "what makes you think you can build this boat? I believe it will be a tough job for a professional carpenter, even a cabinet maker, and you've often told me you're only a wood butcher."

"I'll do all right, Nordi. I've looked around at the market to buy one. The prices are all more than I can rake together. You know the saying, necessity is the mother of invention. Then too, I've learned a hell of a lot in the shipyards."

She gazed at me intently as if I weren't her Clyde. I believe she was trying to envision in me the man it would take to launch the boat that was enlarging in her mind from the plans she now carried.

"Let's get back to the hotel, Clyde. You should absorb as much of these plans as you can, and then we'll go down to the floats and see the finished boats once more. That way you can learn a good deal, don't you think?" She was right and we did just that.

Next day we took a side trip to Friday Harbor. There were cloudy skies, but the rain had stopped when we arrived on the island. In spite of a cold wind, we got in a little fishing before returning to the mainland for the trip home.

Below Chehalis, where we had eaten an excellent luncheon, we talked about Nordi's modeling days, and then about painting in general. As we swept up a long hill we considered a landscape of hers, a sketch of a small red building under some Bay trees. It was really great painting in my estimation, but she did not acknowledge the praise. Instead she deflected our interest to Virginia.

"You chose the perfect empty canvas in Ginny," she remarked. "You know, a lot of you men fear intelligence that comes so close to equalling your own. What you've done—well, in a way it proves my point. You don't want mature competition. You want a fresh canvas. You want to go through kindergarten again with an innocent looking up to you."

I didn't answer her. I said, "Ginny tells me I asked her to marry her someday."

"I don't doubt it," Nordi replied. "Art said it often. Love seems an arrangement by the powers-that-be to make papas and mamas out of us," she smiled bitterly. "You were right about going back to Waterspout Point. I see that now. It's a little late, though, isn't it, Clyde?"

"Yes, Nordi. I should have forced our going. I'm weak, I guess."

"No, it's your honesty about the main factors of life, as you and I see them."

She changed the subject abruptly.

Later where the road parallels the Columbia River Highway

she roused from what, I thought, was a nap, though it was really a sad reflection on things as they were.

"Husband," she said, "we've got to face the fact that you'll have to choose."

"I can't," I said. "I love her as much as a man can and you— why, we are one, you and I. Even death can't change that."

"I know how we are, but eventually the family will find out, the neighbors and our friends, Ginny's folks, Teddy and Tek, your family. You're going to have to decide. Oh, Clyde, there's hell ahead of us. That's sure!"

When I got back on the job, I was surprised to see our superintendent had increased the number of my co-workers on this cold ship. My bosses now treated me and paid me as if I were a leadman, but left me on my own. I had a machinist and three helpers, and now Lendel showed up again to work with me. We really were doing much of the hot end's inspection and work. On the hot boat now only three machinists and their husky helpers took care of the journals and bearings as the engine was run in.

Lendel and I soon ate our lunch together and not in the lunchroom, for we found a great deal to talk about and the noise of the others was distracting. Up at the hot end he had seemed opinionless and lacking an interest in things. His reticence, I found, was born and bred into him, for, though it didn't show, he was, he announced pridefully, "half Indian—Cherokee. My family was related to that of Sequoyah, the great chief."

"That march!" I said with shame. "How you must hate us!"

"Not so much, Rice. The Japs paid off what we've owed you at Bataan."

"Yes, I guess you could see it that way."

"You're damn right. It somehow soothed the rankle in my guts."

"Didn't the oil soothe your people?"

"No, it was a break, but Bataan did the job." The heat left his eyes, he achieved that impassive air and remarked, "My father was a Norwegian, came from Alaska. The oil fields attracted him.

They killed him when I was six, crushed in an equipment mishap. Just before the depression I left Oklahoma, sick of the oil fields I worked in. Never been back."

"I'm asking too many questions," I said. "By the way, some Cherokee blood runs in my veins too." We shook hands solemnly. "But let me ask one more thing. Where have you been living since then?"

"I traded chiggers for mosquitos in Alaska and British Columbia. How about you?"

"Later," I said and we tied into our dim-lit work.

After that we often conversed over coffee, sandwiches, celery and bananas. He told me quite a bit about Alaska. "You should go there sometime. Get a job as crew on a fishing boat for a season. I often have and there's money in it too."

·

I phoned Madam Zinger's next day and was informed "Miss Broms is no longer in my employ."

I stopped and became very neighborly when I saw Olga, bundled up in the chilly day, doing cleanup yard work. Since Ginny and I had become lovers we both affected an air of disinterest about each other's affairs. I wondered wildly what had happened to my dolly. Olga was full of news about everybody and everything. A huge owl had been seen flying through the twilight with one of her white Leghorns gripped in its talons. Mrs. Telarino fell down her stairs and broke a leg, and: "Did you know that Ginny Beans (her name for my nymph) has had a fine job handed her on a platter. A school teacher of hers had gone to college with the manager of a distributor of eyeglasses and laboratory glass. He mentioned he wanted someone young, preferably shy, and dully honest. 'That way,' he went on, 'I can build a secretary the way I see fit.' The woman thought of Ginny and, the long and short of it is, our Ginny Beans got the job."

Olga smiled provocatively at me. "So she's out in the business world now, Clyde, and won't need your tutoring anymore. I feel," she continued, "that I have been a good influence for Virginia—four years of piano—and I've taught her to always hold her legs close together, except of course in swimming. Otherwise," looking at me archly, "men will just get wrong ideas."

I thought of moonlight playing on the curving white of Ginny's parted thighs. "A girl can't be too careful," I said.

"Just what I told her," agreed Olga, "and when I did, she smiled. I thought she started to laugh, so I told her as well as I could, circumspectly of course, how some men are."

I also learned from Olga that Ginny's sister, Dory, was spending her vacation week at home. That closed that waxed hinged door to me. I reminded myself that Nordi begged me to hide the fact, so embarrassing to her, that Ginny and I were more than casual friends, so I avoided chances to see Ginny within the family, feeling my love would burst its bounds and give us away if I got closer than ten feet from her. I had not seen or communicated with her since I told her that Nordi knew. That was fourteen days ago. Now there was a great want in me to hold her.

I wrote her a letter. I was standing at the entrance of the building where she worked and handed it to her as she passed in the morning. The letter said:

Dear Ginny,

And now that I'm able to write down all the torrent of things that pounded through my mind after I left you; now that I am alone and unfettered by time or circumstance, I want for words.

My heart says it's no use, my reason makes diagrams, which all prove it is impossible. Do not write, reason says to me. You cannot convey, you never have conveyed to her really what she means to you, and what you want to mean to her.

Still, I now tell you that I want to bring pain to you and ecstasy. I want to tie all your tendrils to the very trunk of life, so no storm could shake your conviction in its richness and worthwhile-ness, but also that you shall bloom upon the trunk for all to see.

For myself I want whatever you can give me freely. Say to

yourself: this man has needs that only I can succor without degrading him. Only in me can he find peace, for I am his true love. I am the one his heart has chosen in the face of all things against it. My smile warms him as the sun warms the meadow. My body is his heaven, the cleft where I bloom inwardly, the home of his ecstasy, my breasts pillow his heart. When I walk before him on the pathway, my movements are as music to him. The grace of my legs is strong melody, my slender arms the cadences of flutes, the beauty of my hips, the pear-shaped buttocks, the canted flare of pelvic splendor are to him as full of portent as the deep restlessness of some master's symphony. Then he lusts, that, through some art, in marble perhaps, he could convey my beauty to others, that, though not knowing me, they yet could find richness in my effigy.

When I walk beside him in the gloaming and put my arms about him, he is content, and he is a man who has long sought to snare contentment, but, when I am there, it is there, and the sackcloth of circumstance turns to velvet.

There were inaccuracies in the letter. It was traitorous to Nordi. Thinking of it afterwards, I wondered about myself and all men. True, I love them both, but the thought of lying in bed with both of them, one on each side of me, sickens me. We men, Caucasians at least, must defecate and love privately. At either end of the spectrum of our activities we pull down the curtain. How could this mere child, still tinged with innocence, bring about in me such a hunger, not for her body or her beauty alone, but for something more—a bud of awakening personality that I nurtured? Was I claiming ownership for fertilizing the opening flower of her mind? I must watch that in me. I must not be unworthy.

On the back of the letter was a postscript:

Dear Ginny, Monday night around one I will be waiting for you by the lower pool. Hope you can make it. Love, C.

She came, but didn't throw off her heavy kimono to greet me. We stood embraced by the pool, her head snuggled against my throat, her tears on my skin. The sound of the river was faint here. There was only this winter moonlight that shone down on the column of Ginny and me, as we stood clinging to one another. She raised her head and offered her lips.

"I thought I lost you," she whispered. "You should leave me, you know. I'll hate that, but I do expect it."

"No, no, Ginny, I can't leave you. It's too late now."

Still whispering, she said, "The need for loving was beginning to make me nervous, but I could take that. The worst was the thought that I couldn't burrow for the center of you anymore like I'm doing now—that scared me. Your letter—oh, Clyde, dear! That goddess is not me. You see much more than is here."

"You can't see her in your mirror," I agreed. "Other girls and women can't see her, but men see her. I see her. Love helps me see the real you. All I said is true."

There was just the moonlight and the warmth of our embrace. She took a step away from me, "I've got to go, Clyde. Dory might waken. This wet ground, everything is sodden—can we make love standing? I want you doing what you do, while I press you with my breasts." She fussed with the stuck zipper of her robe, when a mad urgency made me reach to tear it from her.

She spoke out then, "No, darling, no," and raised her arms high and I slipped it up over her head. . . .

I was an hour late to work, "too late to punch in," the timekeeper said. "Fine," I said, "don't pay me. I was detained, but I've got work to do."

"Can't let you in," he said.

"Call my machinist superintendent, Joe Hendler. I've got to be there. Getting her ready to turn over the engine in the morning."

After the call he let me in and soon I was working. My old refrain came to me—there's no way out for me. I can't even quit this damn shipyard. If I could, I'd go someplace, get away from everything. Maybe there I could see what to do. It would be easy, if it weren't for them. I said it, as if Nordi and Ginny were the enemy. Them—Jesus God!

I began to see a season on a fishing job in Alaska that Lendel had spoken of would be a godsend for me. I'd be able to decide up there what to do about, well—them. By God now!

But how? If I quit, they could throw me in jail or put me in the army on some miserable job.

Several nights before I had accidentally driven a sliver of steel into my hand. I had gone to the first aid station and had it removed. They had to whittle a bit and, in spite of the disinfectant used, it became infected, so after lunch I visited the doctor for further care. There were a couple of guys ahead of me and I watched the doctor take care of them. He was young and green, a tall thin fellow, very concerned about his patients. When he worked on me, he was careful to cause the least possible pain. After bandaging it we chatted, for I was his last patient.

He told me of an old man who had come in earlier and an X-ray showed him to be dying of tuberculosis. From the ravage of his lungs the doctor thought it had been going on for years, yet the old man had been brought into the station for a slight chest wound received over on the ways while handling planking. He was completely unaware that he was dying of the dread disease.

"I don't know how he continues to exist," said the young doctor.

"Sometimes ignorance is bliss," I remarked.

"Ignorance is the norm," he said and looked dejected. As we talked I saw he was much more naive than I. I should get back on the job, I thought, but this earnest young man . . . I hung onto him with gossip about the yards. Why? Far back in my mind some inner planning said, *get acquainted with him*. Well, I was trying to.

A week passed. We were asked to volunteer to work a shift on a large ancient English ship on the drydock. Of course, I volunteered. On the ship they wanted someone to crawl in one of the stern tubes and adjust the lignum vitae blocks of the outer bearing. I offered to do it. I crawled half way through and got stuck. I'd been told that fear makes you swell if you're in such a spot. Panic hit me, panic that turned to futile fury. My leadman at the other end of the bearing outside peered in and told me that after the panic abates, the swelling will stop and and I'll be able to worm out.

His assurance helped, though it didn't help my arms that were thrust ahead of me and cramped. I lay there raging at the grip the steel tube had on me. Then a midget arrived on the scene, crawled in and tied a rope around my feet and I was dragged out, and the midget slipped in and adjusted the bearing. I was very embarrassed.

We four men lined up then (not the midget, of course). The job was to pound on a massive nut wrench fitted on a gigantic recalcitrant nut—this on gear I can't bring to mind. The hammer weighed seventy-five pounds. You swung it from over your head and brought it down to crash on the outsize slugging wrench—seven times before handing it weakly to the next man, then you would go to the end of the line to wait for another go at it. None of us could put the zip in the blow as we were supposed to, for starting the strike, battling the inertia in that seventy-five pounds of steel turned what zip we had into a plodding blow. Finally, loosening several such nuts, we staggered to the truck that brought us there, stopping for a couple of beers on the way back.

Driving home that morning I thought of the young doctor and then forgot him. My arms and stomach muscles ached, strained from trying to put power into the downward blow of the awkward maul. The car skidded on a stretch of ice. I counteracted, but slowly, shook myself, wondering if it was grogginess of a night worker or the careful rehashing of the past that was getting between me and the now of the road.

The over-conscientious doctor came once more on my screen, as it were. *Then it came:* how I could use him to get to Alaska. The rest of the way home was joy—theorizing, planning the angles. God, yes! I would fake insanity, a coming explosion of insanity. Imply I hadn't been like this before, but the wild activity, the bedlam of noise of the yards was too much for me—if I somehow could get away somewhere, I might regain my ease.

Dory, as a student nurse, had access to books that would give information on the early symptoms of insanity. I nearly ran off the road I was so excited over this new idea. "Time is of the essence," I muttered.

Nordi had her coat on to leave. "You're late, Clyde. Now we'll miss our chat." I explained my delay—working at the drydock, etc.

I found that the doctor was immensely interested in all that was going on around him, but would not or could not leave his post to see. I got him to come early with me in the swing shift. I showed him around the ways, walked with him the full length of the outfitting dock, explaining as we passed each ship, and took him down into the engine room of the hot boat. We stood with others and watched that great engine turning the shaft, then back to his first aid station.

"Gee whiz," he said grinning at me and said, "Gee whiz," again. "Thank you, Rice. Now I know what's going on around my bailiwick. Thanks. Thanks again."

In this manner I started my small, peculiar campaign. Then I got the book and decided, after a few hours of reading, I would be bugs in the schizophrenic manner. The trouble is that anything I act out, if handled well, tickles me and I have to laugh. I'm unable to keep a poker face. My grinning ego gets in the way when I should appear depressed. Several times I had to leave his office to laugh outside, but passed it off as one of the symptoms.

By now we were on a friendly basis. I visited him every other day. Though the infection had cleared up, the constant irritating I did to the wound, kept it from healing. Each time I appeared I dropped a symptom that I read of in the book and always dejectedly. Before many visits I had completed the picture of an incipient schizophrenic about to explode. I felt I was doing very well. I almost patted my back in his presence, as I over-appreciated the virtuosity of my act of slowly going crazy. In a week and a half he had become very concerned, in fact, primed for the question.

"Do you think," I muttered very down at the mouth, "that if I could get out of this bedlam and go home to Alaska and take my old job in the stationery store that the confusion that now distracts me might disappear?"

Oh, the solicitude on his face, as he said, "Well, it certainly could help. The war is almost over," he continued, and he didn't think "there's need of so many people in the shipyard now."

"But the way it is, I can't get out," I muttered hopelessly, "I can't leave."

"Well, I can fix that for you, Mr. Rice. I'd be glad to."

I told Lendel while we were taking the top off the big low-pressure pump (the bottom was rigged with some hidden scrap iron by a guy who loved Germany or Japan, or maybe just hated us). One stroke of the pump in the morning would have wrecked it and they were difficult to replace. He had put this scrap where casual inspection would have missed it. With my tiny mirror and the flashlight turned a certain way I found it.

"Guess that was somebody's solid achievement," remarked Lendel.

"Yeah," I pontificated, "if a guy finds he lacks stature as a doer, he still can loom large in his own estimation with a few matches in a dry forest."

Lendel made no reply. He was as tired of my comments as I was.

"Alaska," he said, "we talked of you going up there. If you are, Rice, you'll have to hire up in Seattle by February fifteenth, that's this month. The cannery fleet leaves about that time."

"I'm going," I said and told him about the doctor.

"Fine." Lendel said. "You know, when I was introduced to you back on the hot boat, I noticed your hand was thin. You lack the plump fingers and hard suet-covered palm of a fisherman."

Remembering Bunky's hand, I said, "My son's hands will fill the bill."

"Sure, and, of course, the canvas gloves you'll wear will help," he said, "but I'm talking about you. When you fished before did you personally ice down the fish each night."

"No, Cordoza did it, but I cut the bait and baited all the hooks."

"There you are," he said. "You couldn't scoop your hands around in the crushed ice burying the fish. How you figger to get by?"

"Why I'll bring a scoop," I said.

"Unh-unh. I'm going to get you a set of scoops. You sure you're going to be here tomorrow?—Fine."

I rushed home. Nordi was cooking our breakfast. We embraced in the kitchen. "You're early," she said with a sweet smile and kissed me. Then her smile faded as she continued looking at me. "What is it? Tell me? What happened?"

"I'm going away to Alaska for the season, dearest, to learn more about fishing and boats, but mainly I'm going to get away from here and all this place implies, and from you and Virginia. I'm propped up here by those I love. I've got to find if I'm—well—still my own man."

She smiled through her tears as she caressed my hand. "Of course, you've got to go to prove yourself once again and make your decision. Clyde! You said 'dearest'?"

"Yes, as long as I live, you'll be dearer to me than anybody, even Bunky. I swear it on the gentleness of my mother."

My leave-taking of Ginny was as brief. As I was leaving, I said, "I'll write and I'll be back. Until then, I'll remember you dancing in the moonlight for me."

Next night I brought my tools and gear home. I handed my medical discharge to the timekeeper at the gate and was through with the shipyards.

I saw Lendel as I was gathering my things. "Rice," he said and came over to me. "I know you're leaving wondering why you were sent to the cold boat."

"Small hands," I said.

"Yes, but that's only part of it. Mostly you're not Irish or Catholic or heavy on the booze. They were, leadman and all. You didn't fit in and, on top of it, you're not bigoted enough."

"Yeah," I agreed, still sick that I hadn't been able to really belong, but I smiled at Lendel. "So long," I said. "It's been great working alongside of you. I've got some advice to leave you: hide your breadth, fella."

I phoned a big cannery Lendel had spoken of, asked for a job in Alaska on one of their boats, and was offered a job on the *Fairweather*, an eighty-foot fish hauler and barge tug in Southeastern Alaska. So I found work in Alaska, though the pay was much less than in the shipyards. He said, "Bring your clothes and rubber boots, that's all. We take care of everything else."

The *Fairweather*, he told me, was docked at Alki Point along with other cannery boats. "You must be there Monday, February eleventh."

As I brought my tools and things home from the shipyard, I stopped at the bus station and bought a bus ticket to Seattle. Nordi brought me into town after dark. Now it came time to leave her. Our togetherness wouldn't let go. Finally I flung myself out of the car, Nordi reaching after me stretched out across the seats with a cry so lost, I wavered, but somehow got a hold of myself, took my toolbox and walked away.

How can we do these things?

VI

The Steps   Charles E. Heaney

In Which
I Face the Family Music, Build a Boat,
Lose and Gain a Wife,
and
Attempt to Beat Some Sense into My Head

1944

WHETHER YOU WILL BE pleased or relieved to hear that I am not including my Alaskan adventures in these pages is not my call. Like *Night Freight*, the account of my trip to the Siskiyou mountains in search of gold, the Alaska narrative is complete unto itself. Moreover, it adds little to the events that the present book attempts to recount. Unlike my trip to the Siskiyous, my Alaskan sojourn did produce gold of a kind—people, places, and memories that I treasure to this day. It did not, however, provide any of the answers that, perhaps foolishly, I went there to find. For all of these reasons, I have decided to save the pages about Alaska for another time and, if my publishers are willing to continue in their own quixotic brand of folly, another book.

I stayed in Alaska for six months—from February to July—and would gladly have stayed longer had fate, or reality, not intervened in the form of a telegram and a letter. The letter, I assumed, was from Virginia, and I set it aside to read at my leisure. The telegram, which I opened immediately, was from Nordi. It read:

> Dear Clyde: Come home. Our son has run away. I expect you to find him.

Like her wounded cry when I had left her, Nordi's telegram echoed in my mind as I boarded the *George Dolthrope*—steerage, and lucky to get even that—for my journey home. We sailed at dusk, and I lay in my bunk wondering where I'd find Bunky and about the strange tone of Nordi's telegram. I was eager to read Ginny's letter, but saved it to read in the morning.

The next morning, on the deck for steerage people, I pulled out the letter, only to find that it wasn't from Ginny. It was from her sister.

"Clyde," it said,

> little did we realize that we sheltered a wolf in sheep's clothing until I unintentionally opened a letter that I thought was mine, but found that my unwed sister is no longer a virgin, instead, the helpless pawn of a married man. I could not believe it, but my parents do. They know now that we've all been duped by a vicious scoundrel living in our midst.

Christ! Maybe she was right. At least that was the book on it. Who was I to confront these unsparked people? I had only one thing working for me and that was *fait accompli*. But good God! What of Nordi and Bunky? Ginny had been a simple child of a backward family. I was now tied to her sensually, but I was not when I first became aware of her. It could only have been her eyes that enslaved me, but what had they to reflect—certainly no great volition, no intense seed of being.

The times she had danced before me in the moonlight, there had been a sense in me that she fitted the pieces of the puzzle we all ponder over wordlessly and that her inchoate solvings slipped them into place. How? I knew of no background for this. Once she had said as she rested bedside me from her dancing. "I'm not a thinker, Clyde, but when I dance I can look down from a high place on thinking. Words do something to thought, I can see that then. They push thoughts around, make them fit square places."

I saw her with no saleable ability. Instead she was an untrammeled human creature, more like a young doe, cognizant sure, but gentle and quiet, open to music and poetry, marvelling at beauty and things that flower, pliant, without a mad drive. She accepts exquisitely, I remembered, but seldom offers herself unless she is dancing for me. Where do her dances come from? I pondered. Not from the movies or from the ballet. Maybe from Swedish dances old lady Nordstrom taught Tek, Olga and Nordi. Could it be that these dances she did for me with coquetry and passion and with happy laughter expressed by rhythm—could all this derive from my old mother-in-law?

How could this young doe . . . ? Ah, yes, I see it now. Her dancing is an expression of her joy in being loved and adored. Here! Stop this! I was thinking of Bunky and sweet Nordi and instead I've slipped to Ginny. I'm leaning toward Ginny and away from Nordi. I must never allow it. Enter my mind, Bunky! Help me with this unfair imbalance! I'll find you, boy, and hold your mother in my arms once again. Bunky, when I find you, we're going to build that boat.

Ketchikan—we layed over a day there. I wandered the town and ended up in a bar sipping whiskey thinking of the manifold problems that awaited me in Carver—not Nordi. "Nordi is civilized," I said, "but the rest of them were . . ." Could it have been Minnesota that did it to them, I wondered, or because their God was a jealous God? A Swede who came west directly vaulting Minnesota, would he be less stodgy? I was never to know.

"Are you talking to me?" asked the barmaid.

"No, I'm talking to me," I said, "and my glass is empty."

I remembered vaguely that later I had a hard time with the ship's gangway. I got past the officer stationed there, but after showing him my ticket, I fell off it but clung to a stanchion so that they could reach down and get me back and, I suppose, help me on board.

Much later, I awoke in my bunk. Every muscle in my body was strained and store. When it was time to eat I stumbled off to chow, got in my place in the long bench and started to eat. I found I couldn't; it was too hard to open my mouth. Then the man next to me said:

"Do you always get so damn mean before you pass out?"

"Not me," I said, "not me."

"Took four of us to hold you down," he went on. "You bit and kicked and yelled till one of the mates come along and caught you one on the jaw, cold-cocked you, he did, for your own good. You kicked my hand when we was quieting you and that's all I want of you. Just stay away from me." I did. I felt like a pariah before that mob in the steerage.

I left my tools at Acme when I got to Portland. Nordi wasn't there. The girl in the office said, "She took a couple of days off." I hurried on, caught the bus and went to the end of the line and started walking through the scenes of my childhood, past Grandma's house on the hill and through Happy Valley where I first made love to Nordi. Strange, how a fellow is! This familiar country was clearing the cobwebs from my mind. Then I was crossing a pasture on the north side of the hill back of our place, yes, and their places too. It all lay between the hill I was on and the river. I climbed out on the rocks of the cliffs atop the hill and looked down. Our houses were hidden by trees, the road directly below me I could see, and the Bromses' field and ours, each separated from the blue of the river by a string of cottonwoods. Ours was planted in alfalfa and in it I saw four horses. Horses in the alfalfa field—how strange!

For some obscure reason my inner eye saw a boy of eleven with a pole and a can of worms and a broad-brim straw hat trudging toward the river. "You damn sentimental jackass!" I said out loud and was back in it. That callow part of me had no right to be here today. Hidden below me was the home we'd made, Nordi and I.

I stayed on top of the cliffs for several hours, looking down where unseen below were the three homes that held old lady Nordstrom's clan. The hell of it was I loved them all. We had camped together and farmed together, put up hay together and, when the sun went down, sat all leaning back against the warm, sweet smelling hay shock and sung to Teddy's small accordion, sung until the moon was high and our clothes were damp with the dew of the summer night. They had gathered around me, the "oddball," who, with my ongoing studies, was moving farther and farther beyond their hatreds and weevily conceptions. Nordi and Bunky and Ginny were sprung from them, were my tie with them. At least they were preferable to my own family, who were also fanatics but of another sort.

Then I was leaving the cliffs. I found a remembered deer trace and headed down. No answers, there was just me approaching people whom I had hurt.

I came to our house. The door was open and it smelled strongly of paint. A man, a painter, came down the steps from the bedrooms. "Yes?" he asked. "What can I do for you?"

"Tell me where I can find Mrs. Rice?"

"Why she's right up above here." He pointed where I could see the tip of her tent, so I went up and found her. We embraced. I held her hungrily. We didn't kiss or say anything. We just held each other tightly for a long time.

Then, stepping away from me, she said very quietly, "Don't worry about Bunky. We found him. He's working in the ship-yards and is staying with a friend who lives near the yard. Let me get you something to eat." We hugged again. "How about a French omelet?" she continued.

She had a little cooking place—a steel plate over some bricks. She built a fire and prepared the meal, not looking at me, her head bowed. (I did this to her! Oh, God!) But she hadn't sent me to Alaska like this.

"Tell me, Nordi. What is it?" She raised troubled eyes. "Bunky has been away for two weeks. Both of you gone! I hated it. I had the house repainted inside. I did it so I could get out of that empty house. Believe me, this tent's cozier."

"If he's through downstairs," I suggested, "we can put the furniture back, make it homey again."

"No, not yet," she entreated me. "I've come to dread those rooms empty of you and Bunky and friends. They seem to mock me and tell me I've failed! Oh, Clyde, stay with me here in the tent, at least for awhile. Let's play we're camping in the saddle on Sugarloaf near Tiburon—remember—or by the great stone tab-leau that you were fond of." So we stayed. "Don't let the others see you yet," she said. "We'll camp here tonight just as we did in California."

I agreed. She relaxed then and we kissed. We sat close, patting each other from time to time and talked of our days in Tiburon.

"Clyde, think back to the camp we had on the Russian River. Oh, how happy young people can be. They should not waste a moment."

"We weren't always camping in our Tiburon days," I reminded her. "How about our house? It was small but just right."

I felt a little reminiscing might dispel her depression, so we talked on awhile about the past.

She told me she had stood up well to this trouble I'd brought her until the family found out about the letter. Instead of being sympathetic, Old Lady Nordstrom and Olga had come down hard on Nordi, saying that she had sought her own counsel instead of that of her church. They'd warned her, they said, all along. "And you had a lover in Tiburon," said covetous Olga, "and now you're paying for it." Nordi could understand Olga's vexation but her mother's ugliness astounded her. She loved her mother and was deeply hurt.

A sudden bitterness shot through my gut. So the old lady and her own sister came down on Nordi like vultures, huh? Yeah—yeah! How about me? I'm snarling at a simple old gert and her daughter, when I should be mutilating myself, chop off my damn cock, shove these caressing hands into the cogs of some machine! Ah, God, to what avail! I've got to remain useful, got to be of some value to whomever in this world.

But Nordi and I were smiling at each other and kissed again and drew closer with memory. "Remember some of our tomfoolery—playing Dickensonian characters?" she said. "I was Mrs. Thubish and you were my Nailby."

"Yes, I was Mrs. Thubish's Nailby. I even learned to walk like a Nailby. Remember, dear?"

"Sort of an ungainly hick," she said.

"Yes, an earnest stumblebum," I agreed and hid the gall in my heart.

I brought up the horses, then, that I'd seen in the meadow.

"Jack's been doing a little horse dealing and I've rented pasture-land to him and he agrees to have them off by August fifteenth so that the grass can come back before the winter floods. How was Alaska?" she asked with an inevitable change of subject. "I mean you wrote me about it, but now you're away from it. Tell me how it seems to you now."

"You mean did I find an answer to my dilemma?"

"I was going to lead up to that, Clyde."

"No, dear, I didn't. I couldn't. I'm stymied. I love you every way a man can. I loved you as much when you left me for Art as when you were with me."

"I know, Clyde. We are one, nothing can change that. When you took me away from Art, I was so happy but, of course, I had to act as if I wasn't. How do you feel about Virginia now?"

"I love her deeply, Nordi, and she loves me. It's too late to grab you and run. We should never have come north. Relatives—Jesus—mine and yours!"

"How about Virginia, Clyde? She's a relative too."

"She's like you, Nordi, she's worth putting up with all the relatives in God's green earth, but I'm not worthy of either of you."

At dusk we retired to the tent and, after joining, we lay holding one another throughout the night, just holding. With morning she became worried. "You'll have to face the family."

"I only hate facing Ted. I love him for a kind, honest man."

"How about Jack? He says he'll beat you up."

"I'll have to use tools."

"Tools?"

"Yes, after that wrestler went after me in the shipyards my neck has never been the same. It still pains me. Now the guy who beats me up automatically puts me in the pen. That's final."

We were eating breakfast when Tek, passing through on her morning visit to her mother, saw me and scooted on and told her mother. At once they came back, Olga with them, arms akimbo, the three talking all at once. They reminded me of bluejays worrying an owl. Nordi tried, uselessly, to bring quiet to the harangue. Her mother kept saying I was the devil: "Utterly evil, ruining our poor Virginia."

"You'll pay for this," Olga cried out. "The Bible says—"

"Leave the Bible out of it," I begged.

"You're a dirty Communist to say that of the Bible," Tek shrieked. "You ought to be thrown out of the neighborhood." They glared at Nordi.

"It's that Acme Flavoring Company," accused Olga. "If you'd have been home, this never would have happened."

"Acme paid for getting us out here and it still pays me."

"He's a no-good husband. I told you that twenty years ago," said the old lady biting down on the words in a futile fury. "He isn't God-fearing."

"Clyde has his ups and downs," said Nordi. She came over and took my hand and raised her voice over the babble. "He's a passionate, hard-working man. I've had twenty-two years with him and I treasure those years. Unlucky, yes, he is unlucky. Foolish, sure, but I know how this trouble happened. We unknowingly set a trap for him, a trap for a lusty man and he got caught—by his balls, at that, poor guy—and anyway, I've forgiven him."

They were all yammering at her, but her mother caught the last of her remarks: "Ev-a-lyn, I'll not have you talk that way in front of Tekla and Olga."

"Don't their husbands have testicles, Mama?"

"Testicles—balls—you're vulgar, Ev-a-lyn. I won't have it. Clyde made you this way, that devil."

Arms akimbo, glaring at me, Tekla stepped close and placed her feet in the manner of childhood, daring an attack, "And how about my daughter, Mr. Rice?"

"Tek, you have no idea how sorry I am."

"I'll bet you are!"

"I love your daughter."

"No kidding," sneered Tek.

Later, I drove to town and picked up my toolbox. It was

Saturday, so I went over to my father's. The Little Lady answered the door. "No," she said, "your father does not want to see you. Definitely," she added.

Well, I couldn't blame him. On the way home I saw Jack's car at the beer joint in Carver. I stopped and parked. I had a bad beating coming to me and I'd take it from the right guy like Ted, but not from the likes of Jack. I went in and ordered a beer. I sat a seat or two from Jack. He'd been talking, I could see that in the expressions of the faces of the fellows at the bar on the other side.

I said, "Hello, Jack." He didn't answer. I had another beer and left. That was tended to. Talk is cheap.

Driving home after the beer I drove on and into the Bromses' driveway and was ready to knock when the door opened. Ted looked me over. Finally he said, "You want to come in?"

"No," I answered. "Please come on out."

He came, "How come?"

"Look, Ted, I've done you and your family harm. I've come to take an earned beating. I won't fight back unless you try to kill me."

"That letter proves you've been carrying on with Virginia."

"I've loved her since she was fifteen."

"Why?"

"I don't know. I've been trying to figure it out. Guess I was moved by the male urge. We all know it comes in many guises, but that must be the reason. To me it came as love, admiration, pity, tenderness and finally the thrust of my loins."

"Don't you get all that from Evelyn?"

"Yes, I do."

"Then why Virginia?"

"It seems God often favors polygamy."

"Not in the Bible."

"To hell with it, but, yes—in the Bible."

"Our people don't."

"More people do—Mormons, Mohammedans, Chinese, Buddhist. They're all God's people, just like us. Ten percent of them don't—the Christians, and divorce runs high among us

Christians. I didn't choose this situation, Ted. I was deep in it before I saw. Then I saw whatever I did someone I loved would get hurt. I went to Alaska to figure it out. I drew a blank on it up there, now I'm back. Let your fury at me get what satisfaction it can. I love Virginia. I'll always love her and I love Nordi. Come on! Here I am! Maybe I should take a poke at you to get you started."

"Too much of what you say makes sense for me to sock you, Clyde."

"Well, I didn't come over here to be patted on the back. Maybe I should bat you one so you can flare up?"

"Lots of what you said goes over my head, Clyde, but you've studied a lot. I haven't. I've always figured you're honest inside. Tek's pretty upset. Well, so am I, I guess, but you made some points that she wouldn't understand. I want to ask—why Virginia? But, of course, you don't know why anymore than I do. I'm sore, plenty sore, but I don't hate you. And, Clyde, look out for Jack! Well, Virginia's in the garden with her mother."

When I approached the garden, Ginny saw me and came over. She gave me her hand and I kissed it. "I see you've been through hell because of me, Ginny."

"I always knew it would come," she said. "I was relieved when it did; no more hiding. Poor Nordi, they chewed on her, not me."

"Will you walk with me to the river?'

"Not now, Clyde. We've waited months, we can wait longer."

She was right, of course, and with her mother standing yards away I decided to wait for a better time to find out how things stood with Ginny.

I went past her down their road to the bottom. For seven years I had taken care of the bottom, not just mine, but Teddy's, Jack's and Mr. Giesek's. Giesek, and Brown, who owned the land before him, both told me this particular bottom was losing its small eminence above the river by the loss of the topsoil when the annual floods rushed over the land, too closely cropped. The river removed topsoil faster than plant residue could build it up.

They pointed out that the bottom must have an ample blanket of grass or weeds or willows as each winter approached to protect it from the scouring floods.

When Bunky and Dave, Dory, Virginia and I found a spot where the topsoil was gone and subsoil deeply eroded, we would shape the ragged edge pit into a shallow bowl shape, then fertilize and seed it. Over that we would toss straw and pin it down with small bundles of willows, laboriously wired to stakes. It worked beautifully, catching the mud, sand and debris in flood times. In a few years the holes filled and the wound on the bottom was no more. To keep the horses and cattle off of these places, I fenced them temporarily. The kids and Virginia gave me a great amount of help on these. I maintained that one tiny ravine, if let go, could cut the bottom in half.

When I left for Alaska, I once again warned Jack of a break on his land so big we could not fix it. It would take money, labor and concrete to handle it—twenty-five bucks' worth.

Now I found that the fence around the spot on Teddy's land that Ginny and I had worked on for a year was gone, the stakes pulled up and our work trashed. I went to the other places where we had worked and found all of them trashed. My relatives and neighbors were getting back at me for stealing Teddy's daughter. Well, so be it!

•

Nordi had said that Bunky was not aware of the Monk blueprints of the boat. She'd been hiding them from him for fear that his enthusiasm would soon wane if no action was forthcoming. Now, she wanted him home so that we three could consider how we should go about building it. I must look for work, but not before we had our meeting.

Bunky was employed at Swan Island Tanker Shipyard. I came to the yard as a visitor and found him idling around a three-wheeled truck with which he moved small stuff around the yard. He seemed glad to see me, but a bunch of orders came to him just as I did, orders marked "rush." He promised to come out home after his shift ended. Then I went to Personnel to see if they were hiring. They weren't at the moment but would be in the following month.

Back home the painter and I moved all the furniture back, both upstairs and down, and when Bunky and Nordi arrived that night, I had the table set and a chowder and some steaks ready. After dinner we proceeded to flabbergast Bunky with the plans. I had set up a big panel where we could thumbtack each plan up easily, including the intricate detail prints. There were six in all and we went over them thoroughly. Then while Nordi made coffee, Bunky and I settled back in our chairs.

"How about it, keed?" I grinned at him. "Were you thinking along the same lines as those plans?"

"Yes, Pop, only I didn't believe it possible."

"Well, if you want to, I'll build it with you. We can do it, I know we can."

"To fish or sell, Pop?"

"To fish, of course. You said you wanted to fish. We've taken you at your word."

"Okay," he said. "I certainly think fishing is the place for me. How will we handle it?"

"Fifty-fifty," I said. "We'll both work in the shipyards for wages and we'll spend the money and all the energy we have in building it. It'll be a rough one, Bunky, and a long one. You think you got the guts for a long haul? You're pretty young."

"Can't think of anything I want to do more. Try me."

Nordi came in with the coffee. "The next thing is where will we build it?" I said. "We need to be near the shipyard and near the water where it can easily be launched. We can't be coming out here each day. I've inquired," I said; "until the war's over they will not allow such a thing to be moved on the highway. Before I get a job I'll look around for a boat building site."

Nordi spoke up. "I'd like to see you both home every night but, you're right, you should be near your job and someplace along the Willamette or the Columbia. I saw an item in the newspaper," she went on, "about three or four shipyard workers who were building some boats on Tomahawk Island. Maybe you could get work in the Vancouver shipyards—no, I guess not, the commuting jam-ups on the bridge would waste your time. Let's go over to Tomahawk Island tomorrow and scout around. I'll take the afternoon off."

Tomahawk was ideal, a small sandy island off the Columbia's Oregon shore. We took a twenty dollar option on a fifty by a hundred lot; the owners would bring in electricity and water with a rent of fifteen dollars a month. With the option paper in Nordi's purse we grinned as we headed home. Bunky's enthusiasm was kinetic and it was hard riding with him in the pickup.

"Have we got enough money to start?" he asked.

"Yes," I answered, "but I won't start until I've got a steady job, and I believe I'll try Commercial Iron Works right now." While Nordi and Bunky waited, I went in and got a job as machinist's helper, graveyard shift.

My work was to disentangle the extension cords, twisted into a sinuous mass. It looked like a snake pit in the confines of a sixty-foot hull. The drills and other electric tools had been removed at the end of the second shift. Fourteen men working in the hull on each shift had somehow produced this gorgon knot. Well, I wanted a job! It was good to be working again.

Ginny and I were able to meet by the river and slake our thirst for each other and to listen to the sibilance of the Clackamas. We said little about our condition; we accepted what little we could get. My intimate hours with Nordi were similar. Either Nordi or Virginia was going to end up alone and I was to suffer for it intensely a thousand times and for the rest of my life. Only the boat for Bunky lightened my burden of guilt.

Nordi came to the yungrubarn to see Virginia one night. They wept, embracing one another. Though they were willing to share me, they agreed that convention would in the end make it impossible. I didn't hear about this meeting right away. After making a few forays into the countryside I found a mill whose timber came from a tract the mill owned, and the old growth

Douglas fir logs from it were of extreme hardness and weight that appealed to me. It would be difficult to work, but once in place it would be stout against the sea. I made inquiries in the nearby town and was told that the owner was honest, a religious zealot and hated boatbuilders, as one of them had left in his boat to the south seas without paying for the lumber of its construction.

I don't like being devious, but would have to be here, if I were going to get his excellent lumber. The planking favored by boat builders was vertical grain long lengths, free of knots—the same material as was used in building silos. When I brought Monk's material list to the mill owner, a Mr. Wanster, I included what was needed for a shack for Bunky and me to live in and enough lumber to make a shed fifty feet long, twenty feet wide and tall enough to build the boat in. I led him to believe that I wanted to put up a barn with two silos and a shop. He fell for it. An agreement was made, we signed a contract and I gave him my check to cover the complete order.

Sunday Nordi wanted to search for oaks. Following Mr. Monk's lead, we had worded our contract with Wanster to include sawing and planing of what oak logs we brought to his mill, and I had specifically warned him not to dump our oak logs into his millpond, for green oak will often sink. We drove out Molalla way and had not reached the town before we saw an oak, not the spreading tree of poetry, but a tall one, limbless for at least thirty feet and with great bulk of trunk. Monk had warned me of overripe trees where the lack of flexibility of the wood would be expressed in a certain condition of the bark.

The tree was in a small pasture near a house and the owner was hoeing in his house garden. I asked him for permission to examine the tree. It was without a fault. I bought it from him for twelve dollars and at that price he cut it down and cut two logs out of it, one fourteen and the other sixteen feet. There they waited for a hauler.

In my scouting around on my time off I found a grove of oak

near Eagle Creek. They were not as large as the single tree but
with perfect trunks. I could get one good log from each tree. I
bought them and Ted and I chopped and sawed all day until in
the evening we had six fine logs and, from the limb wood, several
cords of firewood—Nordi and Bunky helping us with bucksaws
we brought along.

On a farm some distance away a fellow was plowing his field
with a large tractor. I got him to drag the logs out of the woods
and truck them to the mill. He would do the same with the two
big logs at Molalla and bring the firewood to Carver all for the
right price. We were all pleased. Our need for oak lumber was
half solved.

That night I had to work, though it was Sunday, for the
extension cords should be in order when the machinist cord-
tanglers came on Monday morning.

The guards in these defense plants were nifty in their military
uniforms. They were not workers and were disliked. The guards
at Commercial Iron Works carried sidearms very much in evidence. Not only that, but those loafers swaggered. When I came
on to the job at midnight, the guard in the parking lot was
parking the cars in a diagonal fashion in the row. It was a tiring
night and I wasn't through when the whistle blew. I stayed on a
few minutes more to finish. When I came out to the parking lot
the guard for the day shift had arranged the parkings square-to
and my pickup was askew of the others. The guard came over
roaring at me. My truck was cockeyed to the pattern, he said. He
was a big fellow, well over six feet, and he wore two 45s in his
low-slung holsters. He bellowed and gestured, and he called me
a son-of-a-bitch among other things. I don't let that pass, never
have, but I was very tired. I just wanted him to shut up; his noise
bothered me. I listened dully. He kicked the fender of my pickup.
Oh, God! What you have to put up with these days, I thought.
He kicked the fender again. A piece of dirt dropped from underneath the fender. That did it! I had him by the throat bent back
over the fender and hood, banging his head on the hood as I

choked him. I was half aware that his eyes stuck out, his beefy hands were futile at pulling mine away, but tears were running from his eyes. I let him up.

"You go too far," I said.

He felt of his throat that was plainly bruised. "You choked me," he muttered.

"I told you, you go too far."

"Let's say this didn't happen," still muttering, he looked wildly around.

"Any way you want it," I answered. "I can take a certain amount of shit from you guys, but you went too far."

"Okay," he said, still massaging his throat, "I won't say nothing if you won't."

I got in my pickup and drove home. When I got there Nordi had already left for work. I cursed the imitation tough guy for absorbing those few moments I had with her each morning. I phoned Wanster's mill. Wanster answered. I explained that the oak logs were coming and not to put them in the pond as I had told him before.

"You telling me how to run my mill, Rice?"

"Okay, okay," I said, disgustedly. "I'll see you later."

When I reported to work next midnight I was met by seven impeccably attired guards. I was handed my paycheck and then they formed around me and I was escorted to the gate. In front of me their lieutenant stepped blithely forward. Farther back I too wended my way toward the gates. On each side of me three guards saw to it that I didn't lose my way, while behind me, further confining me, strode another bastion of law and order. I didn't know they had so many guards in the plant besides the big one that I made contact with in the morning, who was absent, probably indisposed. I hadn't known he had a tender throat, but even if I had, forbearance at that time was not mine to pass around. When they left me at the gate I advised the lieutenant if he and his crew ever lacked for work, I felt sure they could get it with any comic opera company that came to town.

So I was out of work, was I? Well, I was going to give myself a week arranging things for boat building. The first stack of lumber that we would use to build the shack and the boat shed arrived at Tomahawk Island on our lot. It was a week well spent. There was a carpenter on the island who, with Bunky and me, spent Sunday raising tall posts and the framework of the shed. There was enough of the shack and boatshed up by Monday so that I could finish them myself.

The keel timber came and the keelson and the timbers for the stem of the bow, but that was all. It did not worry me. I was busy looking for work and fitting out our cabin, which we called "the shack." It was soon almost liveable.

I received a notice from Swan Island shipyard that the swing shift superintendent on the outfitting docks wanted to see me. I went looking for Adolph Hannemann and came on him in his office shack. He was wiry, of slight build, and with sharp grey eyes. He looked wise and weary of the world. That was the look of Adolph Hannemann. He was arguing with several other men when I came into his office. I stepped over to his secretary. "I'm Rice," I said. "I understand that Mr. Hannemann wants to see me."

He heard and came over. "Yes," he said. "On account of the war they've got a dossier on everybody. Yours interested me. I just want to check with you on some of it. Is it true that you quit Oregon Ship three times because they didn't provide you with enough work?"

"That's so," I answered.

"One more then, Rice. Is it true that you choked a big guard who became abusive and that he was off work for three days?"

"Yes, I was tired and he went too far. Anyway the bastard swaggered."

"Well," he said, smiling broadly, "you're just what we're looking for. You know, you might be able to take the sag out of Hank Anderson's crew. Here, I'll give you a note to him."

And so I began working again at the hot end of an outfitting dock but this time on the swing shift. It worked out splendidly for Bunky and me. We bached together at Tomahawk Island.

The boatshed was now complete and our shack was warm and cozy, and my bunk with my son's over it were roomy and filled with fragrant oat hay covered by a canvas. It was primitive but we liked it that way. We were going to build a boat.

We of the the trial crew here had it much better than we did on the Liberty ships at Oregon Shipyard. We hovered over various electrically operated auxiliaries. Two men of Anderson's crew were loafers and Anderson allowed it, though he was about to lose his job because of it. Hannemann knew something was wrong and asked me to point out any malingerers.

"I'm no squealer, Hannemann," I said, "but you won't need a telescope to find them yourself."

"Them?" Hannemann inquired.

"Yes, two."

He questioned Anderson carefully and found that the dead-weights on the crew were his favorite cousin and his cousin's sidekick. Though it would make trouble in his family, he fired them.

I made a trip over to Oregon Ship and got Lendel to quit there and join me with Anderson and we soon became a pretty good crew.

For a week Bunky and I worked on the keel by day, shaping it and chiseling out the exact notches where the boat's ribs would join the keel, the backbone of the boat. We needed more lumber to set up the temporary forms on which to bend the long fore and aft timbers of the hull. I phoned to find out why the material was not forthcoming. Wanster would not come to the phone. Next day I drove out to his mill and asked him what was causing the delay.

"Why?" he yelled. "Why! Because you tricked me—that's why! You're out there building a boat! Silo—huh—my ass! And I'm against boats. No more lumber for you. You tricked me." He was right.

"But you didn't tell us you were bothered about boats," I said.

"Makes no difference," he answered, wrathfully.

"Still, you cashed the check," I countered.

"Yeah, and then I spent it," he agreed, "but for a good cause and you're out of luck 'cause you tricked me."

"We'll let that pass," I said, "temporarily. But where are my oak logs?"

"In the bottom of the pond, you fool, that's where they are."

"Well, get them out of your pond."

"Can't. The pond's shallow and right after I had them dumped in they sunk, like you said, but after your tricking me, I figure everything you say is lies. Anyway a load of big butt logs was trucked in and dumped on yours, drove yours down in the soft mud bottom. Can't even see them when the water clears over night. They're buried in there solid and what good are they anyway. I'm through with you and the likes of you."

Exasperated, though feeling a little guilty, I wanted to poke him, but that would bring his crew down on me and I wanted lumber cut from his tougher-than-usual Douglas fir.

"Look," I said, "you're getting noisy and noise is hard for me to take. You've talked, now let me talk. I'm not building this boat to sell or for my own use. We're building it for my boy. He doesn't want to sit behind a desk. He wants to make a career of fishing; and me, well, I want to be a writer, but I've got to see him settled on this boat first. He's my only son and I'm going to need special lumber from special trees so he'll have a good boat under him when he's out there. You've got what I need and I'm buying it from you for cash. I've heard you profess to be a Christian and I've done you a slight disservice that shames me. Well, a real Christian would turn the other cheek. Forgiveness is built into Christianity. As for boats—well, St. Peter was a fisherman, and though Christ occasionally walked on water, I believe he usually preferred to use a boat."

That got him. "Well, I am a Christian," said Wanster, "'a pillar of the church,' I've been called hereabouts. I suppose I could mend my ways as a deacon should."

"How about the oak logs?"

"Okay. I got a crane you never seen," Wanster answered. "I'll get them logs out after work tonight, 'cause I'm following *His* teaching. You do the same and we'll get along fine."

Driving back from the mill that day I thought of Nordi. I had worried about her constantly for the last several weeks. No matter what I was doing or what was happening, Nordi was in my mind. Now, driving along I tried a pet name I called her— "my own little Pee-ang." God! I must see her! I curved my route to the island to pass Acme Flavoring, but I was stopped in the office by the Little Lady.

"Yes, we employ her here," she enunciated coldly, "but we can't have our employees disturbed," she said, as she arose and walked me to the door. I laughed.

"May I ask what you find funny in this situation?" asked the Little Lady in the same affected tone.

Can't the woman ever be herself, I wondered, as I said, "I find an amusing similarity between your escorting me to the door and my being escorted to a gate by seven culls of your stripe last week."

She slammed the door, but Nordi opened it after her and came out in the street. "What is it, Clyde?"

"You," I said, hugging her. "You may not have known it but you've been with me all my waking hours and you're getting into my dreams, so I thought I'd better come over and see you, and I'll come out this weekend—Saturday or maybe Sunday. Bunky and I are kind of busy, Nordi, or I'd have been along sooner."

The following week we received a load of long clear vertical grain material, enough to completely plank the hull, and soon after, the extremely long heavy pieces that, when steamed and bent, would be the fore and aft members that with the keel would shape the boat. Over them the ribs would be bent, making the frame of the boat complete—ready for the planking, or so I explained to Virginia one Sunday a month later.

When I made the same explanation to Nordi, she said: "You make it sound too easy."

Nordi had gone over the boat plans with a fine-tooth comb while I was in Alaska.

"You and Bunky have taken on a complex assembly. How about the shaft log, the horn timber, the stem and keel assembly, deck beams and stern post?"

"Sure," I said, "but I'm talking about the main features of the hull."

"And that's the mistake of simplifying. The simple conception is fine for the classroom or in games, but not in living or in constructions other than those of the classroom."

"Okay, darling, you're right. But if I bother Bunky about butt blocks and calking angles and a hundred other angles, well, it would cool his enthusiasm." Nordi agreed with me.

•

Hank Anderson came to me one night as I was cleaning a reducing valve, "Clyde," he said, "seems no one around here likes extra jobs unless they're paid extra. Now I can't pay extra, but will you take on some extra stuff besides what you're doing?"

"I'm bored with what I'm doing," I answered, "even though I know it has to be done this way. Sure. What's on your mind?"

He grinned, "It's the stern gland, you know, where the main shaft goes through the stern to the propellor on its outer end. The bearing that holds all that weight is made of hardwood lignum vitae blocks, water lubricated, but we stop the water from coming into the ship around the shaft with a stuffing gland of many wraps around the shaft of a thick flax rope saturated with oil and lard and a retainer. It works. I want you to take charge of it, yeah, and the reducing valves. In fact, I will relieve you of your other duties. How about it?"

"Swell," I said, "it's a deal."

I found the introduction of the flax packing had been negligently done. Welding slag had been allowed to cling to the greasy flax, scratching the polished steel surface of the shaft. I cleaned the whole area around as best I could, then covered the deck and the equipment about with butcher paper before I would lay the packing on the inboard part of the shaft. Adolph was pleased when he saw the mistakes I corrected. I worked with an air hammer, the business end of which was an oaken mallet that would not damage the perfection of the shaft in the gland area.

•

I was visiting Nordi as I had promised. "An empty house sounds like an empty house, Clyde. This boat business is training me for living alone. I don't like it, but for Bunky's sake I accept. I feel this war will never stop until it grabs Bunky."

"Maybe it'll be over soon," I said. "Patton is approaching Berlin, and the Japanese posture has sure changed."

"I'm glad they didn't take you, Clyde, but there's times, living here alone, when I hate you as much as I love you. Damn you and your sweetie. Oh, don't misunderstand me, I love her too. Sometimes I almost wish you were lying shattered far away on some battlefield. Oh, let's go to bed again. I'm sated, I mean, my body is, but I still need your touch—not of your hands, I mean the touch of lying close beside you."

•

On Tomahawk, Bunky and I spent the next couple of mornings piling the lumber that continued to arrive in small loads. There was planking and decking and lumber to sheathe the boat inside and there were timbers from which we could hew out the slightly curved deck beams. We were stacking the narrow strakes of our decking, when, easing a tired back by standing, I saw a man approaching. He seemed a bit stooped and round-shouldered and as he came near, the expression on his face was as if he was tolerating bad news recently received.

"Hello," I said, "fine morning. My name's Rice."

"I'm Bill Nagel, fisherman and boatbuilder. Say, can I be of any help to you, not that I'm so much, but maybe I can show you an angle or two?"

What luck, I thought. "We are stacking our stuff here. Have you an angle on stacking?" I asked. He had. He showed us how to put lathes between the layers of boards to let air to each piece as it seasoned. He was full of these angles, as he called them, the result of an inquiring mind and wide experiences. In his unassuming way he eventually helped most everyone on the island. When I brought our old privy with the half moon carved in the door over to the island and placed it so all could use it, it pleased him and he proceeded to offer me his bandsaw to use until our boat was complete. With Nagel, Bunky and I wandered among the other boatbuilders and, under his aegis, got acquainted with them. There were seven of them besides us. We were, to a man, shipyard workers, but we were also a fiercely individualistic scattering. Four were rather oddball, including me. One was a little squirrely, and one called Mel, who addressed everyone as Bo as if this was a hobo jungle, became my friend. The boats being built ranged from thirty feet to a fifty-five-footer. Our own plans were for a forty-six-footer.

We were settling in to the new way of things. Nordi, of course, took the brunt of it. Bunky slipped away at least once a week to his tugboat friends with whom he had spent so much of his time when we thought he was safe in school. Later, I learned there was a girl in this, his secret life, but that was all I ever found out about it. He worked vigorously with me on our project and, strange, though knowing of Virginia's place in my life, he was without comment.

We received a note from Wanster telling us that he had sawed one oak log, the smallest one, he said, and would wait until we came to the mill before he sawed more of them. Bunky and I talked the sawing over and drew possible ways—diagrams—for in rib wood slab grain is needed, the opposite of the grain best for planking and decking. Well, we devised a sawing we felt would get the most slab grain ribs and next morning brought our diagram to Wanster and his sawyer.

We spoke of it to Nagel first. "I don't know," he remarked, "but how are you greenhorns going to make a professional sawyer see it your way?"

"We'll go easy on his dignity," I said to Bunky as we parked by the mill. Wanster brought us to where that great man, the sawyer, stood near his monstrous whispering bandsaw. I explained to him that we were asking him to saw out ribs that, after they were planed, would be three inches square and clear of sapwood. And I said they were to be steamed and bent, and that slab grain was the best for that. We showed him our diagram. He looked and then laughed, but in a way that included us. "It's the pattern I use," he said, "unless I'm whacking up inferior timber. This is going to be duck soup. Four cuts to remove the sapwood then slice it up in the size you want and throw away the heart-wood. How many you want?"

"Eighty pieces," I answered. "Some of the ribs will be broken in the bending." I gave him a list of the sizes of the stern timber, the horn timber, the shaft log and the engine bed. Going back to the island, Bunky said, "Pop, you win by anticlimax. You're always getting ready for trouble that, when it comes, is so small that it makes you look silly. I'd have said we want eighty three-inch squares, no sapwood."

"You're right but, Bunky, I've been caught too many times with my pants down."

Next day when the frames arrived (ribs I always say for I see the anatomy of a boat better that way) we realized that we had enough material on hand to start building. I went to a ship chandler in Portland and purchased some kegs of square cut nails, and bolts and rods. Coming back with them, looking around, I saw that it was late fall.

I took Ginny out to lunch soon after—so near and yet so far—we both felt that. The following day I took her for a drive on her noon hour. We stopped to admire the last of the bright autumn leaves and we clung for awhile wordlessly. Ginny was penitent but said our love had shown her how relating enriched people. She was trying to come closer to her parents, but that they drew back from the tiniest gesture of affection, perhaps because her mother felt Virginia had learned of caring from me. She spoke of me always as "that viper." Ginny admitted that she would like me to come to the yungrubarn some night but not yet.

"You're busy, awfully busy," she said. "You haven't time to spend on me and love. Daddy said you've bought yourself an impossible setup. Goodbye, Clyde. Kiss Nordi for me but don't tell her where it comes from."

Bunky and I decided we would start building the boat in earnest on November tenth, only a few days away. Bunky wanted to go home and do some fall chores for Nordi.

"I'll be away for four days, Pop. Don't start the work on the boat till I get back." I agreed.

"You know I think I'll make the steambox," I ruminated.

"Why don't you coast for a few days?" wondered Bunky.

"Beat it," I said.

I had the planks for the steambox of an inferior grade of lumber. I would make a very narrow box thirty-five feet long. It was easy to make. I supported it chest-high with a door at each end and a hole in the middle where I could ram a heavy hose in, then I laid an old oil drum over a pit for a fire, ran a hose over from the drum to the hole in the steambox, first filling the drum with water, and I was set. I put a twelve-foot oak frame in the box and built a fire in the pit. An hour later I drew the oak frame from the box. I held the middle of the frame waist-high and both ends drooped to the ground, but only for a minute, then it became stiff as before.

During the recent luncheon with Ginny I tried to answer some of her questions about boats. "They're so graceful the way they curve. Why are they curved?"

"For a number of reasons," I replied. "One is that the sea has tremendous power when it hits a large flat surface, but a curved surface can accept much more wave force and there's very few places on a boat that are not curved in some way."

"But how can you bend the boards? Won't they break?"

"Steam bending is the way, but you must move fast when the board or whatever comes out of the steambox. You have only sixty seconds." And so on.

Hank Anderson came apologetically to me on the job. "Clyde," he said, "I don't have to worry about the reducing valves anymore. You kept them in tip-top shape on the last ship and this one too. I've got a job now that no one who's not deaf can handle. My deaf man quit last night—back to Kansas—and it's a job that's got to be done—a federal requirement. You can say no, man!"

He led me into a narrow complete cross section of the ship, at the bottom of which were five electrically operated transfer pumps that handled the cargo of oil in the ship's many tanks, but for tests they pumped only water. They crouched down there, those pumps, sullen and incredibly powerful. All five could, by manipulating great valves, pump into a large pipe discharging overboard and the flow could be altered or stopped by another immense valve. On the test, after all pumps were putting out through this discharge, I'd constrict the flow putting a strain on the pumps for an eight-hour test run. Fine, the trouble was that the constricting valve screamed—shrieked is a better word.

I once started the test while painters were finishing there. They ran out like panicked sheep, and I found that they went without their lunches rather than reenter to get their lunch-boxes.

After eight hours of harrowing shrillness I was more worn—frazzled as it were—than I'd be from cutting down a large second-growth fir with a dull axe. Also I'd taken on the testing of the tanks of this tanker and others that followed. The rest of the crew clung to their simple duties and I should have done this too but there was a war on out there. I hate war, but I hated even more seeing that it was killing some of my friends and neighbors and that chief engineer on the *Samuel Decker*. For him alone, with his steady regard of things as they are, I must work harder at what was called the "war effort."

On the island, Bunky and I had earlier on chiseled the rib notches in the keel protected by three smoke smudges. It had been a damp summer and waves of mosquitoes swarmed outside of the smoke, humming furiously at being thwarted from their vampire feasts, but fall was kind, ridding us of these pests and chilling us if we didn't keep busy. We turned the keel right side up and erected the stem on it, tapering the stem to split the sea, and backed it with a large oak knee, the three bolted together in the approved fashion. Then we turned to the stern, bolted in a big filler block (deadwood they were called) and then the shaft log and stern post, all in massive oak. We were lucky to do this work under the critical eyes of Bill Nagel.

We made our own bolts from galvanized rod procured in twenty-foot lengths, threading them ourselves for the nuts and tightening it all down to a rugged mass that looked like it had grown together. Mel approved of this, but he felt that the half-inch electric drill we bought was an extravagance. He on his boat was drilling all of the holes with a hand drill. One day he challenged me to a race—I with the electric drill and he by hand—and he was able to come out slightly ahead of me.

"I tell you why, Bo," he growled in his slow bass voice, "I got the know-how and the muscle." It was true. He was small and wiry and still very muscular.

We now made the temporary forms for bending the long narrow timbers that ran the length of the boat and shaped it. The forms took a week for I was uncertain in this, but Nagel set me right on it. That weekend we steamed the long members of the boat and with Mel's help rushed them from the steambox and bent them around the forms.

Bunky had brought word from Nordi that my father wanted to see me within the month. Nordi said that he was having trouble with the vanilla percolator. She appeared, almost an apparition to me, and as always so pert, reminding me of a small bird—a thrush.

"Good morning to you two," she smiled. "Your Pop drove me over, then he drove back across the bridge and is waiting over there. Says he doesn't like this damn island."

By then I'd extracted myself from the various braces and had her in my arms and Bunky was prying them away from her, so he might embrace her as exuberantly, for he was proud of our shack and boatshed and beginnings of the boat. With due ceremony we showed her into our shack. She glanced around.

"You've kept it clean; I was worried about that. Everything in and out of your establishment is orderly," she smiled puckishly, and said: "I guess I'm willing to pay for your arrangement here by living alone like an old spinster."

The coffee was hot though a little bit old. She had some with us, making faces of imitation distress. "Bunky," she said, "I want you to go over and visit with your grandfather. You haven't seen him for some time and he mentioned he'd like to see what you've grown into."

When he was gone, she turned to me and her kindness filled the shack. "Clyde," she said, "what are you going to do about our problem? I know you well enough to know that, after your mistake, you've been rearing back, the soul of rectitude—but with two ladies? I know why you can't make a choice between us—because of the harm you'd do the one not chosen. So you can't allow yourself to follow your secret heart, but you've got to, dear, you must. I'm afraid this will end in your having to make an honest woman of Virginia. I almost approve, even though that would mean my divorcing you. Well, we'll solve it somehow, honey." A horror came over me. "I've got to go," she continued. "I can't keep your Dad waiting any longer." We were out in the boatshed. "You know, all that you've done here makes me very proud of my boys." We embraced and she scurried away with that hurried little scamper of hers.

At the shipyards later I hungered for a job complex enough to involve me completely. There were none that shift needing my small abilities. With the others I monitored the auxiliaries, but guilt and sorrow possessed me.

The following day I repaired my father's percolator. When it was finished he glanced coldly at me and handed me fifty cents. "We don't require more of your time," he said and opened the door for me. I closed it and found Nordi and hugged and kissed her and then left.

Saturday Bunky left for his tugboat friends and I took the bus home and spent the day with Nordi. It snowed intermittently and thawed almost as fast as it piled up. Nordi baked some sweet-dough scones and served an omelet filled with several things, including grated peanuts. Like most of her experiments it was a great success. We relaxed before the fire and got out some of her old drawings and paintings and it seemed we were back in Tiburon. In the evening as I stepped out in the slush to leave Nordi pulled me back. "Stay," she urged, her hands on my arm, "it's a night to cuddle through if one can, and we can."

Bunky phoned me at home the next morning saying that he was going to help his friends move a short tow of logs down to St. Helens, so he wouldn't see me until Monday afternoon at the shipyards. After a sumptuous breakfast Nordi sent me back to Tomahawk with kisses and vegetables from her garden.

I began to shape the heavy oak members of the deadwood of the stern with broadaxe and adze. Our minds work in strange ways. As I hewed at the oak, my mind concerned itself with a novel—I think one of Lloyd Douglas's—which had been a popular book some years before. The title of it escapes me, in fact the gist of the story didn't enter my mind. I was musing about part of it now as I adzed, refining the work of the broadaxe, and then I was feeling the fury I had felt about one of the incidents in it. The main character had been discovered by his wife as having a mistress. The young girl and the man had been close for a number of years and were deeply in love, though the man loved his wife too. The wife was a fine person, highly thought of in the community in which they moved. The man's decision to abandon the helpless girl was, I felt, callous—more damaging than if he'd left his wife. I was disgusted with him. The girl needed his support in every way. His wife was bolstered by their home and her grown children and her status in the community. She was quite sophisticated and probably would be able to remarry well. I swore back then, slamming the book down, muttering that I could never do such a thing. Now it all came back to me, though until this moment it had been unrelated to my life. I still had the adze handle in my hands but no crumbling chips were flying from its blade.

"No," I said in anger, "not to Ginny! No! We'll protect her—

we? We! Who is we? My God!" Consternation overwhelmed me.

I thought in words. I heard the words clearly as I thought them. I can't ask Nordi to be part of me in this, to destroy her marriage, deliver her husband to a mere girl. God no, I'm no paragon of a man. Why don't they get Ginny a better fellow to consort with, force me aside, the damn shipyard worker always stumbling around the bottom of the ladder. I dropped it. Which one, I wondered covertly, can handle the hurt with less damage to herself? Nordi is stronger! What am I thinking? Christ! Get on with your chopping, you bastard. Hew oak, don't pick on Nordi.

I chopped at the deadwood on the other side, too scared to think, too lily-livered to make this cruel decision. Remember the book. Let it be my guide! Ginny is timid, so shy she needs me. In me she has a way to face the world, for she is loved. Nordi is not only loved by me, there is Art who has adored her for years. I know she had two other lovers when we were without resource. How she must have despised me in those years. Anyway, I believe she understands the world of men.

All right, I said to myself, dutiful to whatever sense I found in this preamble, I'll ask her to divorce me.

I went to work later and luckily I had to stay with the pumps on the pump test. As the painful hours passed and the scream of the valve entered my very being, I exulted in it.

"Yeah," I said to the vibrating walls. "Whatever is coming, God knows, I'VE GOT IT COMING!"

•

Bunky and I worked on the stem next morning. I was sick with knowledge of the damnable decision I'd made. Bunky, above me working away with his chisel, asked, "What are you muttering about, Pop?"

"Nothing," I responded. "Say, how's the blade of your chisel? I'm going to sharpen mine right now."

"Still good, Pop. I'm cutting to the line like you told me. When we get this shaped, are we going to start bending ribs?"

"Not yet," I answered. "We've got to build a long vat so we can put the ribs to soak in this new wood preservative that the inventor sent a bag of—pentachlorophenol, it's called. I'll dump the ribs into a mixture of it and fifty gallons of paint thinner and after they've soaked overnight, we'll steam them for bending."

"Boy, that steam will force the stuff right into the wood, I bet. No rot in this boat!

"Pop, it's getting too cold to work on the boat. Yesterday it snowed and my hands are freezing now. Bill Nagel says we can't get much done for the rest of the winter. Everybody else around here is just sitting tight."

"Well, warm your hands by the fire in the shack. We'll try to push on through these colder months. There'll be some mild days. There is usually."

The next time I saw Ginny I asked her if she had done any thinking about our situation.

"Not really," she answered. "Looking back to last year, Clyde, and the year before, I saw I was often, well, blue for Nordi's sake. Still, all and all, I was happy most of the time. You claimed me some way back there when I was a kid. I saw that I'm yours all right! Anyway I haven't looked ahead much either, but you taught me to when you said that someday you'd marry me. That made me look into a future that I'm afraid I can't have."

I was stricken still. I didn't want to say it, but I did. "Ginny," I said, "I'm going to ask Nordi for a divorce." At that we both looked down at the floor saying nothing.

Finally, Ginny suggested that perhaps Nordi's hurt would be lessened and our consciences salved if we agreed that, after two years, we would separate and I would go back to Nordi.

The idea seemed vulgar to me, but we were now far beyond such conceptions and, after a time of consideration, I came around to thinking maybe that was the way to handle it.

It was Saturday. Bunky was away with friends. Bill Nagel appeared at our shack bringing a great steak from a sturgeon he'd caught and news. Bunky had told him he wanted to join the Merchant Marine before his eighteenth birthday.

Bill said, "He wants to avoid a three year stint in the army that would mess up your plans of fishing the boat when it's completed. There's a friend of his on a tug whose going to apply for a K.P. job in the Merchant Marine and Bunky wants to join with him. He asked me if I would break the bad news to you. He hates letting you down on the boat building."

I was ashamed. I'd been so busy stewing about my own problems that I wasn't aware of his approaching birthday and its significance. "What do you think of it?" I asked Bill.

"I think he's right. In a month he'll be eighteen and he'll be taken out of your hands either by the military or by the Merchant Marine. In between trips in the Merchant Marine he could give you quite a boost on your boat construction."

"I'll speak to his mother about it."

"He already has," Bill said. "It'll put a big dent in your timetable on this boat, but it can't be helped."

When I got to Swan, I called Nordi. Yes, she said, she was aware of Bunky's upcoming birthday, had been worrying about it for the last year. His decision was obviously the right one. With the war over, three years in the navy or army would be ridiculous and ruin our plans for his future.

"Pop," he said as we drove home from work that night, "I told Bill to let you down easy. It's going to play hob with the boat. But, Pop, why didn't you figure these possibilities into your long range plan?"

"I thought the war would be over much sooner," I said. "Hitler held out two years longer than I thought he could, and Japan—! Well, there I was just plain ignorant. I thought Japan had bit off more than it could chew in Manchuria. What were your guesses about your near future, Bunky?"

"I don't do that, Pop. One day at a time is enough for me. You got me looking ahead a bit on the boat, but I only halfway believed it until you rigged that steambox, then somehow I knew this boat will be launched 'come hell or high water,' as Nagel puts it. He believes you'll carry it to completion, but Nagel says only one out of six small ventures of this kind survive. Did you know that, Pop?"

"Yes, I did, Bunky."

"Then why did you go out on a limb on this?"

"Careless of me, I admit."

"Nagel wouldn't, I'll bet."

"Oh, I don't know. Nagel's just another guy. We all make mistakes."

"Not the kind of mistakes you make. Nagel's only got one woman."

"I see."

"So do I, Pop."

"You got any more points to make?"

"No, not really."

"Okay."

We drove in silence the rest of the way to our bailiwick. There, adding chips to paper and a lot of kindling, we soon had the stove roaring. Then I thought to ask: "Say, how much time do you have before your ship leaves?"

"I've got three more days to get some ribs on the boat."

In those three days we bent seven ribs in on both sides. We worked from the bow back where the bend was slight. We put the more perfect stock to one side for the midship belly of the boat where the curve from the bottom to the side made the most abrupt bend and where we expected the most breakage.

Too quickly the day came when Bunky's ship would plow down the river to the sea. Out at the farm he declined our offer to to drive him into town, seemingly anxious to be off on his own. Cheerfully he bid us goodbye and boarded the bus waving from the window to us at the side of the highway.

He was gone and Nordi turned to me and smiled at the tears in my eyes. "Clyde," she said, as we walked back down the driveway, "our boat on Tomahawk Island has already initiated me into being a solitary creature." And abruptly, "Clyde, have you got your message for me. I've known it was coming ever since the night you inadvertently confessed your love for Virginia. You said 'two years,' and I knew."

We entered the house. She motioned me to a chair. With her voice serious and steady, she began again: "They talk about the mid-life crisis, all manner of excuses and incriminations. Oh, it happens all the time. I'm like most women, instinctively wanting to hold things as they are, but I know how you men are driven to range and to impregnate one more woman and that she must, by nature's selection, express the current foibles and the best physical characteristics of the race. Let me put it another way, Clyde. Men must seek for other qualities in other women, and also must find what is across the sea and over the hill. You men are made that way.

"As you see, I've been doing a lot of thinking, trying to understand what my place is in this. Well, searching doesn't heal the hurt. The wife is the loser, but the man in his secret heart may eventually suffer more. The cure for this is polygamy, but that would destroy a certain delicacy in our relationships that we cherish." She turned from her philosophizing, "Now, Mr. Rice, speak your piece."

I nodded. "It seems neither one of us can have a speculation but it reverberates in the other's consciousness." I went on, "I came over today to see Bunky off and to ask you for a divorce so that I can marry Virginia. Ginny and I have decided that after two years we will separate and, if you want me, I'll come back to you."

We sat there silently. I had just struck the lowest point in my life. "I'll get it for you at once," she said finally. "Clyde, I'm getting very angry in spite of myself. You had better go! But remember you're always welcome wherever I am. Now go! Get out, you miserable, miserable man!"

Dumbly, I plodded out through a drenching rain. I was in the pickup starting the engine. Thought came! With what was left of me I thrust it aside and drove away numbly aware of the streets and roads that led to the shack on Tomahawk Island.

Next morning, sick at heart, I nevertheless shoved six boat

ribs into the steambox filled the drum with water and built a fire under it before I started a fire in the shack for my breakfast. I had drilled a small hole in the ends of all the ribs where they would fit into their notch in the keel and, before I put them into the steambox, I drove spikes into the holes. So I had only to hurry the rib up into a loop of a rope to steady it, and then forcing the lower end into the keel notch, drive home the spike. I was free then to pull on the rope and bend the limber rib to conform to the shape of the boat. I got three ribs in that way and now I broke two ribs, for they stiffened before I could get all my arrangements for controlling them placed just right, which included a temporary narrow steel band fitted on the outside of the rib.

The broken ribs showed me I would have to get a helper and be much more careful or I would run out of oak. I approached Hank Anderson, my leadman, at the shipyards. To my tale of woe he said he would have to come over and see. He did and tied into the job in a manner that brought a smile through my glumness.

Hank pointed out, "You get another fellow to work with us and we could get this done in a couple of days."

I got Ernest, the Little Lady's brother, to pull on the rope, clamped on the temporary steel bands before steaming and three days later we were through steambending ribs, losing only two more. Hank turned out to be a wonderful worker, as jolly as I had become grim, and eager to work on the boat.

In the winter the boatshed without sides offered little protection from the rain that was brought in when the west and southwest winds blew. Wind from the east blowing down the Columbia River thickened the ice on the puddles and skiffs of sleet hurtled horizontally under the high, broad roof. Then work slowed almost to a standstill, for I was forever slipping into the shack to warm myself before the stove. I knew the shack as a haven from more than just the winter weather. Guilt ridden, I would have sulked there if I could afford the time but the shipyards and the borning boat took all I had and a little bit more.

One day Adolph told me that I looked gaunted. Chip on my

shoulder, I asked him if he was satisfied with my work. "Can't kick," he replied, "but you wear a sour face and I think your muscles and your patience are strung out. You ought to eat and sleep more."

Christmas came. Bunky came home from Coos Bay where his ship was waiting for a cargo of lumber. He spent the time with his mother and her family, Ginny with hers, and I thoroughly enjoyed the awkward bolting in of the floors.

It was now time for me to start working on a curved part of the stern often called the horseshoe. I had Wanster saw seven heavy timbers. They were, however, from green freshly-downed fir trees. They would shrink as they dried out and, in the manner that this type of stern is made, there must be no shrinkage. What to do?

One night after my swing shift duties I was hunched over the stove in the shack trying to get warm, my mind messed up with my darlings and the slow but sure decline of my bank account, and how I could possibly bend in the first plank, down next to the keel, the garboard strake. And the idea came to me to clear my mind of all this slurry and think just one thing, perhaps something from out of the past. My lips whispered, "Miss Crippen." I had never called her Ethel, just Miss Crippen. In San Francisco she had been my father's bookkeeper and a friend of mine and finally sex partner. For several months our relationship was fiery indeed, though we never spoke of love. She was at least ten years older than I and knew that I was happily married. We parted the best of friends and, as the years went by, I forgot her, except that every so often the words, "Miss Crippen," would come into my mind and then her favorite perfume and the faint musk of her arousal would be in my nostrils and a frantic and grieving nostalgia would shake me before the present with its thousand compromises would take over again.

"No," I said out loud, "No!" And then between the thoughts of Miss Crippen came the answer I was seeking, for I saw a simple way out of my horseshoe timber dilemma. I drank my last cup of coffee and went to sleep as lightly as though I had never caused harm to anyone.

In the morning I borrowed a long trailer from another boatbuilder and took my green timbers to where I remembered the county kept its store of timbers for small county road bridges. I hunted up the bridge crew foreman and told him of my need for seasoned timber and why. He came, saw that my timbers were of good stock.

"Why shore," he grinned. "Glad to hep you. It'll only set you back two fifths of bourbon. Make that Grandad."

He even helped me load them. That handled that. Soon I unloaded at Tomahawk with time enough to mark out the curved sections of the horseshoe's pieces—six strakes of them—wow!

While I was chalking out the big awkward sections Mel came visiting. After watching me for several minutes he rumbled, "How about me helping you on this, Bo?" and added, "no filthy lucre required." He snickered over this. I agreed and told him that I hoped to do some of the job with Nagel's small bandsaw that I had set up under cover. Mel brought over a sharp two-man crosscut saw. We cut out the three pieces and were able to run them through the bandsaw following the curved lines by carefully taking the weight off the table onto our hands and watching the blade cutting along the chalk line while keeping an eye on each other as we manipulated it. We cut up two of the timbers in this manner without mishap. By then I had to leave for the shipyard, but not before Mel said he would see me through on the sawing tomorrow.

"Pay me back in stuff later on," he said and I did before I left the island, most adequately.

For two weeks I spent my mornings chopping with the adze and axe on that horseshoe stack of timbers, bolting, refining, beveling until one day I was through with it. Mel helped me the first two days. From then on it was hewing with a broadaxe that only one man could do at a time.

As I mentioned before, now in the shipyards I had the oil tanks of the tankers, a line of work that I gradually cut out for myself and I had two helpers. Then one quit—Kentucky beckoned. The other was a drunk who kept his bottle near at hand. One night there was a test run and he hid out and those in the engine room were sharing a bottle or two and weren't paying much attention. You were supposed to spin the big wheels on deck which operated the valves down in the tanks and for leverage in turning them jam a four-foot club in the wheel, but I hadn't time for that. I tugged at those wheels until I thought my deltoids would melt. I shut off seventeen valves before I quit. I couldn't make another move. I was doing what two men would find hard to do. Finally a tank on the side near the wharf filled up and spouted a great stream of water fourteen inches across and twenty feet high.

Adolph rushed over. "What can I do for you, Rice?" he asked. It was obvious that he should get news to the engineers that the tanks were full, the ship low in the water.

I looked at him standing there so concerned but useless and suggested that colored lanterns would make a gala scene of this fountain! He hurried away then to tell the engine room to slack off. After that I had two sober helpers on deck for the tank test.

On Tomahawk I was ready to start planking the boat. Bunky came home for a two-week stay from San Pedro where his ship was docked. We had heard of old Ole Lind who, they said, could plank a boat with only a broadaxe if necessary. His charge was two dollars an hour and one for his young grandson who helped him a bit. I was glad to get him for I was plenty leery of the garboard strake that lays along the keel. It is the widest plank in the boat.

He came—a broad, short, squeaky-voiced Norwegian. He shaped the planks, one for each side of the keel. We steamed them, then with many of the other boatbuilders looking on, old Ole and his grandson tied into that long, wide important plank. He squeaked orders to Hank and Bunky and me over his shoulder as he warped and twisted and finally spiked the garboard strake to the rib ends down there jammed against the keel. We repeated the process on the starboard side and, though he used us four helpers and a lot of clamps and props to accomplish this feat it was still quite a display of Ole's famed ability to brutalize a plank.

At the after end of the boat far below the horseshoe of the stern, where the tapering in from the swell of the midship ends, is the arrangement of oaken members—the stern post, shaft log and under it the deadwood. Through the stern post and shaft log there is a hole two inches in diameter to accommodate the propellor shaft. This hole is usually produced by making up the stern post and shaft log in halves, then gouging it out in each their share of the hole in careful alignment to the angle of the engine. After this the halves are bolted together and presto— well, sort of presto—you would have it.

I felt this was inherently weak and decided to drill right through the four feet of oak and have a stronger, simpler setup. Alas, I didn't do this when circumstances would lend themselves to the job, I was too involved with the rest of the building. Nagel and Mel saw the danger after all ribs were in and the garboard strake in place, for I'd have to be right in drilling that hole or I might as well use the rest of the boat for kindling because, if I drilled off center in any way, I couldn't correct it. It was an engineering problem and I'm not even a mechanic, and Nagel didn't want to have anything to do with it, feeling it was now too late to correct my oversight. Gee whiz! I'd have to fall back on what ingenuity I could lay claim to.

So first I established from the blueprints where the hole should come out of the stern post, high enough so that the propellor could swing clear of the keel that projects a bit there for the lower rudder bearing. On the forward bulkhead of the engine room space at a point shown on the blueprint I placed a tack dead center. Then with kite strings, sticks, tacks, small boards, even drops of water from above, and a series of home- made devices, I went to work. Eventually my yokel summations became verities in my mind and I bought a two-inch auger of the barefoot variety, famous among those in the know as not deflecting from a knot or whatever. I had a six-foot shaft welded to it by an expert machinist, rented a one-horse drill motor and was in business. I set it up with some boards to guide it and commenced, feeling certain in my calculations. I drilled in about five inches, then brought the drill out and cleaned the chips away, and again and again. After a very vigorous hour and a half, wrestling with that powerful drill, it broke through and the shaft hole was complete.

I did not look through the hole. I put careful crosshairs in both ends, then sighted through at the tack on the bulkhead. The crosshairs zeroed in on the tack perfectly. I had won. I let out a warwhoop and began dancing under the stern of our boat and the other boat builders who had somehow sweated it out with me came running to pound my back.

After that, Bunky and I did the rest of the planking ourselves. Each long boat plank had to be tapered, for at the bow where it begins it must be narrow but where it lays on the ribs midship it must be the widest and taper again toward the stern. This is because a boat's greatest girth is amidship. So each long plank, being narrow at the ends and full at midship is a curved thing, rather cigar-shaped and, when these cigar shapes are fitted to the curve of the boat, a marvel comes about. They fit close together needing only caulking and paint to face the onslaught of the sea. There's a book on planking a boat called *Laying Down and Taking Off* (sounds erotic but it's not). Bunky and I studied it, then had at it with the endlessly tapering pieces. With the bandsaw we removed the surplus and with hand plane brought them toward perfection ready for steaming. After that we would get the piece in with clamps to hold it in place, then starting at the bow we would pin it tightly to the ribs. Often they creaked and groaned at the stress put on them but seldom broke. Bunky was excellent at this. He would fight a plank in place, drilling and counter-sinking for the square-cut nails that held the plank to the oak ribs. When he had to go back to his ship he left quite a hole in the proceedings. But I continued the planking, planing away,

moving up and down the long plank sighting in, planing, measuring, standing almost up to my knees in the rich scented
shavings that came from the tool like the curls of some fair-
haired girl. There was the grand feeling of forcing the plane
along the edge of the plank to carve away that tiny, thin ribbon
redolent with the fragrance of fir. How I exulted in the days as we
planked the boat, guilt driven far away like a small vaporous
cloud disappearing in the sky.

.

While I was working so, I was often visited by knowing men well
past their prime who gave me pointers on how to draw the planks
tight against each other. Finally I learned that they were caulkers
and were looking our boat over for a caulking job—tarred oakum
driven into the seams in a very special way. We planned to do it
ourselves. Nagel said he'd done his own boat and had a bad time
with it and wanted no more caulking the rest of his life.

On his next leave Bunky saw I could not finish the boat by
myself without a great delay in our timetable. When I introduced
Hank to him and when he saw Hank's enthusiasm for the boat
and the way he went about things, he went to see his mother. He
came back saying that we should bring Hank into it some way, as
a partner perhaps, if it worked out that way.

Then one day the mailman brought me the divorce papers.
Now I was free to marry Virginia, and I knew the price was too
great, not only for me but most for Nordi. I went home to talk to
Nordi but she was adamant. I'd asked for it. I got it, she said. She
closed the door on me.

I had not seen or communicated with Virginia for weeks—
gross conduct indeed, but I was unable to celebrate Nordi's loss.
Still, by not calling, I was adding to the insecurity Virginia must
feel. I took her to lunch and afterward told her of the divorce. I
had the paper with me but she would not look at it. She wept
bitterly, loving Nordi as she did.

"Because of Nordi's hurt, how can we ever be happy?" she

mourned. "Can other people who do this ever be free in their hearts again, Clyde?" As she got out of the car, she did not meet my eyes. Tearfully she said, "Don't come around for a long time, Clyde."

"Do you still love me?" I asked.

She raised her eyes and looked long at me. At last she turned her gaze away, was still and then said, "Yes," but quietly. The word was poised in space. It seemed bereft of meaning, but it was an acknowledgement. To me it was a fact—a definite, irrefutable fact.

I watched her as, after turning away, she joined the pedestrian parade, watched until she disappeared in it. My eyes didn't remark her comeliness. No! As she disappeared another weight seemed lifted from my shoulders. Not only that but I was able to slip off the harness of guilt for awhile.

Time to head for the shipyard? Hell no! Instead I drove out to the stump ranch. I looked around. How drear. Did I ever slave here, I wondered. It was hard to remember but, yes, you did, memory said, and you lost it, Mister, you lost it! Yeah, I remembered. I lose everything as I go along. Quit talking to yourself, fella. Come on. Let's have a song! Okay, I said, we'll sing awhile. (Sung very slowly):

> "Last night when the mockingbird woke me,
> Last night when all was still,
> I stood in the silvery moonlight
> From out the windowsill.
> I opened the window so gently,
> I looked on the dreaming dew
> And oh! oh my heart that b–i–r–d was
> S–I–N–G–I–N–G
> Singing of you–ou, of you."

Oh, the melody of it! My throat ached with love, not for Nordi or Virginia, or even Miss Crippen, but part for my mother and part for the lovely girls who pass me in the street.

I came back by way of Estacada. It was dark when I stopped at

Carver to be near the place once again. Nordi wouldn't be home for an hour or so. I didn't go in the house. This homestead was Nordi's now. So be it! I had bought that. Still, I loved our little farm, always would, and I knew it. I once more fondly stared through the dark at my old home, then hurried away, for I had been trespassing.

On the island I spent the evening with Mel. Mel was a veteran of the first World War. The wounds he received, while serving his country, were psychic instead of physical. A year in the mud of the trenches with death and explosions all around him had altered his view of things and still colored his existence. Before the war his life had been sheltered. He was in his second year of college when he enlisted. He came out of it, a man who saw only the larger aspects of things. He saw the framework, not the foolishness or splendor we drape upon it.

"The human race is a bunch of bums," he would say at every opportunity, "and most of us are worse than that—we're frauds— and worse than that, we don't know it."

He left the war vowing to never do an honest hour of work for any man. By various small and devious ways he had survived. He ended up teaching welding that he knew very little about in a shipyard school and he dropped that, after he had stolen enough small steel blocks to ballast his upcoming boat. Several tons of metal blocks he carried out sequestered in special pockets he had sewn into his coat. The absurdity of it never entered his mind.

·

That stale, indefinite time, the last of winter, was upon us, but there was so much to do I hardly noticed it. Nordi would not see me at Acme and let it be known that I was not welcome out home. And Hank, who had been helping me, took leave of the shipyards to go back to Minnesota for two weeks. Then on a Saturday evening Virginia knocked at my door and when I opened it, just stood there saying nothing. I pulled her in, closed the door and, holding her, began kissing her. She put her finger to her lips signifying silence. I obeyed. I took off her hat and rumpled her hair. It was warm in the shack. I was helping her out of her coat, when she drew it back on and went out in the dark again, returning with her weekend bag which she put beside the bunk. Again I took her coat and seated her on my best box. She still signified silence. I made fresh coffee for her and warmed up my famous mulligan.

After we had eaten wordlessly she stepped to my bunk, then still indicating silence, she started to remove her clothing. I helped her as she was helping me. Naked, we embraced and celebrated once again the bond that held us. Then we were looking up and out at the shack's rough interior.

I spoke, "The silence was full of sibilances."

"Yes," she agreed, "the whispers of other times."

"And the murmuring of the Clackamas," I added.

She reared up in the bunk staring down at me. "Did you hear it too?"

"Yes, because it's often been part of our bliss."

"Clyde," she said, "I've been afraid that words were destroying what we had. I came here to find out. Mother and Daddy, Olga and Grandma and other relatives who'd been told, their words came at me every which way and they got to me finally, but no—we've proved them wrong."

The next day she wanted to help me on the boat. So, jokingly, I set her to hacksawing bolt stock. I was soon busy planing a strake when Mel, who didn't see Ginny, called to me to come over and help him raise his boat off its blocks so he could place more substantial ones. It took us more than an hour and, when I came back, I expected to see a very tired Ginny in the cabin. I called and she answered from the boatshed. She'd moved the bench the pipe vise was on to another location and she'd cut not only the piece I'd set her on but twenty-three others, all hacksawed out laboriously. I found it hard to believe. It was drudgery of a most wearying sort. Surprisingly, her hands were not blistered.

"Remember," she said, "when the whole family were out

shocking hay, my hands were the only ones that didn't blister. Clyde, I want to put thread on these bolts. How do I do it? What tool?"

"It's a tough row to hoe," I said. "Why do you want to do it."

"To help you, of course," she said, trying to look grim. "So far I've been nothing but trouble to you."

So I gave here the threader with its most inadequate handles and showed her how to adjust the dies. She threaded half of them before dark, and left happily next morning on the bus that passes at the other end of the bridge.

When you build a boat you attract men and boys. There are many reasons for this. One, a boat is a conveyance and, to ranging man, it is the ticket to elsewhere and curved like a woman. It is both practical and pleasing. Men were always hanging around our boat. They couldn't help it and we couldn't blame them. We accepted them as men. The boat proved that, and they were always eager to help. They regarded me as a priest of sorts—the guardian of a dream that men have dreamed since prehistoric time.

The other boat builders on the island, though we were grouped in the same area, seldom appeared at our boat. They used the privy I had brought from home and, when the howling east wind of winter stopped all work out of doors, they would come and partake of my mulligan. But in the main they had as little time as I for lounging, for we were all spending our vitality to the limits in the two shipyards—Swan Island and Tomahawk. So most visitors were strangers. Oh, I got to know the caulking team and the friends of Bill Nagel.

Several boat builders would not allow people to view their efforts and two had made such horrendously awkward things that men turned sadly away. But Edwin Monk's fine design was already showing through in what we were so slowly evolving.

Among the strangers were two who appeared to be twins, though they dressed differently. They were so quiet, so restrained that I decided they could both be Sunday school teachers. They came often. One day one of the twins asked me why I steamed the planking. I explained that we were using vertical grain material instead of the usual slab grain and that slab grain bends easier but it's not so strong and we were trying to make a very strong boat.

"Yes," he said, "we can see that all right," and then impulsively said, "we think yours is the best of the lot." At which his brother said, "He means on the island here, Mr. Rice."

I was at a place in the planking where I had to force a piece about eleven feet long in a spot with such a twist to it that they would break each time I put the nails to them. Five times I did this and Nagel watching me fight them, disgustedly said, "For Christ sake, Clyde, put an easy slab grain piece in that spot. It's so small and narrow. What the hell! It won't matter there."

I broke one more and followed his counsel and got on with the job. I was already considering the launching for it was not too far away, and I had talked to the Small Business Loan people for money enough to buy the engine, tanks, propellor and to make the house. In fact, I was asking for enough to finish and furnish the boat and the insurance paid for six months. With what I had left in the bank I figured four thousand should cover it, and their man surveying the boat, seemed pleased. The vertical grain planking a full two inches thick and the oversize ribs convinced him.

I had a chance to buy a thirty-foot piece of steel ten inches wide and three inches thick for eighty-five bucks including delivery. They would angle one end and round it and blow ten three-quarter-inch holes in for bolting the piece to the underside of the keel. Probably its use saved four lives in the boat's first trip out—that and the bait tank I built below deck instead of setting it on top as is almost universal.

A couple days after delivery a slight fellow, tweed cap jaunty on his yellow hair, appeared around the corner of the boat and said "Hi." He looked down at the long chunk of steel I had drawn up alongside of the keel and after several moments he said, "You know, I need a few days of work. I'm good. You'll see. I'd like to help you with your butt blocks—real handy there—and we could have that slab of steel hung under your keel. I've helped with that job on the east coast. How about shipyard leadman wages?"

He was as good as he said, miraculously so, and I had worried a lot about the butt blocks. He quickly completed that job and with a couple of big jacks from Nagel and a rented hydraulic we raised the boat and slid that ton of steel onto the foundation blocks then lowered the boat down it. In the midst of it the twins came around and gave us a hand.

After the steel was bolted tight to the keel I paid Ernie and he took off, back to Maine where his father needed him in their small boatyard.

Just one more strake on each side and the planking would be finished. I bandsawed what I could away from one of these and was planing the final camber, trying to get it ready for steaming the next day when the twins appeared again. I waved to them. It was a very significant day in my life, but I didn't know it then. I do remember that I was standing deep in the rich scented shavings that fluffed gaily from my plane.

"I'm just about to leave, fellas," I said, "I'm going in town on a borrowing trip today." They said nothing but, after a moment went to the other end of the shed to mutter a bit, then came back. Their talker, the one his brother called Simon, trying to appear offhand said, "Trip to the bank, huh?"

"No," I said, "to the Small Business Loan Administration. Their inspector looked her over and didn't find her wanting."

"How much and what interest?" asked Simon. "Excuse me for asking but Gideon here and me might be interested." I didn't like their prying but I answered anyway. "Four thousand dollars, four percent, excellent terms."

They disappeared again and I continued to work on that long camber until it was done then went into the shack to change for my trip to town. When I came out they were still there and came toward me with more purpose in their movements than I'd ever seen before.

They both looked at me a moment saying nothing, and again it was Simon who spoke. "We'll do it for two percent if you pay us to help you finish the boat and keep us in your fishing crew for one year."

I was really surprised—these men with their Sunday school aspect—but two percent—well. I said, "I'll think about it, but offhand it sounds like a dandy offer."

I looked them over as crew material. They were well set up with large fleshy hands and I guessed them just under six feet. Neither one had a belly. Yeah, not bad, I thought to myself, and wondered about their boat building capabilities, what lines of work they were in.

The next day the men came back (their last name they said was Swaggart) with this offer as a contract for me to sign. I called my father's lawyer, Mr. Alderton, after they'd gone and told him I had a contract I wanted him to examine.

"Rice, right now I can't help you. I can't squeeze you in for another ten days. I'm snowed under. Call me in a week and maybe I can give you a bit of time."

I decided to hunt up another lawyer and get this tended to. I looked the contract over again. It was simple and direct and I don't like lawyers anyway.

"Hell's fire," I said, when they returned, "time's a-wastin'," and impulsively signed it.

After that things moved faster. Before I could finish the remaining strake and have the planking done Simon, who turned out to be a fine machinist, had enlarged the stern tube as needed.

The brothers then left with their wives and children for a visit to the midwest town where they had come from, and I was left to garner all that was needed to make this fine hull into a sea-going fishboat.

First though, I went out on Sunday to talk to Nordi, whether she would or not. Winter was past, spring was melting the snow in the mountains. It seemed a happier world, but with a wan face Nordi answered the door and drew aside to let me in. When I sought to embrace her, she stepped back and held up a restraining hand.

"No," she said, "leave me alone." With a most woebegone

expression she said, "I don't think you have any conception of what you've done, Clyde."

"Perhaps not," I said, "I've been terribly busy on the boat."

"I haven't such an out with which to avoid things, Clyde," she said. "I only know that I've been cast adrift. Yes, I have. You see, I didn't know how much of my life was just being your wife. You aren't so much, you know, but you were my husband. You backed me, well, spiritually, I guess. Anyway, I suppose you'll say that hasn't changed, but that divorce paper—! Oh, Clyde, some-how it seemed to deny that we are as we are."

"Not to me, Nordi. I swear it. I'll never change toward you. Circumstances can change, already have, but not our relation-ship, not my love for you. Let me hold you?"

"I've thought of nothing else, dear. Still I want no salve. We've changed all that. No pats on the back, no sex. They'd only do harm in the long run. I'm getting along all right, but I've found that a widow, even a grass widow, is fair game to cheat and steal from. Even my own mother is getting in on the act. I don't want to talk about that now. Have you heard from our son?" she asked.

I told her of my last note from him from Valparaiso. She'd received a similar one. She wanted to know all about the boat. I went into the building at great length, even the drilling of the stern tube. I followed her movements with my eyes as she went to the stove and realized how much I'd missed being near her. Our closeness, our every activity and discussion together was so much of my life. How could we continue being apart? She brought the coffee to the table and I grasped her hand in mine and she did not pull it away.

"I want you to name our boat the *Bunky*. Please, Clyde." I agreed. I told her of Mel and Nagel and of Ginny's bolt making. That hit her. "Fool! Ass!" I berated myself silently.

But she perked up. "Hurry up and marry her, Clyde," she said wryly. "That was what this divorce was for." And then rather forlornly, "but you'll always be my Nailby, won't you?"

"Yes, I am, and you'll always be Mrs. Thubish." We laughed.

"Dear," she said, "you must leave while we're laughing. I'm going to the bathroom. You must be gone when I come out. Good night, dearest!"

I took a couple of days off from the shipyard and drove down to Astoria. I had placed an ad in the *Oregonian* and the Astoria paper for a used diesel of sixty horsepower, one that would take the scrutiny by its manufacturer, local branch, whatever the make. Of the responses I decided on one a fisherman offered—a sixty-horse four-cylinder Caterpillar. We made our arrangements and he shipped it to Portland to the Caterpillar people, who pronounced it little used and sound. I bought it and had it delivered to a shop down river from us. The same week I ordered two wing tanks for the diesel oil, three hundred gallons apiece, and a bait tank of my design. We had the templates Monk had given us of the tanks and I made a drawing of the bait tank. They were shaped against the curves of the boat. Oh Lord, I was deep in spending, a thing I abhor, but it was the time for it.

I got Virginia to take the day off and come with me to Stevenson, Washington, to get married. We got our license and were married by a Justice of the Peace. I saw that she was so excited she had trouble signing her name. We had a lunch smiling at each other conspiratorially because she was not going to let her parents know. Then we hurried back to Portland deciding to keep the marriage a secret for now. She went back to her parents in the evening, I, to the shipyards. Again it was one of those nights when I was not called on to do more than the others, so I brooded as I monitored the equipment. I was remembering the help Ginny had given me, protecting the tears in the bottomland's turf, shoveling away at a great rate, bringing the stakes so Bunky and Dave could lash the willows down. I was remembering our walks—how she looked that time on the Roaring River trip, her help at haying time when Nordi and Olga dropped out, weary. I thought of her quiet companionship or, when no one was around, her swimming before me in the pool, naked and beautiful, cavorting about in the water, a creature of laughter, entrancing her lover. I called her my dolly.

I'd received no word from the Swaggarts and hoped they'd come back and help in the launching of the *Bunky*. I needed help with the engine and tanks too. But onward, onward. Now it was time to drill through the horn timber for the rudder stock. Well, I had luck with it. I thought of building the rudder of fir, but put it off. Maybe we could make a hollow steel one. Gideon was supposed to be a fine welder. I'll wait a little bit.

The caulking foreman came Friday, a purposeful look about him. He pointed out that planking, steam-bent, shrinks more than slab-sided planking and that such planking needed a professional caulker. They had decided to do it for me very well and very cheap.

"Now is the time to do it, Rice. We'll turn up tomorrow morning and Sunday night your boat will have a perfessional job done on her. Come on! It ain't just the money. My men is set on doing it. The caulking will sound different, planked as you are. You'll see."

Finally I agreed, too tired to argue. I hadn't been feeling up to snuff since I saw Nordi last. I had a stomach ache all the time. But there was a lot to do on this boat before it would be ready for the sea and time was, after all, wasting. I was looking over some heavy plank from which I'd make the rudder, when Simon and Gideon turned up with broad grins on their faces. Well, I put them to work immediately, Gideon to make a hollow aerodynamic steel rudder. Included in the deal with the fisherman was the propellor shaft and propellor. I asked Simon to fit the stern gland to the shaft hole and to fit the shaft in that and secure the propellor on the shaft ready for launching.

Next morning I was awakened by the sound of the caulkers tapping the cotton and oakum into the seams of the *Bunky*. It was a fine sound. The caulker's strange wooden mallets, short of handle and long of head, make it as they tap or later beat on the steel caulking irons which drive the tarred oakum into the seams. All this produced the peculiar resonance that, once heard, is remembered and identified against all other sounds of the world.

It did not affect Gideon as much as Simon and me. We were

excited by it. Simon smiled broadly as he installed the stern gland that would keep the sea out and allow the shaft to turn endlessly. It was exactly the same only miniature by comparison to the ones I watched over on the tankers. Gideon was quietly assembling the parts of the rudder and proving that he was an expert welder and could also handle a cutting torch. All was activity on the *Bunky* but I left, for I had to scrounge for timbers, dragging them back to the boat with the pickup. We would need two big rails for the boat carriage to roll on when we dumped the boat into the river. The Columbia was slowly rising. "An early warm spell in the Canadian mountains," the *Oregonian* maintained.

There were enough old timbers on the island scattered where floods had left them, some jammed into smaller trash and some under rotten logs on the beach. It took me till Saturday to drag the necessary long pieces to where we needed them between the shed and the river bank. Sunday I drove out to the farm for some short pieces of pipe to make rollers to put under the boat carriage. The field looked strange. I knocked and when Nordi came out to greet me, I asked, "What happened out there?"

"Part my fault," she said, sadly, "for trusting relatives. Clyde, another one of your pet projects has gone down the drain. High water came in February. You've been coming out here after dark and I didn't have the heart to tell you what happened, because there's nothing you or anyone can do about it now. Go on down there and look at it."

I did. First, I saw there was no field of alfalfa, just a sea of mud. From Jack's problem spot a small canyon thirty feet wide and fifteen feet deep ran across our place and I could see it continuing through Giesek's and Teddy's and farther on through Brown's. When I got to Teddy's, I found the canyon had a branch that went to a place where an acre was washed away. The center of it would have been where Ginny and Dave and Bunky and I had worked so hard to save the turf. I was sick to my stomach. Good God! What devastation! It was hard to recognize what had been a lovely bottom. Now a wide canal split it, the full length.

Eventually I came back to Nordi and we had a cup of coffee together. She looked repressed. There was bitterness in her glance as she scanned me over the rim of her cup. Finally she set the cup in the saucer definitely ending our silent perusal of each other.

"Clyde," she said, "I'm going away. I'm going where I still have friends."

"Nonsense," I said, trying to carry it off with a laugh. "I'm your friend, Nordi."

"Oh, yes," she answered dolefully. "Your friendship has brought me to a point where I see only enemies when I thought I was surrounded by friends."

"I suppose it's so, if you find it so. Still, what's got you talking up a riddle for me—'going away,' 'leaving your home.' You're exaggerating wildly, aren't you, dear."

"Well, as long as your love of my sister's daughter was hidden, everything worked around here, but Clyde, you're a do-gooder and on top of it you trained yourself not to hate, so you're fair game for the average guy or guys. You're simply outside the 'pale.' When that letter was found, every gutless wonder around was after you with weasel teeth."

"Nobody approached me to take that bite."

"No, of course not, but they undid one of your good deeds on the turf of this bottom and the thing kicked back on them. We lost but they lost too. Still, they couldn't come at you direct, so they slipped around to me. Just look at that alfalfa field. I'm not talking about Jack's canyon. I'm talking about my hard-earned alfalfa field.

"Well, enough of that. Madeline is bedridden, Clyde, with a bad heart. Zimmie asked me to come back to Tiburon. He'll pay me very well for it and I used to have a lot of friends down there, not the back-biters I have here, and I can get away from you. Oh, Clyde, how could you do this to me?"

"This about your enemies, dear. Aren't you a little bit over-excited? Who are you talking about?"

She looked out of the kitchen window at the great gash that bisected her meadow. "I hate to say," she said, "but I'll tell you if you give your word that you stay out of it. In fact, if you love me, you'll stay out of it. Well, it isn't Virginia, strange as it may seem.

It's Jack and my own mother, and Olga always follows Mama's whim, but Jack wanted to go in the horse business. He's shoed a hundred riding horses, I do believe, in the last couple of years and it paid well. It's practically a lost art, so trading around, he bought three horses and he already had one. There was no pasture on their place, oh, maybe half an acre. Anyway he asked me if he could pasture them on our alfalfa. I didn't want that to happen, but he was in a tight spot, so I said: 'All right, Jack, if you take them off my field August fifteenth, but only on that condition. That'll let the alfalfa build up before the rains.' And he was to pay me for the alfalfa. When the time came, he didn't remove them. I was upset. I asked him to every week. The horses had eaten everything, weeds and all, and I found that they'd eaten the button that is the base of the alfalfa plant. That kills the plant.

"There was the making of four more good years of alfalfa. Now it's gone forever. 'Don't worry,' he said, 'I'll get some alfalfa seed and scatter it around,' but the horses were still there. He came to me saying that our place was too big for a woman and that he would buy it. I didn't want to sell but Mama said I should. Finally he named a price for the place—a little over a thousand dollars.

"All this time Mama and Olga were berating me because they couldn't snarl at you. You were my fault, they inferred. And because I would not join their church. The same eternal squabbles that you took me away from when you married me twenty years ago.

"I decided to rent the place. I wanted to be out of it now with Bunky and you gone, but I laughed at Jack's offer. A family was going to rent it. I had shown it to them, but they wanted to look at it once more before they brought their furniture. They came to Acme and I gave them the key. When they got here, Mama appeared. 'Get out,' she said, 'you're trespassing.'

" 'No,' they said, 'we're renting this house. We talked to Mrs. Rice.'

" 'No, you won't. You get out of here,' Mama yelled. 'We're buying the place and we're going to tear down the house. It's the house of the devil.' And she carried on in that manner until they left and returned the keys. Said they didn't want to live next to a mad woman. Now I've rented it to my cousin Judy and I'm leaving Sunday night for Tiburon. Tell Bunky where I am when he comes in again.

"First you, then Tek and Olga and now my own mother. I want to be free from all of you and I'm going because you set me adrift. I still see how and why but right now I hate you. Get out! It's you who are trespassing."

"But, Ginny," I implored, getting mixed up. "A . . . a . . . a . . . Nordi, dear—"

"Shut up, you fool. Ginny, Nordi, ugh! Your Dad was right. You're a born fool, Clyde. Go away!"

I left. I was sick with impotent loathing of myself. I drove to the shack like a beaten dog to lick my wounds. I was dazed, destroyed! As if I were drugged, I fell asleep. All afternoon and all night I slept.

In the morning I called the railroad. Yes, they had a train leaving Portland at eight P.M. I wanted to go with her. If she had only gone with me while there was still time. Bob had offered me a partnership if I would go down there. Now she was going alone. It was too late.

I crouched over my stove, weary of life, chewing dully on some short rib bones. I went out and started to move the driftwood timbers into place. The river brushed by the island, creeping higher and higher on the bank. Monday, we'd have to put up all the decking, all the lumber on the levee, all the oak, all the incidental lumber with which to finish the boat. It had to be up there by the following night. I staked down the runway timbers so they wouldn't drift away if our low part of the island flooded.

I didn't dare to really think, but it came as fear: I'll never see her again! I can't accost her in the depot. She's sick of me! I tried to picture how she looked yesterday. I couldn't. Good God! When I try to see her, my memory plays tricks on me—it won't see her.

I drove more stakes, gnawed at more bones again, warmed yesterday's coffee and cleared a place on higher ground where I could stack the mass of lumber that would go into the finishing of the *Bunky*—the bulwarks, the rail top, the house and the five bunks in the foc's'le. I stacked some of it in the pickup and ran it over and piled it. I looked at my watch. The day had worn through to six o'clock. Far back in my mind was the wish to see Nordi, to refurbish my memory of her dear face.

There must be no ugly scene at the depot, but maybe I could see her on the train. Perhaps at Oregon City. The trains go slower as they pass through Oregon City. She might be at a window on a side I choose or she could be at a window on the other side and I'll lose again. What of it, I'm a loser anyway. There's a fifty-fifty chance I might see her anyway.

I throw off the lumber. Do I have enough gas? I test the tank—almost full. I drive through Portland and finally reach Oregon City. I go to a place where the road crosses the railroad track at the base of the cliff that bisects the town. There's a cove there and I park in it and wait. My watch says eight o'clock—the train is leaving Portland. She'll be in a seat on the left side of the car so she can look east. When the train crosses the bridge over the Clackamas, she'll be on this side so she can look up the Clackamas toward—oh God! How did this all happen? We're blown askew by every ill wind that comes our way.

Far off I hear the locomotive scream for the crossing at Clackamas town. Be alert, my heart pleads of my muddled mind. When you see her in that split second, memorize her sweet features so I can mark them indelibly on my soul. The engine is blowing for the town. I rub my eyes, dash tears away. Stare, my heart says—search!

Now the passenger coaches are passing. I search each one as they slowly go by. Maybe she's on the other side, maybe she wants to be shut of the Clackamas country. I don't see her. Car after car, I search as they slide by. So she sat on the other side. I don't blame her, and this—this is the last car. I've lost. But there she is on the observation platform. We see each other the same instant. She rises in a crouch, a tentative hand out, as if to wave me away, or as if to beckon me to her. The space between us is lengthening. I jump into my pickup and head after the train on the road that, at places, parallels the tracks.

I race through Canemah and onto the flat beyond and draw up beside her, the tracks and the road beside each other. Oh, Lord! I can see her so clearly. Now the road and the tracks curl between the river and the cliffs in tight curves. I still see her. Oh Nordi! Nordi!

The train is gaining speed—well, so will I, the gas pedal to the floor. Then we draw apart, I over a hill and down the other side and there's the train and my darling, staring back at me as we course along. She is waving me back. She knows that my tires are rags—wartime shreds. I can't think about them. If I smash up, hurrah! I've got it coming. The train slows through Canby, curves down to cross the Molalla River, then another flat. We're side by side. Ah, darling! Love is here with us. I've got this rig moving with the pedal to the floor. Nordi! Nordi! I see you clearly, though I'm bouncing all over the road through rain, through streaks of heavy fog. I come close and rush along beside you for awhile, anguish and love are on your face. You smile me love! Oh, dearest, dearest!

Along about here the tracks go away from the road. I know it and you must too for you are holding that smile for me, when the tracks and the road part permanently. Soon I roll to a stop, the long race over.

Next day our work goes on at Tomahawk Island. I build the crude carriage that will support the *Bunky* on its trip from the shed to its launching. I won't think. In monosyllables I address the crew. The carriage absorbs me. In the afternoon it surrounds the boat. It's done.

I don't go to Swan when it's time. I tell Hank I have something to tend to. At dark I head for Oregon City again, but this time I don't stop at the cove. I head on past Canemah and Canby slowly. I'm seeing her as she was last night, illumined by the overhead light on the observation platform. I absorb her image.

I hold her picture in my heart. It's still here; my death may erase it. Nothing in life can.

On I go, slowly, until arriving at the place where we parted, where the rails and the road separate, going by different routes to Salem. I know this place. I bought some sheep here once. There's a vast field across the road, maybe a thousand acres of grass. I wander out in it, away from the lights of distant farms. Now I must know the vast curve, the endless belly of the earth that separates me from my darling. I stare southward through the long Willamette Valley past the Calapooya hills, down the valleys of the Umpqua and the Rogue, down over that great belly tracing the Sacramento Valley to the Bay, near the Golden Gate to Tiburon where my wounded Nordi seeks refuge.

Then, still looking south, I seek for light on the vague horizon and there is a very faint glow, probably of Salem, but I must envision the lights that encircle the Bay, those of Richmond, Berkeley, Oakland and San Francisco. My darling must have illumination however vague when she steps from the house at night for a breath of the Bay's salt air.

But I came here goaded by another urge than yearning down across the endless miles. I came here to bring to a close these selfish acts of my philandering nature. I will not leave this field while still able to inveigle another woman into a sexual relationship with me. If there is no other way I haul out my cock and sheath knife, hoping that there is another way, but certain that I will not leave until a permanent change is made in me.

How I hate and despise myself, but I put the knife and my penis away. In futile hatred I pound on my head. I'll beat on my head until my inner life will abhor sex with anyone but Nordi and Virginia. So I instruct myself. *Pound it so!* I hammer my head everywhere with all my strength. A madness seizes me. I black my eyes, smash my nose, batter my jaws, crush my ears. My knuckles are torn and raw. I no longer have strength to continue.

Staggering about to face south, I shout, "THAT'S FOR YOU, NORDI!" And to me I grit out, "YOU REMEMBER," knowing that I will.

VII

In Which
I Become an Ineffectual Fisherman, Visit Nordi,
Learn to Appreciate Spike Jones,
and
Have to Sell the Bunky

1946

SOON WE WERE READY to move our boat to the river. With pipe and wooden rollers we got the *Bunky*'s carriage on the wooden rails of timber at the same hour that the river invaded the boatshed. The timbers sank into the sandy mud. The river came higher. Mel gathered what lumber we had left floating and piled it on the high spot on the levee.

Darkness came. It seemed impossible to move the *Bunky* in these conditions. Bill Nagel rounded up the other boatbuilders. They'd not go to the shipyards this night. One of our own must be launched. Knee deep in water on sand that melted away underfoot, with big jacks against foundations that also melted away, they strove. I didn't know their names; enough that they were boat people.

In the morning, after an hour of sleep, I stepped out in much deeper water to see in daylight what we had accomplished in last night's floundering win over the river's inundation. Man! The *Bunky* looked grand. The small tug I'd ordered appeared, put a rope aboard. I put smaller rollers of wood where the hull would brush the timbers and looked around.

Hank and the brothers had just arrived on the jetty. I signaled and the tug gave a slight pull and the *Bunky*, with its keel already in three feet of water, took to her element like a duck. (I wonder where she is now. I know she's in the Atlantic, but whether on it or beneath, I'll never know.)

Well, we anchored near the levee and, with lines ashore and a wide plank walkway, she was ready to receive our further efforts.

Not a drop of water did she leak. My hat was off to the caulkers! We towed her down to where the engine waited and lowered it into the boat and came back to our berth by the levee.

Soon Simon was happily bolting the engine to its beds, placing the fuel tanks on each side of it in the bellies of the boat. At this time we also put the bait tank in its assigned place.

After we got the tanks set and stoutly secured for capsize, if need be, we bolted in the six-by-six deckbeams. We spiked the deck over them and caulked it under Nagel's sharp eyes.

The cabin of the *Bunky* was to be a bit over eight feet wide and fourteen feet long. It contained the pilothouse and toilet, each with outside doors, a roomy double bunk, a table in a booth seating four, stove and sink. I got my friend, Neufer, to build it.

All my time, it seemed, was spent finding materials and small equipment for our vessel. The war was over but still many materials were in grievous short supply. One bit of piping—the street ells—was not to be found and yet, because of their position at the bottom of the fuel tanks, I had to have two and they were suddenly nonexistent. Portland, Seattle, San Francisco—I tried by phone and wire, uselessly. I tried to get machine shops to make two, but they all were busy filling orders that had been put off since Pearl Harbor. Two weeks and still no street ells.

I went out to see Wanster to saw out one special piece that we had broken. While there, I told him of my street-ell predicament. "You mean these?" he asked, reaching into a grab-all box that was handy. He came up with three street ells with his compliments.

Carrying live fish aboard for tuna fishing meant having a second engine on board to continuously pump a six-inch pipe of sea water into the tank to keep the anchovies alive. These six-inch pipes were hard to get. Various sections, like an ell shape with supports, had me hopping. I finally had several short sections machined out expensively, only to have them knocked overboard. The shop refused to make another. "We did it as a favor and you were careless with them. Get it done somewhere else."

And always I drank milk, for the doctor at the shipyard had told me I had a stomach ulcer. I drank two quarts a day, but it didn't seem to help. I was sick all the time—guilt and tension and dwindling cash. I couldn't sleep—and Ginny? What of her? I hadn't time to think of her. What must she think of me?

Hank was bewildered by the odd way Neufer began work each day. He described to me, laughingly, how Neufer carefully laid out his tools and the materials he would use every morning, and with those strange heavy, black brogues he worked in (the kind that the comrade worker wore as pictured on radical sheets), he would proceed to walk backwards over all scuffing the tools as he clumped on them. After this display of the working class, dulled by labor but honest, he would miraculously turn out the most delicate joining of wood with dovetailing, dowling of mortise and tenon joints, almost microscopically perfect. Hank shook his head in wonder.

Neufer passed his fine craftsmanship off as nothing to remark about. In Neufer, wood—any wood—found its master. For him, wood never split or checked or even sulked, nor did it pull the mean tricks it plays on us lesser mortals. He sculped in wood, brought out the beauty of fine wood's grain. And this close relationship with wood down through the years affected him. His sense of humor, free in youth, was gradually becoming a bit wooden.

The trouble was, he made the cabin eight feet high, put the curved roof beams in, covered that with five-eighths plywood, glued the canvas cover to that and gave it a coat of paint—this, while I was in Seattle buying an engine and bait tank pump. The plans read six-foot-six-inches for the height of the ceiling, but Neufer, a land man, thought it was a mistake by Monk, the architect, and Neufer was used to eight-foot ceilings. I thought of having it lowered; it looked unseaworthy, but thought it best to wait and have it done later, for it was through-bolted with the ten bolts through the roof beams and down through the deckbeams.

I hired Nagel to build up the bulwarks fourteen inches high

and cap it with two-by-eight oak bent to fit. With Hank and me helping, he did a fine job. Nagel said the oak cap was still kind of green and to let the sanding and varnishing go for awhile.

One afternoon Nagel asked me to come to his house, which was close to where our gangplank came ashore.

"Bring along your contract with the Swaggarts," he said. I got it out of the shack and stepped into his house. There were five other men there, four of whom I knew. "We're going to butt into things, Clyde," Nagel said. "When you brought in that privy for you and other boatbuilders and placed it like you did, I knew you were a public-minded guy, so I want to help you. I think from the signs, you're being had.

"You know these other fellows here, but I want you to shake hands with Mr. Clarence Adams. Ever' so often I do some work for the Portland Yacht Club across from us here. He's their legal counselor. I've got him to come over and look at your contract with the twins. I suspect something. No fee, Clyde. You're amongst friends. Mr. Adams's hobby is boats, any boats. He watched you with glasses as you built your hull."

I handed Adams the contract. "It's simple and concise," I said, "so I never took it to a lawyer."

He studied it for a minute. "Too late, now," he said. "Mr. Rice, you're in a very tough spot, if what Nagel has seen is true. A good attorney could prove with this contract that you have to provide paychecks for each of them for one year. What if the boat isn't finished to fish this year? As it seems, from what Nagel says, they're doing everything to make that happen. They'll break you. Stall you to death, take the boat in lieu of wages."

Nagel spoke up. "They're stalling the work when you're away. These guys—Bob and Jerry and Art—they've seen it too from my window here."

"It's strange," I mused, "that I haven't noticed this, or that Hank hasn't nor Neufer."

"They don't do it when Hank is around," said Nagel. "You and Neufer rant about mankind. I know your sort. You both love your neighbor but, I think, Clyde, neither of you wants to see how tricky some guys get to be. But believe you me, I keep my eyes and ears peeled and still I come out a loser ever' once in awhile. I didn't want to bother you with just my hunch, so I got witnesses."

"Which one is the leader?"—fury rising in me.

"Can't tell 'em apart," answered Nagel, "but Simon, the bossy one, chews snooze. Gideon does what he's told and rolls his own."

We all looked at boat-loving Mr. Adams. Finally he said, "Finish the boat for sea and get out there. The season will be almost over, but try. I understand these fellows are not seamen. They might not be able to take the rough weather you'll hit, and if they won't go out with you when it's rough, that'll cancel their hold on you."

"Let's see," I said, "it's September twenty-eighth. I planned to fish her in the spring."

"You can't with that contract. I've shown you why. Get her out fishing now. It's your only option. I'm no fisherman, but if I were in your position, I'd head south. They'll still be getting a few tuna when the salmon season is over up here." I came out of the session at Nagel's furious. I grabbed Simon's arm where he was working on the rudder quadrant.

"Come along with me, Simon," I said, and he did.

I led him down into a cul-de-sac behind the levee and took off my coat. With his size and youth I knew how it would end but I must have at him. I just had enough sense to tell myself not to grab his throat. Punch low, my anger said. Get him in the gut! Get him down and kick him in the gut! I was wild enough to walk through a brick wall.

"Get your damn coat off!" I yelled at him, but he wouldn't take off his flimsy working jacket. Instead he just stood there, weeping, big tears streaming down his cheeks, looking at me with his big watery eyes.

"I know what Nagel told you," he wailed. "I don't know why but Nagel's got it in for me. Gossip!" he blurted out. "You've been listening to gossip and now you want to fight with your friends," he sobbed distractedly. " 'Tain't so!" he cried out. "It just ain't so!"

The tears confused me. My wrath—where was it? I felt sympathetic toward him. It didn't make sense, but I did. Seemed like I was being unfair and on hearsay at that. Still, I should be wary.

"I can buy off your contract. You and your brother are paid up on wages."

"How would you do that?" he inquired.

"A loan from the Small Business loan people. How much more would you need over the contract?"

"And us already sending our families back to Peoria? Nope," he said, "sorry, but a contract is a contract. Don't pay any attention to that Nagel," he went on. "Everything is on the up and up between us. Let's keep working together on building the *Bunky*."

While we were behind the levee Neufer was busy marking out a line for the lower cabin. Now I told him to leave it as it was, for I was realizing what a jam I was in and that California and tuna were my only hope and to hurry the completion of the *Bunky* was all that I could do about it. So I oiled the decks with a penetrating compound and gave the bulwarks the first coat of paint.

Next day the brothers ran the cables from the quadrant through the quarter blocks and onto the drum of our excellent steering wheel. I took off for the mountains, but not before I found time to go to Vanport city, an enormous housing project nearby for shipyard workers, and rented a furnished apartment, though I was not communicating with Virginia yet. I needed time and I had the excellent excuse of endless work. Later I found she understood. Now and then I sent her a card about what we were doing at the moment.

I went up the Oak Grove fork of the Clackamas River where there was a stand of fir poles I'd been watching grow for years. Here I got the *Bunky*'s mast and four slender, very long ones for trolling poles. What luck! They still would peel. I wrapped them in a bundle, lashing them to the right-hand side of the pickup on some braces that stood up from the bumper and hurried back. Peeled, they were perfect for our needs.

Raising the mast two weeks later I temporarily guyed it while bolting the chain plates to the hull and bulwarks, then stayed the mast with proper cable.

When I told Nagel some time later what had transpired between Simon and me, he grinned, "What I figgered. Glad you didn't bust your hands on him," and still speaking of the Swaggarts: "knowing as how they're watched from all sides, they'll have to work for their money. I put Hank wise and they know it. That monkey business is all over with now.

"Say, Clyde, Clark—you know, he owns the island—needs your shack for a rich sturgeon fisherman. Wants to put it over on the Columbia side. Says the guy will pay five hundred for it, if he can have it there tomorrow."

"Great," I agreed. "I've got a place for my stuff at Vanport."

"Do tell," said Nagel with a grin, "haven't you settled in with your new wife yet? Not yet! Look, I'll help you move it," he said. "Clark will pick your shack up with that crane he has in the morning. But what you gonna do with that big boat shed?"

"I'm going to give it to a friend of mine named Nagel," I answered.

Next morning Simon and I boxed in the batteries, while Gideon fitted the thirty-gallon freshwater tank in its place and finished piping it to the galley sink handpump. It was time to put in the cement ballast as hold floor of the boat, but not before we filled the tanks. We got a drum of diesel and put some in the two tanks and tried out our engine, Gideon acting as engineer. We also tried out our rudder and the wheel and the operating levers in the pilothouse. Everything worked beautifully. We made a slow careful trip to Vancouver where we filled our tanks. That done we moved over to the cement plant and took on cement in our hold till she sank down to her empty lines. After that we cruised back to our berth and gangplank below Bill Nagel's house.

And so it went, month after month. Neufer eventually finished the cabin. He'd enjoyed building it, he said. One evening after the Swaggarts had left, Hank long gone to Swan where they still employed a skeleton crew, Ray continued to hang around.

"I don't like to see the day end," he said, "everybody going home."

"Why is that?" I asked.

"Because I hate to go home."

"You should be happy with that new home you built," I said.

"I'm not," he said and wept.

"What bothers you?" I asked.

"They don't welcome me home," he answered, still weeping. "My mother-in-law lives with us. She's a foxy old lady. She's taught Catherine and our son to sneer at everything I do."

"You ought to throw her out."

"I suppose so, but the three of them got me backed against the wall."

"How old is your son now?"

"Eleven," said Neufer. "He's a very bright boy."

"Well, if it was me, I'd make them toe the mark." I said.

"Look who's talking," Neufer replied. "I certainly don't approve of what you did to your wife."

"Neither do I," I said, suddenly depressed. "It's a long story. It goes back too far." I let it go at that.

Then we had trouble with the engine. An expert from the shop who had examined it first came. He found they had changed a part around in putting it back. In fact, there were innumerable hangups.

It seemed the harder I pressed, the slower the job went. Gideon and I spent days and weeks, it seemed, sheathing the hold and building the heavy pens to ice the fish in. They had to be husky in case we ran into a school of big tuna. A frozen hundred and fifty pound tuna, if it slipped when you were unloading, could smash in the side of a frail pen, we were told.

We stationed our big compass carefully in front of the steering wheel. The compass adjuster came and the Federal Documentor of Ships did too. October was all but past, but we had our

lights, port and starboard, and the masthead and all the para-
phernalia needed for five men to live aboard for a season. And the
trolling poles were in place and the fishing gear, the plugs for
salmon and tuna that we bought long ago when we laid the keel
were aboard. I was broke. The five hundred for the shack never
got to rest in my wallet.

I went to see my father for a loan. He agreed to loan me two
thousand and he gave me five hundred and was quite sour about
it. He said it belonged to me. Years later I found it was money
that the Little Lady had filched from me back when she was
doing my bookkeeping. She couldn't help boasting about it to a
friend, who inadvertently spilled it to my father.

My father came out to the island to see the boat. By now it
looked the hefty craft it was from any viewpoint, but he refused
to step aboard; said he'd never stand on anything that I built—"it
might fall to pieces," snarling but impeccably, as always.

Now we made cruises up the Willamette and down the
Columbia, breaking in our new equipment, especially the new
engine and pump that supplied the bait tank. We finally weeded
out weak spots and were ready for Astoria and the Pacific. We
decided to leave in three more days. I wondered if Bunky, who
was due any day now, would make it.

I took Ginny out for lunch. She looked serene, no longer a
hidden lover, but my wife and helpmate. It showed in her face,
even in the way she draped her coat on her chair.

"I know you've been frightfully busy," she began, "so don't
apologize. How's it going? What's happening on the island?"

"Three more days, Ginny, and we'll leave for Astoria. She's
ready to fish. Will you make the trip down to Astoria with us?"

"Why, Clyde. You mean the boat's all done—finished?"

"Ready to go," I answered.

"But I thought you were going in the spring."

"There's been a necessary change in plans. Oh, here's a key.
I've got an apartment at Vanport. Could you call your folks and
tell them you're spending the night in town?'

"Of course. They don't know I'm married yet, but I do. Pick

me up after work." She leaned closer and looked me carefully in the face. "Clyde," she said, "you look like you've been run through a wringer. What's wrong?"

"It's been a wild year for me, Ginny, and I've acquired an ulcer."

"So I've been right. I've been so worried about you."

"I'll be okay when I have time to get this ulcer cut out."

"Stomach?" asked Ginny.

"Yes! Look, I've got to go now—get the sea charts for the *Bunky.*"

Later that evening, I took her out to see the *Bunky.* She really was astounded. "My goodness!" she exclaimed. I took her aboard and was successful in not pushing her onto the lower bunk. She admired the steering wheel and the booth and its table and marveled at the compass. Then I took her to Vanport and showed her the way to find our apartment, which was plain and a little sketchy. That it was didn't bother her, for it was ours as long as we paid the rent.

She looked wonderful to me, so new and happy and smiling. I felt shy before her. She took off her coat and wrapped her arms around me and kissed me and I forgot everything for awhile—the Swaggarts, the late-start fishing disappeared. All I knew was Ginny's warmth—guilt and tension were not in this sparse apartment, only love.

On the appointed morning, Ginny and I left the apartment at ten and found Hank and the brothers already aboard with their duffle. Bunky obviously was still at sea. It was twelve forty-five before we left the island under the eyes of our ever useful Nagel and went carefully between the shoals on the north end of the island because our trolling poles and mast would not clear the bridge. Out in the main current of the Columbia we were able to pass under the railroad bridge and the Interstate Bridge without touching. I put her full ahead and she forged her way down river. With proud grins we watched endless shores slip past.

For quite awhile we cruised along Sauvie Island's east shore and then we were passing the sawmills of St. Helens and charged on our way by Goble and Longview. The sun was in our eyes for awhile, glittering on the disturbed chop of the water ahead, but with the sun the wind went down.

Through the twilight we seemed in a slow rush past little islands and log booms. Then it was dark and as the different navigation lights appeared we went on until about twelve, when I ignorantly decided to find a harbor of some sort and lay up for the night. None of us knew the river nor the charts. The brothers were somewhat agitated. We had all traded places at the wheel during the day, but now I had it. It was completely dark when I saw a light ahead of us. And, yes, it wasn't going down river, it was crossing it. I kept on our present course until we reached where I assumed it had crossed in front of us, then I turned and followed its receding light and on its course headed into the land that I soon sensed, was close about us. With a flashlight we found we were in a narrow channel between mud flats, but the light still moved on ahead of us. Finally I turned away from it toward a dim-lit wharf where we tied up for the night and ate a spaghetti dinner, the first that Virginia had ever concocted.

Ginny and I slept out on deck that night, looking up at the stars and caressing each other's faces as if we sought to know each contour to remember in the time ahead.

Morning saw us on our way again. I had grown in stature with Ginny and the crew for getting unerringly to a dock in the black night. It was the simple matter of the light and a hunch. On we sailed, and before noon we entered the boat basin of Astoria and tied up. That night under the stars Ginny had told me that she was going home to tell her parents of our marriage and that she was going to take up residence at Vanport and wait for me to come back. She said this with the short finality with which she expressed her yesses that had allowed the first intimacies that soon forged the bond between us.

I searched around through the crews and skippers and hangers-on, who were ever present at the wharves of the boat basin, looking for a temporary skipper. It was necessarily a haphazard search. I was a stranger here.

I struck up a conversation with one guy who was about my age, tall and skinny, a hard-bitten and knowledgeable expression on his face. I told him of my boat, that we were late and hoped to get out and get into albacore, but that I was going to leave the boat and get to a doctor and medical help.

"Time's a-wastin'," he said. "The season hasn't ended yet."

I said, "I thought perhaps you'd know of someone who could skipper the boat for a trip or two up here before heading for California."

He considered me in the manner of an old hand who looks over a neophyte. "Yeah," he answered. "Is that your boat over there?" pointing to the *Bunky*. I replied that it was.

"And your name is?"

"Rice," I answered, "Clyde Rice," remembering ruefully that interrogation in Estacada with the draft board.

"Well," he said, "I know California waters from Frisco to the Canal. I'm a fisherman, by God, and I'll take this skippering job if you will go over to the Custom House with me and get it written out.

"I see you already got a crew. Are they as green as you?"

"Yes," I admitted, "and they have shares in the boat for one year."

Then there was a hand on my shoulder shaking me and Bunky was standing beside me. "I made it, Pop. Hit the island—no boat! Mel told me you were headed for Astoria."

I introduced him to our new skipper, who I found in the introduction was called Wes Dolan.

The noon whistles were blowing. "Chow," said Dolan. "I haven't eaten since yesterday noon."

"Come down on the *Bunky* and let's see if my wife has lunch ready." She had—more of the spaghetti and hefty corned-beef sandwiches and canned beans she'd heated.

"Wife!" exclaimed Bunky when he saw Virginia. He drew me aside. "So you finally did it, huh, Pop?"

"Between the devil and the deep blue sea. I love them both. It worked out this way."

"I figured it would. I've got no say in this, Pop. You're always talking about suspended judgement. I'm going to lean heavy on that for awhile—okay? So you've named the boat after me."

"Nordi's idea," I said, "and I seconded it. Bunky, I can't talk anymore. I got to keep track of this new guy."

"Hard-looking," remarked Bunky.

I went back to the cabin where they were eating. "This is your new skipper, Wes Dolan," I told Hank and the brothers. "And I'm on the sick list until further notice."

At the Custom House as we signed papers, he said, "Now what do you want me to do?"

I answered, "Those brothers have got me in a terrible bind. I hope you can take the boat out in rough going. My highest hope is that when you come back the twins will jump to the wharf and ask somebody else to pass up their luggage, through with the sea."

"I gotcha," he said.

"I hope Hank stays. He'll have a share of the boat if he stays."

"How about your son?"

"It's his boat when he earns it. We built it for him. He's always wanted to be a fisherman."

"Okay," he said, "I'll ice up tomorrow, take on stores, get the tank full of anchovies and I'm going where they're still getting albacore off the west coast of Vancouver Island. Will get in touch with you when I come back. I will say you built yourself a boat, what I mean!"

The brothers accepted him in a startled manner, but accept they did. I saw that, but I also saw that Bunky and Hank were eager to work under him.

Bunky left Ginny and me at the bus station. "Nagel was right, Pop," he said, "when he said you'd see it through. Now we'll find out what sort of a sea boat she is." He kissed Ginny's cheek before we stepped aboard the bus.

On the bus ride we said very little. She did say, "I'll learn to cook, dear."

In the next few days in the apartment I found that her mother and father had taught her nothing. All the household chores and tricks that most girls learn as they grow up had been kept from Ginny and her sister. Her mother had insisted in keeping them as little girls and was terribly disturbed and depressed by their budding breasts and rounding contours.

In the following fortnight I was that creature that one sees in doctors' offices—an embellishment not yet as tattered as the old magazines, that live out their days in such an atmosphere. At least I went home at night. There seemed no immediate help for me. Finally one old physician gave me a box of little pills and said, "Try one of these, Mr. Rice. Come back tomorrow and we'll see how it goes."

I took the instructions on the pill box—three per day—in earnest, but not his desire to have me come every day. I was not going to be addicted to doctors if I could help it and I kept the *Bunky* out of my mind too—another addiction I hoped to control.

One morning, the phone rang. I hurried to it, my mouth full of breakfast. Chewing rapidly and swallowing what I could, I said, "Huwoe."

It was Bunky. "We're in Newport, Pop."

"Grake," I said, "Wha's the plicture?"

"Just a few fish. We were in one hell of a storm off Vancouver Island—and snow—there was two feet on deck before the storm hit. We were fishing when you couldn't see the bow from the pilothouse. Been five days trying to get in a harbor."

"You could have gone into Neah Bay," I pointed out.

"We did. After it had calmed down some we headed out again. It came on worse than before. We couldn't get in Gray's Harbor or cross the Columbia bar."

"I hope you didn't try Tillamook Bay."

"Tillamook was closed. We could see the Coast Guard signal at the entrance. We were two days here before we could cross this lumpy bar. Pop, we built us a boat!"

"You trying to tell me that she is sea-proven?"

"That's it. We've heard here that six boats went down in that storm off Vancouver—two of them twice as big as ours. She's a dilly, Pop! Say, you going to come down so we can take off for San Pedro like we planned?"

"Okay, Bunky. What do you need in the galley?"

"More coffee and, Pop, we need cookies and smokes, and I'll need my fancy shoes down there in California."

That night as she lay in my arms, my so lovely creature, I thought of Nordi. How was it with Nordi at this moment? Ginny stirred against me and I was back in the luxury of her sweet ways. Before we went to sleep I whispered that I would write when there was anything good to write about and sleepily she murmured she would besiege me with notes.

At Newport aboard the *Bunky* the bait tank pump motor was noisy, was going to be eternally noisy, pumping a big stream of water from the sea into the tank to keep the thousand or so bait anchovies healthy.

The skipper seemed a bit disheartened, but said no other boat on the Swiftsure Bank got more fish than he did. "About the coming trip," he went on, "fuel and stores and water is aboard, but we got to get us our bait."

"Are Hank and Simon uptown?" I asked Bunky.

Before he could answer, the skipper said, "Remember what you told me on the dock? I got it half done, but I was low on diesel oil, though I didn't run out of storm. Sorry," he grinned.

Bunky spoke up, "Hank and Simon couldn't wait to get ashore. They were seasick the whole trip. Gideon is a tough one. He handled it like he has a barnacled ass."

"I'm really sorry about Hank."

"Well, the way it turned out it wouldn't have worked out, Pop."

In our first set in the upper end of the bay we snared a seine full of pilchards that we didn't want. Another boat, bigger than ours, brailed them from our net. Said they'd try to sell them to the canneries. We made another cast, got anchovies this time and filled our tank.

We anchored out in the bay that night. At dawn, trying to

raise our anchor, we hauled and heaved, for we had yet to install a winch. Eventually a Coast Guard launch came out and explained that our anchor was caught under the submarine cable and that we should cut our anchor line, leave our name and address with the Coast Guard and the cable company would reimburse us on the cost of the anchor. So without the anchor, we headed out through the breakwaters and found the sea calm.

That day we steered south about thirty miles off the coast. The weather was moderate, but we sighted no tuna schools with the attendant flocks of birds. In the morning we headed in on the long slant toward the coast, for the skipper had a hunch about Redding Rock that came up out of twenty fathoms of water to tower ninety feet above the sea. We circled this great pillar, flinging bait uselessly, and stared at the coast four miles east of the rock. Fishermen learn to be philosophers about the many vagaries encountered in bringing in a fifth of the world's protein. We headed out, setting a southerly course about twenty miles off the coast. I was taking the tiny pills night and morning.

.

In early afternoon the skipper, staring long and hard to the northwest, pointed out a sulphured sky low on that horizon and set a course south-southwest. "We're in for a blow," he said, "and I want sea room."

Soon the wind hit us and gradually the waves built up. In the night the combers topping the seas were startling with their phosphorescent glow. We were lifted before the crests to run down the forward slope of one, hurling us into the back of the wave that had just passed under us. We continued to plow into the back of each passing sea, causing the boat to yaw dangerously, so the skipper put the engine at half speed, and at once the *Bunky* fit its shape to those of the Pacific.

Morning found us laboring in a world of massive breaking seas. In this awesome welter of water I was sure one would come crashing down on deck and wash the cabin and wheelhouse off the boat, but the curved hull of the *Bunky* lifted at the last moment and the wave passed beneath, marching on past us.

There was no respite. The anxieties of the past few days over my problems of Nordi and Ginny now became extravagantly unreal in the face of the cold seas that came hurtling out of the north. The now of the storm blotted out the past and future.

The skipper, a seasoned salt, now had two men at the wheel, one steering, one standing by, to see that the boat was on course. For if a man fainted or, looking away from the compass, allowed the wave to fling us askew of the course, we would spin sideways down its sloping front and capsize.

That day Gideon at the wheel faulted in his concentration and looked wearily away. The boat started to stray into a yaw; Bunky, standing by, reacted in a flash and slugged him and, gripping the wheel, got her back on course.

Once, when the seas between the surges left us caught in the timeless moment, the waters broke away from an immense spotted formless something that was alive, for a huge eye in the mass regarded us, then a comber crashed down on it as we, caught in the surge, swept by. We barely missed striking it. If we had, that would have been a quick end to the voyage. Farther on we ran through an endless school of albacore. They were on the surface and hungry. The water was dark with them. I flung out a jig, a dozen leaped for it. I caught four before the skipper ordered me away from the wildly gyrating stern. "If you were swept over, we would have to leave you. We'd have to go on."

There they were—the albacore—our bread and butter, the reason for the boat's construction. Ah, God! God! But after a few more miles the breaking seas were clear of them. Now my mouth was dry, nostrils cracking, I felt no hunger, but I continued to take the pill. Hell, Doc Gibbs wanted me back next day for the four dollars per visit. I'd call him from San Pedro, but the world for me was turning to the right in a slow spin—probably seasickness.

Our skipper now had us headed for Hawaii. Land! Land was a haven a landlubber yearned for. We were two or three hundred miles off the coast and I had found, talking to him, that the skipper had gotten the variation between the compass north and the true north mixed. This course would carry us so far from the coast of California that we would not have enough fuel to get back. I tried to explain this to him but aroused him to fury, so he grabbed my rifle. I had hired him as skipper and signed the papers in the Custom House in Astoria, and "By God!" he yelled, "until we hit the beach I am in command."

That day he asked if anyone could pray. Finding no adept aboard, he said, "We can't keep this up much longer. It's been hair trigger all the way. Somebody's going to slip up, bleary-eyed as we're getting, and over we go."

I wept. It was my will to get Bunky and me fishing—that would probably be the death of the four of us. Bunky, however, said if his death was near he wanted some hotcakes before drowning and proceeded to mix batter and, holding the frying pan level over the flame in the stove, produced and ate the cakes with lots of syrup and gusto. Then something happened to me. From bewailing my drive to make Bunky a boat owner and boss of others, I suddenly became intensely alive to our situation— more alive than ever before in my life. My life was being threatened. If I was going to die, if we all were going to die, then I would hold off death to the last ditch. Battle! That was it. I was going to put up a fight.

"Give me the wheel," I muttered. It was relinquished to me. This sounds like silly bravado, but it was not. I started fighting the seas, for now cross-seas seemed bent on knocking our bow aside, so the big one behind us could roll us over. I must catch these threats and conquer them with the wheel and rudder, the rudder that I had built bigger than was necessary. I thanked my lucky stars for that foresight.

A couple of hours of the struggle and we were still going strong. It was strange that, after I had demanded the wheel and taken it and spread my legs to take the jerk of driving cross-seas, my three companions relaxed even in the situation that was upon us. A positive thing was happening. A negative guy had become the dominant guy and the ease with which they accepted this was not entirely from their weariness. I had accepted the challenge with sudden fury and they gladly believed in me and sought their bunks. Awakening through the afternoon and the long night, they stole a glance at me there at the wheel and then sought more sleep. I look on that time as one of two or three most excellent times in my life.

No cross-sea slapped our bow, but I was miraculously ready for it and turned the boat in the face of its onslaught. Slowly I changed the course and when I saw the boat could handle it, changed it a little bit more. The wind wasn't quite so strong and the seas, though still enormous, did not seem so savage. The *Bunky* was headed now on a long slant toward land. I now knew we could handle it, so I turned a few degrees more toward California. After four hours, I yelled at Bunky until he awoke and came up from his bunk. I left the wheel to him for half an hour of respite. Standing on the hatch I proudly watched how our boat fooled each sea.

Taking the wheel again, I did not give it up till morning when far on the eastern horizon we saw the tip of a mountain. Hours later we reached Point Concepcion and passed into the Santa Barbara Channel out of the violent northern water. We had made it.

That night at the wheel, the chaos of cross-seas gone and the seas from the north blown flat by a warm west wind, I knew a strange peace. We creased the ocean's dark plain. In the pilot-house the small light of the binnacle glowed faintly on the compass card. If we have souls, it is times like these that bring us closer to the answer. I was the boat, the engine, and our steady progression. I was the phosphorescent bow waves and I was me, warm within the wheelhouse, my land-based problems blotted out as fantasies. There was only the now of me in my new boundaries that reached far out from the secret self—hidden deep as a kernel or its germ. Now there was no need of hurry, no need to scurry about in my thoughts. I had the whole quiet night to live in this larger perimeter of being.

All at once our little ship was brought high above the water plain, then dropped into depths only to rise again and again, as three monstrous rounded sea swells passed under us coming out of nowhere or from some fierce typhoon that had pounded Guam or the Philippines days before. And these too somehow were included in the boundaries this night allowed me.

Next night, before we got to Pedro, I was at the wheel but no longer hogging it, when Bunky came in and lounged beside me.

"Pop, what do you know about Catalina Island?"

"Well," I answered, "from what you and I have read in the boating magazines, it has a small town on it called Avalon and the gum magnate, Wrigley, once owned it. He put all manner of wild animals on it and made it a sort of a game reserve for exotic creatures, cared for by Mexicans. But what happened after that I really don't know—except there's a steamer that goes there daily from Pedro."

"Uh-huh," he said, and the *uh-huh* was tunnel-shaped and lay deep into his desires. "I've been thinking," he said, "you can swing over that way on the way to Pedro and, if the weather continues, you can drop me off in our lifeboat and I'll row in and have a vacation before I join the army. I know you need the boat, but boats like it are available in any harbor. As a going-away gift, I'd like that."

"Well, we need the skiff."

"Look here, Pop," Bunky said after a moment of silence, "I worked hard building this boat and I've put in every cent that I earned as you did. I figure I've got a couple of weeks of freedom coming before I'm jammed in another routine that isn't mine. I appreciate what you're trying to do for me, but now I want to goof off for a week or two. Give me any cash you got in your pocket. With what I've got in mine I'll make out. Just slow down outside their harbor and give me a hand with launching the boat."

So we did it, much to the skipper's annoyance, though he could get another hand to take Bunky's place. The last I knew of

Bunky was the phosphorescent glow from the strokes of his rowing, as he disappeared amid the riding lights and gloom of the harbor.

On the dock at San Pedro I soon came to realize that I was not seasick, but very sick period, and had been through all the manifold excitement of the trip—though on the night of the three great sea swells, my sickness had not been able to intrude. I decided to return to Portland, have an operation to cut away the problem the medicine seemed unable to handle. Before I left, however, I took our skipper into a place between two buildings.

"Look," I said, "you've been loud and peremptory with me. I've found it hard to take, except that you were the skipper. I think you can beat me up in a scrap for you're tougher and your reach gives you great advantage, but I'm perfectly willing to be knocked about, even out, if I can have at that nose of yours, or at least hang a fat lip on you. It won't change things; you'll still be skipper of the *Bunky*. Anyway, how about it?"

He uttered a gruff "Unh-unh," sizing me up coldly. "I like the boat and I like my job on it and I carried out your orders on that first trip north."

"That's right, you did." I thought a moment. "And a swell job it was. I haven't got a kick. Only—oh hell! Let it go. Now I've got to go to Portland to get this ulcer taken care of. While I'm gone, see if you can wangle a couple of trips for fish," I said, turning away.

"Yeah," he said, grinning, "just keep your balls out of the way of that knife when they're whittling on you."

In Portland, Ginny was somberly affectionate. The bills on the *Bunky* (there was a sheaf of them) had her worried. We would be unable to pay the coming quarter's insurance. We were behind on the payment for the diesel and Portland Marine, which had supplied most of the equipment, was insisting on the final big payment due months before the launching. True, we could draw on an account with Van Camp's Fish Cannery. They backed us on our supplies for trips but so far no money was coming in. The salmon season had failed. Everything depended on how much fish the *Bunky* could bring to the dock, as the albacore tuna season was drawing to a close.

In an extremely troubled mood I went to my doctor and told him of my condition on the trip.

"You mean you're still taking that atropine?" he asked.

"Yes, I am," I answered.

"My God!" he exclaimed. "That was only a trial. It has been used effectively sometimes, but it's a wonder you didn't get convulsions out there. It's obvious that you're allergic to it. Why didn't you come in next day and let me know?"

"I would like to be at your beck and call, but my life doesn't allow it."

"Well, I have another pill for you to try."

"No, I have had enough," I said, getting to my feet, "see you."

I had heard of a surgeon who was very successful with his whittling and, calling for an appointment, was advised to eat nothing in the evening or morning before. Next morning I was taken into a small room and crowded into a smaller corner by a nurse, who was small too, but still a powerful Brunhilda. Sensually I realized she was without her armor. She ended my pleasure by forcing a tube down my throat and, while I gagged and tried to stop her, she forced it down further into my stomach.

"How wong is?" I asked.

She understood me (part of her work, I guess). Anyway she said, "Twenty minutes." To get my mind off the constant gagging, I asked her for a *Life* magazine from a pile I'd noticed in the waiting room.

"Life?" misunderstanding me, she laughed, "Why you're in no danger. It just feels that way."

Again I asked her for a *Life* magazine. Trouble was that with the tube gagging me, I couldn't say "magazine." I couldn't even gurgle like that. By now I saw she was fed up with me.

With the beginning of a snarl she said, "I told you, no danger. You men just can't take it like we women."

"Wha a *Life* from the yating room," I begged.

That girl had a very short temper. "Here," she said taking up a tube similar to the one she had encased in my gullet. "I'll show you." She crammed it down her own throat, not far but, I'm sure, south of her tonsils, then choked out: "See, nofink to it. Nofink to it for a wongan. We not ninnies, not scairt." But here she hauled up that tube, making sounds that belied her iron will and granite constitution and disappeared.

I left my corner and with the tube still in place and gagging me, went into the waiting room, found the pile of *Life* magazines, went back to my corner and became calmed by pictures and captions. I was gagging slightly and contentedly when the white-coated doctor appeared, shook hands, and then carefully hauled up the tube to make his evaluation. After his thorough examination he told me what I already knew, that I had an ulcer and that it should be removed.

"How much stomach will you remove in the process?" I asked.

"Not over a third," he said. "My book's full now, but I could operate on you sometime late next month, and two months after that you could be up and about."

"How?" I asked. "Wheelchair?"

He laughed with fake heartiness, "You would not be an invalid by then. You could get around nicely on two canes."

I said, "I'll think about it."

One third of my stomach. Jesus! I'm going to see an herb doctor pronto. Yeah, and a couple of chiropractors. Mrs. Eddy, my spiritual nemesis, began to appear bland and perhaps useful.

A day later, as I drove through the flat Willamette Valley, a man crawled out of a culvert up ahead at a turn where I could see him. By the time I got to him, he was up by the highway indicating his desire to be elsewhere.

I stopped and picked him up and, as we rode along, he told me of an injury he had received in the shipyards. He worked at the slab, where men swinging great sledge hammers battered and changed the shape of white hot steel, working in the inferno of the steel's heat. Slugging away he had torn a muscle that encased a nerve and had lost the use of his arm. "A doctor up in Portland is working on it for free, seeing as how I'm broke."

"What's his name?"

"Dr. Lawrence Selling," the man said reverently. "He's kind of a smallish Jew, but I got it figgered he's one of the biggest men I seen. Hey, let me off at the next crossroads."

Lawrence Selling, I mused as I drove along. I'd been introduced to his father, when my father felt I was an old enough Portlander to shake hands with one of the town's great men. I'd heard that the great man's son, Lawrence, had become a famous diagnostician, the rich coming from several states to consult him. And here's evidence at hand he offers his services free to bums. I forgot herb doctors and Mrs. Mary Baker Eddy. This man was the one I must see.

"Good morning, Mr. Rice. Up from California, my nurse says."

"Just temporarily. I took our boat down there."

Selling was a small, vigorous, nut-brown man and I liked him at once.

"You're not new around here then?"

"I was introduced to your father on my fourteenth birthday."

"Ah," he perked up.

"And my great-grandfather was a doctor in Salem about 1859."

"Hmm—well, would that be Dr. McAfee, one of the founders of our medical college here?"

"I didn't know that, sir, but I've heard that he murdered his wife, but went scot-free of it. But why all this?"

We were interrupted by the entrance of his office nurse. "That patient you told never to come back—"

"Which one?" he asked.

"The racist bigot, who got intoxicated and tried to fight the wooden Indian in front of Milford's Cigar Store. He's here again—says you didn't get all the splinters out of his right hand. Do you know the one I mean?" she asked.

"Yes, I remember him. See if you can fit him in this afternoon." Turning to me, he said, "I like to know a patient a bit. Sometimes it helps. Now, what have you been doing to acquire an ulcer?"

"I don't get you."

"Was it too many kids, or too many women, or too many bills?"

"Drop the kids and substitute hunger to create a good book or a statue."

"That sounds glib," said Dr. Selling, "and from the front of your mind. There's where the glib stuff lays. So you think of those hungers often?"

"Yes."

"And the women—how many of them?"

"Two."

"Are they heavy on your mind?"

"Like a plague, but it's not their fault."

"And the bills?"

"About five big ones."

"You're quite a normal guy, aren't you, Mr. Rice?"

"Wish there was a pill for normal guys."

"Well, let's look you over." He did and then said, "It begins to look like our minds and emotions make ulcers. I have had a lot of luck with my ulcer patients by prescribing an evil tasting expensive powder. Its main ingredient is hog pancreas. Anyway, those who stick with it are cured and if you could consider your anxieties as surmountable problems given time, I'm sure that would help too. I don't know, maybe it's the price and the taste, but I'm getting results with this stuff. I'll prescribe it, and I hope you take it. So many of my patients feel having the prescription in their pocket has a healing effect of itself and never go near the pharmacy."

Within a week the ulcer pains were subsiding under Dr. Selling's care and his truly horrible medicine. My elasticity—my bounce—was returning so that I could look a bill full in the face.

Then the telegram arrived:

Skipper disappeared with cash from poor trip. What shall I do?

I wired:

Hire temporary skipper and crew and make a trip. Will be right down to take over.

It seemed the quickest way to get the *Bunky* fishing again. Then I realized if I could get there in time I could be her skipper myself.

•

I phoned Virginia at work and told her I was leaving at once. She told me to take the money out of one of her bedroom slippers—"and be careful with it," she added. For what with the small debts she was trying to take care of, it would be several months before she could send me any more.

"Clyde, remember we'll be together in my mind," she said, "I'll use memories of us to keep you close to me."

The bus I boarded had carried endless thousands of people—people, oftener than not, down on their luck. The odor of anguish and forced hope persisted in the entire interior. I sat down next to a window in the middle of the bus. Soon all seats were taken and, with a few standing, we left for Los Angeles and way points. The man who had taken the seat beside me was only a profile to me until we began to roll through the suburbs, then he turned a face that fitted his profile. He had a long sharp bony nose with no chin to interfere with his resemblance to a bird of prey. He was a small man in a big overcoat. His eyes suddenly glared as he opened his mouth, but for several seconds no word or sound came; he closed it, only to open it once more and say:

"Salem?"

"Nope," I answered him. "Where are you headed?"

"Redding," he said off the top of his head and I knew he lied, for his hands were made for cards. He was leaving trouble, but not too far. Surmises, sure, and probably somewhat wrong, but the scientific approach doesn't help in encounters of this sort, though I did observe that his feet didn't touch the floor. He went into his spiel now about a hotel he owned that had burned—"up in Bellingham," he said—and he was heading to Redding to seek funds to rebuild from a banker he knew there. "I've got plenty of collateral, but that stack of ashes has me on a thin edge. How about lending me ten? I'll give it back to you when the bus lays over for lunch in Redding."

"Nope, I haven't got the money and I never did have the rattle of collateral." I answered. I snickered inside. I'd always wanted to say "the rattle of collateral."

"A rube, heh?" he said, flaring.

"Yep," I said, "a rube. Better try somebody else. There must be some loose change here to be had." I looked out the window. We were crossing the bridge at Oregon City. I looked up river at the falls and when I turned back he was gone and the various bulges in my pockets were intact. At once the seat was taken by a girl, a waft of fragrance from a cheap but pleasant perfume came to me.

"Excuse me," I said, "but you should have the window seat," and I got up with the blanket I expected to wrap around myself that night and changed places with her.

"Thank you, kindly," she murmured and gave me a cautious but pretty smile. On we went, swaying with the curves. Some people began to talk to each other across the aisle making acquaintance to battle boredom.

Every so often bus lines have urinating stations with sandwiches, cigarettes and kewpie dolls. This one was in Eugene. You could tell what it was before you stepped inside. I saw the girl from the other seat before she stepped into the filth of the "Ladies" and I did the same with the "Gents." Afterwards I saw her looking wistfully at the sandwiches. I ponied up fifty cents wastefully and, with two lettuce and cheese sandwiches, boarded the bus in time to save her seat beside me from a fat fellow in a straw boater coming home from a convention with B.P.O.E. in yellow on a purple band on it.

"My wife—it's her seat," I said as he tried to sort of crawl over me to it. He backed off but laid a sweaty palm on my shoulder.

"Why sure, friend," he said, "I thought I'd get me a window seat all the way to Yreka. Was worth a try, like they say."

As he moved on, I saw behind him my seat partner, with an understanding smile driving wistfulness away for a moment.

"I really was a wife a month ago," she said. "Anyway, thanks for saving my seat."

Sheer boorishness and boredom made me ask, "For how long?" It should have offended her, but it didn't, for she answered sadly, "Only eighty-seven days. A car accident killed him."

"I'm sorry. Really, I shouldn't have asked, you know. It's a long boring trip, but that's no excuse. You ask me one now," I went on.

"All right," she answered, "where are you going?"

"San Francisco—really Tiburon. And you?"

"Atascadero. I'll stay with my sister. I had to get away from Portland. It kept reminding me of him. He was gone 'like a light' they said. 'Never knew what hit him.'"

"You've had a terrible experience." I offered.

"Yes," she replied, "and the car was totaled—an Imperial Stiletto, this year's model." She lapsed into a sad reverie, then said, "Now I'm broke and in debt—the headstone, you know."

Glancing sideways, I studied her. She was small with delicate features, not built for the rough real world.

I suddenly lapsed into sleep, but she woke me. "Have you gotten this far through life without a great sorrow?"

"Some," I answered, "but I can't talk about it."

She reached over and patted my hand. "Sure," she said. "Let's snooze," and we did.

Again I awoke. It was getting dark. We were ascending the Siskiyou Mountains. I remembered the sandwiches and got out the packages. I awakened her and offered them to her. Looking at it with misty eyes, she said: "Oh, thank you," and really meant it. "I couldn't afford breakfast this morning."

"Well, I overate. I hope you'll eat them both."

"Are you sure?" she asked, staring quizzically into my eyes.

"Most sure," I answered, and while she ate I looked over a newspaper I had gotten at the urine stop at Grants Pass.

On we went. The air got colder in the mountains. We could see moonlight glittering on patches of snow. About ten-thirty the driver put out the lights and we became more aware of our passage along the winding road. It became quite chill. I got out my blanket and covered her. Pushing the blanket back to me, she said, "Take it. It's yours." We both were talking quietly, for others were sleeping.

"No, I couldn't," I answered. "Ladies first."

She turned then and through the deep gloom considered me a moment. "Come close then, and share it with me," she said.

We crept close. I wrapped my arms around her and she patted the blanket around my back.

"Please don't take advantage of me," she murmured, "that is, too much." And then, in a timid whisper, she asked, "Can I trust you?"

"It's strange," I whispered back, "normally in such a situation I couldn't trust myself, but now somehow it's different. You can trust me completely." She gave me a little hug and in a few minutes fell asleep.

An hour or so later she stirred. I asked her if she was comfortable. "Drowsy and contented," she whispered and raised her lips for me to kiss.

When we came to Yreka I bought two hamburgers. After we relieved ourselves we hurried back to our seats and sat straight and prosaic, eating the hamburgers, until the bus got underway and the lights went out. We wrapped ourselves in the blanket and kissed for awhile in a sweet but controlled ecstasy.

We snoozed and snuggled. I held my arms around her protectingly, and though we would both have enjoyed my searching for hidden loveliness, I did not, for I was thinking again of Nordi.

Later I awoke. The girl had slipped away. We were stopped at a junction point. I had to hurry to catch my bus for San Rafael and Tiburon.

When I came up from San Pedro, what with the atropine, I was much too sick to stop, but now I would see Nordi. I arrived in Tiburon and walked the old familiar road. A few new houses seemed alien to the scene I had carried in my heart through these many rushing years, but the pebbles in the road seemed the same. "Hello, Clyde," the pebbles, the bushes and the houses and the winding road seemed to say. But no, no, it was me, Clyde, greeting the old terrain, nearing Nordi, trudging through lost familiars—the Grippincurl house, Davercozen's and Stark's houses on the hill.

Then I was looking down from the road on our cottage and Madeline's new house, and in its rock garden Nordi with a sprinkling can bending to the flowers. I was shaken, torn near death, by the storm and turmoil raging through me. Below was my mate, my companion since childhood, my beloved, whom I had chosen to put aside. Why? Because of the three of us, she alone seemed to have the most strength. God, God! Who was I to have been the judge, to choose. With moonlight and nature's urging I had bought into Ginny's life and must needs cherish her while my Nordi pays the cost—not I, who did this harm, but sweet Nordi, my Lail-Lail, my own Pee-ang! Oh, why must a man rage and tear himself to pieces and bring eternal harm to all who love him? Why?

Nordi looked up and saw me where I stood and raised a hand to shield her eyes, to recognize me and to say, "Clyde!" staring, smiling.

"Am I allowed here where I have no right?"

"You're welcome here, Clyde. Come on down," and she came to the gate and opened it and took my hand as I, raging within, passed her with a smile. "This is unexpected, but come on down."

We separated our hands so that she could go ahead of me. I felt the loss and hungered to rejoin hands. Ahead of me she brought up the picture of the many trails we had traveled together. I always admired her twinkling steps moving on before me, so pert and eager she walked along. The sense of fate drawing us apart came like vertigo and lingered. Fate, my ass—I did this! I made this hell I carry with me and I can only guess at the wound of my inflicting that she hides.

As we entered the house, Nordi warned me to be silent, as Madeline had had a bad night. Zimmie came in from his shop holding his hands behind him, smiling cooly as he murmured, "Good morning. Where is the boat Nordi has been talking about—named after her son, I gather?"

"It's fishing out from San Pedro," I answered, "and I'm heading down to join it. We were going to come into the Bay here when we came down, but we were two hundred and fifty miles off the Gate and just holding our own against the storm. I wanted to show it to you. You'd have gotten a kick out of the way we solved some engineering problems."

He didn't answer, but stepped back into the corridor that led to his shop. I understood. Once we had been friends. Now all my friends were my enemies, including Zimmie. They cut me whenever they could. I had hurt Nordi, abandoned my mate for a young girl. Most of them had been derelict in some way to their marriages, but Nordi and Clyde had stood firm. We had showed that the old ideals were possible, we had become symbols of a good marriage to our friends and acquaintances. I had destroyed it.

Nordi was watching me as if she was interested in just how I took that cut. "You'll have lunch with us, of course. It'll be just a few minutes."

"I'd rather have it just with you. I can take feeling guilty, but now that I've become a status symbol of guilt, I feel that there ought to be a salary attached."

"It isn't from any saying of mine, Clyde."

"What can I reply, Nordi?" I muttered.

She passed close to me. I restrained myself from reaching out as I had all those years. She was looking over her cooking as she looked up at me still examining me, and she reminded me of a photo I had of her as a baby. I started up with a jerk and walked outside for a moment. I knew now that that divorce on paper couldn't half change things.

In a few moments she brought out a tray and we ate our lunch looking out over the Bay. The house that we had built together years ago stood next door, but neither of us would look at it, though we did remark about the *Delta Queen*, which was passing down the straits as we spoke, and that they were making more roads across on Angel Island. We said little. Christ, what noble restraint! I bought all this. Well, I would go in and say goodbye to Zimmie, which I did, and then Nordi and I were saying goodbye to each other with our eyes. We seemed to come to some understanding—spiritual, I suppose—when I heard Madeline calling from her upstairs bedroom.

"My breasts are as beautiful as they were years ago, Clyde. Come on up and play with them before you leave."

Sex! Jesus-God! What had I done to those I loved? Sympathy for Madeline welled up in me, as I looked at the stilled faces of Zimmie and Nordi. The kitchen door was open. I ran through it, calling back, yelling back, "Goodbye, goodbye, goodbye." Then I was up on the road running half-way to Tiburon before I could control my self-hatred.

•

"Vacate before five," the landlady said. She had allowed me one night more in my room when I could no longer pay. Where to sleep tonight? The *Bunky* was out at sea somewhere. The crew of six, now at chow, would soon be sleeping in comfortable bunks, the galley range keeping the cabin cozy—"rocked in the cradle of the deep," as the old song goes—while I searched for a place to hole up until morning. There were quite a few crannies around the fish canneries, but it they caught you in one, off to the jug you went. So in the end, as it began to get dark, I worked my way along the edge of the wharves and crawled over and down.

Under the wharves the rock walls of the harbor were fronted by a long, thin strand of sand. I hunted for a humped-up place that the tide would not reach and then hurried back to where the free ferry crossed to San Pedro. Quickly, I picked up newspapers left by passengers and back under the wharf again and, in ever-dimming light, I found a box board and then another. These I placed on the high spot in the sand. After putting papers on the boards, I worked several pages of newspaper down between my shirt and me and awaited the dawn that I assumed was crossing the Atlantic to enlighten New England, New York and the Carolinas and was coming toward me. Envisioning this gave me something to hang onto.

When darkness came I tried to curl up on the boards but it was impossible and I realized I'd have to sit up the rest of the night. It's better than standing, I told myself. I also told myself to be thoughtless in the long hours that were coming, but in spite of it, I peered back into the just-past month of November. It had been a wild trip down the coast from Newport—three seafarers and a barnacled captain heading for warmer seas.

A truck rumbled over the wharf above me and dust came through the cracks. When it passed I realized how hungry I was. I felt around in my pants pocket and found a bit of crust left from the loaf of bread I had had in my room. I munched this tiny morsel with great satisfaction. I knew where my breakfast would come from, but at the moment I didn't want to think about it.

What would Ginny think of this? But I must live now, as if there were no Ginny or Nordi. I told Ginny I'd remove her from my consciousness until I could offer good news.

No thought clung to time's passage for an interval. I almost fell asleep when consciousness asserted itself and I was wondering how far dawn was from the coast. Surely it had passed Iceland. Oh, to hell with it! I was shivering; must stand up and slap my arms about, increase circulation.

Standing, I could see the harbor in between countless pilings supporting the wharves. A yacht, all lit up, was gliding by the harbor's entrance. It moved slowly and gave me many glimpses until it passed from view. Comparing my setup with that of the owner of the yacht, I saw that accident and stratification were factors, sure, but desire and order also separated that passing luxury from my squatter's rights on two box boards and gathering newspapers. Am I kicking? No! No, of course not. A bit of irony, perhaps, but I don't want to think eskew the facts—the basic problems that halter and stimulate us. Okay, okay!

I put some of my newspapers against the rock wall at my back. The little breezes that continually played chillily between me and the rock wall were blocked, as I leaned against the momentary insulation of the sheets of the paper, but in a few minutes the cold penetrated the papers and I sat up straight once more. I'd like to get my back against a wall that was warm, I decided—a wall that I owned and had a deed to prove it. Like our place on the Clackamas that Nordi had received, as was her right, in the divorce. Maybe I could buy it from her sometime in the future. If I could, I would make it a haven not only for me, but also for friends who were down on their luck—a place for all of us to get our backs against a warm wall and fight off enemies and circumstances that were part of our undoing. A man could nurture his weakened purpose there and reacquire lost dignity—gird himself once more to tilt with the future.

I awoke chilled and peered out under the wharf into velvet blackness, shook myself, and sagged into sleep once more. I was brought bolt upright by a racing truck thundering overhead, then a police car rattling the planks as it sped after it, siren howling. After that I couldn't sleep. Suddenly furious at my condition, I climbed out on the docks. The God-damn dawn must be hung up in Kansas! But eventually it peeked over the Sierras and what it saw must have been good, for it came right on and I had to hurry and take a ferry to Pedro and get to my trees before people were about.

The night before, the town had been full of hell and strong waters. Now it sagged with lifelessness. I ran into three places where blood had been spilled on the sidewalks. I passed through the tenderloin, then the respectable shops and into a residential area where I reached my trees. They were in the parking lot—a whole block of them with big brown pods hanging from the lower branches. Furtively I gathered a dozen or so, shoved them under my shirt and slipped away unseen; my provender for the day, such as it was, secure. Cautiously I nibbled a pod. It was tougher than peanut shells with seeds in it as hard as rocks. The pods, however, when carefully gnawed, produced a sweet, nutritious pulp.

When the sun was high, I searched the harbor for signs of the *Bunky*, then sat in the sun and dozed, making up for last night's discomfort. Eventually, with evening coming on, I got up and went into town.

I approached the restaurant where I would have the one meal a day that I allowed myself. The sign said OTTO'S SHORTSTOP RESTAURANT. Inside it was sleazy and greasy. On the ceiling and on the walls were crinkled red paper decorations of several years past that were covered with a patina of grease to which ancient dust clung, but the food was cheap so they never lacked for patrons. I slid onto a stool, resting my feet, and ordered my usual—hamburger with onions, half an order of fries and a Dr. Pepper—fifty-five cents. In that condition I watched the waitress slide the platter before me and handed her the two quarters and a nickel as the steam from the food relaxed the tensions of my day I nibbled on a fry, took a sip of Dr. Pepper and regarded the bun, in which was ensconced the hamburger, with reverent eyes. I nibbled on another fry and at last took a small bite of the hamburger. The onions crunched and their grand flavor filled my mouth, as I munched on the bun and meat. I tried to slow down, but I took another bite, not a large one, but one obviously diminishing the size of the main course, as it were. So I put it down on the plate and ate half of a French fry.

Loud, sudden music filled the room. Somebody had chosen Spike Jones's rearrangement of the "Hawaiian War Chant" and put in the dime necessary to find out what Spike Jones thought of its hokum and how to deride it. I believe that half the lore of Hawaii came from the impresario David Belasco and Tin Pan

Alley, but here it was—a wild hooliganism on that noisome chant. I began to laugh. I had felt the need for this hokum, blasting reply every time I heard that war chant—war chant, my ass. I was vastly relieved of my venom and tension by this. As long as there were Spike Joneses in this mucked-up world, I could survive. I laughed louder and louder, tried to suppress it, but it burst the bounds I placed upon myself. People had quit chewing and were glaring at me. My laughter was reaching a higher pitch, still I got it throttled at last and looked again at my food, but another of Spike Jones's blatant musical guffaws at the chant toppled my restraint and I laughed out of control. Hysterics—in a man? Everyone was now staring at me. Even the cook left his kitchen to see what the rumpus was. I was interfering with their meal. I couldn't stop, so snickering and howling with laughter I rushed from the place. In a few moments it subsided.

I went back in the darkness that had reached the door of the restaurant with me and peered in a window and in the steamy light within I beheld my half-eaten sandwich, the fries and bottle of Dr. Pepper and Spike Jones was still at it. I was so embarrassed I could not force myself to enter and claim it. I looked at it longingly and then ordered myself to leave, and on reluctant feet I did so and left to find my room.

Soon after Spike Jones's inadvertent attack on whatever plumpness I still retained, I saw that even my frugal way of starving through the long wait for our boat would eventually take my few remaining dollars. I hocked my watch and, taking the boat to Avalon on Catalina Island, I searched for my son whose time to face his draft board was now a week past. Winter, mild though it was, stopped much of the tourist trade here and the yachtsmen were elsewhere skiing or in boatyards fondly scraping the barnacles off their shore-stored craft. I could find no knowledge of Bunky in the several small businesses of the place, so I approached the Mexican caretakers of the island. They were reluctant to talk.

"Yes, he came here much," finally the top man said from his door. "He come seeing my Rosa."

After some desultory talk I saw that he wanted to tell me where Bunky was in order to stop his affair with his daughter and, through me, to remove him from the island, but Mexicans are close-mouthed with gringos. He solved the problem by pointing and, after that, excusing himself.

My errant son was obviously put out when I knocked at the sleeping place, a small room constructed of opaque plastic over wire mesh. Yes, he said, he was wildly in love with a charming Mexican girl. He showed me a photo of her. Beauty was there. Both of them were trying to obscure with love the fact that, if he did not leave and report to his draft board in Portland, the army would root him out. He had a tiny job of cleaning up some shops at night.

"Her love," he said, "it surrounds me—I hadn't known—a guy shouldn't—a guy has no right to be as happy as she makes me. Anyway, Pop, there's no war on now. They don't really need me."

"I think," I said, "that great beauty is happening here, but the military doesn't give a damn. This wrenching you apart—well, armies have done this to millions of lovers the world over. Face it, Bunky, but if she'll wait for you—"

"She couldn't," he replied, "too much fire. She couldn't."

"Well, then, I advise you to make your parting now. Will you come back on the boat with me—I have a ticket for you—or leave in handcuffs with a blemish on your record?"

"I don't know, Pop. Why did you have to come?"

Well, I got him on the steamer. We were looking down at the wharf and then she was there. Her arms were rigidly at her sides, but no gesture could ever say much more than her eyes, her lips, as they appealed to him not to leave her. The steamer blew a sonorous blast and slowly we started to move away from the wharf, then canned music emerged from some tired mechanism—"Aloha." No canning can kill its poignancy—the loss of parting. I held on to Bunky tightly. I could feel his muscles turn to stone. They were staring hard at each other, the girl with her arms still held so stiffly, but such a flame of love and passion blooming from her countenance. Bunky fought with me to get loose to jump and swim to her, but I held on with all my might until she was a mere dot and then gone. He turned on me then such a look of fury and loathing that I dropped my hold. I suspect that somewhere far back in him some of that same feeling still exists.

When we got to the room, we sat down and ate what was left of my last loaf of bread.

"Is this all you've got?" he asked disdainfully.

"Yes," I said, "unless you want to go out and eat Saint John's Bread pods. Look, Bunky, I think you should get started for home right now. You're a week late with the draft board as it is."

He looked long and sourly at me: "Okay," he said at last, "I'm broke. I need money to get home." I gave him fifty cents.

Again he glared at me, "What's the joke?"

I showed him two more quarters. "That's all I have left," I said. "I told you while we were coming over what the setup is. If that boat of ours doesn't come in loaded with albacore to pay some of our debts, we'll be dead in the water. Swaggarts could foreclose and we'd lose all the dough we've put into the *Bunky.*"

As he went out the door, he turned and muttered, "Shit," then slammed the door shut. Privately I agreed with him, ever since I signed that simple-looking contract. Ah well, soon it would be time for mackerel harvest if the tuna failed us.

After my nights under the wharf I looked as unkempt as I felt. I had grown a beard. I sat on the docks waiting, snoozing. Often I rode the free ferry back and forth between Terminal Island and San Pedro. The movement and passing people gave me the feeling that I was using time more constructively than dozing on the docks. Sometimes I tried to talk to the deckhands, being a former deckhand, but they soon saw I was a loner down on my luck, and the area around Pedro abounded with such people to be avoided as boors. I'd walk the wharves, watch the sardine boats unload, and scan the harbor mouth for the *Bunky.*

One day riding the ferry I noticed a pretty, but forlorn looking girl using the boat as I did. I approached her, forgetful of my slovenly appearance and the thin lacy veil of the seat of my pants.

"Have you noticed we pass time the selfsame way?"

"Sure," she said with a weary smile, "we're both broke, huh?"

"This isn't my town," I answered, "and I'm dead broke."

"Ditto," she said and lapsed into a study of the seat before us, out of which she said without interest, just talking, "Where you from?"

"Portland."

"It's my hometown too," she said, arousing somewhat from her lethargy, and sadly, "or was. What you here for? Aren't there plenty jobs up there for a man?"

"I'm waiting for my boat to come in."

"Like the song," she said, snickering weakly.

Nostalgia touched me. "I went to Franklin High," I announced, groping away from Pedro and California itself.

"Huh," she answered, "so did I. Old Limpy denounced me and expelled me."

I was going to say, "same here," but instead used her "ditto," and asked "Why?"

"I was selling it. Some sneak squealed. Old Limpy even told my folks."

The ferry reached Pedro. There was a rush off of people and cars. We watched them and were dimly aware of the moment when the boat seemed ours (a fine strand of tenuous owning even in such as we) before the next invasion of cars and people headed in the opposite direction. Then the cars came aboard, lines were cast off and we were on another brief voyage. I handed her one of my Saint John's Bread pods.

"Try chewing the pod," I said.

She chewed and chewed and when the strange sweet flavor developed in her mouth, she grinned like a kid, "Yeah," she said, catching my eye, "it's funny but sweet."

I gave her another pod and another, thinking of the hoard I kept buried in the sand of my sleeping place. Rats were my problem.

"How come you're here?" I asked, chewing on a pod myself.

"Well, up there I was a hooker and I was doing all right—no pimp. I don't think there's anybody in the world likes it as much as I do, an' I like guys, most every kind. I give them what they want. Most hookers I've met say all guys are the same. I don't. I see it different."

"You and I see our worlds the same way," I said.

"Yeah. Well, then I got the clap—Jesus! But I had some bucks so I holed up. Did what the Doc ordered and soon I was over it, but broke. Well, I ain't screwing yet, that is, not as a job. Got to be awful sure I'm not passing the clap around, so while I'm waiting I thought I'd see what California guys are like. Hid on a tanker coming this way. They kicked me off here today. Nobody tried to grab off a piece on the trip. Scared of their captain, a killjoy, Bible kind of a guy. I'll have to take up the trade soon or starve. Take you now. You're broke and not interested in me. You're a true blue sort of guy with one or two dames heavy on your mind. Ain't it so?"

I had to admit it was.

"See, I know guys."

"Don't you call us tricks or johns?"

"When I do I'm gonna quit and marry."

The ferry bumped on the slip of the island side. I wanted to scan the harbor, felt the need to. "I've got to look," I said. "I've been away at least four hours."

"What's your name?" she asked. I told her. "Mine's Sandra Plant. Forget the Plant—they threw me out."

"See you!"

"Was fun talkin'."

I turned toward the harbor. Half-way there I met a couple I knew—a guy named Alex and his wife, Elaine. They frequented the place, wandering around, I thought, aimlessly like myself. We had chatted many times. I told them tales of Oregon and they seemed to enjoy them. I felt they must be empty-headed to have an appetite for such stories. In this tremendous gulf of free time that my spirit wasted in, I'd gotten quite friendly with Alex and Elaine. She now ran a few steps in front of her husband, smiling happily.

"Your boat's in, Clyde. They say they got no fish, but your waiting is over."

"Thanks," I muttered, hurrying past them down the dock. The tide was out; just her house and mast showed above the wharf edge. I looked down. She looked dirty and worn, the engine that pumped water to the bait tank still.

The *Bunky*, the wonderful boat we had fondly built, lay below looking tired. I went down the dock ladder and stepped on board. The crew were eating their last meal aboard. I grabbed a slice of bread. Gideon said, "Hi," through a full mouth.

"Any luck?"

The skipper, a blocky sort of a Scandinavian, spoke up: "Sold a few in San Diego, enough to buy bait. Been a long, bum trip. Every boat we've spoken to is in the same spot. Lots of tuna living high on the hog, what with these sardines and anchovy schools. Won't take the bait; they look at it and leave. Hey, you're Rice, aren't you?"

"Sure. How's the boat?"

"Tip top! That bait tank is a doozy. Say, want me to make another trip?"

"I can't afford such trips. I'm going to have to sell."

"Yesh, it figgers. We gave it one hell of a try."

"Had a home and chow. You watched the fish go by while I starved."

"You got a kick?" All the crew were looking at me now.

"None at all. I'd done the same. Now it looks funny, but back under the wharf it—"

"Under the wharf?"

"Aw, let it slide. Luck has been in short supply around here, except for the sardine boats."

The skipper, his sidekick, and Gideon stayed on. The other three of the crew heaved their seabags up on the dock and were gone, all from Pedro, the skipper said.

"Look," he went on, "me and Pinkie here are from Juneau.

After this fuckin' trip we're flat broke, but there's a seventy-footer from Sitka goin' to stop in Ketchikan on the way up. They'll take us on as crew. Leavin' Friday, but their bunks are all full till they leave. What I'm getting at, can we hole up here till then?"

"Sure," I replied, "if there's grub on board?"

"Look it over," he answered. "The last trip we left Santa Barbara and planned to cruise four hundred miles straight out, so we took food for a long trip. Then the radio announced that a big school had been spotted off Catalina, so with everybody else we rushed back only to find it was just a school of porpoises with no albacore along with them—another God-damned false alarm. I came in then, sore at this warm water fishing."

There were forty loaves of bread, case on case of beans, Spam, corned beef, coffee in bulk, rice in ten pound bags. I opened a can of beans and was lost to the world for awhile. It took the tremble out of my legs. My belly at last had plenty to work on. I flopped in the cabin's lower berth. What luxury!

Gideon came up from the engine room. "Hi," he said again shyly, "what's the score?"

"It's a toss-up," I replied. "I'll put her up for sale and, if it doesn't sell by mackerel time, we'll fish it. We could recoup there."

"Yeah, I suppose so. I hear this is a terrible fishing season all up and down the coast. The salmon failed from the Columbia to Kodiak." Sadly, he looked me over. "I hear mackerel is a poor answer." I had heard it too.

Next day we cleaned up the *Bunky* and took the blankets and pillow cases to a laundromat. Gideon had the cash to do it. I put a FOR SALE sign on the boat and arranged for an ad in the *Los Angeles Times* and settled in.

As I placed the sign, two tall fellows strolled past. They headed on up the wharf, then slowly came back, staring hard at the *Bunky*. I was about to speak to them, but they turned away continuing up the dock as before, staying close together as they walked. A team, I thought—I'll bet they do everything as a team—and wondered idly which of them was the boss.

About sunset I saw Sandra loafing along the dock. I waved and she came over.

"Have you got any more of those pods?" she asked me.

"Come aboard," I answered and helped her down the ladder. "How about a thick Spam sandwich and a couple of cups of coffee?" I said it glibly and was annoyed. From starvation to glibness about food seemed to need the passage of quite a bit of time not to sound obscene.

I introduced Sandra to Gideon, but she spoke up: "I'm an unemployed hooker," she said, "but I'm clean and I can also cook." So she stayed.

While I had been back in Portland doctoring my ulcer, Gideon had had some problems. Now he told me about them.

"Well," he said, "we went out on a trip to try and find that big albacore school that we went through in that tough going coming down. It looked to be two miles long. Remember? They were heading south, the skipper said. Said he felt it in his bones that they were a hundred miles west of Point Concepcion. They weren't, but we picked up near a hundred fish close off the point as we came in.

"He got the check from the cannery and cashed it in Pedro. I had a beer with him, then left to change oil and wipe up. He had the money where you could see it in his shirt pocket. I warned him that was a dangerous thing to do in Pedro. You know how he was. He got sore and sneered. 'When I need your girlish advice,' he snarled, 'I'll let you know.'

"Well, an hour after I got down on the boat a fellow came down, said he'd been hired as engineer. I told him the skipper couldn't fire me. I had stock in the boat, so we both went back to have it out with him. The bartender where he had been had seen him going around like a damn fool with those bills in his shirt pocket. He's never been seen since. The cops dragged the harbor for his body. No luck! That's when I wired you and you said get a new skipper, and we made this last trip with this Alaska guy."

"It don't make much sense to me," I mused. "It don't fit him. I think he piled on some friend's boat heading south. Everybody was sure he was dead. Those bills were a plant to make it look as he wanted it to look. Remember he was always talking about Punta Arenas."

The skipper, Vorp Lindstrom, as Gideon later named him, came back from town toward evening with his partner smelling fragrantly of booze, so they had a few bucks stashed away for absolute necessities.

Sandra had washed her dress and the accouterments she wore to feel dressed. I had hung them up to dry while she slipped down with faint ironic modesty into the darkened foc's'le.

Gideon had cooked a big stew of corned beef, beans and rice and had spiced it as no self-respecting Irishman would, more like he had lived a long time under a sombrero. We sat around (the lower bunk made a handy seat for two) dawdling over coffee. Vorp's sidekick, whom he called "Pinkie," was trying to tell of an experience he'd had fishing in Icy Straits, Little Indian Passage, he said (Alaska of course).

Vorp said he'd heard it too many times. "Tell it when I'm not around," he begged.

Sandra wanted to hear it. I noticed she had taken quite a shine to Pinkie. He was big and solid like Vorp, only one shoulder was much lower than the other. He never said how come, and I never asked. To me the evening was wonderful; the nights under the wharf were back there and dwindling already. Gideon was silent as usual, but I knew he had abilities you could count on in a pinch.

The talk was of no consequence now. It went on and on and ceased to make sense, just a pleasant blur to me. I fumbled my way to the best bunk, in the foc's'le, and was gone while trying to enjoy the coziness of blankets.

Much later I awoke with the need to relieve myself. I came up into the cabin just in time to see Sandra climbing out of the captain's upper berth to get into the lower berth with Pinkie. Protocol had been taken care of.

Next morning we had barely finished breakfast before two men hailed us from the dock. Both were tall, looking much alike, standing close together, the same men I'd seen when the sign was put up. A team, I'd thought, and as time went by this proved to be true. They'd seen our FOR SALE sign. On board they gave the *Bunky* a thorough inspection—asked a lot of questions and said they'd be back.

Some time later another fellow showed up on the dock and gazed intently down at the boat. I motioned to him to come aboard. He was handsome, with a small, dark mustache, still wearing olive drabs which appeared clean and neat. He replied to my question that he was not a prospective boat buyer, but, glancing furtively at the still uncleared breakfast table, said that he was very hungry. He'd been unable to find work and was broke. I heated up last night's leftover mulligan and made him a sandwich. It was obvious that he was half-starved, but his eating was deliberate and careful. The cliché, "impeccable manners," slid through my mind.

When he had finished, he turned and thanked me. We talked a bit about general things, the times, the late war. Apparently he had once been a Rhodes Scholar, but after a harrowing ordeal at the Normandy landing, he was left pretty much a basket case. I could see that. There was a confused agitated look on his face. He got up quickly, "I'd better go now."

"Where?" I asked.

"Anywhere," he answered, and started to leave.

"Why not stay here for a bit? We've got a great windfall of food on board and extra bunks."

"I would like to lie down," he said, so I soon had him ensconced in the foc's'le where he fell asleep at once.

The second night on board we were well lit with shore electricity, the radio moaning low as a background of our coming meal. The Alaskans, who had been removing the bait tanks on the Sitka boat, seemed, by their expressions, to find the music of Brahms, later Smetana, irritating. But with free food and lodging, they accepted it with good grace.

Sandra appeared in early dusk in a different dress. "Sorry I'm late," she said, "but a guy needed my attention." She named herself cook and produced supper in short order, contriving to sit next to Pinkie at the table. But when the addled soldier appeared from the foc's'le, she left her seat to help him fill his plate.

Later in the evening she got me out on deck and asked me what I knew about him. I now called him Stevenson, for I felt the kind of mother he would have had would surely have given him a three-syllable first name. It wasn't quite requisite to getting a Rhodes Scholarship but it probably helped.

Pinkie tried again to tell the tale of Indian Passage on Icy Strait, but Vorp again prevented it. So the harrowing story was never told. I was never to learn what almost happened to Pinkie.

Next day I was alone, except for Stevenson. There was something odd about him. You never noticed him among other people. He was the guy that wasn't there. He ate with us and slept on the boat. I'd told him to consider it home until it was sold, but he was not woven into the background of my problems. I noticed that Gideon, as I did, felt very protective of him. Sandra was fascinated with him. Though Pinkie scowled, Stevenson was so unaware of everything that Pinkie soon forgot it.

Stevenson seemed genuinely terrified of the girl, perhaps any girl. Sandra continuously tried to touch him, to brush against him and to see that he got the best parts of the meal.

Now, on this final night of the Alaskan's stay, Sandra was beside herself to mother the boy, to cuddle and caress him, and I had to tell her to leave him alone or get off the boat.

That night, worried about him, I slept in a blanket in the wheelhouse where she'd have to step over me to get down the ladder to be near him. As usual, after she'd paid deference to the skipper in her intimate way and crawled down to be with Pinkie for the last time, I fell asleep thinking all was well. But sometime during the night the most awful screaming startled me awake.

Stevenson had stormed up the ladder, stepped on me, with Sandra right behind him making placating sounds as she rushed over me, tearing after him up the dock. I followed barefoot. He was howling as he ran at top speed down the long wharf, down past the net drying areas. Moonlight showed her following him, now squalling to him that she would take care of him forever. I followed but could not keep up. I caught up to her at the ferry slip, watching the ferry go out, Stevenson obviously on board.

"I warned you. Why did you do it?"

"I couldn't help it. I'll get off your boat. I want to get off. I'll hunt till I find him."

"Don't you see he's in terror of you?" I said. "You'll drive him over the brink if you haven't already."

"Maybe," she said, "maybe, but I've got to be sure. I could do so much for him."

Back at the boat she said, "Please get my clothes. I don't want to come aboard." I brought them to her and she put them on, slipped her feet in high heeled pumps and was off in the darkness without a word.

Next morning, after Vorp and Pinkie had lugged their seabags up on the wharf and away, Gideon and I, over cups of coffee, stared at one another. "It's kind of quiet around here," I said.

Gideon poured a bit more of condensed milk into my coffee. "You don't attract quiet, that's one thing sure," he said, smiling quietly at me. I knew he was beginning to like me, though he shouldn't. He and his brother had been intent from the start on somehow wangling this boat away from me. His silent companionship was good, and I found it impossible to see him as my enemy.

One day Alex and Elaine, showed up and I waved them aboard. They had a bottle of good wine to share with me and I told them my woes. They questioned me about what I would do after I sold the *Bunky*.

"It's obvious now I have made one more failure," I replied. "I'll see if my wife will still tolerate me and if she does, I'll get a job, but really I'd like to take a year off. I've been working darned hard—two jobs at a time for around eight years, and all I've got to show for it is debts." Rather diffidently I went on, "I'd like to take a year off and write."

Alex nodded vigorously, "Yes, I'm sure you could. You impress me as a born storyteller. You haven't been reticent over this—even though we're strangers. You made an interesting tale in the telling. In fact, Elaine and I've been listening and laughing over your great stories ever since we met you on the docks. It's a gift you have. What do you want to write about?"

"Well, there's the lighthearted times in my youth when I worked on the ferries of San Francisco Bay—I'd like to tell of those years. I know I could write about how the little railroad terminal Tiburon was once and the odd, wonderful people who lived and worked there. Gosh, I'd love describing the cave we children dug when school was let out during the flu epidemic, about the log cabin we built and a lot of other things we kids did. I could go on and on."

I told them the synopsis of a short novel that I thought I could do justice to. The short story that seemed to particularly appeal to them was of a sadistic cop on the waterfront, which I called "Hitch Your Wagon to a Star." Anyway as they left they said maybe they had a way to get me in with writing people.

Gideon eyed the long slim legs of the girl going up the ladder, "Umm-umm." Forgetting the girl then, he said, "Hey, Clyde, I like your story about the cop. The name you gave it—sure describes that cop uncle of mine—a mean son-of-a-bitch!"

Later that day the two men who'd stopped by before came down the ladder. "Okay so we're interested in your boat," said one, "but not your price."

"You mean the price in the paper?" I asked. "It's a giveaway."

"No, we see the *twenty-one thousand dollars* on your FOR SALE sign in the window. Giveaway, sure, but look around, all along the wharf, any wharf. Every second boat has got a FOR SALE sign on it. Price, hell! Boats are up for grabs this winter and you know it."

"How about a cup of coffee?" I asked to break it.

"Sounds good. In fact, we were planning on it. Ed, get that bag of doughnuts out of the car."

They resembled one another, but on closer inspection I noted the deep-set eyes and generally more robust look of the one called Ed, as well as the prominent nose and slightly bulging eyes of the other who made himself known as Sam Tolberg and the boss (he wrote it on himself but not in italics). He grinned at me in a way that made me accept him as a very sound person. Neither he nor his companion looked weathered enough to be commercial fishermen.

Sam stepped before me into the cabin and drew his long legs under the table and leaned into the corner seat. I could see he savored the moment. If he could make the *Bunky* his own, he'd lean into the corner of the booth full of contentment but set for adventure. When Ed returned with the doughnuts, Sam introduced him as Ed Bortum. "He was the foreman in my shop during the war," he explained.

Sam complained that the coffee was too strong. "I've had a humdinger of a heart attack and have to watch things like that—always have Ed along now."

We dunked doughnuts and considered each other obliquely.

"Heard you built this boat yourself. Got to admit she's made like a brick shithouse. But twenty-one thousand dollars! Sure, in ordinary times, but not now."

"I'd take five hundred off, if you don't want the bait seine."

He grinned at me, "Hell, that's an awful short drop. I'm offering fifteen thousand cash, not a cent more. Okay, that's a bona fide offer. Like to see how she's built inside if it's all right with you." They gave her a careful scrutiny and left.

Fifteen thousand dollars! There was a twenty thousand debt on the boat. What was I to do? The possibility of making another trip would set me back a thousand dollars more. I decided against the offer, but dreamed wishfully of a great killing in mackerel.

One boat-length past us down the dock was the place where the great sardine boats came stern-to at the dock, with their capacity of tiny fish to be processed and labeled, the cans boxed and wheeled out into the world that was sick of eating fish instead of meat all through the war. At the moment, however, the cannery and the sardine fisherman were doing very well, while all around the harbor and up canals tied to the many docks of the region, the tuna and the salmon boats from Kodiak to Monterey lay idle, listening to vague rumors of great schools of albacore that never panned out. The canneries were just across the dock from us. Our *Bunky* was tied up to the dock along with a dozen others.

It was the main thoroughfare for the harbor. When the shrill noon whistle blew, the office workers and a horde of young Mexican girls who worked in the canneries, coal black hair glistening in the sunshine, poured out. They joined the tourists and loafers and fishermen in boots coming from their nets on the drying racks to their boats for lunch—a pageant of sorts—and classical music, maybe from the *Bunky*'s radio, filtered pleasantly through the throng. This was no ordinary street, for there seemed to be a certain camaraderie. The loiterers, cannery workers and office people were joined indirectly but tenaciously by that product of the seas—fish.

Many of the workers sat with feet hanging over the edge of the dock and, while they ate their sandwiches, joshed with the crews of the boats below them. One young man who sat there called to me as he left and thanked me for the music and the next day when he came, I invited him on board to eat his lunch and to talk of music in which we had similar tastes. Willard was his name and he worked in the office of the port captain. After that he lunched with me everyday, sitting on the hatch admiring the Mexican girls' legs.

Several days later in such a setting the port captain appeared escorting a very important person in Homburg hat and light overcoat, for there was a slight coolness to the breeze. Meticulously attired, like a mannequin in the window of a Frisco haberdashery, he peered timidly down over the edge of the wharf at the boats.

"Which boat in the harbor is the most seaworthy?" he asked.

The port captain promptly named our boat. "One of the best skippers we know of had her up off Vancouver Island. A number of boats were lost in a bad storm up there, some twice as big as the *Bunky*, but the *Bunky* came through without trouble, due, I've heard, in part to a heavy yacht keel."

The peering, important one's face disappeared from view, though the Homburg hat could still be seen as they moved along the dock. God! How proud I was, how I hated to give up our boat, but the feeling of overdue bills soon snowed in my love of the *Bunky* with just plain arithmetic.

Sam, the prospective buyer along with his pal, Ed, made an appearance soon after and I told them proudly what I'd heard.

"We know what the boat is worth, Rice," Sam said, "that's why we're interested, but the boat's unfinished. Like a lot of other people in the harbor you came down with the boat seaworthy, but not quite finished, to try to make enough money to complete it and carry you and your bills through the winter. Sure, I know it's a good boat, and what needs to be done to it Ed and I could do in a hurry with that fancy equipment up in my shop.

"How about all these other people who are coming and looking at it?" he said in a very friendly way. "I saw you showing it to some Mex who haven't got a dime and Greeks who have, but won't be parted with it except by amputation. Hell! We watched one day. You had seven prospective buyers, you thought. They liked the boat, but exchange some of their dinero for it, not a chance!"

I had to agree that it had so far been a disheartening experience. Sam turned to Gideon, who was standing near me: "By the way," he said, "were you thinking of going uptown to buy a necktie in the next couple of hours?"

"No, I'll be around all day," Gideon replied, smiling.

"Well, don't sell the boat till we get back! Come on, Clyde. I want to show you around so you can get a clearer picture of where you stand."

We drove around the wharves to see all the FOR SALE signs on boats. Then we stopped at two boats that were slightly larger than mine and beautifully finished and found that the price was sixteen thousand dollars apiece.

"You're beginning to get the picture," said Sam, "but I want to clinch your view of it."

We drove to a small shipyard where a newly finished boat stood in the ways. He waved to the owner of the yard.

"Same length and tonnage as yours," Sam said.

The hull hadn't been painted yet, to show prospective buyers the craftsmanship used in its building.

"What do you think of those planks and the way they are laid? She's bronze fastened."

I had to admit there was artisanship of high order in the laying of the planking of the hull.

"Two-inch mahogany," said Sam, "and I don't mean that soft mahogany that's been turning up lately. Let's step aboard."

It was a beautiful, practical job. We climbed down and hunted up the owner of the yard.

.

"How much you taking for the *Lena*—cash?"

"Fourteen-five takes her. It's a shame, but with the situation that's suddenly developed here. . . ."

"You mean too many boats and not enough fish?" Sam asked.

"Yeah. I'll not build another one till something drastic hits the market," the builder spat. "Hell's fire, I'm getting so I talk like a newspaper."

"Well, I'll be thinking about it," said Sam and we walked away.

"You wonder why I haven't taken one of them instead of yours?" he said as we drove along. "It's like this. When they made the house on your boat, they made it too high, and we're six-three and -four and we need headroom. Besides that, the way you placed the bait tank and the boat's reputation are the rest of the story. I'll give you fifteen thousand dollars cash, and I'll hold off for a month. I just wanted to show you that you've got a buyer on your hands. You probably won't come out ahead, but it sure will cut your losses."

When they left I tried to look things full in the face, but my mind shifted into hope—hope and the coming mackerel season. Perhaps we could bring in enough fish to get through this winter somehow—have one more chance at the tuna. Just thinking about it made me consider the bills lightly. One was bound to be belabored by creditors while getting started, I told myself.

I sent Ginny a pleasant letter about brighter prospects, though I can't imagine why. Hope can brighten the color of things, sure, but arithmetic does not lend itself to mood.

"Looks like we're having visitors," murmured Gideon, as Alex and Elaine came down the ladder.

"After being completely flotsam and jetsam for so long, don't you find it hard to get used to the comfort of the cabin?" Elaine's remark seemed rehearsed.

"Good morning," I greeted them. "Not so. Living under the dock was much harder to get used to."

Abruptly, Alex started talking, "Some of those things you said you want to write about, your stories—we'd like to hear some more. There are people in the writing field I can get you in touch with, but do you have something you've written down? If it's anything like the way you tell a tale, you've got it made." He was quite businesslike about it.

Here was a chance to read some of my own writing! I felt buoyant. "Well, you know there is a lot of activity around here, but now there are boring times while waiting for possible buyers and I've filled them in by writing about an old friend I knew in San Francisco. David Wheelwright was his name, a strange combination, a large fellow of great physical strength. He threw the great Strangler Lewis for a fall in his training camp and had more than once swum the Golden Gate in December, yet his sometime mincing, prissy ways marked him as a homosexual, which he was not. Here's what I've written, though it's not yet completed."

"Great! Read away. We're good listeners, Clyde."

I read:

"David was addicted to creampuffs and whiskey, though whiskey was certainly secondary to pastry, and as the years passed he become increasingly fat, until he looked out of one wrinkle, took food in at another and generally functioned from crevices.

"To get David past a pastry shop would take three strong men. Once trim ankles flickering up Market Street would have kept him away from his vice, but in later years I have seen him stand, a majestic figure like Balzac, and I'm thinking of Rodin's *Balzac*, in front of the swinging doors of a pastry shop. The owner, intent on acquiring further victims of his soul-dissolving product, had placed a fan in the rear so that the smells of pastry and candied cherries and strawberries, of vanilla and, topping it off, the gently insinuating odors of apple dorper would sail out the doors as customers batted them to and fro and swishing between the legs of newsboys, swirling around the corseted promenaders, would strike our David standing there at the curb, a man defiant. At such a moment I have seen him tremble like a leaf and, when you are built as David was, that's a particularly difficult thing to do. Then in the end, after grimaces of pain and determination and half a dozen flashings of the 'glance defiant,' he would rush through the crowd, burst open the doors and demand a half a dozen large creampuffs, breathing in the airs of the place and snorting them out as do the caricatures of enraged bulls. Upon receiving the creampuffs he would gulp down three or four, leering meanwhile at the other pastries in the showcase. Then, rending and swallowing the last of a creampuff, he would stop seemingly sated.

"There would be about here that uneasy quiet purported to be the advance publicity of storms. It would wrap around David like an unseen wraith that even the salesgirls felt, and such was its force that at times friends who were with him said that the whole bakery would be filled with its foreboding and inertia.

Flies ceased to buzz, gumchewers broke rhythm and stopped, and once when David was being particularly David, the powerful quiet stopped the pendulum of a Seth Thomas clock on the wall and stilled forever the flickering blades of the fan. And then the sense of degradation would begin to prick him here and there before remorse, like a great wave from a septic tank would rear up and tower over him before it bashed him with horror and effluvia. At such times David would stand like a rock, for all this was just, he felt. After all, had he not broken his high resolve? Then he should accept the pain of it like a man, which he would do.

"One of these friends of his, watching him at such a time rooted to the floor of the pastry shop while the commerces of buns and frosted cakes went on about him, said that David in the utter degradation stage looked nobly disdainful, that people drew away from him respectfully, for then he could easily be mistaken for a massive Eastern potentate travelling incognito.

"'Probably the Shah of Smerth,' a small man was once heard to mutter to his wife. 'Probably rammed all his jewels up his— probably hid his jewels somewhere about his person. Them Asiatics has inscrutable ways.'

"He did look, his friends said, as if digestion for the moment was not for him a reflex, but conscious and as if David were working out the complicated procedure as a mental feat like juggling, and to tell the truth David, in self-degradation, did look like a juggler with eight balls; he even walked like one. Then when he had taken his punishment, and part of it was imagining the layer of suet that was disposed between his hide and him as becoming thicker and more dense, David would leave the pastry shop throwing what was left of his bag of creampuffs into a corner, and he would walk that walk of his that told the initiate how he had lost his integrity but still retained, if not resolve, at least some purpose and dignity in direct relation to his fat. However fat, dignity and all, David now moved faster, for he was well aware of where he was going and what he was going to do.

"This was the 'Black Tulip and Blue Dahlia' stage, for David had worked out some not so strange alchemy, a sort of photosynthesis in which he used money as a catalyst, did calisthenics called, 'lifting another one,' and carried out a heavy exercise that required magnetism and verve called 'one on the house,' and ended up with a temporarily drowned and unincumbent remorse."

Alex and Elaine were amused, though not laughing. They weren't the laughing kind. "I'd like to hear more about him," Alex said.

"So would I," I answered, "but he's dead. He had a dispute with a streetcar over the right of way. They say the streetcar cut quite a figure. We who knew him still miss him."

Alex said, "I'm no writer, of course, but I associate with a number of them, and I'm quite certain we can get you a job writing. I notice you have pretty liberal views. Mine are radical. Elaine and I are communist organizers. If you would join the party and carry the card, I could get you on as a writer tomorrow in one of the big studios."

I was surprised. "Just what would I do there?" I asked.

"Really you won't have to do anything but say 'yes' or 'well, I don't know if I'd go as far as that, still'—or something like that when people bug you. Anyway the fellow who would be your immediate boss is a communist too. Several of the writers are. I do know I could get you started at two hundred a week. You could climb out of this hole you're in. Funny, I had a hunch something would come of this."

While he spoke, I tried to take in the picture. Marx in his writings appealed to and influenced me when I was sixteen and seventeen. I had high hopes that the Russian Revolution at the end of World War I would result in a perfect state—the state envisioned by Marx. It would handle the problems of hierarchy and stratification far better than our democracy. But then as I read more of their publications, listened to their apologists, I became disillusioned. I saw it now as another faulty ideology weakened by jousts with reality. Its basic statements no longer had the ring of truth for me, but of idealistic nonsense, extolling values it itself had proven wrong again and again.

The money looked good. A writing job would be heaven, but I must turn it down. I would make a very poor hypocrite while trying to protect what was left of my integrity.

"Need I ask your decision," he said, as he grasped my hand while Elaine slipped a friendly arm around my waist.

I responded emotionally to the warm contact and, feeling very mean, I reluctantly replied: "I can't accept it. It's a wonderful chance that you offer, perhaps better than I will ever get again, but I'd be seventeen kinds of a hypocrite if I took it. Your beliefs and my beliefs are different, still I want to shake your hand for offering it."

"I don't think you know anything about communism," said Alex. "You could learn. We have a school."

"Alex, I read *Das Kapital*, if my memory serves me right, about the time you started grade school. One of my long time friends was an intimate of Trotsky's. He corresponded with all the leading American communists. My favorite aunt brought the *New Republic* and *The Nation* to the west coast. I carried a Wobbly card for awhile and that was when I first became disillusioned with communism."

The both looked at me as if I had suddenly acquired another dimension. Alex asked me: "What does capitalism have that other governments don't?"

Here I was in the harangue that I wanted to avoid, but I talked: "There are too many predatory over-ambitious men in the world, Alex. In a capitalistic democracy they go into business and work up so some of them get to be corporation presidents. Business absorbs them. Such guys are a clear-cut danger in government. The likes of Hitler and Stalin would end up in this country as presidents of corporations that have a corner on the potato chip market or bathroom fixtures."

We stared at one another for a moment, then they turned and silently went up the ladder. With very mixed feelings I sat down on the hatch. The little childhood rhyme entered my head. In laughing irony I sang it:

"Be sure you're right, then go ahead.
Don't mind what people say,
You have a way that you must go
So do it your best way."

I had proven time and again it was a great way to end up behind the eight ball. I mourned that job for years.

•

The mackerel season—the annual canning of the fish—was due. Every boat in the harbor except the sardine seiners and the big tuna boats were ready to go out and harvest that stinking fish and get the last paycheck of the year. Hope was in the air: a manly resolve to make this last-chance fishery the thing that would bring in the beans and pay off some promissory notes. Everyone had their mackerel gear ready for action. Fishermen strutted down the long dock and all around diesels were started that had been quiet for some time, and then came the news.

The canneries would not can mackerel! The problem, they said, was that all the mackerel had a worm in the intestine, and they were not going to fight with the pure food department people over this parasite. Mackerel were canned, as are all fish, with their intestines removed, but on this charge, nobody really knowing, the augmented fleet stayed in the harbor.

The fishermen's union sent committees to the cannery heads and on the various docks groups of men met in frustration. They did not want to realize that the canneries could not possibly handle all the mackerel from this large a fleet. It could jam their warehouses; anyway mackerel was a fish few were fond of and now that there were no restrictions on meat, canned fish hadn't the immense market it had during the war.

There followed a week of useless negotiation. The union

fought an uphill battle, while it was found that the mackerel were sick with an inflamed appendix—hogwash! But fish scientists were brought in to make statements until the season was at last over. I had to face the fact I must sell at once, for my boat insurance would be delinquent at the end of the week.

I went to see the port captain to go over my account with him. He was a fine big brash sort of a fellow who probably played football in college and should have become a politician. Down on the docks they said he had a way with people. He greeted me pleasantly and had my file brought out.

"Well, Rice," he said, "it's been a bad year for you. You couldn't get down the river till almost winter. Looks here," considering the file, "like luck allowed you to keep the bait tank full but the hold empty. It's the general picture down here this season. You forty- and fifty-footers aren't big enough, couldn't carry fuel enough to get down around well below Magdalena Bay where big catches are being made. You haven't had a Chinaman's chance. You still have your boat, encumbered sure, but still able to fish, but very few fish are being caught in the areas you can reach. What are you going to do?"

"Sell her," I answered. "It's a hell of a thing to do, after all the oak trees I cut down, fighting the lumber through the mill, the whole doggoned thing. This last has happened way too quick for me."

"You know Rice, it would have been a lot better if you'd have wintered your boat at Astoria, then got down there about March or May, but that's all water under the bridge. I see why you had to do it. The bills from the construction were immediate, so you come down here half-assed like a lot of other northern boats. Now here is a new angle to fishing I'll let you in on. Those bills you owe the company I can let fly for awhile, that is, if you will go south way down around Point Arenas and fish for us."

"Have you people got a cannery down there?" I asked. Excitement and hope were pushing resignation aside in me.

"No, we haven't a cannery there yet, but it's in the hopper, I hear," he said. "We're bringing the fish catch back up here in small freezer ships. They'd lay in Point Arenas and take on the fish you and seven or eight boats would be bringing in."

"That's a long pull for us just getting down there."

"Yes," he said, "but you could lash a few drums of fuel on deck and fuel up in Mazatlan, and you'd make it easily. Stay close to the coast crossing the Bay of Tehuantepec, but I guess you know about that. What do you say, Rice? It seems to me the only way for you to get out of the jam you're in. You got to be getting down there if you go. You'll need a crew—five would be right."

"Could you let me have an advance, so I can take care of the quarterly insurance that is due next week?"

"Sure, we can do that. You get your stores and oil and your crew on board and we'll take care of the insurance."

The whistle blew in the midst of our talk and I went out into the sunshine to faces and colors and laughter that registered in me as banks of flowers. This possibility probably had been there all along as I'd sweated it out trying to sell my boat. Now things would not come to an abrupt halt. There definitely was a great future for the *Bunky* and Captain Rice would take her down and cross the dreaded Bay of Tehuantepec, not too close to the shallow shore and not too far out where the famous winds of the region would catch her broadside and roll off the drums of oil.

The tide was high. I jumped down on deck and told Gideon of the offer. He was a family man and he saw his chance to own the boat dwindling, but adventure pricked him up and, though trying to hide it, he gave me a wonderful smile and said: "I'll go where the *Bunky* goes."

"It's too easy to be true. I want a couple of days to think it out," I said, grinning widely.

Next day I looked for Sam and Ed to show up, but they didn't appear. In early afternoon I sent Gideon to Pedro to see if he might see some of the crew from the last trip. Gideon came back without crew members. His rather melancholy smile didn't light up when he had given me the split-second examination that we all carry out.

"It didn't go so well with you either, huh?"

"You're right but let it pass," I answered.

Together we cooked up a stew, but were very much in our own thoughts well into the evening, then the *Bunky* tipped ever so slightly and we looked up to see Willard appear at the cabin door. He was dressed casually, his feet in tennis shoes, instead of the usual business suit.

"Got a cup of coffee?" We had. After he'd sipped a bit of that ancient brew he said:

"I'm so used to the dock being a busy place, that this quiet now seems kind of disturbing. I guess it's because I am feeling conspiratorial. If it ever gets out that I came here tonight, it would mean my job, and I'm in line for promotion, but we've been friends, Clyde (anyway you like Respighi's music), so don't go down there. Those little freezer ships were offered to us months ago. We examined them, but never bought. There's seven boats like yours sitting there waiting and have been for six months for a freezer ship the company promised. They're broke and I'm sure they'll lose their boats all because of a big company's fool whim. Don't go down there, Clyde! You'll lose everything. Well, I can't say more." He disappeared from the door and again the boat tipped ever so slightly, righted itself and we knew he was gone.

"Well," said Gideon after a long silence. "I believe your friend. What would he gain by telling us that? He took quite a chance to tell you."

"That's it," I said, "it's got to be so. It adds up. Willard gave us one hell of a break tonight, but we can't let on."

"You know," said Gideon, "when this is all over—the goings on in this little harbor and that parade, as you call it, up on the wharf at noon—I'm going to miss it. Well," he said, "guess I'll turn in."

"We get along pretty well," I said.

"Yeah, considering," he answered, thoughtfully.

Sleeplessly, I adjusted to not being a captain of the *Bunky* in southern waters and put aside once more the notion that I would ever be a screenwriter. I had to laugh at my losses, as I blinked away possible tears, and startled Gideon.

"What's the joke?" he asked.

"The joke's on me," I said with an unmanly sigh, "it's always on me," and cursed myself for harboring this self-pity.

I don't know what time it was when I awoke. It wasn't a sexual urge that bothered me, but hunger to be holding Ginny, confiding in her, laughing with her. She was there wraithlike for me to see. Was it in my mind's eye or did my own wide open eyes build her lovely image against the darkness? One was of a time when I had met her in the bus station in Portland, and in another Ginny was togged for snow, and camping scenes with Ginny at Roaring River. The images passed turning to gossamer which some breeze of the mind wafted away.

Then I was back in reality. How could I lessen my losses by the sale of the boat for more than Sam offered? Going over what had happened so far I realized that, except for Sam, there had not been one serious buyer.

I had gotten a runaround with some Mexicans, which included waiting on the corner of the Los Angeles tenderloin to meet a man (they had said in broken English) who owned a whole fleet of fishboats and was eager to buy mine. He never appeared and, though I sensed I was being watched, I couldn't understand why. My problem battered my mind. I couldn't sleep. Finally I turned on the bunk light and got out all the letters I had received from Ginny and pored over them until at last sleep took over.

I awoke, the light still on. It was morning. Letters were scattered all over my bunk. As I dressed, the eight o'clock whistle was shrill at the cannery. Gideon was up and out on deck watching a big tuna clipper—a hundred-footer—docking.

We watched its slow landing with morning's no comment and moved back into the cabin for rolled oats with some fresh milk from San Pedro. We both hungered for physical activity; work that we could do to make us part of things. Neither of us was fitted to be an idle observer. We scrubbed apathetically in the bait tank, though it did not need it and looked for Sam and Ed but they didn't appear.

I renewed my ad in the paper, a much more expensive ad, fully describing the boat. Surely this would bring in some prospective buyers. No one came, not even riffraff without a dime who put on great airs as buyers and felt the power of working up a deal, though with non-existent money. No, no one came! So went the dread day that the *Bunky*'s insurance lapsed.

Next forenoon as I was passing down the dock, I saw Gideon in one of the open telephone booths. Though it was certainly not my habit, I knew I must listen in on him. He didn't see me standing behind him. I heard enough to know that his brother and their attorney were coming down to take over the boat next day. Here it was! He turned around and saw me, first with a guilty look, then one of relief. Before he said anything I asked:

"When do they get here?"

"I don't know, Clyde, but they're taking the six-forty-five morning flight out of Seattle tomorrow. They're coming right through. Well, now you know!" Looking rather shame-faced, he headed back toward the boat.

I had Sam's phone numbers in my wallet. I called his home and his place of business. No luck! He hadn't been down for a couple of days. A panicky feeling crept in on me and I instinctively rushed over to the *Bunky*, as if to protect it against whatever enemy forces. I was so keyed up that I couldn't think straight. When the noon whistle blew, I jumped a foot. If I tried to hunt for Sam that would further complicate matters. I could only stay by the boat. Anyway, I climbed out on the dock needing the rub of people. I stared about uselessly. I was about to give up looking for them (no tall person had appeared in the crowd), when far down the dock a head and shoulders showed up above the Mexican girls and squat Italian fishermen, and I knew at once it was Ed, but where was Sam? I worked toward him in the crowd and before we met I yelled: "Where is he?"

Ed grinned and pushed on toward me. "He's in San Francisco. His son had a bad accident up there." Then looking very pleased with himself, he said, "but he left me with the power of attorney. Do you want to sell your boat?"

"Yes, I have to," I answered.

"On our terms?"

"Yes, fifteen thousand dollars, not a cent less." I told him of the coming of the attorney and Simon and the immediacy of the situation.

First we paid the Swaggarts' loan. Gideon accepted it, looking hugely relieved. Then we went across the dock and paid off the cannery. We worked on other bills that I had on the diesel, on the equipment, etc. We kept at it till we had used up the money and I found there was the two thousand dollars that Bunky and I had put in it and the three thousand dollars that my father had loaned me.

"Sam said to trust you to clear the boat. I wouldn't, but I'm not Sam."

"The boat will be cleared in two months."

"Yeah, Sam said to trust you. Anyway, if the slate isn't wiped clean in two months, he'll send me up there and don't put yourself in that picture. It ain't healthy."

I looked him over. God, no! It could be dangerous, perhaps fatal not to clear the *Bunky.*

What would Bunky think of all this, and Ginny and Nordi? I'd failed again. What would Bo and Bill Nagel and the other boatbuilders on Tomahawk Island think? Gideon broke in on my reverie. He brought a cup of coffee for both of us. We stirred in sugar and canned milk.

"I want to say something," he started in a manner not usual to him. "When we first got here I was tickled about the failing tuna season. We got here way too late. What a laugh! You were playing right into our hands. If you didn't make your payments on time, our lawyer would come down and take over the boat according to the contract. Fine, but after the mackerel disaster—you wriggling and squirming trying to sell it—we living and eating together in this cabin, it became hard for me to remain loyal to Simon. You've treated me like a friend and I felt cheap about my part in this. I'm glad you got out from under in time, Clyde. Anyway, lots of luck!"

Later, when Gideon was gone, I started to say goodbye to the *Bunky*. I went down in the foc's'le and the engine room and in the hold to see the heavy oak frames, the boat's ribs we had steamed into position. I felt of the deckbeams above my head—six-by-sixes—with the beautiful slight arch of the deck sawed into them. I studied the plank lining of the boat and saw the heads of thousands of spikes we'd driven home, went out to the bow and touched the three-inch square iron cutwater we sharpened above and under water. It was there to defend the bow and was welded down under the water to the heavy steel keel, the ballast of the boat, deep down. In some of the frames I came upon bolts Ginny had threaded by hand.

On deck I studied the tarred seams of the decking, went to the stern and, leaning over, saw what I'd shaped from the massive timbers I'd gotten from the Clackamas County bridge crew. As I leaned over looking down at the curved surface I imagined a broadaxe handle in my hand—the broadaxe with which I hewed them to shape. For an hour I knew my boat, all its parts and all its wholeness. I ended up in the wheelhouse. I grasped the steering wheel as if I was going to make a passage. Christ! My hands fell away. The dream ended.

Then I balled up my personals in three great bags to be sent home in the morning. Walking down the long dock, I looked back once more to see for the last time the flaring bow of the *Bunky*.

In some ways I have never lost her, and though I've looked in many ports I never found her again. Long after, a Greek, who had bought her from Sam years later, gave me a snapshot of her loaded with twenty-eight tons of pilchards. It is one of my dearest possessions.

I looked about for Gideon, but he and his belongings were gone. I often see his face in my memories—a quiet, most likeable guy.

●

On the night train to San Francisco my thoughts were a hopeless jumble. I couldn't go straight home with the guilt of losing the *Bunky*. I didn't know how I was going to go any farther toward home, and Frisco, thank God, was between San Pedro and Portland.

I wondered and wondered what Bunky would think about the loss of our good ship. What would he say to me, for I'd lost his key to a proud future? And what of Ginny and Nordi? I'd failed them all once again—failed the *Bunky* itself. Oh, I was loath to go home. In Tiburon I bought a loaf of bread and a section of salami and roamed the hills while anguish ate at me, wandered Sugarloaf for several days and though, I often gazed down and hard at it, I did not approach Waterspout Point and its inhabitants.

VIII

In Which
I Become a Sawyer, Tinker with Writing,
Get Alder and Deeper in Debt,
and
Learn of Nordi's Decision

1947

GINNY AND I left Vanport after a year. Nordi, in one of her letters, mentioned that her cousin had vacated the house and she'd like us to move in. We were glad to. The vague trumpetings on both sides of us were less loud than the crickets. So much for the distaste of our relatives.

I had a job as a helper on an insulating crew and lived day to day. I moved about as a shorn sheep, bereft of pride, a willy-nilly guy savoring comfort and abjuring the urge "to get ahead in the world." Still, we were happy, in fact, we were gaily following the hounds on weekends, but no "tally-hos." These were cougar hounds and we followed them into the mountains, but they stuck up their noses when we showed them cougar tracks in snow and in the trail.

Three or four days after we had lost our hounds up the Clackamas River, the ranger called saying the dogs had come to the station. I left very early next morning to pick them up, but on my return an accident, not my own, stalled me. I was a half an hour late getting to work and they fired me. Though they couldn't fault my work, I didn't and couldn't belong to their union. It was a funny little union—everyone belonging to it was related to three or four families. They passed the good jobs on only to relatives.

Ten years later, returning to the insulating company to find out about the crew I'd worked with, I was told they were all dead. The asbestos with which we were insulating had killed them all and I, whose job it was to stir up the fluffy material every morning in a trough making a dough of it, coughing and sneezing in its dust, had gotten away from it in time—all because of the frivolous business of following the hounds. Another example of my profiting from my mistakes and gaining nothing in my serious endeavors.

After I was fired, I got on again with my father at Acme Flavoring. The work there was dull for me. Nothing had changed. My father made middling-good flavoring extracts. He was a tradition in the trade, but the trade was changing and he refused to believe this. It didn't matter to me for awhile, for Ginny was in all ways beginning to bloom. Always a reader, she now had devoured the classics and what was good in contemporary writing. This, on her bus trips to and from work. She took an interest in philosophy and government and our conversations were lively and I found I had to bone up and drag out my old assumptions for a thorough dusting. Somehow she was also able to get me to put more time into writing; picking up a chapter I'd written in Alaska and enlarging on it.

Ginny had developed on the marvelous frame she'd inherited from her father. Now, though still a bit on the lean side, she nevertheless became almost sumptuous and I could not get enough of her beauty and photographed her scores of times in the buff around lakes and streams and sometimes somewhat immersed in them. In late spring we made a little garden. What joy! Just Ginny and I and nature. How we flourished. After much thought we decided not to bring a child into this overcrowded world.

Ginny and I were in paradise, whether hiking or loving or just having a meal together. At such times, I forgot that I was doomed to failure and was swept blithely along. Perhaps it seemed such a heaven because we had to reap the joy one person could get from or give another within the two years we allotted ourselves. Though we lamented the thought of being parted, we were firm in our resolve, for had not sweet Nordi given us this time to be together?

I hid from Ginny that I sought a place back in the storeroom almost daily and put myself with Nordi in Madeline's garden and tried to make her feel my presence and my love, trying to be as fair as I could in a world that always seemed arranged to confound me.

When Nordi and I had been together we were often at outs, angry with each other for days. But with Ginny, knowing that our time was short, neither of us wasted it in acrimony. We had few friends and did not seek outside companionship. Oh, a little bit, not enough to interfere with the ecstatic hours we spent together. I was writing more stories now. I became interested in the short story form. I wrote twelve short stories. Four of them, I felt good about, as I had conveyed in them what I wanted to say about the yeast of life.

But to me both writing and making extracts lacked the heavy physical activity I had so enjoyed most of my life. When writing or formulating extracts I felt I should be wearing bedroom slippers. They were inside activities that I somehow equated with feminine pursuits. I knew better, but I couldn't get the notion out of my head.

But then I was offered a tiny sawmill for fifty dollars. These rigs were advertised at two hundred and fifty in a farm magazine Nordi had subscribed to. I bought it and ran it with an old car engine and sawed some small logs into boards and two-by-fours. It was like a miracle. Why, here was something Bunky and I could do when he got out of the military. (I had forgotten how he hated the timber of Western Oregon.) I sold the Belsaw and bought the makings of a larger mill with a fifty-four-inch circular saw. With it I could reduce a thirty-inch-diameter log to lumber. With young Dave Forsythe's help in the evenings and weekends we set it up on the hill near the road.

Two or three months later I found a big Case power plant cheap. Now Bunky had, with the mill, a tool to make money when he got out of the Air Force. I relaxed. Maybe this would partly fill the gap left in his life by the loss of the *Bunky*.

A neighbor gave me some medium size logs, even brought them down to the mill. Another fellow living in the area—a buff and collector of old time steam sawmills—was more than pleased to show me how to inset the saw against the log and give me pointers so that soon I was ready to saw commercially.

At Acme things droned along as usual. Twenty-five percent of my paychecks went to pay on the remaining *Bunky* loan. I thought of going back in the lacquer thinner business, but realized that I'd be up against new paint manufacturing standards concerning the locale and very expensive safeguards. The least I could get by with would take twenty thousand. God no! My fingers had been burned too many times.

I studied how I could make money with my saw to augment my wages at Acme. Ray Neufer came by with a couple of logs on his trailer and I sawed them up for him.

Then a friend of a friend who made furniture came out and asked me if I could cut some alder for him. He would more than pay me for my efforts. The furniture factories of the West like alder—a good furniture wood that takes any finish, doesn't split and holds upholstery tacks well. In this area they buy it rough sawn and air dry it for six months. Green, it cuts like a big carrot or the stem of a cabbage with a cushy sound. Seasoned, it's a tough hardwood.

I procured some alder and sawed the fellow a year's supply. Word got around and I filled five or six more orders. Alder is cut in eight-foot lengths and sawing it is a fast easy operation with an offbearer at the other side of the saw, taking care of the cut lumber. I bought the logs from farmers. Alder was everywhere. When the fir trees are removed, alder springs up. Soon I had as many contracts as I could handle. That summer I did my sawing on weekends and a couple of hours at night. I was soon making as much as I earned at Acme.

So with one man to stack the lumber and another to haul and deliver and a neighbor boy to bag the sawdust, I had an operation. It never tired me.

The farmers brought in their logs and I paid them cash. Each log was a challenge. How to get the best lumber out of it? I'd turn some logs over four or five times as I sawed them. It was a slower process than the usual way, but the furniture plants loved my lumber. Everything was going along too well to last. It became a waltz. Everybody was happy—the farmers and the small loggers and the furniture manufacturers and me in the middle with my whining saw bringing it all together.

Ginny was always fooling me. From the first I felt she was frail. Now she helped out in the mill, offbearing at times when I couldn't get my regular help, throwing her weight into the work like an old hand, proud of her ability.

One morning an enraged farmer stopped by. "You've been cheating us, paying thirty dollars a thousand when you knew good and well, Mr. Rice, that it's worth a hundred a thousand. You've been tricking us."

"Look," I said, "I'm paying what is the going rate in Oregon and Washington, thirty dollars a thousand."

"Yeah," said the farmer, "well I have it on good authority that you're lying and you'll get no more of my logs 'less you pony up the hundred dollars per. We found out that alder is a hardwood like mahogany, and you knew it all along."

Later that day a small-time logger, passing by, said much the same thing. No logs were delivered that day nor the next. I shut down and searched out my suppliers in the country. By evening I found the cause. An ill-informed, or perhaps mischievous, or maybe sinister, fellow, nameless to me, had gone around to the granges of the area with this misinformation. Not a log could I get. They believed him. What to do? I'd have to fill my various contracts or hurt the good name I was acquiring.

I heard there were some fine stands of alder across the Willamette where a big subdivision was going to be built and I got the alder there for eight dollars a thousand standing. With a couple of loggers, down on their luck, and a big Belgian mare, we tackled it. The fellow who hauled my lumber to town, now hauled the logs to the mill besides. I tried to make do. I took leave of my Acme job, getting the Little Lady's brother to take my place.

It became a wild time for me, running the mill and rushing

over the river toward Lake Oswego, where I would fall the trees and drag the logs to their loading place with that immense mare. We were keeping up, though barely, when we cleared out both stands.

I looked around for other alder. There were no more stands such as we had just finished. I spoke to the Forest Service people. They said there was big alder, lots of it, on the coast.

"Look around Hebo and up the Nestucca River."

A quick trip proved they were right. I must move my mill or quit. Quit this well-paying, outdoor free-for-all and stay in my carpet-slipper job? Was there any question?

"Remember the boat, Clyde," my father said. "Where did all that scheming and all that work get you? You're forty-five now. Time to quit this defying-the-ocean, bull-of-the-woods nonsense. You're not built for it. I told you that before, but you can't seem to get that fact through your head. You're stubborn, like your mother, God bless her!"

"Sure, but the furniture factories need my special lumber. The good name that I am building requires that I, somehow, fulfill my contracts."

I trucked the mill to the coast and got sort of a handhold on some land (that was the way out—the only way out) of a vast federally-owned alder stand.

There was also a house. I set up the mill temporarily on the ground on a flat place and hired a logger to cut and haul down a lot of alder logs, making an immense pile before the mill, enough to at least fulfil my contracts for the year.

I was left alone with my pile of logs. "Yeah," I said to myself, "this time I'm not under a wharf chewing on carob pods. I must be moving up in the world that I love."

I was getting my things rearranged in the old house, as a dog takes another turn before settling down. I got a fire going and, as dusk deepened, I lit a lamp. No electricity way up here. The lamp began to smoke the chimney and I turned it down lower just as someone knocked at the door. It was dark on the small porch and I saw only a vague figure before me.

"Come in," I said, "I'll have coffee in a bit." Wordless he stepped in. I peered at him in the dim light.

"Hi, Pop," he said. It was Bunky. "Surprise! Surprise!" he yelled and grabbed my hand. "Good Lord! I've had a deuce of a time finding you. Nobody in the burg down there knew about you. Finally I found out from the ranger. You gonna offer me a half a loaf of stale bread and fifty cents, like the last time we met?"

"You know," I answered, "it got a lot worse after you left before it got better."

"Yeah, I know. Mom told me what you said in your letters."

"Shall we go down to Hebo, Bunk, and eat or will hot corned beef hash do you until morning?"

"Pop, I've seen all of Hebo I need. Have you got plenty of onions?" I had, so we made a fine big hash and devoured it by lamplight, relearning each other's countenances. The old masters knew how lamplight defines character. I stared at my son's illumined face, as he dumped catsup on his food, and was deeply content.

Next morning he looked taken aback, almost sick, when I pointed out the forest of alder on this creek's big drainage.

"This," I said, "is all I could get you to take the place of the *Bunky*. Maybe I could have done better but I'm still paying on the debt to my father for his loan."

"Yeah, I know, Pop, but how did you come to pick this place? It's plain weird. I was out at dawn and took it in. I believe it's haunted. Can you laugh up here, Pop? My God, I can't!"

"Yes, I know," I agreed, "but I've got contracts to fill and I aim to fill them, no matter how spooky the country. You looked at our mill yet?"

"Not really," he said. "I'd rather put it off, but let's." We did. He stared long and disconsolately at it, at the bruised logs in that big ragged pile. "Is this what Ginny's been writing me about?" he asked with a disbelieving look on his face. "Is this what you've been getting ready for me for when I'm clear of 'Uncle'?"

"It's the best I could do," I said. "Look, Bunky, give it a chance. Got an edger coming and an engine for it."

"Pop, tell me—why do Nordi and Ginny believe in you? Seems just women do. Uncle Jack don't and Dave don't, Uncle Teddy don't, and I got to agree. I sure don't either anymore."

That last, well—I've said it all along. I had it coming. Still, I felt like I'd been kicked in the stomach. This should teach me that I'm not needed in their world. Drop them, one and all, and start writing, I thought in a timid defiance of them.

Still, I said, "Have you been home and seen the bottom?"

"Yes, I've seen it and I got Mom's letter about it. So what?"

"Doesn't that tell you anything about Jack and Teddy?"

"They're regular guys and, yeah, they never bite off more than they can chew."

"I see."

I should have dropped out of the whole thing then, accepted the rejection as my lot and started doing what I really need to do, tended to all that chokes up in me pleading for outlet, but I said, "Let's have a little more of that bitter candor, Bunky. 'Uncle Sam' isn't feeding you any longer. What are your prospects?"

He didn't reply, staring his hate, loathing me and the scene. Ah, this so still mill that seems to be begging to be put on a solid footing and set going, cutting lumber.

"I see your candor ends after chewing out the other guy."

"No," he said, looking down toward Hebo in the valley. "I really counted on this, but it's just one more kick in the face. Christ! I should have known better. Okay, so I'm your man until I can get out of here. When do we eat?"

On this we started. After breakfast I got the engine going and rolled a big log on the carriage. The logs were all eight feet long so it was fast going, and I snowed him under with white gleaming boards. Then we put them back on the carriage and edged them. I helped him pile slabs on the slab pile. Still, I worked the tail off him. After lunch I speeded it up, helping him when he must have it. We hardly spoke and he continued to glare at me. We quit when it got too dark to work.

After we ate I handed him a ten spot. "For cigarettes," I said, "here's the car keys."

"Too tired to drive," he muttered. "Where's your radio?"

"In the car."

He went out and slumped in the seat, listening to what there was. He was still there when I turned in.

Next day we ran the mill as if our lives depended upon it. At noon a long semi-truck appeared to haul away our stack of lumber (changed now from white to a reddish salmon color as alder does) into Portland Upholstery and Furniture. We loaded him with five thousand board feet and the driver paid me three hundred and fifty dollars. I gave him sixty dollars for the hauling.

"What's your make on that, Pop?" said Bunky, suddenly interested in the proceedings.

"We get a hundred apiece on a deal like this." Remembering the hate in his eyes, I asked the question (if the answer was negative, the mill would be up for sale tomorrow): "Do you still want to stay partners here or move on, Bunky?"

"Walk away from this, Pop?" he said grinning at last. "This looks good to me. This miserable place don't look half-bad with money coming in."

"Well, we've got to keep at it," I said, much relieved. "I don't like working our mill on the ground the way it is, but we've got to. It'll take all the lumber we can make out of those logs to get everyone satisfied in Portland. It's early October now. I've got a feeling that a tough winter will shut us down in a month or so. Up in here there could be quite a bit of snow."

Several months later with the lumber all delivered, it snowed as it had not snowed for at least ten years. We had wrapped the mill, all of it, in heavy canvas, drained the motors and the waterpipes in the house and then dug our way down to the country road and, luckily, followed a snow plow out of that hinterland to the main highway and eventually to Carver and Virginia.

"I expected you two," she said, kissing my son before me. "Your room's all ready for you, Bunky. Clyde had some oak lumber in there. I threw it out in the snow this morning. I knew you'd come." I had visited Ginny every other weekend, but

Bunky had not come home with me before. He'd found a very attractive girl at Pacific City a few miles away and was far from lonely.

That night, before the fire, we drank mulled wine and avoided mentioning our lost boat. Later in the evening we decided to phone Nordi and each of us gave her our message of love. Virginia demanded that she be last and ended her good wishes by asking Nordi to come home. "It's now February fifth," she said, "and the two years we spoke of are over in April. We hope you'll come home before that."

As the fire became coals we popped popcorn and before going to bed stepped out in the snow and breathed deeply of the fresh chill air. In the night I felt Ginny's tears on my shoulder and crushed her tightly to me, bereft of even whispers.

It was too late to look for dry wood on Mount Hebo. We'd been too busy filling lumber orders to take care of our own needs. My deal with the owners was that we would keep the house heated through the winter. I pried myself away from Ginny and home and, with Bunky, headed back to the coast and our sawmill, taking along some dry wood.

There was no problem for Bunky with his girl waiting for him, and I saw little of him for a few days while he dug her and her invalid father out of a snowdrift that surrounded their house.

Spring was slow in coming, but one day we were able to take the canvas off the mill. While we were locked in by the snow I figured a way to make two enormous sleds (the sort that are used to hold donkey engines), floor them and install our operation on them; the engine and the edger with its motor on one sled and the other drawn up beside it holding the mill, its carriage and log rolls. We would build a temporary roof over them. We needed large logs and we found four large, extremely long Douglas firs in the national forest which we were allowed to cut down.

Meantime I asked the county work crew to make a bridge on our road across the creek where a very unstable one stood. They came one day and I took them up to where the trees were downed explaining how I needed four logs for two sleds and that the rest

of the trees could make timbers to stretch across the stream on
on which to place the bridge.

I don't know why but a jolliness came about between them
and me. Maybe I told a dirty joke that they hadn't heard before or
maybe they told one and my fits of laughter made them feel
expansive. Anyway, they decided to do the job and brought a
great Caterpillar tractor up. They dragged the logs across the
stream, but then I didn't have any planking to cover it. Sort of
snickering, they said they thought it would be possible to get me
some. Shortly after, they trucked up planking for the bridge
three inches thick—all the right length—that I found they had
stolen from another job.

We hewed the top of the logs for a good surface and placed
the planking crossways over them. The bridge had a span of
about thirty feet. They brought out a keg of spikes to fasten the
planking to the logs and tapped all the spikes in so they stood up
in two rows. Then with sly smiles they asked me to race one of
their crew in driving the spikes. I think there was perhaps fifty on
a side. I agreed. My opponent was a young fellow with a broken
nose—evidently a prize fighter of Tillamook County who worked
with the crew. The hammers were long-handled, of maybe eight
pounds. They are called butting sets. There was a normal hammer at one end; the other end was long and pointed ending with
a flat place about the size of a spike's head. You would have to be
good to hit anything with it. While everyone stood around and
watched, we started out driving them in the conventional way
with the big end, me over one log and my opponent over the
other. Then, with the crew urging him on, he turned over his
hammer and began driving the spikes with the pointed end. A
cheer went up from his partners. They were really going to show
this city guy how things were done in Tillamook County. But I
turned mine over too and just as adeptly drove them with never
a miss. Ole Lind had taught me on the *Bunky* how to handle a
butting set. My rival began to go faster, so did I. There were
more cheers and bets. They were quite excited. Both of us were
worn out before we reached the other side, but neither of us

missed and we ended in a dead heat. We turned dripping and shook hands and the crew accepted me, by God!

"What else you want done around here now we got the Cat up?" the foreman asked, so they dragged my four logs all the way to where I was going to work on them in a meadow, and graded the road into quite a boulevard.

We had a chance to get a crew of three fellows to harvest the alder—horse loggers they were—but they had an opportunity to get another job in fir instead of alder, so they gave us two weeks to make the sled or they'd leave.

It was one of the accomplishments in my life of which I'll never cease to be proud. First we had to hew the logs so they turned up on each end—sledwise—then we took the bark off. For each we made three crosspieces that were dovetailed into the logs, then rod holes were drilled through the logs and the crosspieces and heavy rods driven through and bolted tight. It had to be a tight fit and the crosspiece dovetail joints we pounded into the log with a heavy nine-foot ram of maple.

When the two sleds were done in the two weeks allotted I had lost about fifteen pounds and Bunky had lost a few himself. We were able to do it by shifting from one job to another, so that our muscles were not harmed by staying too long at one task. The drilling of the holes that amounted to seven and a half feet each was the hardest task of all with the equipment we had.

Bunky and I grinned at each other. We were now indeed partners. We'd done the impossible, considering the limited time. The joints never moved but stayed ironfast until the logs rotted away years later. With the mill seated on the floor of these two sleds we were ready to operate on the alder of that big basin.

We began sawing alder in a little draw, the sleds drawn into a cove near a pool in an intermittent brook that disappeared below us in a swamp. The extensive grove of large alders swept up the hillside and eventually over into some cliffs. The ranger had said, "You get that private right-of-way into the valley and you can cut in there and the alders will spring up behind. You and your son can harvest a new crop on the same land. A twenty-five-year-old

alder is a good saw log. If you have trouble with the owner, we'll
run a road in beside him to make your outlet to the valley."

The ranger believed in me, for in making a survey of the basin
he found I was as good a woodsman as he, finding my slashed
trails and markers where I'd laid out logging roads during the
winter and cleared future mill locations for our portable mill.

In the mill I sawed the logs to get the widest boards and avoid
the black knots that are the bane of alder lumber. I never grew
weary of getting the best out of each log. Perhaps it was foolish in
this world of "to hell with quality, up your production," but I
never lacked for customers, and others did.

I bid on the whole basin and got it. There remained only the
visit and confirmation of the top man of the whole Northwest
Forest Service.

Bunky and I now had another man running the edger, a clever
fellow but tricky. We fired him when Bunky caught him messing
up the carburetor on the edger's engine so he could rest while we
were fixing it. The next man, Giles, could keep up with us easily.

We had been expecting to get word from Nordi that she was
on her way home, but now we received her letter:

My dear family,
    I miss all three of you very much and it would be so wonder-
ful to see Oregon again. I've been planning to come home as
Madeline has done well all winter—was really looking forward
to being back—but she has had a setback. As much as I want to
see you again, I cannot bring myself to leave Madeline. I've
been happy here—she and Zimmie have been so good to me
and now I'm desperately needed. Madeline has such a horror of
nurses, so I will stay. Zimmie has been doing well at the office.
His firm has made him vice-president of production with his
salary more than doubled and he has doubled mine. It will be
next April now before I get back.
    Well, my darlings, I hope that things at the mill site are
going well. I'm so pleased that you, Bunky, and your Pop are
partners in the mill. Besides what is reported about the good
work you do in the mill, Ginny said in her letter that you do a lot

of the cooking, Bunky, when your Pop's legs refuse to work and cramp up at the end of his day of sawing. He should use the log turner instead of using his legs just because it's faster.

Today, Clyde, as I gazed out of the window at the Golden Gate Bridge I thought of the battle with the tide's whirlpools you put up years ago before there was a bridge, and the injury to your arms. Finally you did get us around Lime Point, but our lives were hanging on a thread for awhile.

This past winter I've had a chance to see many old friends down here and now have started doing ceramics with the help of my good friend, La Bess, whom I see frequently. I'm anxious to show you some of the pots I've done. I enjoy it so much.

Bunky, write and tell me about your girl. I liked her looks in the snapshots you sent of her and the two of you playing in the surf. Send me more pictures of all of you, a dozen at least. They will have to do me until I get home again.

Love,
Nordi

It rained intermittently through April and May. The hillside was always sodden. Where the loggers dragged down their logs it became a mire, a mire that stunk of rottenness as some earths do on occasion. Then in early June the streamlet dried up and we couldn't replenish the water in our small log pond, though the hillside mud did not dry up. It was on our boots and into the mill, and the log pool became more fetid than a sewer. Even the lumber began to smell at the ends. I wanted to move to another setting, but the ranger did not want his assistant to mark more trees before the supervisor came and inspected the basin and my operation. Ranger Anderson said the head man would be along any day now—another week at the most—and we could get away from that malodorous place.

The pond had become a soup in which we scrubbed the logs to get the clinging mud off of them. We had reached an impossible condition when Anderson appeared with a tall, dark man dressed for the city, his shoes nicely shined (though he at once stepped where he shouldn't and got the mire on the cuffs of his trousers.) I saw his nostrils dilate as he took in our sad condition.

Ranger Anderson introduced him as the new Northwest Supervisor, a Mr. Stone. The man looked around as if startled. Was this what he had been led to expect? We were a terrible comedown, a horrid picture in the land of the majestic Douglas fir. Later we found this was his first survey. He was just in from the East taking up new duties. He didn't speak to me after the introduction. He stared around at the basin bereft of evergreens, alder taking up country that should be filled with conifers. Alder must be destroyed—the area planted to Douglas fir, Western red cedar. He moved away, glancing down to his befouled trousers, still looking back at the mud-caked mill, the hideous soup of the pond. I knew things were going badly, but the saw was whining. I tried not to think. I stopped the saw and sharpened its teeth. That gave me time not to think. The loggers came down with more mired logs. We all looked at each other, all six of us, and apprehension was on each face. "We should join the sewer workers' union," Bunky said disgustedly.

My friend, Ranger Anderson, admitted later that we'd been turned down. It seemed to the supervisor that our operation was of no consequence.

Next morning I was in Portland at the Forest Service headquarters seeking Mr. Stone. I'd spent the rest of the day before gathering facts and figures. Again he seemed startled. I was neat in a business suit and brought with me no stench of the befouled log pool. He did recognize my face.

I was abrupt. I removed the injured-party-seeking-redress look from my face. "I understand you're new here," I said.

"Yes," he agreed. "Of course I've heard a lot about the timber of the Northwest, but this was my first time on the coast."

"Well, I came up to tell you about alder," I said, "if you can give me a few minutes?"

"It will be my pleasure," he said, so I told him of the Western furniture factories in Seattle, in Portland and Los Angeles. I told him how many men were employed on the coast in furniture manufacture and that the main wood used in its production was alder. I explained how it took a finish, would not split, and air dried in nine months.

"It's an industry out here, Mr. Stone, and we who produce the lumber are rather ill-paid, but we're proud to say we're not digging into the remaining supply of Douglas fir, which can't be replenished in time. I wonder if you know it? Anyway, alder is a weed, a short-lived tree. Unless it's harvested it rots. Harvested, it's the excellent wood I've been telling you about. When you shut me down, I don't think you were aware of its uses and the many families that alder supports one way or another.

"The first job I had was in 1920 working in the Reforestation Experiment Station. There wasn't an American then who knew anything about reforestation, so the Forest Service hired Mr. Hoffmann from Austria. We got to be friends and I learned a great deal from him. Now, what I tell you are facts and I brought them to you so that you could use them in your new job. I also hope you will rescind your order so that I can get on fulfilling the contracts I have with the local furniture factories."

An aware and very sensitive man, he had tears in his eyes. "From what you say, Mr. Rice, I see that I've done you an injustice. Let me think a moment."

"It's eleven-fifteen," I said, "and I'm hungry. Will you be my guest? There's an Italian restaurant where I've eaten for years. We could consider what to do about this over a bowl of grand soup. This is Thursday. They always have boiled beef with horseradish sauce on Thursday."

The minestrone was excellent as always. He liked the boiled beef, and the strength of the horseradish sauce made his eyes water again. We talked.

"Mr. Rice," he said, "listening to you, I notice that you're still fond of the Forest Service, though it has disappointed you in many respects. Now, I'm a career man in the Service. I understand your complaints about the willowy spine of our national directors, and that offends my loyalty, but really our directors are a product of Congress. Congress will not pass on them unless they are as they are—they are chosen that way. It's pork barrel thinking! Do you understand?"

"Yep, too well, and you have my sympathy, Mr. Stone." I answered. "By the way, I'll never repeat what we're saying here."

"Well, then here it is," he said, "in my position I'm open for all to see and my first move on my new job was not well founded. If I rescind it, that will be a bad way for me to start out here. Still, if you ask me to, I will, but we could do it another way. I could get you another little valley of alder around Hebo somewhere and if you do well—keep sawdust out of the stream and the nominal things we ask—after the second year, I will see that you get the Cedar Creek basin and I'll help you all I can. It's up to you to choose which you want. Think about it a bit. Maybe you can decide as we drive back to my office."

As we drove back, I decided to take his offer and save him from the smirks of his subordinates, for I knew him for a just and sensitive man and there's too few of his breed around.

After a bit of scouting, I chose Oldorn Creek several miles toward the coast from Hebo. A gravel road passed close to the entrance of the valley, however I would have to cross private property, a tip of which ended at the Forest Service boundary. The owner, old man Lindquist, agreed to allow me through at a price. I offered to run my road through the brushy corner of his place, fence it and pay him three dollars per truckload passing over.

"Yes," he said, "that's swell, but will you pay for the fencing and the gate?"

"Certainly. Five strand fence and a plank gate with a padlock."

"Okay," he said. "Payment on the first and don't cheat. Me and my Missus will be watching every load you take through to the county road."

I swamped out the brush on the three hundred foot cut through his land. I didn't have to grade it. All it would need would be a gravel base. An early day lane had gone this way to a homestead, now long abandoned. Bunky was digging the postholes for the fencing and I was building the gate when old man Lindquist came, a sardonic grin on his face: "Say, fellas," he said, "I've changed my mind. No reason. I just changed it. You know, I might cut that alder up there myself."

"You can't," I replied. "I bid on it and I won and it's mine."

"Why, you dirty stinking bastard," the old man yelled, as if he was stung by yellowjackets. "I was going to let you make the road in for me, but I couldn't wait. You damn city scum! Get out!"

I went to Ranger Anderson. They would not be able to help me at Oldorn Creek, he said. "You'll have to get another road in somehow. The alder stands in there have got even Cedar Creek beat for size of trunk. Trouble is it just hasn't got enough area for us to put a road into it. Sorry!" And he was sorry, but he had to act according to the book.

Bunky and I held council and, with misgivings, swamped out a right-of-way through adjoining property. There were two deep ravines to cross, one a veritable canyon. It looked impossible. Well, we could quit and go home. "No sir," Bunky said, "we'll hang in here."

With a team of horses our two loggers, Al and Pete, (the third man had quit when we moved to the new site) plowed away knolls and the side-hill side of our road as it wound around obstructions, while with axes and shovels and picks and dynamite Bunky and I cut roots, dislodged stones and blew up tenacious stumps. We plowed and dug at the high end of steep pitches and moved the dirt down with a scraper to the bottom, that way modifying the pitch. When we had done so with the worst one we had changed it to twenty-two degrees, slackened it by four degrees, then we came around a sharp turn to the left and faced the ravine of canyon-like proportions. We dropped two towering firs into the bottom of the canyon. They lay side by side, just where we needed them, and over the narrow interstice that lay between then we placed a third log—not so hefty, but long. The canyon stream ran under this. We covered it all with brush and debris.

We hired a man with a big D8 Caterpillar tractor—wow! He

dug our road deeply on the edge of the canyon, forcing all the dirt and rock into the chasm below, covering the logs. The land was still spring wet and it rained continuously. Then he came around another way at the bottom of the canyon. The following day he was on the other side digging our road over there and dumping the stone and clay down on his fill. Finally the roads met over the buried logs and there he made an immense fill for the road to turn on. He was doing fine when his machine slumped into some of the soggy fill and started slipping down the lower face of it. With its own power he tried to get it out and was at once foundered in it. I was away at the time. He got another fellow with a like machine to pull him out and it too sank in the waterlogged mud of the fill.

I heard about it that night and in the morning got a third man with a smaller machine to come and see what he could do. He trespassed on the edge of old Lindquist's place, got into the bottom of the canyon and, on firm footing, was able to winch both the big ones off the mudslide and eventually out. Lindquist filed suit, though nothing ever came of it.

In time the road across the canyon was done and we came on around another bend to the lesser ravine. We treated it the same way with logs so that the stream could run free underneath our fill and this fellow with the little Cat filled to the roadbed level in two days. He was a miracle man, seemed always to be delivering at the fill. The D8s had been too slow and ponderous. A little grading with the small Cat and we were ready to gravel the road, but now we were almost broke.

I got the county to gravel our road from their quarry nearby, but they received orders to clean up the floor of the quarry and put their slurry along with the crushed rock on our road. When they were through, I complained to the superintendent of roads and, with one look at the mess, he had them lay down solid crushed rock over it and with the gravel trucks rolling it down as they spread the gravel, it soon could support any load a truck could carry.

We had our mill sleds trucked in and now, completely broke,

we started turning out our bread and butter and that of the offbearer and the loggers too. We brought in an enormous work horse, a Belgian, to help the horse loggers. With their chainsaws and with the extra horse, they brought in all the logs we could handle, though the mill with the new log turner and a new placement of the edger speeded up our production. For months Ole, our trucker, complained of being overworked.

From the logs Al and Pete snaked out of the woods I sliced great flawless white planks, sometimes four inches thick, fourteen inches wide. How the furniture makers loved pieces of that sort! It was ecstasy to find among the other boards in the log such a perfect wide plank. The search for the best in the log always held my interest, and the days rushed by.

There were problems, of course, problems that led in time to my undoing, for the profit was slim. I could not hire a trucker who could also collect for me. Ole was steady and cheaper and I liked him, but he would not quibble over payments for the load, so twice a week I must head to town to collect. I'd found that if I didn't get the money within the week, it would be several months or longer before I was paid.

In offbearing it was important to handle the big planks just so or they would split. Bunky was good there and he was excellent with the lesser pieces. His use of the edger retrieved narrow boards that were the difference between profit and loss. My other problem was that when I was away collecting and drumming up business, Bunky would not take my place as sawyer. He was completely adamant about that. This from my fearless steersman and that wild trip to San Pedro. Of course, he had hated the timber and farming for years. The town and the sea were his chosen habitats. Even so, I could never quite understand his strong aversions. Here at the mill he stood loyally up to our adversities. He would do anything in or about it with a great show of zest that I knew he didn't feel. He was a great help in the evening when I was completely worn out. My legs cramped, then I'd be useless. Bunky took care of me with hot water bottles, cooked the meal and was off with his girl or the young fellows thereabouts. I guess I was asking too much. It cut down our income but gave the loggers a chance to catch up.

Had I been able to hold onto the good ship *Bunky*, I believe he would have skippered it well and I could have gotten a job of no consequence and written every night, saying things I wanted to say.

Driving along to the city there was one story that I was working up in my mind about an itinerant shake splitter who wandered into a book shop in Sacramento looking for a pamphlet he'd heard of purporting to teach a man how to train his eyes by diet, only so they would have X-ray values and could see through women's skirts, even corsets. He could not explain to the young lady in charge what he was looking for and moved slowly toward the door. But, dawdling as several others were over a table of scattered volumes, he peered into this book, appraised phrases in another. When he finally did leave, he had had his first taste of the richness of books. He came back next day and bought four battered volumes, one of which was *Leaves of Grass*. My story was about how books affected him and how they fitted him for his death when caught in his own wolf traps years later.

On the long drives to town I built the story piece by piece as a memory trainer. On I went, hurtling past other cars in my rush to get to the city. That was part of me, but within the car alone with my thoughts it was the values of words that dazzled me. Ah, the gliding sibilances or the shock of them. They come in all sizes and can speak as well of the shattering spars of a sailing ship's demise as of the remembered breast of your mother, relating in you deep down to the delicacy of those of your first virgin.

Good God! My mind wanted to write so much that I could leave my consideration of Bunky's future, caught away by dulcet phrases. What a pitiful father I was for him!

Bunky and I had been camping in a large tent near the mill. I found it difficult, but cheap. Still, Bunky had a strong need to get out of the woods at five. He pressed me to rent a house near the lower end of the road. We moved in. He was delighted, but then so was Ginny. She began spending the weekends with us. She had become a good cook of bland dinners, though the meals soon became spicier at our urging, and Bunky beamed. He wasn't proud of the plain fare he fed us on week days. Bunky had always been fond of Ginny.

He remarked one supper time, "You're not my mother, but you certainly are something," and he rolled his eyes appreciatively. He was seven years younger than Ginny.

Ginny loved to scout around in the valley for wildflowers and strange plants that she brought home to transplant in our wooded barriers. Bunky or I always accompanied her armed, for there were many black bears in Oldorn basin and, wandering in there, we were liable to get between a sow bear and her cubs. Each night, bears fouled our spring beside the mill. We had to abandon it.

Deer season came around. My God! Have we been here that long? I asked myself, remembering the sounds of rifle fire when we were first sawing the alder of Cedar Creek. Both Bunky and I downed a buck. We rented freezer lockers in Hebo and fed sumptuously each weekend on saddles, rump roasts, and dainty backstrap sections. This time we had plenty of dry fuel with which to face the winter.

That winter, the snow was never heavy but an intermittent nuisance. Still, we produced a sizeable amount of lumber. We were holding our own and looked ahead for a good year, though we expected Nordi to return in April, and Ginny and I clung to each other, albeit sorrowfully. She wept in the night and when we embraced. At odd times I must hunt her out wherever she was to grab and encircle her with my arms for the time grew ever shorter. I could not understand how we could part. Part? A searing anguish ripped through me.

The previous fall, the price of fir lumber had increased. Huge amounts were shipped to Japan and Korea. A moderate housing boom developed here in the States and logging in the West became hectic. Loggers circulated in Portland's suburbs and bought backyard firs and with the new equipment were able to remove them with little damage. We saw that if we were ever going to continue with our mill, we must somehow get the donkey engine and the rigging for the spar tree and the cables and blocks, in fact everything necessary. We were told it would up our production. But how are we going to afford a donkey when we are still paying on the edger?

I tried our bank. They pointed out that the trouble I had had with overdue bills on the *Bunky* would certainly not induce them to offer me a loan and my father would not loan me a cent. He wanted me out of the woods and under his thumb at Acme.

I told our loggers to hang on. Somehow I was going to get the money for the donkey. Then I heard that Dave was home between fishing trips and he heard about my problem from Ginny and lent us three hundred dollars for the donkey engine. That would help. I would have to have it in three weeks.

I received a call from Ranger Anderson to come over to the station. The Forest Service experiment station at Corvallis wanted a load of special alder. They wanted to load a dry kiln with it for an experiment. The planks must all be between eleven and thirteen inches wide and two and a half inches thick. They would pay me five hundred dollars a thousand and they needed five thousand board feet and would take six if I could produce it in time.

While I thought about it, Anderson said, "You won't have to pay our usual stumpage fee on the trees, because it's a forestry experiment, and you can sell the lesser boards to your customers."

The boys were just getting into a stand of big alders that did not lean as alders usually do. "Can you get it down to me before our deadline?" I asked. "Because then with what I've got, I can get the donkey."

"You bet," they said, "we'll go for it."

Oh, it was beautiful stuff that they brought in—three big logs to a tree. From each butt log and the second log I got five of the planks they wanted and plenty of side cuts for my customers. Bunky and the old man were very careful how they handled these big planks. Usually one of ten would burst, but here the standing trees were so straight they didn't have the internal stress of leaning trees and we had no problems. In a week we delivered the order and received the Forest Service's reimbursement. I never heard how the experiment turned out, but it certainly was great lumber to begin with.

Now we had enough for the down payment on a second-hand donkey, so we shut down the mill and went shopping. Dave was home from his fourth successful fishing trip off Colombia and Peru. He was making such money as he had never dreamed of. He went with us to the various sellers of logging equipment. We saw some muscular machines, one a big beauty that cost twenty-seven hundred. He wanted to buy it for me outright, but I refused. I couldn't grab a kid's first big money. I bought a smaller rig, but no midget by God, with a Cadillac v8 engine for power. Then I went to a rigging house and bought the enormous main block, or pulley, that would be at the top of the spar tree and all the other ones that were necessary and a large spool of the heavy cable with which to drag the logs in and a smaller cable, much longer, with which to haul the heavy cable back into the woods for another log.

We had Ole truck in our heavy plunder and under an old timer's direction set up our spar tree and bolted the donkey to a log sled, similar to the mill sleds, cabled it down, and began logging, much to the pleasure of Al and Pete, who felt they were now professionals, working on a first-rate logging show.

While they set it up, I was in Portland and Salem picking up new accounts and contracting for all we could possibly cut even with the donkey engine working for us. But the trouble was that with the new equipment they brought in about the same number of logs that they had horse logging. We tried bringing in sixteen-foot logs and cutting them in two at the mill, we tried dragging whole trees minus their limbs in and production seemed the same. The three of us in the mill could have turned out three thousand more board feet a day if we could only get the logs, but we took what we could get for awhile and were happy.

The sawing—the way the saw bit into the log, tasting it and revealing to me in that first cut what the log was going to be like, the sound of the carriage rumbling back and forth, the roar of the engine, the smells and the enormous piles of sawdust turning red in the sunlight—hellity damn! And me on the sawyer's platform with my levers and canthook, bouncing around like a jumping jack, making the cut as the log sweeps slowly past, to hurtle back and then to slice away another beautiful board (sweet Jesus!) and Bunky, grinning at me across the saw, yelling, "More wood, more wood! Give it to me! To me!" And Ole coming in at mid-morning to pick up another load. I never ceased to wonder at my overpowering sense of really fitting into the world while sawing, for then I forgot Ginny and Nordi and Bunky, and the writing that I was going to do some day, and was encapsuled with beauty and significance as the sawyer in a small mill.

On a late Friday afternoon I'd been working on some small knotty stuff, jumping around like mad, changing the log's setting on the carriage every cut, getting some mediocre boards out of the cull stuff. I turned to see my next log. It was really a beaut! I rolled it on the carriage, grinning with anticipation, dogged it down and removed a slab deciding, as I brought it back, to turn it onto its new flat surface and slab it again, and was ready to make some virgin white planks. As the carriage wafted it by, the saw went through it like the log was butter.

Hey! Bunky wasn't there to receive the plank. Relieving the old man at the edger, I thought. No! The old man was staring back of me where I turned to see Bunky holding—Nordi—Nordi, in a sleek dark suit, smiling up into Bunky's eyes—Nordi turning her head and smiling at me! In one awkward leap I cleared the rollway and dropped down beside her and she was in my arms and we were kissing and hugging, tears in our eyes as we laughed and got a better grip on one another and I reared back so I could look into her beloved eyes, stare at her beloved features.

"Clyde, easy," she pled, "Oh, Clyde dear, Bunky darling—I'm

back and I can't believe it quite yet. Bunky, another hug, please? Give him room, Clyde, but not too much. Oh, what a lovely, lovely day!"

Finally I stepped away from our celebration. Bunky asked if I was going to finish the log. I shut down the engine. The old man stopped the edger engine and all was quiet in the woods. We were free until Monday—no, Tuesday. I asked the old man to tell the loggers, Tuesday.

"How did you get here?" we asked Nordi.

"The bus and a twenty mile taxi ride. It came high, but was it worth it." More hugs and kisses.

"Did the taxi bring you all the way up to the mill?"

"He did and then backed so that he could turn around. Ginny told me where to direct him."

We were driving back. Nordi was impressed with our road. We had to explain how we were able to cross the canyon.

"This road makes life around the Bay seem stationary," she said. "Oh, it was all right, but everything is set there, glued in place. Looking back, golly, I want to cap Waterspout Point with a doily and forget it. Clyde, the Bay isn't what it used to be." She was animated. How wonderful! "Even Tiburon is trying too hard to be Tiburon," she said. "It's being quaintly. Quaintly used to be one of your sneers, Clyde, at self-conscious posing. Mmm— this Tillamook air is marvelous! I was a little kid down here once, you know, and it's still the same moist salt air carrying the smell of conifers everywhere. Say, let's get along. Ginny is waiting for us with supper—a Carver supper."

"Did you come by plane, Mom?" Bunky wondered.

"No," she answered. "I went down by train and I came back by train. Seemed right," she murmured to me and then: "Clyde, I want to thank you for seeing me off that evening. This is certainly belated, but I hope you know how I mean it." She gave my arm a squeeze.

We were sitting in the pickup in front of the house. "Go on in you two and clean up, so we can leave," she said, suddenly appearing very tired. "I'll snooze here until you get back. It's been a long, long time since I left Waterspout Point."

We got home an hour before sunset. Nordi slept most of the way, pressed between Bunky and me. For me it was a puzzling ride. Each scenario that I made for the future soon seemed windy and silly. I finally decided to let time and fate play it out. Of Bunky, who now held his mother so tenderly, I saw he would never never fit in this sawmilling business no matter if we got the whole Cedar Creek drainage and became big and prosperous and he was set for life. The boat was right for him. I cursed myself for signing that contract. Now I wish I had brazened it out somehow on my own ground here in Oregon, finished the boat during the winter, and fished it the following spring. Instead I lost Bunky's chance to be what he really wants to be, but that's all water over the dam and I can't do anything about it.

Nordi shifted her position and laid her head on my shoulder. Sleep on, my tired lady! We reached the turnoff to Oregon City and bumpy pavement for a few miles. I slowed the truck, but she awakened. I murmured, "Dear Noagy, it's not far now." She snuggled against me and soon was asleep again.

After a good supper, Nordi admitted that she had hardly slept for several nights before departing Tiburon and could find no sleep in her berth on the way north. "May I be excused, dear people?" she asked. "I'll see you in the morning." The need seemed contagious, for soon Bunky and Ginny and I sought our beds. Ginny and I held each other closely and sleep saved us from our thoughts.

We ate a late breakfast and Bunky hurried away to see friends. Nordi broke in to our desultory conversation with a smiling, "Though it's been three years, I'm in no hurry to bring about the agreed change in relationship. I love you two and I want to see how things are going before we make any more changes. I'll keep my bedroom downstairs and not bother Bunky for his upstairs room."

And so it went. At times I hungered for her even while

sleeping with lovely Virginia. After all, I loved them both in all ways.

Nordi had decided to become a practical nurse for young wives who were having their first baby. She'd been taking classes in that particular kind of care. "It's a jolly time for the couple and the baby will be adorable and I know I'll feel useful."

It was a pleasant and relaxed weekend, though I went back to the mill with unsettled mind. Still, I was glad she was home.

The loggers had finished the flat above us and were working nearer the stream. These were splendid trees, the largest of the area, but they leaned toward the brook as alders do so that there was a great deal of inner stress in their trunks. They grew on steep terrain where footing was chancey at best and now the boys began to have trouble with rupturing tree trunks. These great fat trunks of soft brittle wood would rip open when the faller's saw cut into tensed wood. There were ways of handling the problem, cutting in the notch this way and that as you severed the tree from the stump and Al and Pete used them artfully, but still there were trees that would burst in spite of the best of the handling. A great chunk would suddenly explode from the faller's cut up into the tree twelve or fifteen feet. The thousand-pound slab would slam down on the hillside or on the faller without warning. It would smash down where Pete, say, who did most of the falling, stood on precarious footing with a heavy murderously whirling chainsaw in his hands. Wow! Could be bad news.

Now, there was a simple way to avoid this, but one that no self-respecting gentlemen of the logging industry—no timber beast—would ever perpetrate and that was to put a chain or light cable around the tree above the cut, the severing point, and fasten it tightly with a truck chain tightener, stopping the split before it started. Any fool could conceive of this cure for sudden death, but apply it—never! In polite society there are things that simply are not done and in the hinterlands, in the tree-studded hills and mountains the same concept obtains, and certain sissy things like chaining a dangerous alder is certainly one of them.

We had not had splitting trunks at Cedar Creek nor on the

large flat here where they had been harvesting, but now in the steeper going where the bulk of the finest timber trees grew, it began to happen. The boys never spoke of it, feeling, I think, that it would never happen to real woodsmen, but if they were particularly solemn as we ate our lunches, I knew that soon a shattered log would appear on my rollway.

Finally I broached the subject and mentioned the obvious cure and was met with silence. When I continued to press them, Al turned and said, without the strut that I always met with later in similar statements by other loggers, "Look, you're a millman, see. We're loggers and we know how to handle whatever comes up in the woods, see. We're bringing in your logs and you're sawing them up, so let's let it go at that." —No swagger, just the facts.

Day followed day. We were not producing enough lumber. I began going to town only once a week to get the payments and a couple of my accounts got into me for several loads apiece. That hurt! And then, still not paying, they got their alder from other mills—that sort of thing. I put an ad in the paper for a trucker who would collect. As I had before I could get one all right, but all charged the same as they did for fir. The profit on alder by the thousand was much less than for fir but it weighed the same for the trucker.

I could not raise the price. Some mills were selling for less and hurting the trade and going broke doing it. With the payment for the edger and the loan I had on the donkey I was in a high-sided slot and I had to let Al and Pete go while I could still pay them.

We had to change to a new stand, a new spar tree, farther up the creek. We shut down, then Bunky and I winched the donkey up to the new place with its own power and with it dragged the mill sleds up. We put the mill in place and then sat on it for a couple of days wondering just how to go on from there. There must be some way to make things click; maybe if Bunk and I worked ten hours a day instead of eight and cut more lumber. I spoke of it to him.

Sure, he said, he'd do it. "But, Pop, I don't think you yourself could. You work at the sawing too hard. You turn out better lumber, but then they pay you the going rate, no more. Oh yeah, I know, it holds your customers but that's not enough. Why don't you just slice it up, black knots and all? You could cut more in a day that way and, Pop, why don't you get some old time loggers who would bring more logs to the rollway?"

I traveled the taverns of the county and came up after several days of beer-slurping with three guys. It appeared that logging was all they knew. One confided to me that he was a whistle punk at twelve. The other two said they were teethed on peavey handles. Two were in their late thirties, tall lean men, faces scarred from Saturday night brawls. The third was middling plump with quick eyes, small hands; "lots of savvy," said one and the other one affirmed it. "Yep," he said, "he sure is!"

"Call me Murph," the plump one said and, pointing to the rangy two, "them is Beany and Skitch."

At the mill, with his small hands in big gloves, Murph took to the donkey engine like it was a long lost pet. He ordered the other two around. First, they topped the spar tree and then stayed it to stumps with the old wire as we did before. Two days and they were ready to log. Logs began coming to the mill and back up beyond the rollway.

Bunky and I and the old man we hired worked ten-hour shifts and Ole made three extra trips each week and wonder of wonders, Nordi collected for me and got on famously with the Jewish owners of the furniture factories. For two weeks, three weeks, it went on like that before we hauled Skitch up out of the brush, knocked silly by a small falling alder slab.

Next day I told Beanie and Murph about the choker cable and the truck tightener and I handed them one I had made up, saying as little as I could about it and changing the subject. I asked if they knew a third man who could take Skitch's place.

"No," they said, they'd work, "as is, until Skitch comes back. That whack didn't bother him much. Skitch can take a helluva

batting around. He was K.O.'d on a Wednesday 'stead of a Saturday night," explained Murph.

He did come back on a Monday, but Beanie, they said, was in
jail along with some companions for trouble they'd had with a
couple of guys who came down from Garibaldi. "Askin' for it,"
Murph said.

At the mill we got enough logs to continue, but lamely. I
drove up to Tillamook that night and bailed Beanie out. He had
a cut over his right eye. "They never touched me," he boasted.
"I'm plenty handy with my dukes. This cut over my eye came
from stumbling over Skitch. They had him down. I came down
hard on the back of a chair. Don't worry," he answered me, "we'll
all be back swamping out logs for you tomorrow." They were
and did.

Murph was bringing in two at a time, except the butt cuts.
Their chainsaws howled down in the woods. Things weren't so
bad; weren't bad at all. In this big stuff you just squared the log
and then sliced it up into clean handsome planks. It became
monotonous. I needed some more small knotty stuff to get me
riled and awake. Then twice in a day they brought me slabbed
logs. I broached the collaring of big leaning trees. "It'll protect
the butt log so that I can get those wider planks." I said."

"Unh unh," they answered. "We got ways to handle them
kind of trees."

"Sure," I said, "I know those tricks, but sometimes they don't
work on a big leaning alder and I don't mean collaring every
tree—just those that your woods know-how tells you might
screw up a damn good saw log."

"Look, leave us do our stuff," said Skitch, "we're old hands at
logging. Tell ya, I'd quit the woods and take up sawmilling
before I'd wrap a chain around a tree I was bringing down."

Well, they kept my mind off my personal problems. Murph
never entered into their conversations about their safety. In fact,
I couldn't figure him out. He seemed completely out of place in
the woods, except in his handling of the donkey. Three times I

bailed one of them out of jail before they told me they had a chance "to grab off a big stand of second growth fir back county," and they disappeared. I went down next day where they'd been cutting and found an immense tilted alder with the saw cut into it that had thrown nasty slabs out both sides. Either one could have crushed the faller.

With no fallers, Bunky and I wrapped up our mill. We hadn't been home for two months. The sawing shift and the clean up around the mill and machinery maintenance made for a fourteen-hour day. Well, we ate like horses and gained no weight, I'm sure, but our bills were paid on time and our bank account was okay. Neither one of us took more out of the till than we needed. Down here Bunky could make a ten-dollar bill last for four nights of sparking.

One day when I was about to go out looking for new loggers, I received a note signed by Nordi and Ginny demanding our appearance for the weekend. There was some fencing to replace and some wood for the fireplace to be cut.

We were exuberantly greeted. The doors were open, a warm breeze came through. All the windows allowed light everywhere and Nordi and Ginny, in flowered gossamer dresses, moved about like dancers. Maybe it was our long grimy work-filled days in the mill—the dark of the woods—but Bunky and I were exhilarated by the extraordinary airy light at home and by the gay femininity of our ladies.

Bunky took his fishing pole to the river. Luck was with him. He came back soon with ten large pink-fleshed trout. Nordi produced a great pan of apple dorper. I forgot there were tense emotional problems just beneath the party air of the day, for the kisses I received from both of them were sweet, but promised nothing.

After an hour or so I brought my latest writings to Nordi, wondering what she'd think of them. She read them and asked for more, saying, "I'll make my comment in the evening." Then she asked for still more and I showed her a story and a poem.

When she finished her reading, she seemed quite withdrawn. "Any more?" she asked, so I gave her a story called "Oasis." After supper, Ginny and Bunky and I went walking by the river where we met Tek and Teddy. We all went down toward the rapids.

"Where's Ev?" Tekla wondered.

"She begged off from the walk. Said she had something to tend to."

On the other shore an otter came out with what looked like a large crawfish. He consumed it there, then, giving us his quiet concern, slipped into the stream and disappeared.

Teddy turned to me, "Would you look at that!" His eyes twinkled. "Pretty tame," he said. "Too many people for the wild things. They are acting out that old one, you know: if you can't lick 'em, join 'em. Even the beaver aren't so wary as they were when we moved here."

Ginny had her arm around my waist. It bothered Tek. She turned from us. "Funny Ev isn't along," she commented again.

"She's reading Pop's stories over again," Bunky said, "or she'd be with us."

"Stories, humph!" Tek said. "Such nonsense, fooling around writing stories! Real guys don't write stories when they should be working around the house."

"Doing what?" asked Bunky, mischief in his eyes.

"Why—like—whatever needs to be done—tack down where the carpet needs it. I could find him plenty. That's all they're good for anyway, except going to the job."

"Tek, you're talking like your mother!" Ted exclaimed.

"Depends who I'm talking about," Tekla said. "Let's go. We can't stand around here all day."

We came back to find that Nordi had raided Virginia's garden for some early corn. After we had eaten, Bunky excused himself and drove off to see a movie with friends. We lingered rather wordlessly over our coffee. "Let's sit in the living room," Ginny said. "I don't want to clear the table yet."

"Me neither," agreed Nordi, so we sat around the cold

fireplace, paying deference to absent ritual fire. Nordi began questioning me about the *Bunky*. I told her briefly what I had told her more fully in letters.

"When it was all over, Clyde, and you left San Pedro, weren't you in Tiburon for a few days before you went on home?" she asked.

"Yes! How did you know?"

"Don Barkley's sister thought it was you. She was about to have a baby and couldn't hike up to see. She watched you with binoculars, though she wasn't able to tell me till days later. I hurried up there, scoured Sugarloaf, and even went down to where Art had his tent. It was our trysting place. He planted violets and maidenhair ferns all around it. You knew about it, but never said a word. Am I right, Clyde?"

"Yes, that was a long time ago, Nordi."

"Well, I went in there," said Nordi. "The tent is gone, of course. That was eighteen years ago, but Clyde the banks of violets and ferns were still there and they had been watered recently from the sump in that trickle that seeps by there, and I think you were the one who watered them?"

"I didn't have much else to do up there," I answered. "Sure, I soaked them. Seems a guy can't have secrets."

"I'm proud you did."

"It was too damn sentimental," I muttered.

"No," she responded, "I don't think so. That's the whole point of what I'm talking about. No—look how long I've known you—sentimental doesn't cover it. You have an inner life full of mirth and kindness. In an odd way, you're a mystic, Clyde, and in the two senses of the word: as a connoisseur of the beauty of the world and your habit of stubbing your toe on the threshold of psychic phenomena. These qualities are your strengths and I see them in what you've written—the writing you've done as Ginny's husband. They surpass anything I was able to inveigle you to do, so I definitely don't want to change things around here. I want things to stay as they are."

"Are you saying, no divorce?" asked Ginny, hesitantly.

"With your permission, we'll change nothing, dear. I will always have a womanly, call it motherly, regard for your husband, so please let me always be near you two. I'm sure your love will sustain me and, if I have an urgent, though temporary, need of your husband, will you remember when our positions were the opposite of now?"

"Oh, Nordi, I'll strive to be as gracious as you were!"

Laying aside that matter, Nordi turned to me with, "And you, Clyde, forget fishboats and sawmills and write, Mister, write! I'm deeply pleased with 'Dim Remember' and 'Oasis.' At last you've found your medium. It took you forever but you found it, even when I'd given up on you ever doing so. I've gotten over the pain of separation. I see you, Clyde, in a different way now. If I chose to stay in California, Lon Curtis wanted to marry me, but he hates the Northwest and this area particularly, while for me there's no zest in life unless I'm living in Western Oregon. You know, even the strictures of my Seventh Day Adventist–bound family looked rosy from California and I'm going to try to see them that way in the closer view."

Whispering in the night, close by me, Ginny admitted to the same frightened qualms that Nordi had just freed us from. Whatever my flaws—and they are many—Ginny still adored me as I adored her. Slowly life had woven us into a web unseen, but we felt it all around us. So, willing slaves of each other, we gloried in each strand of our confinement.

That night I wafted through intermittent sleep, while out the window I could see each time I awoke that the moonlight was full on the land. My mind was awash with vaguely related scenes. The wheatfields of Bruegel's masterpiece *The Harvesters* were mixed with a movie Ginny and I had once seen—an orgy—bare bodies twisting about with abandon, and that was all wound into Hieronymus Bosch's *Garden of Delights.* I suppose I was asleep and it was a dream. Garlands of svelte bodies were emerging from Bruegel's field of wheat, large-breasted girls with baskets of fruit balanced on their heads by upraised arms swayed by, strong-limbed youths snared a big stallion with ropes to trip him. It was as if the sculptor, Rodin, was molding my dream, and then I was awake and outside the moonlight still beckoned. I woke Ginny—no whispers—I led her from our bed out into the strangely compelling light.

In house slippers and nightgowns we gently trod the meadow. The warm night was fragrant with the odor of recently cut oat hay. It seemed we glided through the milky light and we both knew where we would come to the river. There the bedsprings were still evident, locked in by branches that had grown through their interstices. We put our nightgowns down on the grass and lay on them entwined, but far from arousal for we shared the same exalted mood.

Finally, I said, "To me, it's corn or was, but tonight I glory in the cliché: 'till death do us part.' Had you thought of that too?" But my poor darling was weeping—why, I didn't inquire.

"Why did you come that night, Ginny?" I asked.

She was looking up at the moon now and didn't answer for a moment. "I guess," she mused finally, "it was because I had come to depend on you."

I looked over at the bedsprings—a moonlit web above the water.

IX

*In Which
I Trade the Mill for Vanilla, Settle Accounts
with My Father for Good,
Gain Some Familiar Neighbors,
and
Suffer My Greatest Loss*

1955

I GOT BACK TO THE MILL to find that we were losing our latest team of loggers. They stated the problem as it was: "We can't wrap no cable around them trees that look chancy, not and hold our heads up in this here neck of the woods. Bringing them big leaners down ain't real logging anyway and we're loggers. We got to draw the line somewhere and we're doing it."

Bunky and I held council. "Maybe we should hire somebody to run the mill and get out and do our own logging," I said. "At least we'd have sense enough to collar the trees before we cut them down."

But here it was Bunky who drew the line. "Pop," he said, "this setup that you got for me to take the place of the boat—well, you can see for yourself. It's panning out piss-poor and, knowing you got into it for my sake, I'll stick with you in the mill, Pop, but I'm proud to say I'm no logger and I aspire not to ever be one."

The days when the saw was still in the mill, the weeks when I searched for other crews, were bringing us ever closer to bankruptcy. Each time one left, it was more difficult to snare others. The fir lumber market was at an all-time high. There were more jobs open in the woods than men to fill them. Wages had risen and I had to offer a bonus to get workers to look my way. The weeks of idleness were maddening and we were losing Ole. The furniture factories now paid more but not enough to cover the demands of the loggers.

As we waited, Bunky and I worked on a shack. When we had cleared around the spar tree at the new setting, there were four lofty firs that were in the way and had to be removed. We made them into excellent lumber—enough to make a fine shanty. It was big and roomy with a large window facing the basin of Oldorn Creek. I'd gotten a fine cooking stove for a song and installed it.

While we were idled, Ginny, and Nordi too, when she was not on a job, came down on weekends and saw the shame of our inactivity. I grew sick with a hundred aches and pains. I loathed myself. Finally we got a crew of three rheumatic old timers, forced out of regular logging by their slowness. They came up to stumble about for us and we were plenty glad to get them. They lasted three days, the steep terrain too much for them. The biggest one fell, skidding down into a hollow. It took his mates and Bunky and me with ropes to get the two hundred and eighty pounds of him unhurt and out.

One day, licked, but unable to admit it, I stepped into the local pub at Cloverdale to inquire about loggers. It was that time of day when the place was empty. I asked for a mug of draft. The owner's calm eyes looked me over in an appraisal carried out in a brief split second to affirm what he'd heard. It was a kind face and one that could be thoughtful, I decided, in an equal modicum of time. He set out a special bottle of German beer.

"It's on the house!" he said, as he opened one for himself. "Rice, I'm interested in your mill up there on the creek and the reason is that before you came I planned to do the same thing. My bar was not doing so well—that was the year before last—and I was itching to have at all this alder that's stacked up all around the side streams of the Nestuc'. I had a little dough and I figured I'd try my hand at it, then you showed up on Cedar Creek and I've had my eye on you ever since.

"I hear about everything you do up there along with everything else that happens in the county. Local news and beer flow in about equal amounts in here." He sat two more bottles before us.

"It's on the house," he said, "and I'll tell you why. It's because if you hadn't come down here and started first, I'd be in your shoes now."

"Great," I said. "Look, you've given me your best beer. How about a small draft of your candor?"

"Yes," he replied, "I hear what the loggers say about you and alder. 'He's okay,' they all say, 'but alder, what a laugh!' You and that throttling of the butt cut, they think is very funny. 'City stuff,' they say.

"Mark my word, it's the way they'll all be doing it, say in five years, but now, no way! You asked me to level with you—well, here it is. I looked it all up on account I figger to maybe get in your game when this fir boom wears thin and loggers are a dime a dozen again, but you won't be in it then. I can't see you hanging tight for a year or so to get to the better going. This year it's financially impossible. I know of four alder mills that's closed up the coast and two in Washington. To take alder's place the furniture makers are buying tulip wood from the Midwest. It ain't so good but they're using it till this fir boom ends."

I told Bunky what the bar owner had revealed to me. When I was through, Bunky agreed with him completely. "It isn't your fault that this heavy dough in the woods had to happen, but we can't stay in the game any longer. You can sure see that, Pop, you'll have to sell the mill."

"I hate it. I love this mill and it's been a tie between us."

"Sure, Pop, and it's proved that riding on your coattails doesn't pay. I've got to get out on my own."

"I'll put an ad in the Tillamook papers and the *Oregonian*," I said. "But what will you do, Bunky?"

"Anything until I can get on a boat—tug or a fishboat, or shipyard. I haven't had a fit for over three years now; you can stop worrying about me. And, Pop, I've got no regrets. We gave it one helluva try."

I explained to my customers that I could no longer supply them. They were pleasant about it and thanked me for the fine lumber I'd brought them.

Nordi and Ginny took the news with relief. "We saw what was

happening soon after the lumber boom started. Welcome home!"

Nordi was just leaving for two weeks' care of a young Jewess who was expecting to give birth in the next day or so. She was frightened and so was her husband. "They are new out West," Nordi said, "I'll have to be several things for them for awhile, but it will be gratifying. Clyde, please write while you're waiting for a sale." She kissed me and left.

I was suddenly seeing into an odd and an indefinite future.

"Ginny," I pled, "Don't come to see me until the mill is sold. This failure, added to all the others, well, I've got to have time to come to some understanding of what my life's all about."

I drove up our road in the dark, no moon or stars, my lights picked out the shambles of our old mill site and passed it to the cabin. Eyes showed in the car's lights to disappear and appear again. I shut off the engine and darkened the lights and sat still listening to the silence. After awhile I got out of the car and with my feet felt my way over the bouldered hillside to the door of the shanty and stepped into its inside stillness. After searching I found a lantern and watched the wick catch from my match. I made a fire and heated the cabin and drank coffee and drowsed until dawn came.

The results of my first ads in the papers were nil. Each morning after the mail had come I hurried down to my box. I got the usual answers from penniless coots spelling out grandiose futures, if I would but permit them absolute control. They were very secret about their formulas for our success. One spoke of it as "xx-100." Another admitted to the "sork factor."

Eight times I had failed in my life, though I only blamed myself completely for the loss of the good ship *Bunky*, and partly for this last fiasco. After days of disgust and fury I was physically sick with raging headaches.

Walking down for the mail one day I decided in mid-step to become a non-person. I went back from the mailbox empty handed. "So what?" I grunted out. I refused to think, but that was like holding my breath. Gradually, though, my mind escaped the usual flurry of impressions, hatreds and memories. I denied myself any memories of Ginny, Nordi or my son.

I continued to run ads in the Sunday papers. A month later when a farmer bought the mill he wrapped it up, at least until things settled down in the woods, as he knew they would. I only know that as I left, walking away from the richness that was always there for me, I wept. Very reluctantly, I left my road at the bottom and stepped out on the highway, got my car from the grease rack in Hebo, and drove home.

I applied for work at various places and at one of the firms I had a definite promise of a job in three months. Meantime I continued trying for something more immediate. With Nordi and Ginny both away working I got the soil in shape at home for a big garden now that I had the time. The season was warm, unbroken by our usual cold spring showers, and the seeds came up quickly. Though we hadn't water piped out in the bottom where I put the garden, I got out my old yoke from California days and with it hauled two big buckets of water at a time from a nearby waterhole.

In the midst of this, my father appeared one day. It turned out that he wanted me back at Acme. He said he had a good woman in the backroom and a first-rate salesman. I would only have to take care of shipping, deliveries and making of the extracts and keeping up the plant premises. "Yes, and the emulsions," he said, "I can't get anybody who handles the emulsions like you do."

"Pop, working there is a frustrating and no-win situation for me. You give me the impression that you'll be retiring and I'll run Acme, but the Little Lady is able to convince you I'm completely irresponsible and unable to handle things. She has the time to work on you and pretty soon you're believing it. I'd prefer not to go back to where simpletons treat me like a half-wit. Sorry, Pop."

Finally I succumbed to his begging and crying, his promises that things would be different. He wanted me back the worst way, he needed me desperately and so on. As soon as I came back he became suspicious that I would steal the secrets of his business. Instead he got me to put a new roof on his house, paint the damn thing beige, and so I was again the general choreboy.

Eventually I was back with the test tubes and eyedropper and vats amid sweet smelling barrels and drums of corn syrup and grain alcohol and little vials of orange-blossom-petal oil. It was a sweet and cloying place with an atmosphere that impinged upon my manhood insidiously.

The thing was I could close my eyes and see my big whirling saw flashing through a log, hear the thump of logs being turned down on the carriage and the edger saws screaming through bark-edged boards, while behind me the donkey engine strains at a log caught momentarily out in the brush.

"Now, this formula," says my father, "calls for eight drops of aldehyde G to tone the Messina lemon oil in this emulsion."

"Yes, sir," I say, "gotcha. Ten gallons finished product, yes, sir," but part of me is with the whine of saws or from further back but still vivid with the majestic following seas or the lordly billy goat of yesteryear, back there with Art Coulter and Miss Crippen and the ferryboats. But the real, the present, is vanilla, man, vanilla and you better like it!

Later I laughed inwardly, stirring a vat of concentrated maple flavoring, for all of that isn't behind me. It's all here with me, in me.

Nordi was away as a nurse for another young Jewish couple's first baby. This was the third similar case. Why Jews three times in a row? I'd have to ask.

Nordi came back radiant from her last job. Each place where she had worked, she left as a close friend. "The Jews," she said, "usually have more money, so they can look around more, while we with our meager funds are always bent over our lasts, as it were. These young women I've worked for are as well-read as I am. We find interests together in the passing scene, interests in history, and we try to apprehend the future. We have long conversations and I work in their gardens, trim their roses and enjoy myself vicariously. It seems strange, Clyde, but I get a great deal out of it.

"They're clannish and interrelated and tell one another about me. The wife of a rather famous doctor called me up just before I left the Spindler's place. Her husband was sick of and irritated at condoms, but she would not let him impregnate her until she had my word that I would take care of her in her confinement.

"I asked her what her interests were. I'm getting shamelessly picky, Clyde. 'Camping out in the Cascades,' was her reply, so of course that made us kindred spirits and I told her to throw all those thin rubbers away, that I'd be there when she needed me."

Nordi brought home a big pork roast. "Now that I've been unable to have it with them, it becomes precious in my foolish thinking."

Bunky was working now for a fellow who wanted to build rowboats on an assembly line and this on a long barge that was tied up in the Columbia slough, so Bunky was happy. "Boat, Mama, boat"—these were his first words.

Of course, Nordi got the place in the divorce proceedings. She would not charge us rent. "We're a big happy family, Clyde, and I want you to put every cent you can on your debts. You fought a losing battle down there on the coast and I'm proud of Bunky and you. You knew the odds when you went down there and both of you lived on pocket money, didn't you?"

"Worse than that," I answered. "I owe you and Ginny and the balance on the donkey."

"Sure, Clyde, that's the way it is when you try to raise yourself by your bootstraps. It's just the way of things; still some win through. I don't want you to pay me. Pay off the donkey engine.

"By the way," she said, "I saw Catherine Neufer the other day shopping at Meier and Frank's. We lunched together, talking about our days at art school. Ray has built them a big home near Oswego Lake, far enough back in the brush to avoid the stink of the lake. I told her to bring her family out for lunch some day when I'm between cases."

We lived a year in this odd domesticity. Near the end of it Bunky married his girlfriend. They stayed with us for awhile and then moved to San Diego, where he got on a distant relative's large fishboat and made a trip in it. His last letter told about the trouble they had with its diesel out on Tanner Bank. Bunky had been working with the engineer and another hand on the engine. The engineer asked Bunky to go up to the galley for coffee and while Bunky was gone, started the engine. It ran all right; it ran out of control and exploded. It blew the engineer through the deck, but the other fellow was unhurt. The ship sank at once with the captain rushing up to the pilothouse to send a mayday, but too late, the pilothouse was flooding and down she went. The crew were all in the water supporting the injured engineer.

Then some oranges came up from the sunken ship and the boat's skiff pulled loose from an entanglement of line and broken beams and popped up. We were able to bail it out and all get in. The sea was calm. Some distance away we saw another fishing vessel. I must hurry, Pop. This boat is taking off. I'll post this and tell you what happened in the next letter. Kiss Mom for me. Love Bunky.

We got some guinea fowl. Why, I do not know. They roosted in the trees around the house. About two-thirty in the morning they would begin cackling, all seven of them. The noise that they would keep up for half an hour was like breaking up glass— brittle, sharp and clashing in the extreme. It set your back teeth on edge.

Maybe the garden plants assumed they were in the tropics because of the racket of the guinea fowl each night. Whatever the reason, our garden prospered as never before. It was luxuriant in many colors and many shades of green and flavor and weeds that we attacked relentlessly. Otherwise the ladies did their thing in their chosen fields of babies and correspondence. And I, my suits reeking of vanilla, quit cigarettes and puffed cigars, and affecting a basser voice hoped to dispel wrong assumptions about me, as I followed the waft of vanilla, sweet cloying vanilla, that came before me wherever I went.

During the next few years there was a sameness in our lives—Ginny as an office worker, Nordi as a highly-esteemed practical nurse of young Jewish mothers, while I was interested in producing a more fruity red raspberry flavor, synthetic, of course. We paid off debts, we bought things, and continued our forays into the mountains.

Back at Acme was as flat as that sounds, still it was a living. Pop was glum whenever I returned from a weekend mountain backpacking trip. He hated vacations, believing they were a waste of time and on him they would have been. Around this time ossification set in for sure. Instead of moving ahead with the times as other extract makers were doing, using the new substances, he continued with the old materials and his archaic ways. He converted his business into a little papa-and-mama venture and dropped Spokane and Boise and way points from Acme's territory. Any possible big customer whom I brought to him he found means to avoid, and the Little Lady helped him in this. But, as I said, it was a living.

I was writing nights. Knowing that I was, infuriated my father. It absorbed energies that he was buying, he maintained. My writing was slow, my output small, for my aims were toward art and I was ill equipped for it. That and the weekends on the place and at night with Ginny more than paid for any provocation I received from my father and the Little Lady, for to me Ginny was simply a delight. The hours we spent together, whatever the activity, were exquisite and we both flourished under one another's regard.

Nordi had received several proposals of marriage but seemingly could not make up her mind. Along about here her friend, Catherine Neufer, hired her to look after her mother who'd had a bad heart attack. Catherine worked in a doctor's office and could not care for her.

After Nordi had been there for a week, Catherine asked her to come for a walk. She said she had something important to say.

This Nordi told Ginny later. The gist of it was that she was going to leave Ray. She had a lover who she wanted to marry. He was rich and owned a ten-story building. This impressed Catherine. "Imagine Ray ever owning a ten-story building! I want a businessman for a husband, not a wood carver.

"But you, Nordi—why don't you marry Ray? I've noticed how well you two get along at parties. I don't know if you've had other marriage offers, but give some thought to Ray. He is more your kind of a person. But don't wait for him to make the advances. You make them, because Ray is quite shy. You do like him, don't you, Nordi?"

"Yes, I always have," she replied, "but I hate to see you two split up. You should reconsider."

"No," Catherine answered, "we've been planning this for over a year. My boyfriend is hot in bed and he has the money that I need to move me along."

Nordi continued relating the events to Ginny. A few days later Catherine left. She had also pointed out that because she had helped Nordi in on the ground floor, so to speak, that Ray and Nordi should care for her mother and her son.

The mother, of course, couldn't keep her mouth shut and guyed Ray about what was happening. It was her kind of fun.

Nordi liked Ray a lot and when he crept into her bed one night, he was received as he'd never been received before. The next morning he asked her where she learned such loving ways and, she explained to Ginny and me, she had replied, "Mostly from Clyde," and she grinned impishly at me, her eyes twinkling.

Catherine filed for divorce and Nordi and Ray planned to marry as soon as the divorce was final. Some time later Catherine showed up one day and asked to come back. The man who owned the building had suddenly died. But Ray would have none of it, Nordi told us.

Reid, Catherine and Ray's son, was a freshman at Reed College when this exploded around him. He blamed it all on Nordi and was bitter about it, theatrically so. Nordi was very solicitous of the old lady's comfort, but that evil creature made her life as miserable as she was able. Eventually she moved to her other daughter's home in California.

Nordi and Ray, with Reid appearing at odd times, rattled in their big house. It was encumbered with a large mortgage so they decided to sell. Ray had heard of an older house near Council Crest in a fashionable district, which he could get at quite a reasonable price. The land fell away on all sides steeply. Four or five homes clung with Ray's chosen one to the backbone of a spur ridge of the great ridge that backs Portland, a very awkward home site, and so choice. Ray saw that he could make some changes, add rooms and some brick walls to retain enough soil for a brief lawn.

I was not jealous of Ray, for Nordi and I were one. He did, however, absolve me from my dog-in-the-manger guilt, one of the many that I carried in those years.

Ray was a constant producer of fine furniture. His house was loaded with it. Catherine had taken all she wanted; so did the aged vixen and Reid. In the carved panels of chests and cabinets I felt Ray reached the epitome of his art. The furniture was not produced for sale. What he did not keep he gave away. He was a man with little leisure; his free time he spent on and with wood. His sense of the austere, of grace, of the sublimely sensuous he was able to say in wood—with mahogany and teak, with our own Douglas fir and myrtle.

Soon after the decision to sell, Ray was able to do so—glad to, as his son would say, rid himself of bad vibes.

Now that Nordi was Mrs. Neufer, we began to visit back and forth. We got along very well. Ray and I had many interests in common. Eventually we spent all our weekends as a foursome.

We continued making trips into the high country on weekends, though they were no longer backpacking trips. Nordi had always been mad about camping, but it took awhile to get Ray out of town. He was a city person and looked on camping or even our place at Carver as a bore. In fact, Nordi was distressed at his discussion on more than one occasion of selling the farm at Carver or turning it over to his son.

There was a great friendship between my father and Nordi, that my father and I never had, and finally after worrying over what could happen to the property, Nordi took the problem to him.

"Clyde would be lost without the place that he loves so much and has spent so many years working on and improving. I can't sell it to him. Clyde made an offer to Ray of forty-five hundred, but he would not accept it, though it's the most Clyde can raise at this time. I'm filled with dread that the place will be lost to him, so I'm asking you to go to my husband and buy it from him. Clyde can add the cost onto the amount he owes you now and pay off the property so much a month. It should be done now because Ray needs money to work on our house. I'd be so relieved if the property was back in Clyde's hands, then eventually it will go to Bunky."

"Why does he always have to be doing things to a house?" my father asked.

"Because that's the way he is. He gets tremendous satisfaction working a house over."

"I often wonder about people," mused my father. "My father was a printer—lead and alcohol killed him. My grandfather was a doctor and, I guess, a murdering son-of-a-bitch. Some fellows are interested in shows or horses, stuff like that. To me, well, I put people into two categories—customers and the competition."

"How about the rest of us?" asked Nordi.

"They are the garbage and I don't mess around with it. I got just so much time, that's all. You mess around with the garbage— why it uses up your force. A guy that's going somewhere in this world has got to have his force pointed."

"How about his head?" put in Nordi.

"It could help," answered Pop. "I've seen fellows with pointy heads get to be somebody. It don't matter, so long as you get up there where you can tell other men—'do this, do that.'"

My father agreed to Nordi's request. "I certainly wouldn't do it for Clyde, but doing it for you—why Nordi, it's a pleasure."

What happened was never explicitly told. One day Pop said to me, "I own your place out there, Clyde, and I got a notion to have you thrown off. Still, I guess I don't want to do that. I'll sell it to you for three thousand. That's what I paid for it. We'll set up a schedule and if the payments aren't Johnny on the spot, out you go."

The Little Lady, when she found out, was furious, but for a month after, Nordi moved among us most spritely with a pixie look in her eyes.

With the marrying of Ray and the constant companionship he wanted from her, Nordi discontinued working out as a nurse. Instead she took a job at the nearby studio of Alda Jourdan, an outstanding photographer—a portraitist in the true sense of the word. Alda Jourdan and her late husband had at one time hidden the writer, Thomas Wolfe. He had become a Communist and was under the impression that the F.B.I. wanted him.

In her spare time Nordi took up her painting again—portraits and landscapes—which she continued doing throughout her life. About this time Ginny changed jobs too. Though she dearly loved the crew at the wholesale optical firm, she wanted a change. She found an interesting job for an old firm that had at one time made all the harness and saddles for the area and now handled sporting goods and manufactured custom leather goods.

We received a brief letter from Bunky. It said:

Pop, I'm in oceanography and they supply me with a tape recorder on this island. Pop, enclosed are a couple of tapes I've made. Get yourself a tape recorder and see what I've got to say, and we can communicate with tapes after that.

Ray knew a fellow who dealt in recorders and I bought one, then we spent the evening familiarizing ourselves with the machine and recording our voices. Ray sounded pompous, Ginny shy. I sounded immature—a sophomore voice—Nordi, an octave higher than I expected. Hers was an explaining voice, as if she spent her time informing oafs. Then we the quorum, as we spoke of ourselves, gathered 'round waiting as the spools turned and then suddenly Bunky's bass voice bellowed into the room. We adjusted the sound:

"Hey, Pop, is Mom there with you? Hello, Mom. I'm hugging you in my mind, Mom. It's late evening and I'm gazing at the gentle scene here and I almost think I'm looking out over the meadow at home, only that the lovely green is sword grass and I stay away from those sharp saw blades. And there's one-clawed crabs wandering around in it and rats. This tiny island is really an atoll, a couple hundred miles from Eniwetok. Bikini is closer. I'm all alone here watching a gauge, checking the atomic pollution in the water. My buddy, the scientist, well, they took him out after three weeks. He'd gone nuts from the solitude and the heat and the crabs rustling in our moat each night. They sent out another expert—a real 'intellectool'! He lasted three days before he began to go batty, so I'm the sole human on this place.

"I'm an able seaman for Scripps Oceanography and we've been at the Bikini blast. Our ship was the first to go in and take measurements, temperatures, that sort of stuff. The engineer made a boo-boo and we were stuck in there. The navy was in a perimeter beyond the horizon all around Bikini and we asked them to come and pull us out. They radioed back: 'You and your ship are expendable.' The lily-livered bastards. Finally we got out and we're still alive, but according to the navy docs who looked us over, none of us will ever father any children.

"I'm in a tent with a dry moat all around me. What drove the brainy guys into tizzies was the one-clawed crabs and the big rats trying to get at us in the night. There's only a few coconut palms here and they're starving. Maybe they eat each other. We fixed it so the crabs and rats can't climb the sandbank of the moat. Each morning I clean them out of it, shoot 'em and feed 'em to an enormous grouper who stays in a coral cave just under the shore. He's my friend. When I get really lonely I take my tank and gear and go down and visit with him. We seem to communicate.

"Hell, the batteries are running low. Have to wait till next time to tell you what happened after the fishboat sunk on Tanner's Bank. Well, I'll sign off."

·

All the winter before I'd been writing. I knew there was to be a writer's workshop in Missoula where the writer I much admired, Walter Van Tilburg Clark, would be teaching. I talked Ginny into taking her two weeks vacation and go with me and I begged time off from Acme so that I could take over my latest writings to Missoula for criticism.

The lectures and the criticism were perfectly logical and I could see that people were getting a great deal from them, but I found that I couldn't apply them to my own work. I'd have to do it my own way.

We had an enjoyable trip and came back over the mountains by way of the Lolo trail, then a long, rough primitive road—the Lewis and Clark route and later the sad trail of the Nez Perce and their chief, Joseph—so high that one looked down on the mountain goats.

Ginny and I built a small barn. It was in two levels, the lower part for the animals that we wanted and the top part for hay, tools and equipment. The top we painted a reddish brown and the bottom white.

After we had bought a couple of weaned Hereford calves and put them on the bottom enclosed in an electric fence, we got a pair of peacocks. Wowie! Then we got chickens, twelve geese and more guinea fowl. I brought home fourteen day-old turkeys and put them in the bathtub with a heat lamp over them until I could figure out what to do with them. We got a couple of little pigs and a stray sheep. We turned rabbits loose, way out on the meadow and they did what rabbits do. We soon had pets among all these animals. It seemed all right with them if we ate their relatives, so we did. We were extremely happy. I believe Nordi enjoyed it most.

"It's a little bit like the goat ranch, Clyde," she said one day, "but we only had chickens and goats and a beef or two."

Our male peacock was sort of the overlord of our bird population. Nests were scattered about—a guinea setting on eggs here, a Rhode Island hen setting there. Each day the peacock went to these nestings and stood a moment beside the squatting lady with a proprietary air before going to the next nesting fowl that he felt needed his consideration. We got to be friends, he and I.

The turkeys grew to be pullets and all acted almost as stupid as the young goslings that were now appearing. One Saturday Virginia and I were sitting contemplating a stairway I was making beside the barn when a little turkey pullet came and stood looking up at us, then flew up and sat down between us on the sawhorse and made appreciative sounds. This was Isabelle, who, in the next seven years, was to be the major-domo of the place who took care of things and ordered us around in no uncertain terms. Eventually she took a mate, a big cock we named Mr. Thud because of the noise he made when he strutted. As his consort, Isabelle put on all the airs of a very distinguished matron. She probably would have gotten into politics in her later years, but instead one night an opossum ate her. Would there were some big hungry 'possums in our capital.

The other lordly animal on the place was George, the pig. He loved his food, but would leave the trough to separate fighting turkeys, opening his mouth wide, pressing it on their entwined necks until they desisted, at which time he would resume his repast, at least until they started at it again.

The twelve geese were in Ginny's special care and would follow her fondly across to the far edge of the field in a long-strung-out pompous procession, then come marching back.

Ray was an excellent photographer and loved taking innumerable pictures of the geese and the rest of the feathered and furry inhabitants. He and Nordi had joined a group that specialized in making movies and they became enthusiastic in this as well as black and white stills.

Watching Ray, I realized I had a job to do. We men, at least our brains, seem ill-constructed to handle jobs like this, at least when sober. I rectified that with a bottle and staggered into Ray's presence.

"Ray," I said, "I wanna talk to you. I love your wife and she loves me, but it's platonic love. She loves you, Ray, and you and Nordi are better fitted than Nordi and I were. And, Ray, I like you a great deal. Now I'm an agnostic, same as you, and swearing before God hasn't the meaning for us it has for others, so I'll swear by what I feel was fine. Hear me! On the gentleness that was my mother I swear I'll never lay hands on your wife nor kiss her or ever speak words of love to her till death takes me."

After a long moment Ray resumed chiseling on a post he'd been working on, saying nothing, and I staggered out and lay in the field until moonlight seemed cold and I sought Virginia.

The Little Lady became intensely jealous of the companionship my father had with the woman he worked with in the backroom and forced her out. I took her place bottling the goods. Very soon I had built up an excellent stock in the storeroom and then there was nothing to do, nothing to fool around with. I ran a controlled and sensible backroom. He missed the silly foolishness that he was always so busy with and was upset because he wanted a woman to work with, not a man. He advertised the business for sale. Of this I was entirely unaware.

·

I came to work one morning to find I was out of a job. "I sold the business yesterday," my father said. "We won't be running it any longer and the new people don't need you."

I was dumbfounded, much to the great satisfaction of the Little Lady and my father. The buyers, two partners, Pat Patterson and Dick Meiling, walked in the front door. I was introduced and they asked me to show them around. I showed them the mixing room and the bottling room and the pitifully inadequate lab and the storerooms, then left them poking around in the room where we did our shipping and kept our supplies. In half of it I had built a mezzanine or balcony where the cartons and paper supplies were kept.

I saw that they were not too interested. They exhibited a humorous attitude toward whatever I showed them, as if they knew they were buying a papa-mama business that they were about to modernize. Our ancient printing arrangement made them laugh. They stopped and studied the complicated bunch of cubbyholes built into one wall where my father's over-meticulousness was self-evident. I had built it to his instructions, the nature of the contents written before each cubbyhole in large letters: *Small Bolts, Large Bolts, Spigots, Small Spigots, Faucets, Washers, Little Washers, Hose Clamps,* and for my own amuse-ment, *Middle Size Bent Nails,* and *Ham Sandwiches.* The shorter one of the two started laughing.

"This place is sick," he said, "but putting *Ham Sandwiches* in that 1894 arrangement is good. It acknowledges the cupboard for what it is, and if Mr. Rice's son did this, he can't be all that bad. Let's hire him."

"No," said Dick, the taller one, "the Rices definitely want him kicked out of here."

"Who's buying this?" said Patterson. "I hope they're not attempting to take our right to hire whom we please. There's something sick here," he continued, "and I don't think it's the son. Maybe it's why we're getting it so cheap. Let's find out how we can use him or how we can carry on without him."

"Well, okay," said Dick, "but I don't like to irritate the old man."

"I got a hunch you'll be irritating Mrs. Rice much more."

I stood by, hearing all this. Patterson came up to me. "Look," he said in an undertone, "stick around, will ya. I think I get the picture."

Next morning Pop and the Little Lady were in the office with the partners. They asked me to come in. Patterson was speaking again. "Who will produce the flavors when you're gone, Mr. Rice?"

"Why, either one of you," replied my father. "I'll show you how and you have my formula books."

"We'll be out selling and running the office," Patterson said. "I wouldn't take a chance on it. I can't even fry an egg. How about you, Dick?" he said to his partner.

"Let's look at some of the formulas."

He looked. "Okay, let me make one."

I watched. Though the old man tried to tell him, the technique was lost on him. Almost immediately he had twenty gallons of insoluble knots.

Patterson said, "Throw it out. What'd it cost us? Twenty bucks. Okay, we'll try it again."

They did try and under my father's hurried explanations, it went wrong again. Dick turned to me.

"Can you do it, Clyde?"

"Of course," I said, "I do it every day. It's the way I make my living."

"Are there any tricks here in the trade you don't know?"

"No, not one, but there are a lot of tricks of the trade that should be practiced here and aren't."

Patterson took me to one side. "What would you do if we hired you?"

"Modernize it? I hear that everywhere—it's too glib. However, if I go to work for you, not only do I know the value this place has, but more important, what it needs. I advise you to hire me. You're going to need me and how I'd love to straighten this mess out."

"Okay," said Patterson, "You're hired!"

Later I continued my work of drawing off a batch of pure Mexican vanilla from the percolator and was starting it through the filters, when Pop came to me in cold anger: "I sold this place out from under you. Get lost!"

"I'm not working for you, Pop. I'm working for Mr. Patterson."

"I'll stop that," he said.

"I wouldn't fool around with Patterson too much if I were

you, Pop. He's about got your number already and I believe there's some heavy backing behind him. You made your deal. Why don't you go home?"

The Little Lady came down to the plant one day. "Clyde," she said, "I feel you're not aware of what's going on. Your father sold this business because he hates you and wanted to get you out of here for good, but you're still here and he can get no rest." With that she whipped around and left.

Even though my father threatened, in the event of a late payment, to close them down if I received a raise, they gave me one anyway. In that period of my life I felt I had never been of such value to other people. We had great harmony.

But then Patterson and Meiling got into a row and Meiling bought Pat out. There was just Dick and me and a boy, Biff, in the factory.

After Patterson left, business went on as usual. We were busy, but it became increasingly clear to me that *I was Acme Flavoring* and that my wages were way lower than they should be. I produced all that Dick sold. I did all the buying. I would be impossible to replace. I went with Dick in my linen smock to difficult customers and played the weird genius of flavors. We picked up our largest account that way. I felt that I should be paid as much as Dick for my efforts for the Company.

One day he came in early and stood talking to me as I scrubbed the floor under a rack of drums. "Dick," I said in the midst of some desultory gossip, "you've got fifteen minutes to make me your partner or I'll quit. And I'll form a new company of three other men with whom I've discussed this several times. I will up the formulas ten percent. With our markup that's easy and that'll clear the law. Each of them have agreed to put up fifteen thousand against my know-how and formulas, but I'm going to give you this chance to keep me on at a fifty-fifty basis. What do you say?"

He wilted. In his shoes so would I. Finally he said, "Let's go over to your father's and talk."

When Dick had told them what I proposed, the Little Lady

led off with a, "Humph! After all we've done for you, but then I've often told Jim I expected it of you. Let me tell you, you can't do this. You'll be breaking the law and we'll sue."

"Don't you understand?" I said. "Think. I'll up the strength of the formulas ten percent—a good selling point, by the way—and with the enormous make there is in flavors, that will be easy. Ten percent difference in a formula clears the law. Doesn't it, Pop?"

"Yes, it does," he said. "Clyde, will you tell me the names of the gentlemen involved?"

"Certainly not. Not knowing them, you can't slander me to them." He looked like I kicked him the face. I let go then: "Pop," I said, "why did you turn down every break I found for the Company, every suggestion that would have increased the Company's make? Yeah, and why didn't you let me do the job I'm doing now? Instead by ignoring good suggestions, by denying me a chance, you were proving to yourself I was incapable, which seems to have been your whole aim. Why? Why, Pop?"

"I'll answer you with another why. Why haven't you talked this way to me before? You've been so damn filial, that's the word, ain't it, son?"

"Yeah. You're my father. I love you. Keeping Acme going has been a goal for me as well as you, but you made doing it a constant frustration. Now I have joy in handling the work I'm fitted to do. I'm not trying to show you up or change things just to be changing them, Pop."

"Well, the Little Lady didn't see it that way," he said. "Dick, sorry to let you in on this family squabble." He went on, "She's hid all your good qualities from me."

At this point the Little Lady jumped up, very red in the face, "Clyde Rice," she said, "you made me out as a liar. Nobody can do that to me in my own house." She rushed to the front door and threw it open. "Get out!" she said dramatically with gestures.

"Ah, Christ!" yelled my father. "Shut the God-damned door and get us some coffee. But, Clyde, I don't think you understand. She's my last woman. Don't you see it or do you have to get old to see the shrink of opportunity and feel the crush of age's vice on you? I let her confuse me, Clyde. Kinda liked it, I guess. I didn't want you to loom up too much as I got weaker. I can see that now. I was wrong! Dick," he said, turning to him, "he's got you in a bind. You'd be smart to take him on as partner. As the saying goes, his light, at least until lately, has been hid under a bushel of my and the Little Lady's making."

Then he grinned happily. "Well, Clyde, when I die, whatever you still owe for your share of the Company will be paid up. After all, the way we treated you I guess you've earned whatever's left of Acme. God, once we had twelve fine salesmen on the road. Yeah, Clyde, you can have half of what's left, and I'm not belittling you, Dick. You're first rate. I've seen that all along.

"Say, this has been quite a morning. Chirked me up a lot." He laughed, his old eyes sparkling.

One morning some months later, before Ginny and I left for the city, I received a call from the Little Lady. "Your father is sick and he wants to see you."

"Go," said Ginny, "I'll take the bus."

I wondered as I drove in why we hadn't communicated and then realized how busy I'd been. Still we'd had no word from them, though usually we were in contact by phone several times a week. As she let me in, I noticed that she looked wan. My father, abed, was obviously a sick man. He lay without speaking until she left the room, then he moved closer to me in the bed and whispered: "Clyde, I've asked her to call you for three days and she refused. I've been hellishing sick and I wanted you by me."

"Well, I'll stick around, Pop. By the way, is your practitioner doing you any good?"

"No, I can't say she has. I've been vomiting for three days and nights now. Tell you, I'm getting weaker."

"Sure, Pop, that's been an awful strain on you. I want to get my doctor to look you over. Pop, remember how you looked up to Ben Selling. Well, my doctor is Ben Selling's famous son."

The Little Lady, who'd been snooping outside the door, stepped in. "A doctor! Not in my house you won't! Do you realize how many bodies are hauled away from hospitals under cover of the night? Jim, say no to him! I should have never allowed you to come here, Clyde. You want to disrupt this home with materia medica. Oh, they'll want to operate, Jim. Do you want to be cut up with razor-sharp knives?"

"Pop, look! Your practitioner isn't helping you. Something's wrong. Something's got to be changed. We've got to find what's keeping you this way. Knives, my ass! You thought the world of Ben Selling. This is his son, with the same honesty. Please, Pop, let me get him."

I prevailed. Doctor Selling couldn't come. "Clyde," he said, "I'm sending a very good man, one I personally trained. He'll be right out."

When he came, the Little Lady let him in with a barrage of insults. He closeted himself with my father, who also treated him with as much contempt as he could muster. When the doctor came out of Pop's room later, he said, "I'll see you in my car," obviously furious at the treatment he'd received. "Mr. Rice, you have obnoxious relatives."

"Religious fanatics," I said to mollify him.

"Worse," he said, "here's what I found. Your father has had a rupture for years, with the colon, of course, extended into it. A caking has built up in there for a long time, heavily coating the colon. It's poisoning him. In fact, it's killing him."

"What can be done?" I asked.

"Plenty, and it's simple, but I refuse to do it or even enter their house. Bring in a trained nurse. Have her give him six high enemas, but if they won't allow a nurse in, you could do it yourself. That's all that seems to be wrong with him. Good luck!"

I told them what the doctor said. "The very idea," said the Little Lady. "How common can a doctor get."

"Too many enemas brought on my mother's death," my father declared. "I never had one and I never will."

"Yes, but, Pop, don't you see? What he's saying makes sense."

"How could he tell that, feeling a little bit on my stomach like he did?"

"They're trained, Pop. Won't you get a nurse?"

"We'll have to, Jim," said the Little Lady. "I can't stay up another night with you. I've got to get some sleep."

"Okay, but no, and I mean it, no enemas! And, Clyde, I feel much better. Telling that damn doctor off helped, I guess. I won't need you. Go on home!"

That night he died. The nurse said that along about two he clambered out of bed, talking. At first she couldn't make out what he said. On hands and knees he swiftly crawled toward the bathroom, but collapsed, dead at its door, the nurse said. On this, his last trip, he was counting—two hundred thirty-four, two hundred thirty-five, two hundred thirty-six and he was gone. His voice, the nurse went on, was that of a little boy. Evidently my father died happy.

•

We made the final payment on the farm and could afford to have a well drilled. We told ourselves we needed it, but we didn't. We had an excellent spring. Finally the drillers hit water at one hundred feet. It was just slightly artesian and we capped it.

We asked Nordi and Ray to come and have dinner with us. Then we showed them the big building lot that we once arranged for Teddy Broms and told them, "This is yours. Won't you put a house on it and come live near us and share our garden?"

Nordi was thrilled, but Ray held back. "That spring barely gives you enough water. You won't be able to share it with us?"

We took them down and showed them the capped well, removed the cap and water welled up. "There's your water. It's a hundred feet deep and we'll own it jointly," we said and handed them the copy of the legal paper we had drawn up making the place theirs.

"Now we can have a summer place," said Nordi. "Oh, Ray, you're always building something. Build us a cottage here."

It was a great day. Finally Ray began to smile and to figure. I lent him my beloved hundred-foot steel tape, a gift from Ginny before we were married. Ray was soon engrossed in measuring where the cabin could stand and Nordi came smiling to Ginny and me and gave us each a vigorous hug.

"As a reciprocating gesture," I said, "we offer you a third of an acre and a well for thirteen acres and a house. Oh, Nordi, we can't ever repay you."

She turned and looked at me with the "we are one" look. I was flooded with it. That look was another dimension to me. "Sure," I muttered, "sure is a nice day." We broke the spell then, being considerate of Ginny.

"Yes," Nordi replied, "yes, it is a nice day."

"But I don't deserve this," I blurted out.

"I think you do," she answered.

"Deserve—what do you mean?" asked Ginny, as she turned and saw our faces. "Oh, I'm sorry," she murmured and turned to Isabelle who had wandered over. She made a turkey sound that Isabelle answered, as Nordi started toward Ray who was driving pegs where the corners of the cabin would be.

They made a lovely home that hugged their ground as if it grew there with the trees.

Bunky returned to Oregon and worked in Milwaukie, but we saw little of him. He brought up from California a lady friend who had a flaming temper and sunny hair. It could have been the other way. She hated the Carver tribe on sight and produced violent, screaming scenes each time he brought her out. Nordi and I occasionally had lunch with him near his job. We were all too busy to fuss about it yet.

Dick wanted a new flavor—something to use as a leader. I went to work on that. I find great joy in listening to a full orchestra tuning up. There are combinations then that should be in compositions. In a part of Beethoven's "Waldstein" sonata there is this utterly free quality. I find bits of wild freedom here and there in music—it's grand stuff—and the same is true sometimes of what happens in the backrooms of flavoring and extract houses. Strange combinations of fragrances achieve chords, blends you might call them—fragrances—never produced intentionally or used out in the world.

Lately one had happened in our own plant that I liked. We were working with grapefruit oil on the same day that we put up pistachio flavor and imitation cherry. The odors clashed and yet they didn't. I decided to develop this oddity. I kept working at various relationships in the combination. Finally using the one that to my mind was the best, I made a little ice cream. We had purchased a small ice cream making machine and a hardening cabinet, for testing our products. From the ice cream I saw it needed more grapefruit oil and added a bit of vanilla to take out some of the harshness, but not too much, for the harshness of the flavor was intriguing. You kept having another spoonful, trying to decide to dislike or like the flavor. It was a fine and different thing. I named it *Respighi* but I didn't patent it. I learned that was a sure way to advertise to the big guys you had something they should look into and maybe use. No! I did not show the formula to Dick or anyone else. It was something to hang onto and not chance disclosure.

If I did it today, I would improve it with the essence of fir, not much, but I always felt it needed a resinous tang that balsam of Tolu couldn't give it.

Dick liked the ice cream we made from it. Mrs. Scott, the bookkeeper, often got herself a dish of ice cream from the hardening cabinet. One day she came to me. "All my life I've loved vanilla ice cream," she said. "Now I like Respighi better. I'm just an old lady, but listen to me: I'm sure you've really got something there, Clyde."

Then Dick took some to a famous restaurant. They used it and swore it was the greatest thing since peanut butter was invented. That strange dissonance seemed to endlessly intrigue and you savored it while telling yourself you didn't like it. You wanted to try it once more, but you never quite found it, and your taster was always searching, fascinated with Respighi.

One of the nation's biggest creamery organizations with a creamery in every city of any size was the one I picked to sell my new flavor to. Though I didn't know much about them except that San Francisco was their headquarters, I did find out that the name of the president was Job Cable. How to get to him? More than that, how to get *at* him? How to get by all those vice-presidents, superintendents, and buyers and how to interest Cable, who probably had a jaded appetite, in tasting our Respighi?

I inquired at some of the essential oil houses. "You just can't do it. Nobody can get to him."

I solved it. I had one of our favorite ice cream makers make a batch of Respighi with some tasteless chopped nuts in it to add the quality of nibbling. I sent him two quarts by frozen air freight, a mode still in its infancy at that time, and pasted to the side of the package a letter:

Attention Job Cable:

Here is Respighi. From a standpoint of semantics Respighi is a very good name. Customers take to it with that right kind of curiosity and when they taste Respighi, they smile, for they have made a pleasant discovery. The name has a rasp to it that makes one, hearing or reading it, take notice—a bit sinister: Respighi. It is a name that fits the flavor. Respighi is not a marshmallow pink lady sort of thing, which is all to the good, for ice cream as a field certainly needs a new note. Consider it in a list of advertised flavors: Lemon, Custard, Vanilla, Respighi, Peppermint Stick— "What is that Respighi, young man?"

Cherry Respighi . . . Fig Respighi . . . Pineapple Respighi . . .

It's a subtle come-on, a conversation piece, and the flavor delivers all the name promises. We feel it will soon be one of the great flavors. The name is Italian to fit in with the pizzas, spumonis and Gina Lollobrigidas.

We offer Respighi flavor for your exclusive use, nationally, at $10.30 a gallon in sizeable orders. We know of nothing like it. Why don't you taste it! A spoon is in the package.

The letter was aimed at Job Cable's young secretary: the spoon inside—why don't you taste it! Yeah, I guess there's a little snake about me. The way the package came and was delivered was auspicious to the effect I wanted. It was easy to unwrap, the spoon was handy. She couldn't help herself. She tasted it. The flavor was unusual and interesting. I could hear her:

"Hey, Job, get a load of this! Try some of this funny ice cream."

"Unh unh, I don't wanta."

"Jobie . . . as a favor?"

"Oh, all right, darling."

So Job called me up. "Say, that was interesting ice cream," he said. "I suppose you want me to buy it, huh? Well, it won't be quite that easy, but I'm thinking. Give me a ring tomorrow."

Next day I called Mr. Cable. He answered but was going to hang up and, realizing it, I yelled "Respighi" into the phone.

"Oh," he said, "you're the Respighi man from Portland. I'm going to put your deal on hold. I handed your sample over to our taste panel. Some liked it a lot, but then there was those that didn't. As I said, I like it. Still, I'm going to put it on hold for two months. Don't take a chance and offer it to our competition. I'll talk to you—in sixty days!" I put down the receiver with a grin.

Dick was perturbed, however. "I'm doing good with it among our customers."

"Well, hold off. This could be really big. Stall the local ones for the next two months. Say it's on account of a squabble over patent rights."

Sixty days was a long time, but if Respighi went nationally that would pick Acme up out of the small time stuff. Then the time was up and I called Cable. His secretary answered. "Respighi," I said. "May I speak to Mr. Cable?"

"One moment pliz."

"That you, Rice? Say, a guy on my taste panel says he tastes citrus in this stuff."

"Sure," I agreed, "ask him what combinations of citruses he tastes. There are seven available, but what combinations? How much mandarin oil, how much bitter orange does it take to produce that side of the flavor?"

"Yeah I see it won't be so easy to figure out your formula. Okay! Rice, the best ice cream man of all our superintendents runs our Portland plant. I'll ask him. If he goes for it, so will we. If he doesn't, goodbye. Either way, that spoon in the package was a nice try. Give him a sample up there and I'll let you know."

I did and in a week Cable called me. "I'm sorry, Rice, but he don't think much of it. As far as I'm concerned I still like the flavor, but I'm no expert."

I don't recall who gave me the background facts of Job Cable's refusal of Respighi. The reason his manager made that statement, I had found out in the meantime, was that he himself was buying Respighi through several of our customers. He was mixing dates in it instead of nuts and selling it strictly as a side business in Texas as a new spumoni. He was doing very well.

I went to him and asked him to reconsider his thumbs-down reply to Cable's request and to admit that he knew it for a fine flavor.

He replied sardonically, "Yeah, I do know a good thing when I see it. You're in a bind and I'm keeping you in it for my own profit. I'm not the company's pawn to move as Cable sees fit. My retirement comes up in six months and I'll need something to play with like this deal down in Texas. It's a natural. Respighi started it for me. Business is business," he said and jumped up, left the office and got in his car and drove away.

After that I tried to get Cable on the phone. His secretary said he did not want to speak to me. "We're not going to deal. That's final," she reported.

I wrote him a note describing the situation. I received no reply. Sometime later Cable's local manager called, placing a big order for Respighi. I told him I'd discontinued it and that it would no longer be available.

He was upset. "Rice, you can't do this to me."

"I can and do with great pleasure."

A couple of years later I tasted a poor imitation of Respighi. It was pitiful. They called it *Amber Blossom*. It was tricked out to appeal to children, which is, of course, the greatest market for ice cream but what a comedown.

Then we hit a slump. It was a time when innumerable small

ice cream manufacturers were making very special ice cream products. Thirty-two flavors was their advertisement. All these little ice cream stores had talked of combining and starting their own creamery to take care of their own needs, but they didn't. The big creameries where they bought their cream and ice cream mixes decided to raise the price of the cream for them and lower the price of their own ice cream produced in thirty-two flavors. Numerous small outfits went broke, except for the stores that turned themselves into ice cream and hamburger joints. It was a tough time for many of our customers. We were carrying a lot of them and we felt it. It hurt Dick. Dick, by nature, must always go ahead, must always be riding a wave of his own production or others. To sit tight was for him a matter of stagnation. He must leap to something that was on the go. He saw such a chance in his old occupation as salesman for a chemical house.

At last it dawned on me, considering his wilted appearance, that he wanted out. The Little Lady saw it too and together we bought his share. That was a very sad day for me. He had been a marvelous fellow to work with. He gave me full support and I was not used to it. I still hear his footsteps as he came in each evening. He rather dragged one heel at times as he walked. I always told myself it was because he was loaded with orders.

After Dick sold, the Little Lady, to protect her interest she said, for I was buying the business from her, ran the office: "To recoup," she said. She took no salary and I reduced my salary to half. She brought in her brother to help me. Now I was the only salesman and still produced all the products.

Acme was an empty place with Dick gone. He was big and robust and jolly, twenty years my junior. There was only the Little Lady, stout and squat, crouching over the books in the office and the ancient still somewhat serviceable brother she'd brought in to wander around the large echoing rooms.

My hands began to shake as I fumbled through formulation of some intricate flavor—like the way I achieved that tiny sense of must as an overtone of dead ripeness in the Strawberry H emulsion. I soon felt I had lost all of my abilities. Perhaps Dick left because he doubted my talent with flavors. And there was the Little Lady's attitude toward my innovations. She made fun of Respighi and the imitation vanilla that had won the pure vanilla prize at a convention. Yeah! At last I was president of Acme Flavoring, but the echoes were disconcerting.

Since Ernest would not clean up after me when I made the goods, I would have to spend an hour tending to that chore before I could get away to call on the trade. I got rid of him. Nordi had been an old hand here and she offered to help. I had lost very few of Dick's customers and was bringing in quite a bit of new business, some large accounts, and Nordi couldn't handle it all, so I hired Ernest back to help her.

There was objection then from the Little Lady, about the expense of hiring another person but I was adamant that we needed them both if we were going to take care of the new customers.

The significance of Nordi's remark that if the Little Lady wouldn't pay her, she would work for nothing, didn't sink in then for some reason. She said she didn't need the money. I wouldn't hear of her putting in time without payment.

Nordi had lent me money for the donkey engine when we were running the mill. Now that the farm was paid off, free of encumbrances, I was in a position to start paying her so much a month. I got out my checkbook and told her how I planned to do it.

Handing me a cup of tea and looking quizzically at me, she questioned, "Do you really want to pay it?"

"Of course. Now, at last." I answered.

She said nothing for a long moment, then shook her head, "No, I won't take it," then paused. "But, Clyde, there is something—Bunky—I worry about him. Will you look after Bunky?"

"It's obvious I do a terrible job." I replied, "Look at the boat and the mill."

"But will you keep an eye on him?"

"What a thing to ask, Nordi. He's my son."

"Well, I just needed to know that for certain. The money—forget it. I don't want your money."

What could I say! Nordi gave the place back to me in the only way she could and later when I tried to pay her on the debt, she would tear up the checks or if cash, she'd return it to Ginny.

"Well, come on now," she said. "What have we to make today?"

"We're low on butterscotch emulsion and imitation vanilla concentrate. Tomorrow we have to make cherry flavor and imitation almond."

She got out the formula book and started to work on the butterscotch emulsion from it. Suddenly she was in a rush, where in our conversation a few minutes before she'd been so calm and considerate. She was getting the materials together harum-scarum when I checked and found she'd made an error on the work sheet and from that mistake she was gathering the wrong amounts of the ingredients. I pointed this out to her. One of the factors of our flavoring business down through the years was that we allowed not the slightest variation in the finished product. I scolded her about it and she said it wouldn't make any difference. "After all," she said, "I worked for your father for years."

"Then you know how meticulous he was."

"A waste of time," she said. "Let's get on with it."

"No, Nordi, it's got to be done exactly right."

She used a saying then that her sister, Olga, used when faced with the facts: "Well, I don't care!" Then added: "What I've put out here will work just fine."

"Nordi, this isn't like you. What's wrong? What's bothering you?"

"You should be out calling on the trade," she announced vehemently. "We can whip this out and you can be on your way."

Next day there was a similar occurrence, and the next. She kept butting in with a rush to get everything done at once. After a week of it I had to tell her I couldn't allow her to participate in the making of the goods. It tortured me to tell her that. I felt like an abusive oaf, but she was acting with a wildness precipitated by her knowledge that I was trying to do more than one can do. Vaguely, I saw that she was also unconsciously competing with me, as she always had, whether it was chimneys or statues or who could row a boat the most hours without stopping. Somehow though, it made me love her more than ever, but I couldn't understand these rapid swings of mood. She often said she didn't think she had long to live—must get everything possible done, just in case, she said. Her nervous energy would not let her rest.

When Nordi remarked one day that, though I'd been coming to her for years for guidance, there'd be a time when she'd no longer be around, I was preoccupied and it wasn't till later that I remembered what she said: "Listen to Virginia, Clyde. She has the wisdom you lack. You may have the facts, the knowledge, but you don't know how to use them. Talk to her as you've talked to me and listen."

She planted trees and flowering bushes on all our places, consulting with us first, of course. She planted some forty tiny trees, pines and others on the edge of our field against the cottonwoods along the river and elsewhere on our acreage. Later we were to find, sometimes years later, where she had planted some slow growing fern in the narrow stands of barrier trees. She began doing morning favors for Forsythes and Bromses and most of all for Ginny and me before she drove in with us to work in the city. Ray and Nordi went early to bed and awoke before daybreak and after a quick breakfast searched out jobs to absorb their early morning vigor. She cut our lawns, weeded in our gardens, swept our backdoor stoops and this was all done gaily. We all wondered at her new ways. "Energy is to use, not to store," was her comment.

Nordi was all around me, wound into my work by day and into the joys of our country life each evening. The four of us still had our meals together and, after eating, Nordi and I took a stroll or went to the barn where we talked over our day as we always had.

My oath to Ray still held. He was so kind in allowing me this unrestricted relationship with his wife. I must adhere to the tenets of my promise, so when she passed close by me at work, I held myself in strict control to keep from grabbing her and covering her dear face with kisses.

I had found a beautiful melody that somehow reminded me of our unspoken love and my thousand memories of her. I did not know the source of the melody, but once when it came into my mind, I whistled it over and over and tried to write it down on a painted board as a vertical thing with horizontal marks of different lengths conveying the length of each note. I got so I could look at the board and remember the tune and whistle or hum it.

I wanted to whistle or hum it to Nordi. I was sure that we were so attuned to one another that this simple melody would unite us in some psychic way and all our unspoken understandings would become sublimated in that tune, so that after she heard it she would look into my eyes that way she has and say, "Yes! Yes indeed, Nailby, dear!"

The day came when Nordi and I arrived at the plant early. We were standing about in a sort of pleasant limbo. Love was there, our never-to-be-spoken love. Now, I thought, I would hum my song to Nordi. I looked at my board and heard it in my mind.

"Listen to me Nordi," I said, my gaze moving from the board to Nordi's expectant face and back again. I can hum loud enough, I thought, and anyway she was standing very near to me. Now was the time I had dreamed of, but at that moment the front door of the office slammed and then Ernest appeared. I was devastated, unstrung, and though she had no way of knowing, the look in Nordi's eyes was as if something had been taken away from her.

After that, my full schedule kept me from humming the song to her. I fretted about it but an opportunity did not come again. Later, with the pressure of work, in spite of all my thinking about how the beauty of the melody exactly expressed what we felt for each other, it rather slipped my mind.

With Nordi helping me and Ernest assisting her, the goods

were going out on time and the customers were pleased with our extracts and syrups.

She wore a series of smocks, plain in pastel colors and heavily starched so that they stood out about her. When she walked in the open space down the laboratory through the mixing room and into the bottling area, she came like a little ship, her feet twinkling beneath the broad skirt of the smock. I got tremendous satisfaction in watching, and atop this little ship of sweetness was her smile. That smile, that told she had been kicked but not hindered by it, a bright quirky smile that found your eyes in full confidence, though the harm that I had done was there too. It was a smile I still see way too often on the faces of wives and widows as they pass me on the street. Oh, I was guilty. I could take that, but to see it on her face caused me great anguish.

So she moved about the plant, with kindness for all and especially for me, who'd harmed her and loved her to distraction, my promise to Ray too well remembered. I'm a forgetful fellow. Why in hell couldn't I forget that, at least momentarily? But I'm a fool. I hug to myself tightly all those things that twist my life askew. I'm unable to seek smooth sailing. Okay! But it galls me when those I love also pay the price.

At the sixty-gallon steam kettle on its platform six feet above the floor of the mixing room I would stand and stir the vanilla or root beer or crushed strawberries and watch as Nordi moved about at her duties, especially when, at my call, she would come sailing down the long corridor and from my view from above, she seemed to float toward me, but always smiling up expectantly as if I could reply in kind. I would be filled with love and adoration and desired only to humble myself before her, to come down and kiss her little high-arched feet, but clogged with these feelings, inchoate and dulled with my repressions, I stared down at her helplessly. Did she know of the hungering going on in me? Did she know of my oath to Ray? I don't think she did.

On such a morning I called to her from the kettle platform that the crushed strawberries were ready to can and turned to see her parade the alley that seemed to me to be made for her dear progress and it was too much for me. In the height of frustration I looked down at her smile and cursed her. I told her she was causing trouble with her inexact attitude toward formulation.

"At least," I said, "you had nothing to do with the flavoring of this crushed strawberry, which I've spiked with my imitation strawberry flavor."

I continued to berate her, my emotions clear out of control. I saw a hopeless look come on her face. I couldn't stop myself. She was aghast, unknowing that it was love, sheer love, that drove me to carry on in this manner. Oh, it was a bitter moment—the twisted why of it hidden! I climbed down and left the plant, driving furiously to the mountains, unaware of the beauty about me, seeing only the hurt look on her face.

Next morning she didn't come to work. Ray said she'd spent a bad night and I, who knew the cause, poisoned with my guilt, wished that I were dead. She was sick for several weeks. Ray took her to a doctor, not to capable Dr. Selling, but some inferior one out in the sticks.

As she grew better, she was able to go on with her planting. Some people are said to have a green thumb, but of Nordi they said she had a green foot. With her long-handled little shovel she made an opening in the earth, dropped in the seed or young plant or whatever it was, and pressed the spot with her foot and it grew. They always grew.

Just the other day I found an exotic in a deep clump of trees that Nordi had trod there once, still keeping its secret place to say finally, "Nordi planted me here."

Nordi in time was able to take up one of her favorite activities—camping. It was decided that she and Ray and others in the family who were able to go would take off for the coastal sand dunes near Florence. There they could walk the wide beaches, play in the surf, and swim in the warm lakes nestled in the dunes. Ginny had some vacation coming, so she happily joined in the plan.

It had been a wet June; but now it was July and the morning of the trip showed promise of fair weather ahead and while others loaded the cars, Nordi dropped down to bid me goodbye before I left for work.

As she came in the door, Ginny beamed, "Nordi, how pretty you look this morning with that pink ribbon in your hair and your flowery print top, real sparkly."

Ginny was rushing around getting ready, bouncing in and out of rooms, upstairs and down, as Nordi came into the living room all smiles and greeted me. I took note of her appearance, agreeing that she looked perky. She glowed with early morning freshness. Never before had I hungered so much to take her in my arms. How could she help but be aware of the rage that went on within me?

She followed me into the kitchen and asked if I knew the words of a certain tune and then she sang a bit of it:

"I'll be seeing you in all the old familiar places. . . ."

Well, I had heard it, of course—a popular war-time song. Then she turned to me, turned on me her full person: "Clyde, listen to me!" and grimly, staring hard at me, "I want you to learn the words and think about what they mean! Please do that for me, Clyde?"

"Well, sure, I will," I answered, wondering at the odd request.

Then Ginny burst in on us. "I guess I have it all together," she said. "Sorry, if I kept you waiting, Nordi." At that they both left, Ginny throwing me kisses from the porch, and I, suddenly sick from the inner turmoil, went out and fed Ginny's geese before driving to town.

I had been at work about an hour lining up the day with Ernest when the woman who was helping the Little Lady in the office called me to the phone. It was Bunky.

He said, "Pop—Mom's . . . real sick . . . she . . ."

I dropped the receiver and burst out the door. I've no memory of the drive home, but no cop hauled me over. Down on the road before our lane were a lot of people and an ambulance and several cars. Olga was among the women. "You've asked for this for years. It should have been you, Clyde Rice," she said. I felt the hostility of the other women for an ex-husband as I pushed on. "How is she?" I asked a neighbor.

"She's been took pretty bad," she answered, with a sly sneer at me, the oddball.

They stared and didn't seem to want to make way for me.

"They was just going on a picnic," I heard someone say, and, "Mr. Neufer done all a man could."

I pushed on past the ambulance and came to an open-ended vehicle. It seemed like a bad dream. Several men were handing something into it. They had their hats off. I went toward them, but people seemed to hold me back. "Jesus! What is this?" Then Virginia was holding me by my arm.

"Why don't they put her in the ambulance?" I asked her.

Ginny still restrained me. "Clyde—" she said, but couldn't continue.

Then Bunky, in tears, was standing before me. "Pop," he said, haltingly, "our Mom is dead."

A great gale beat me down, sought to blow me away, but I clung to a wheel of a car. Nordi gone! It tore through me like a thousand arrows. I tried to go forward then to her—to the hearse. Ginny held me back. "That's only the shell, Clyde. Nordi's no longer there. I want you to remember her, not the shell." And later, "The doctor says it was instant, Clyde, a blood clot caught in her heart. The expression on her face was so serene."

No! No! Gone—I couldn't conceive of it—*gone forever. No! I'll never be able to tell her how it was! Oh, God! Where is she now? Nordi! Nordi! Nordi! Can you hear me?* I try to reach her with my mind, uselessly. Words come into my head: *Nordi is no more!*

EPILOGUE

I<small>T HAS BEEN</small> TWENTY-FIVE YEARS now and I mourn Nordi's passing every day. Her presence is still here and sometimes I talk with her about our latest effort. I'm sure Ginny and I have her approval for the fruits we planted, the studio we built, its use for painting and writing and the books I write. In the pain of my grievous loss I decided that Nordi's passing would not go unsung and someday I would show in print what an exquisite creature moved among us.

That night after Nordi's death, Ginny and I slept one on each side of Ray in his new house, for he couldn't stand to be alone with his loss. For a week we three were inseparable, sustaining one another. We saw little of sorrowing Bunky because he was facing a continuous uproar and trouble from his cantankerous woman.

Several days after Ray gave me her ashes to scatter on this land, I stopped everything to consider the words of the popular song and hunt for their meaning: *I'll be seeing you in the old familiar places....*

I began to see that she was aware that death was about to take her, and that memories of her were all that I would have and she wanted me to garner the richness of her companionship from things and places we saw together. For some reason I tried to find her in her paintings. I don't know why but more and more I came to believe that she put a great deal of herself into the painting of bushes—the hazels and willows that she so often put in her foregrounds. It seemed that I was getting closer to her. I went to the locations where she had painted, saw the scene, and was drawn to the bushes themselves. In studying them, staring, trying to see them as she must have seen them, they began to glow as I continued looking. They shone in an otherworldly light. How could this be? Was she communicating with me some way? I talked to Ginny about it. Was it metaphysical or a psychic phenomenon? Gradually I realized it was not. Looking with Nordi at the bushes and at the world didn't change anything.

What was happening was I was seeing things as Nordi or children see them, not as a worn and weary fellow who only half looked about or heard or, for that matter, only for business reasons, tasted. I began using all my senses to their utmost and such a world came alive to me. Where I'd only seen the gnarled trunks of trees, I now looked up at their gay tops, so young in their fresh green leaves and twigs and branches. Like the bark of old trees, my senses had become weathered and somewhat scarred. Nordi gave me the world again in all its pristine beauty and after her many gifts and great love, this was her final gift to me.

About a month after Nordi's death, I finally managed to leave Acme Flavoring for good, though not without a showdown with the Little Lady. When I entered the door at Acme one morning, she handed me a bill—a bill for seventeen hundred dollars.

"What's this?" I asked staring at it. I turned then and found Ernest by my side. They both looked worn, but on Ernest's face there was a look of controlled exultation. He held his head high—a superior-to-you look on his face.

"You've been cheating this Company for years," he said. "A cheap trick, Clyde, I must say. I always suspected you. You've been cheating my dear sister."

The Little Lady broke in on him. "You've been giving away some of the profit of the Company, Clyde Rice, with every bottle, a willful waste of Company material. You must pay me at once or I'll take you to court."

"Calm down, you two," I said. "What's your charge?"

"Why—that you've been overfilling every eight ounce, quart and gallon bottle for years."

"That's not true. Show me what this is about."

"I aim to show you," said Ernest. "I have a pint bottle of vanilla we saved that's typical of the waste you carried on for years."

I took it to the laboratory, brother and sister following, and measured it with a tall slender c.c. graduated measuring tube. It was exactly sixteen ounces—a pint—exactly 473.176 c.c.'s. Ernest's mouth fell open.

"I suppose," I said, "you used a flared-mouth old fashioned pint graduate to measure that and carried out a similar procedure on the quart and other sizes. Why didn't you measure with this?" I asked, holding up the straight-sided graduate.

"Oh, it slipped my mind," he said. The Little Lady said nothing.

"Bring me a gallon of vanilla," I said to Ernest.

"They're all the same," he answered. "We took a half ounce out of each gallon in the cases."

"All of the five-hundred-odd one-gallon jugs in cases in the storeroom?"

"Yes," he replied.

I was flabbergasted. I couldn't believe it. I turned to the Little Lady then and said, "I want out of this madhouse, now." I stopped and went into the next room, completely nonplussed. Thieving was bad enough but stupidity with a dose of insanity was too much for me. I came back to where they were still standing.

"As of this moment I am no longer associated with Acme Flavoring Company. I'll take the company car I've been using and a five thousand dollar cashier check. I've had a clever auditor going over your books nights for weeks. He says you're slick, but he's caught slicker. Come on, Little Lady, let's go over to the bank. I want that check cashed and in my account or I'll bring my auditor into it and it'll cost you a lot more when we go to court. He found evidence that you'd been milking the Company for years before Pop sold." It was a bluff, but it worked. After the bank I let her out at Acme and drove away. Neither of us had spoken.

I drove past Carver up the Clackamas to its source and on into the mountains. Finally I stopped the car and stepped out. I was in a forest of towering trees—Douglas fir, cedar and hemlock. I opened my very being to them as I had countless times before, always receiving reassurance, but now they haughtily regarded me with distaste. They let me know in my grieving heart that my insane cursing of Nordi had destroyed the bond between us and caused my darling's death. I drove home, my belief in myself shattered.

"Ginny, what am I to do? I'm man enough to never seek forgiveness, but what am I to do?" At a loss for words she held me tight. For weeks I wandered about, bereft of volition. Bunky, who had inherited his mother's kindness, came frequently trying to get me to go fishing. His vitriolic lady friend had spread her leathern wings and now, with other harpies, resided in L.A.

"Guess we should never have left the mill, Pop," he said one day. "You were hell on wheels down there." Often he conversed with Ginny in whispers.

Ginny had him over to dinner one evening and after we'd eaten they looked at each other in silence. Then Bunky said, "Well, I'll start it off, Ginny. Pop, we think you should build another boat—a little sailing yacht. Ginny says she'll help you and I'll come over whenever I can. You really need a project, Pop. You've been collecting all those boat designs over the years—what for? Now's the time to carry out one of those fantasies of yours and build a boat. Have you forgotten those long evenings at the mill when we had discussions about the newest thing in boats and how we pored over *Sea* and *Rudder* magazines and your admiration for that old 'None Such' design?"

As I sneered, Ginny interrupted: "Listen to him, Clyde! There needs to be something of meaning in your life to replace the flavoring business. This could be it."

Bunky went on, "In Seattle there's that naval architect—hell, you know of him—William Garden. Pop, go see him, get a design—something over thirty and under forty feet."

Ginny said, "Please think about it, darling. I could work with you on the weekends. I'd love to help. After we got tired of sailing the boat we could sell it."

I got up and walked out. I sulked around for several days, but in spite of myself I was thinking about the footing for a mast down on a keel. One day I decided I wouldn't take such chances on the shaft hole as I did on the *Bunky*. This time I'll drill it as soon as I get the keel assembly together. Hey! What am I talking about?

But I was hooked. I began thinking of the wonderful boats of old Herreshoff—he had been sort of a God to me once   and the designs of Olin Stevens. Ah, it was crazy   the building of a boat, all that it involved—but I was growing more and more excited by the idea.

I reminisced how the wind and sea rose up to overwhelm the *Bunky* and how the curves of the *Bunky*'s hull flung off the attacking seas as it rode over and through them, and I thought how the shape of a boat is so sleek and yet so powerful, how the bow is shaped to split the water yet glides on it and is sustained by it. The boat's gentle curves add up to a form able to fend for itself in raging waters. God, yes! And to build such a boat with the wood of trees! Man, oh, man! Yes, I was seeing the symphony of wooden parts—the keel, ribs, and floors, the shaft log and rudder and a hundred others. What a welter of shaped wood is wrought together to make a boat!

I finally drove to Seattle and got excellent plans from William Garden plus the list of materials needed. I acquired a great timber of eucalyptus, which was to be kept soaking wet until the actual molding of it into the stem and stem knee, and also a smaller piece of ironbark for the skeg and some fine planks of Honduras mahogany.

I shipped them home and put up a temporary building to house the budding thirty-four-foot *Swallow*. I involved Ray in my planning. He knew little about boats but he followed each new step of the building with his camera.

I built the ketch slowly, Ginny helping me nights and

weekends. Bunky and Dave worked hard and long at the steaming and bending of the ribs. From a tunnel beneath the boat building they wrestled big bolts through the three-inch flooring and then up through the ballast keel and up through the true keel and into great washers and nuts. That job ended at three in the morning lit by flashlights because of wiring malfunction.

We sailed the lovely *Swallow* on the Columbia and the Willamette, and a few years later, after a shoe-string trip to Alaska was aborted by the suddenly rising costs of everything, we sold her. The sailing in it was fine. Looking back we found building the *Swallow* had made me once more a whole man, no longer concerned with the problems of Ernest, the squat Little Lady and Respighi, and we found that the slow, steady progress of boat building was much closer to our liking than lolling in the cockpit. We are doers, unable to sustain a laid-back posture for long.

In time Ray married a widow and moved into her home nearby and Bunky took over his place next door as Nordi had wanted. After a couple more tries at marriage, Bunky happily met the perfect mate. Their joy in sailing each summer in the San Juans brought about their decision to quit their jobs, buy a larger boat and use it as a bed and breakfast business in Friday Harbor. It was a success. They bought a sport fishing boat and a home, completely happy to spend their lives on the island.

In my seventieth year I took a job with a big firm that made bank and corporate office furniture. I got on well there, but had to leave after two years. My feet and legs could not take the long hours on the cement floor. As I left the superintendent remarked, "Wish we could find young men to turn out work like you do at sixty."

"Seventy-two," I announced with a smirk of repossessed ego. "I spoofed you about my age. I wanted to work with fine woods once more."

One summer Virginia, following Nordi's lead, started painting. I soon saw that she was a natural at landscape painting and decided, why I know not, that she'd be a painter of large, maybe immense canvases and would need a big studio. I tore off the roof of the addition in which the bathroom, hall, laundry and shop were housed and with a second story built her a more than adequate studio and got Ray to make her a fine easel that would hold these large projects. Virginia is not a contrary person. It just looks that way at times, for in this vaulted edifice for spacious art she began doing miniatures, but what of it? She was painting.

Then I had an accident in the hayloft of our barn and injured my left knee and the ensuing operation on it was not a success. I was in continuous pain and unable to do my outside work. Before the operation I'd been too busy to write, but now I started again.

Ginny had often asked me about my life in the years Nordi and I spent in California, so I wrote about those years—the twenties—when we were wildly in our twenties ourselves.

Steve Ollie, a doctor and new neighbor, became interested when I read him the first five or six pages. He said, "When you've got more written, I'll be over to hear it." He liked the second batch and the third.

I bought a fine table from Ray, a great slab of redwood, wide, thick and long, polished so you could look deeply into its grain. I moved it into Ginny's studio and began writing in earnest. Steve had liked my writing. Maybe more would. After two hundred pages I felt I should seek professional help and find what was wrong with the borning opus. I was told there was a fine writer-teacher at Portland State University. I phoned him. His line was busy and I thought, while I'm waiting, I'd see if Reed College had anything to offer. I called and asked if they could connect me with the poet or novelist who they had teaching there.

In due time a voice answered. It was Gary Miranda, then poet-in-residence at Reed. I told him what I wanted and that I was willing to pay more than adequately for his assistance.

He was wary, which I thought spoke well for him. Teaching at the college and writing his own work kept him pretty busy, he said. Then: "But why don't you just come by for a chat." Yeah, I figured, probably in the middle of a boring day.

I leaped at his suggestion, however, and brought him a sheaf of my current writing. He read them slowly while I watched his young son of nine months, Nicolas, playing on the floor. Nicolas crawled across the room and raised himself onto a windowseat by a casement window, which he unlocked and opened and looked out. Then, as it started to rain, he closed it, got down on the floor, and crawled away.

Well, I thought, if Mr. Miranda can help produce a kid like that, he probably has more than average abilities, and I turned and looked to see evidence of it on his face. Well, it certainly wasn't strewn around there. I did see a handsome, well set up, baldheaded man with a beard. He smiled. He liked what I'd written: "This is exceptional writing. You have a lot to say, and you say it very well."

Most people, when they read my stuff, advised me in all seriousness to take up some other line of work, and now here was a professional writing man patting me on the back. Hey! Hey! I'd imagined things like this, but how was I going to snag the guy so he'd be around, maybe even admire some more of my writings? He was looking at me. It was my turn to speak. I was in that position where you make do with what you have, so I asked: "Mr. Miranda, do you fish?"

"I love to fish," he replied. "That is, when I can find a place where the fishermen don't outnumber the fish—and such places are getting scarcer. Why do you ask?"

"Because I've got a pool on my place on the Clackamas River that is pretty much off limits for most bank fishermen. A fine fishing hole—'Citation Hole' they call it; some fisherman evidently got caught there with more than his limit. Why don't you come out and try it?"

So it was that I hooked Gary Miranda and, with his help, came to publish my writings. Call them "the confessions of an inveterate Oregonian." I've sailed a thousand miles upon the Pacific in boats my son and I constructed. I've traveled the Columbia and love its broad reaches. I made my living for awhile on Alaska's sounds and straits, and coursing the world of concrete and asphalt with signs here and signs there directing me, I am still a

Western Oregonian. A creature of the woodland—like my inti-mates, the ferns and brush—I flourish best under trees. Now, though, at eighty-six, my wanderings are inward, or at least over long-familiar terrain.

Ginny, much younger than I, will probably be around for a long time after I'm gone, if she takes after her grandmother who lived to be one hundred and two and her mother, who died at ninety-eight. I thought she could have a fruit stand on the road, with each fruit being so aligned in time in the long summer and autumn season she would always have something of the moment to sell. Anyway, we put in eight different kinds of plums, seven kinds of apples, six different kinds of pears with the marvelous comice finishing the season. Four kinds of cherries and twenty kinds of dessert grapes also grace this land of ours, which has given us so much over the years.

When I think of God—not a Muslim one or a Christian one or a Buddhist, but the precursor of the great bang that uses chaos as a larger pattern and puts pattern in the tiniest buttercup—I'm overwhelmed, inadequate before such a realization. So I seek signatures of the precursor in glades and along leafy pathways. I stop to rest, knowing that the end of my quest is here within me, and, with the leaves and branches and the primeval moss, I am content to be finite.

CLYDE RICE was born in Portland, Oregon, in 1903. His first book, *A Heaven in the Eye*, winner of the Western States Book Award for Creative Nonfiction, was published when the author was eighty-one. *Night Freight*, an autobiographical novel, was published in 1987, and in 1990 Clyde Rice was included, along with Dee Brown, A. B. Guthrie, Jr., David Lavender, Wright Morris, Wallace Stegner, and Frank Waters, in *Growing Up Western*. Mr. Rice lives with his second wife, Virginia, in the rammed-earth house he built fifty years ago along the Clackamas River in the foothills of the Oregon Cascades.

This book is set in a digitized version of Janson, a typeface of the late seventeenth century. Its creator, at first mistakenly identified as the Dutch punchcutter Anton Janson, now is known to have been a Hungarian, Nicholas Kis. The revival of interest in early types led to the first modern cuttings of Janson in the 1930s.

The chapter title pages reproduce woodcuts and linoleum cuts made by Charles Heaney, who was a friend of the author's when they studied art together as young men in Portland. He became well known for his paintings and prints of Oregon landscapes. Charles Heaney died in 1981.